M000281444

Dyadic Data Analysis

Methodology in the Social Sciences
David A. Kenny, Series Editor

This series provides applied researchers and students with analysis and research design books that emphasize the use of methods to answer research questions. Rather than emphasizing computation or statistical theory, each volume in the series illustrates when a technique should (and should not) be used, how to recognize when a technique has been misapplied, common errors to avoid, and how to interpret the output from computer programs.

Dyadic Data Analysis

David A. Kenny
Deborah A. Kashy
William L. Cook

FOREWORD by Jeffry A. Simpson

THE GUILFORD PRESS
New York   London

© 2006 The Guilford Press
A Division of Guilford Publications, Inc.
72 Spring Street, New York, NY 10012
www.guilford.com

Printed in the United States of America

This book is printed on acid-free paper.

Last digit is print number: 9 8 7 6 5 4 3 2 1

Library of Congress Cataloging-in-Publication Data
Kenny, David A., 1946–
    Dyadic data analysis / by David A. Kenny, Deborah A. Kashy, William
L. Cook.
        p. cm.—(Methodology in the social sciences)
    Includes bibliographical references and indexes.
    ISBN-13: 978-1-57230-986-9   ISBN-10: 1-57230-986-5 (hardcover)
    1. Dyadic analysis (Social sciences)   I. Kashy, Deborah A.
II. Cook, William L.   III. Title.   IV. Series.
    HM533.5.K45 2006
    300.72′7—dc22

                                                                    2006001437

To my wife, Marina Julian
—DAVID A. KENNY

To my sons, Daniel and Aaron
—DEBORAH A. KASHY

To my wife, Lori, and my daughters,
Gillian and Jessica
—WILLIAM L. COOK

About the Authors

David A. Kenny, PhD, is Board of Trustees Professor in the Department of Psychology at the University of Connecticut, and he has also taught at Harvard University and Arizona State University. He served as first quantitative associate editor of *Psychological Bulletin*. Dr. Kenny was awarded the Donald Campbell Award from the Society of Personality and Social Psychology. He is the author of five books and has written extensively in the areas of mediational analysis, interpersonal perception, and the analysis of social interaction data.

Deborah A. Kashy, PhD, is Professor of Psychology at Michigan State University (MSU). She is currently senior associate editor of *Personality and Social Psychology Bulletin* and has also served as associate editor of *Personal Relationships*. In 2005 Dr. Kashy received the Alumni Outstanding Teaching Award from the College of Social Science at MSU. Her research interests include models of nonindependent data, interpersonal perception, close relationships, and effectiveness of educational technology.

William L. Cook, PhD, is Associate Director of Psychiatry Research at Maine Medical Center and Spring Harbor Hospital, and Clinical Associate Professor of Psychiatry at the University of Vermont College of Medicine. Originally trained as a family therapist, he has taken a lead in the dissemination of methods of dyadic data analysis to the study of normal and disturbed family systems. Dr. Cook's contributions include the first application of the Social Relations Model to family data, the application of the Actor–Partner Interdependence Model to data from experimental trials of couple therapy, and the development of a method of standardized family assessment using the Social Relations Model.

Foreword

Albert Einstein once said that good theories determine what one can see and discover in nature. The same is true of good scientific methods. Cutting-edge research methods and statistical techniques can influence what scientists see and discover in their data. What may be under-appreciated, however, is that new methods and data-analytic techniques can also inform and change the way in which scientists think theoretically.

During the past two decades, few methodologists have had a more profound impact on what relationship scholars have been able to "see" and "find" than the authors of this remarkable book. This book not only stands as a testament to this legacy; it extends that legacy in several new and important directions.

In the 1990s, I had the very good fortune of being at Texas A&M University with Deborah A. Kashy. At that time, William L. Cook was only 2 hours away at the University of Texas at Austin, and David A. Kenny was a short 3-hour plane ride away at the University of Connecticut, occasionally venturing down to Texas to visit his protégés and to search for the ideal golf course (especially in January). I spent valuable time with all of them, and a great deal of time with Kashy in particular. And, similar to most people in the field of interpersonal relationships, I read virtually everything that members of this team wrote on the design of dyadic studies and the analysis of dyadic data from the mid-1980s onward. The methodological and especially statistical advances that members of this trio made, ranging from the Social Relations Model to the Actor–Partner Interdependence Model, changed not only how I designed and analyzed dyadic studies, but also how I conceptualized relationship processes, derived predictions, and thought theoretically about relationship issues.

The introduction of the Actor–Partner Interdependence Model (APIM) is an excellent case in point. The APIM permitted investigators to properly model and test not only actor effects (i.e., the impact an actor's independent variable score has on his or her dependent variable score, controlling for his or her partner's independent variable) but also *partner* effects (i.e., the impact of the partner's independent variable score on the actor's dependent variable score, controlling for the actor's independent variable). The capability of modeling and testing both actor and partner effects brought the dyad into the mainstream study of relationships. Suddenly, one could conceptualize how relationship partners influence one another while simultaneously modeling the statistical interdependence that often exists between relationship partners. The same was true of the Social Relations Model. By allowing investigators to tease apart actor effects, partner effects, and emergent actor-by-partner or "relationship" effects from round-robin interactions, relationship researchers could ask, test, and answer genuinely *relational* questions that were the province of armchair speculations just a decade earlier.

These developments had a tremendous impact on my own thinking and research. The introduction and rapid dissemination of APIM techniques, for example, motivated me to reexamine some of the major theories in relationship science, including one of the grandest and most comprehensive theories of personality and social development ever devised: John Bowlby's attachment theory. I embarked on this task assuming that Bowlby and most other major relationship theorists must have theorized about how the thoughts, feelings, behaviors, or attributes of "partners" should impact "actors." Thus, I reread Bowlby's classic 1969, 1973, and 1980 books, searching for partner effect predictions in any way, shape, or form. What I discovered was surprising. I found few passages in any of Bowlby's books that offered clear predictions about partner effects per se, including how a partner's attachment style might be associated with an actor's attachment-relevant outcomes. Why were partner effects absent from one of the most comprehensive and important relationship-based theories in the history of psychology?

I thought a great deal about this question. Perhaps Bowlby thought about partner effects, but never derived formal predictions about them. Perhaps he derived a few formal predictions, but never included them in his trilogy. Or, perhaps like so many other theorists who worked during the dawn of relationship science, Bowlby's expansive theoretical vision might have been constrained by the "individual-centered" research methods and statistical techniques that were available before the revolution launched by Kenny and his colleagues. From a theoretical standpoint, it is difficult to think broadly and divergently in the absence of methodological and statistical tools that allow one to test and model *dyadic* hypotheses and processes. Perhaps Bowlby's grand theoretical vision was partially obstructed by the individual-centered methods and statistical tools of his generation. Cutting-edge research and statistical methods do more than simply facilitate better or more precise research; they can also broaden and deepen our theoretical understanding of important relationship phenomena. This book contributes to that critical process.

Dyadic Data Analysis is written in a style that is a quintessential trademark of Kenny, Kashy, and Cook. The writing and examples are clear, direct, and succinct. Rather than overwhelming readers with trivial details and minor side notes, the authors present a straightforward "how-to" approach to understanding and implementing recent advances in the design and analysis of dyadic data. In places, one witnesses the authors creating new ways to conceptualize and solve long-standing data-analytic problems with dyads. Their refreshing approach gives readers the confidence that good and clear solutions to thorny data-analytic problems are but a turn of the page away. Providing this sense of clarity and optimism is challenging for any statistics book, let alone one that tackles so many complicated topics and presents so many state-of-the-art data-analytic techniques.

So read on. Some of what you learn from this remarkable book may actually change the way in which you theorize about, design, and analyze dyadic data.

JEFFRY A. SIMPSON, PhD
University of Minnesota

Acknowledgments

This book has been a long time coming. About 10 years ago, we decided to write a book on the topic. The time seemed to be right. Many investigators had dyadic data and they were having difficulties using methods that were developed for individual data. It seemed like an easy book to write. We were confident that we knew everything there was about dyadic data. Ten years later, we now humbly recognize that the analysis of dyadic data is not so simple. As we wrote the book, we learned a great deal and, honestly, we could have continued to revise our book for several more years. However, we decided to take what we had written and share it with others.

It may seem odd that a triad has written a book about dyads, but it worked very well. We met only once as a group, in Boston in 2004. However, having three of us was beneficial. For most chapters, there was one of us who knew quite a bit about the topic (or at least so we thought), one who knew something, and one who knew almost nothing. With all three of us reading and revising the chapters, we could attempt to have the chapters speak to both experts and novices alike.

We did receive extensive help from many. First, we want to thank those who provided us with data. Kenneth Leonard let us use his data on intoxicated dyads to illustrate over-time analyses. Linda Acitelli generously provided us with part of her data set on dating and married couples. We would also like to thank Kelly Klump, William Iacono, and Matthew McGue for providing us with access to data from the Minnesota Twin Family Study, as well as Jeffry Simpson, Steven Rholes, Lorne Campbell, Jennifer Boldry, and Julie Nelligan for providing us with access to their data from dating couples.

We are especially grateful to Max Blumberg, Niall Bolger, Lynn Cooper, David Gartrell, Thomas Knapp, and Joseph Olsen, who provided us with extensive and helpful comments on one or more chapters. We appreciated the help of Josephine Korchmaros, who worked on the survey of 75 studies described in Chapter 1. Tessa West read several chapters and did extensive data checking. We also got useful feedback on several topics from Joseph Bonito, Regan Del Priore, James Dixon, James Green, Jae Hong Ko, Larry Kurdek, Rudy Thayer, and Mahnaz Charania. We also thank the book's reviewers: Linda Albright (Westfield State College), Starkey Duncan (University of Chicago), Richard Gonzalez (University of Michigan), and Thomas Malloy (Rhode Island College).

We are grateful to several people who helped with the production of the book. In the early stages Virginia Carrow's work was very helpful, and more recently we were helped by Kara Taliento and Stephen Arnold. Marina Julian read the entire book and added a multitude of commas and removed many a "so." At The Guilford Press, our editor, C. Deborah Laughton, was helpful in so many ways that it is impossible to list; however, we must thank her for soliciting excellent reviews that were very helpful. Additionally, Laura Specht Patchkofsky was very patient during production. Finally, we want to thank Editor-in-Chief Seymour Weingarten for his continual encouragement on this project.

David Kenny would like to especially thank members of his department and his chair, Charles Lowe. Deborah Kashy would like to thank her department chair, Neal Schmitt, and her colleagues Richard Lucas, Brent Donnellan, and Jeffry Simpson for their support during some of the most challenging stages of this book. She would also like to thank her parents and her children for their patience and support. William Cook would like to especially thank the Maine Medical Center Research Institute and Department of Psychiatry for their support for this and other work. He also would like to thank the National Science Foundation for the support of his study of attachment security in families.

Finally, each of us wishes to thank each other. We not only have learned from each other, but our friendships have also strengthened through the process.

Contents

14 • Over-Time Analyses: Dichotomous Outcomes

15 • Concluding Comments

Web address for the authors' data and computer files
and other resources:

http://davidakenny.net/kkc.htm

1

Basic Definitions and Overview

The dyad is arguably the fundamental unit of interpersonal interaction and interpersonal relations. Although we commonly think of dating and marital partners when we consider dyadic relationships, friend-ships are also often experienced as dyadic phenomena, even though they may be nested within larger friendship groups. Even family rela-tions have a strong dyadic component in that we have different rela-tionships with our mothers, fathers, and each of our siblings. Beyond the domain of close relationships, everyday interactions with acquain-tances and strangers often occur in pairs (Bakeman & Beck, 1974; DePaulo & Kashy, 1998; James, 1953; Kashy, 1992). This book describes the methodological and data-analytic approaches useful in the study of dyads. The methods that we present in this book can be applied in a variety of contexts that involve two individuals, from rela-tionships between a doctor and a patient to interactions between two people waiting for an experiment to begin to dating couples, pen pals, best friends, siblings, and coworkers. Our focus is on quantita-tive, as opposed to qualitative, methods.

Many of the phenomena studied by social and behavioral scientists are interpersonal by definition, and as a result, observations do not refer to a single person but rather to multiple persons embedded within a social context. For instance, Harry's response when he is asked how much he likes Sally does not simply reflect something about Harry. Yet because the check mark on the questionnaire is made by Harry, researchers all too often make the fundamental attribution error (Ross, 1977) and treat the measurement as if only Harry caused it. The error of thinking that a dyadic

1

measure refers to only one of the interaction partners has been called *pseudo-unilaterality* (Duncan, Kanki, Mokros, & Fiske, 1984). Almost certainly, the liking that Harry feels for Sally is driven in part by characteristics of Sally herself, such as how friendly or agreeable she is, as well as by the unique relationship that Harry and Sally have established. The measurement reflects both Harry and Sally and, therefore, is fundamentally dyadic. In general, a dyadic measurement reflects the contribution of two persons, although the function of those contributions can be quite different (Bond & Kenny, 2002).

The intrinsically dyadic nature of many of the measurements in social and behavioral science research means that they are often linked to other measurements in the study, and the strength of these links may be one of the most important research questions to be examined. Consider the following examples:

- Both members in a romantic relationship evaluate whether they are satisfied with the relationship (Feeney, 1994).
- The amount of self-disclosure made by two people interacting is measured to ascertain whether there is reciprocity (Reno & Kenny, 1992).
- Two persons are asked to describe a common target person to determine whether there is agreement in person perception (Park & Judd, 1989).
- Members of a family describe their attachment relationships with one another (Cook, 2000).

In each of these cases, the issues of stability, consistency, and correlation between related measurements are interesting phenomena worth studying in their own right. However, none of them can be addressed easily by standard methods developed for the study of individuals.

Why has social science research tended to focus on individuals? Although there are many reasons for this focus, we think that three are key. First, no doubt much of the attention given to the individual is cultural. The United States is the most individualistic country in the world (Smith & Bond, 1994), and because the United States has dominated social and behavioral research, the prevalence of research concerning individuals is hardly surprising.

A second factor that has contributed to this individualistic orientation is the reliance on standard statistical methods such as analysis of variance

(ANOVA) and multiple regression. Although these two data-analytic approaches are very useful and, as will be shown, form the basis for many of the techniques described in this book, in their standard forms they both make what is known as the *independence assumption*. The independence assumption requires that, after controlling for variation due to the independent variable, the data from each individual in a study be unrelated to the data from every other individual in the study. As discussed later in this chapter, dyadic data typically violate this assumption.

The third reason is that psychologists have dominated research in the social and behavioral sciences. The discipline of psychology emphasizes the individual before higher levels of analysis (Bond & Kenny, 2002). So it is hardly surprising that most methods of analysis focus on the individual.

In spite of the individualistic focus of social and behavioral science research, many theoretical concepts intrinsically involve two persons (e.g., love, conflict, person perception, helping, aggression, attachment, relational competence, communication, influence). The need for a book detailing dyadic data analysis is highlighted by the fact that most of these interpersonal concepts have been studied by examining individuals in isolation. Before we can have a genuinely interpersonal social science, our theories, research methods, and data analyses must take into account the truly interpersonal nature of the phenomena under study. One of the major goals of this book is to provide social scientists with methods that focus on relationships and not individuals.

In this chapter, we define the fundamental concepts for dyadic data analysis. We begin by defining the most essential concept in relationship research: nonindependence. A series of other basic concepts are also defined, including distinguishability, types of dyadic variables (between dyads, within dyads, and mixed), and levels of measurement for dyadic variables. In addition, a typology of dyadic designs is provided. We also offer advice concerning the organization of dyadic data files. We then describe a database that includes 75 studies of relationships from five major journals. This database is used throughout the book, and a catalog of the types of relationships examined in these studies is provided. Finally, we give the reader an overview of the remainder of the book.

Although much of what we discuss in this first chapter is rather elementary, it is essential that the reader thoroughly understand the terminology presented in this chapter, because those terms are referred to repeatedly throughout the book. Thus we encourage all to read the remainder of this chapter, even those who are quite statistically sophisticated.

NONINDEPENDENCE

Perhaps the most fundamental concept in dyadic data analysis is that of nonindependence. Two members of a dyad are not simply two independent individuals. Rather, they share something in common that we refer to as *nonindependence*. The focus of this entire book is, in essence, the study of nonindependence.

Although we postpone our statistical definition of the concept of nonindependence until the next chapter, it is useful to develop a conceptual definition here. A formal conceptual definition of dyadic nonindependence is: If the two scores from the two members of the dyad are nonindependent, then those two scores are more similar to (or different from) one another than are two scores from two people who are not members of the same dyad. The heightened similarity (or dissimilarity) of scores from dyads is the critical issue that is central to this book. Our discussion tends to focus on nonindependence that results from close interpersonal relationships such as friendships, married or dating couples, and roommates. However, similar issues may arise when the two individuals are initially strangers who have just met in the laboratory or on the Internet. Nonindependence can even occur when two people never actually interact but share a common experience; for example, two patients of the same physician.

The preceding definition presumes that the data are structured in what we define as the *standard dyadic design*: Each person is linked to one, and only one, other person. In Chapters 8, 9, 10, and 11 we investigate other, more complex patterns of nonindependence. In addition, nonindependence can occur as a result of factors other than relationships. For instance, measurements from the same person may be nonindependent, something that we discuss in Chapters 12, 13, and 14.

Nonindependence, or linked scores, can occur in several ways, and it is helpful to distinguish among voluntary linkage, kinship linkage, experimental linkage, and yoked linkage. *Voluntary linkage* is the link between friends or between members of dating couples. We normally think of these persons as having some sort of bond that develops over time. *Kinship linkage* is a linkage that occurs between family members, such as siblings, cousins, or parents and children. *Experimental linkage* is a relationship that is created in a laboratory, as when two persons are asked to get to know each other. Finally, in *yoked linkage*, the two individuals never interact at all and are not even aware of each other, but they are both exposed to the same environmental stimuli. Very often linkages are combinations of two or more types of linkages: Married couples are linked both voluntarily and by kinship.

Kenny (1996b) and Kenny and Judd (1986) describe four sources that may generate nonindependence in dyads. The first source is simply a *compositional effect*: The two dyad members may have already been similar even before they were paired together. Compositional effects are likely to occur any time dyad members are paired together in a nonrandom way. For example, compositional effects are to be expected with dating and married couples because, even before they meet, members of such couples typically are similar to one another on a wide range of variables, including education level, age, socioeconomic status, religion, and so on (Epstein & Guttman, 1984). This similarity of married couples is sometimes referred to as *assortative mating*. Nonrandom pairing is typically an issue in naturally occurring dyads. For example, married couples likely have similar political attitudes because, in part, they have similar educational backgrounds. Moreover, similarities in political attitudes may have been a factor that created the dyad.

Once dyad members have been paired together, even if the pairing is random so that compositional effects are unlikely, there are three processes that may produce nonindependence between the two individuals. A *partner effect* occurs when a characteristic or behavior of one person affects his or her partner's outcomes. The amount of housework that one roommate does may affect the other roommate's level of satisfaction with his or her living arrangements. Similarly, how much a woman trusts her dating partner may affect the partner's level of commitment to the relationship. *Mutual influence* occurs when both persons' outcomes directly affect one another. Thus mutual influence involves a process of feedback. In a study of initial interactions between strangers, mutual influence might occur for a variable such as liking, so that the more a person likes his or her interaction partner, the more the partner likes that person in return. The third process that may produce nonindependence is *common fate*. Common fate effects occur when both dyad members are exposed to the same causal factors. Consider again the example of roommates living in an apartment complex. If the complex was poorly maintained and the environment unpleasant, then the two roommates' satisfaction might be similar because the unpleasant environment affects both of them.

BASIC DEFINITIONS

Distinguishability[1]

One important question in dyadic research and data analysis is whether or not the two dyad members can be distinguished from one another by some variable. Table 1.1 presents examples of dyads in which members are distinguishable and indistinguishable. In heterosexual dating relationships, dyad members are distinguishable because of their gender: Each couple has one man and one woman. In sibling dyads, the two siblings can be distinguished by birth order. In both of these examples, a systematic ordering of the scores from the two dyad members can be developed based on the variable that distinguishes them. However, there are many instances in which there is no such natural distinction. Same-sex friendship pairs, homosexual romantic partners, and identical twins are all examples of dyads in which the members are typically indistinguishable. If dyad members are indistinguishable, then there is no systematic or meaningful way to order the two scores. Thus, by distinguishability, we mean the following: Dyad members are considered distinguishable if there is a meaningful factor that can be used to order the two persons.

Distinguishability is critical to a discussion of quantitative methods for relationship data because the data-analytic techniques appropriate for distinguishable dyads may not be appropriate for indistinguishable dyads. We shall see that the statistical analysis of data from dyad members who are distinguishable is relatively easy. For this reason, researchers sometimes create a variable that can be used to distinguish dyad members. If

TABLE 1.1. Illustrations of Distinguishable and Indistinguishable Members

Dyads with distinguishable members	Dyads with indistinguishable members
Husband and wife	Gay couple
Boss and employee	Coworkers
Older and younger siblings	Twins
Person and his or her best friend	Best friends (mutually chosen)
Winner and loser	Opponents
Parent and child	Roommates
Waiter and customer	Pen pals
Teacher and student	Study partners
Sadist and masochist	Business partners
First and second author	Colleagues
Pet owner and pet	Acquaintances

such a variable is theoretically and empirically meaningful, this approach is not problematic. However, if the distinguishing variable is not meaningful (e.g., the person who is in the front of the data storage folder is assigned to be "X" and the person who is in the back of the folder is "Y"), this practice engenders an arbitrary component in the data, and it should be avoided.

Technically, the decision of whether or not the dyad members are distinguishable is both empirical and theoretical. Notice that the definition refers to a "meaningful factor" distinguishing the two persons. Sometimes a factor is designated as theoretically "meaningful" (e.g., parent and child). Other times distinguishability is an empirical issue, and the defining question is whether there are differences in the data (e.g., if there are no mean or variance differences between the two members) for the two "types" of partners (Gonzalez & Griffin, 1999). We discuss empirical tests of distinguishability in detail in Chapters 6 and 7.

Between-Dyads, Within-Dyads, and Mixed Variables

An important distinction that is often made in research is to refer to variables as either *independent* or *dependent* variables. An independent variable is usually assumed to cause a dependent variable. In this book, we use the terms *independent variable* and *outcome variable*. However, we do not necessarily assume that the independent variable is a variable that is manipulated by an experimenter. In some circumstances, the relationship between the independent variable and the outcome variable may be predictive rather than causal.

The nature of the independent variable plays an important role in determining the appropriate data-analytic approach for dyadic data. In this section, we introduce the concept of between-dyads, within-dyads, and mixed variables (Kashy & Kenny, 2000; Kenny, 1988a). Although this distinction can be made for any variable, including outcome variables, it is most important for independent variables.

Between-Dyads Variables

Scores on a between-dyads variable differ from dyad to dyad, but not within a dyad, and thus both members have identical scores on the variable. For example, in a study of the effects of stress on romantic relationship satisfaction, couples might be randomly assigned to a high-stress condition in which they are asked to discuss a difficult problem in their relationship, or they could be assigned to a low-stress condition in which they are asked to discuss a current event. For this example, the level of stress would be a between-dyads variable, because both dyad members are at the same level of induced stress: Some dyads would be in the high-stress condition, and others would be in the low-stress condition. Other examples of such variables are:

- Gender, in a study of same-sex roommates that includes both men and women.
- Length of a couple's marriage.
- Opinion, when the members of the dyad are asked to come to consensus on an issue.

Some variables that we might think are between-dyads variables may not necessarily be so. For instance, in a study of married couples, the question of whether a couple engaged in premarital sexual intercourse may seem to be a between-dyads variable. However, Liu and Detels (1999) found in one survey that 5% of couples disagreed. In some cases, the scores on an independent variable from the two members can be combined to create a single between-dyads score. For example, if members of dating couples disagree on when they first met, an average, or the earlier of their two responses, could be used. However, we discourage the routine averaging of the scores of dyad members (see Chapter 7 for empirical criteria for averaging).

Within-Dyads Variables

The two scores of a within-dyads variable differ between the two members within a dyad, but when averaged across the two dyad members, each dyad has an identical average score. Gender is a prototypical within-dyads variable in heterosexual couples, in that every couple is composed of both a man and a woman. A less obvious example of a within-dyads variable is the actual proportion of housework done by two roommates. With this variable, the average of the two proportions always equals .50, yet within each dyad the amount of housework varies across the two partners. Examples of other within-dyads variables are:

- Family role in a study of fathers and sons.
- Role when one person is asked to persuade another person.
- Reward allocation when each member of a dyad is rewarded separately, with the constraint that every dyad is assigned the same total amount.

Earlier we discussed the notion of distinguishability of the dyad members. Dyad members are distinguished by a within-dyads variable.

Mixed Variables

The third type of variable in dyadic research is a mixed independent variable in which variation exists both within the dyads and between dyads. A mixed predictor variable is probably a new concept to most researchers. Kenny and Cook (1999) and Kenny, Kashy, and Bolger (1998) present extended discussions of mixed variables. Age is an example of a mixed independent variable in marital research because the two spouses' ages may differ from one another, and, in addition, some couples on average may be older than others. Many variables in dyadic research are mixed in nature in that the two partners' scores differ and some dyads have higher average scores than others. Additional examples of mixed variables include satisfaction and individual productivity. Most outcome variables in dyadic research are mixed. Chapter 7 presents an extended discussion of the analysis of mixed independent variables.

A variable can be a within-dyads, a between-dyads, or a mixed variable, depending on the design of the study. Consider a study of friendship: If only same-sex friends were studied, sex would be a between-dyads variable; if only opposite-sex friendships were studied, sex would be a within-dyads variable, and if both types were studied, then sex would be a mixed variable.

Level of Measurement

Much of our discussion involves variables measured at either the nominal or interval levels of measurement. S. S. Stevens (1946) invented the concept of "level of measurement." The interval level of measurement is defined as measurement in which the interval between the numbers is constant, so that the difference between a score of 4 and a score of 6 is equivalent to the difference between a score of 12 and a score of 14. Generally speaking, the interval level of measurement does not assume an absolute zero (i.e., where a score of 0 implies a total absence of that variable), and so it is not possible to say that a score of 8 is twice as large as a score of 4. Most scales developed and used in social-science research are assumed to be measured on an interval scale. For instance, relationship satisfaction is usually treated as if it were an interval measurement.

Stevens (1946) defined the nominal level of measurement as measurement in which the numbers refer to discrete categories and are meant only to differentiate those categories. When there are just two categories (e.g., experimental and control or male and female), the variable is called a dichotomy. As an example, Hazan and Shaver (1987) defined adult attachment as a nominal variable: One was either secure, avoidant, or anxious–ambivalent. Griffin and Bartholomew (1994) expanded on this definition to create four categories: secure, preoccupied, dismissing, and fearful. They also presented two variables (model of self and model of other) that are measured at the interval level of measurement.[2]

Throughout this book, we generally assume that outcome variables are measured at the interval level. However, in several chapters (see especially Chapters 11 and 14) we focus on methods that can be used when the outcome variable is measured at the nominal level. Chapters 2, 3, and 6 also discuss the analysis of nominal variables. We usually consider analyses appropriate for both nominal and interval independent variables.

Idiographic and Nomothetic Analyses

Two key issues in dyadic analyses are the unit of the analysis and the unit of generalization. Most often, the dyad is (or should be!) the unit of analysis, and the analysis is called *nomothetic*. In nomothetic analyses, research is conducted across many dyads, and the focus is on establishing general laws of behavior that apply to all dyads of a similar nature. Questions such as whether mothers are more responsive to their children than fathers can be approached from a nomothetic perspective by measuring mother and father responsiveness for many families and then testing for mean differences between mothers and fathers.

Idiographic approaches are encountered less frequently: An idiographic analysis is conducted on each dyad separately, and differences between dyads are examined. Thus, in idiographic analyses, an analysis is conducted for each dyad, and the unit of analysis might be time points in a longitudinal study or measures in a study of personality similarity between dyad members (see Chapters 12, 13, and 14). Using the parental responsiveness example, an idiographic approach to this question might involve measuring mother and father responsiveness every time they interact with their children over some period of time and computing mean differences in responsiveness for each family.

Dyadic Designs

In this book, we detail the statistical analysis of three different types of designs described by Kenny and Winquist (2001). They are the *standard dyadic design*, the *Social Relations Model (SRM) design*, and the *one-with-many design*. The basic structure of these designs is illustrated in Table 1.2. In the table, persons are designated by uppercase letters, such as A, B, and D. It might help to think of person A as Alice, B as Bob, C as Cindy, and D as David. Note that *actor* refers to the person who generated the data point, and *partner* refers to the other member of the dyad. Thus Alice and Bob might be a dyad, and when Alice rates or interacts with Bob, an x is placed in the A-row, B-column. On the other hand, when Bob rates or interacts with Alice, an x′is placed in the B-row, A-column. So in this table the x score refers to the outcome score for one member of a dyad, and the x′ score refers to the outcome score for the other member of the dyad. In some dyadic designs, only one member of the dyad is measured, and the design is said to be *one-sided*. A one-sided design would occur if only the x scores (or only the x′scores) are collected. When both members are measured, both x and x′are gathered, and the design is said to be *two-sided*. We also refer to designs in which both members are measured as *reciprocal*.

The standard design is one in which each person is a member of one and only one dyad. In Table 1.2, for the standard design (the first panel of the table), A and B are members of one dyad, C and D are members of a second dyad, E and F are members of a third dyad, and G and H are the final dyad. In this design, there are n dyads and 2n individuals. When the design is reciprocal, there are 2n observations per variable (both the x and x′observations in Table 1.2 are obtained), and when only one of the two persons is measured, there are only n observations (either the x or the x′ observations are obtained). Generally, in this book we assume that the standard design is reciprocal. As an example of the standard design, Acitelli (1997) measured 148 married and 90 heterosexual dating couples on satisfaction. The study consisted of 238 men and 238 women. The x scores might then represent how satisfied the 238 men were, and the x′ scores, how satisfied the 238 women were. Based on our survey of dyadic studies (see later in this chapter), the standard design is used in about 75% of dyadic studies. Note that in the standard design, both persons are measured, and, at least for some of the variables, both are measured on the same variables. If father and child were measured, but only the father's child- rearing philosophy and the child's respect for the father were measured, the design would not be reciprocal.

TABLE 1.2. Three Major Types of Designs Used to Study Dyads

Standard design

		Partner							
		A	B	C	D	E	F	G	H
	A		x						
	B	x'							
	C				x				
Actor	D			x'					
	E						x		
	F					x'			
	G								x
	H							x'	

SRM designs

Round robin

		Partner			
		A	B	C	D
	A		x'	x'	x'
Actor	B	x		x'	x'
	C	x	x		x'
	D	x	x	x	

Block

		Partner							
		A	B	C	D	E	F	G	H
	A					x	x	x	x
	B					x	x	x	x
	C					x	x	x	x
Actor	D					x	x	x	x
	E	x'	x'	x'	x'				
	F	x'	x'	x'	x'				
	G	x'	x'	x'	x'				
	H	x'	x'	x'	x'				

One-with-many design

		Partner							
		A	B	C	D	E	F	G	H
	A		x	x	x				
	B	x'							
	C	x'							
Actor	D	x'							
	E						x	x	x
	F	x'							
	G	x'							
	H	x'							

Note. Designs with both x and x' measurements are reciprocal designs, and designs with just an x or an x' measurement are nonreciprocal designs.

In an SRM design, each person is paired with multiple others, and each of these others is also paired with multiple others. As shown in Table 1.2, the prototypical SRM design is a round-robin design in which a group of persons rate or interact with each other. In the table, A and B are one dyad; A and C are also a dyad, as are A and D. Similarly, B and A are a dyad; B and C are also a dyad, as are B and D. For example, Alice may interact once with Bob, again with Cindy, and a third time with David. Bob also interacts with Alice, Cindy, and David, and so on. The round-robin design is inherently a reciprocal design, and all the observations, both x and x', are gathered. In other words, in the round-robin design, each person serves as both the actor and the partner. As an example of a round-robin SRM design, Miller and Kenny (1986) asked members of a sorority to state how willing they were to disclose information to each of the other members of their sorority.

The other major SRM design is the block design, which is also illustrated in Table 1.2. In this design, a group of persons is divided into two subgroups, and members of each subgroup rate or interact with members of the other subgroup. In Table 1.2, persons A through D form one subgroup and E through H form the other subgroup. The block design is reciprocal if both blocks (the x and the x' scores) are gathered. As an example of a block SRM design, DePaulo, Kenny, Hoover, Webb, and Oliver (1987) had one group of persons try to guess how another group of persons perceived them. In Chapters 8 and 9, other variants of SRM designs are presented.

The final design presented in Table 1.2 is the one-with-many design. In this design each person is paired with multiple others, but these others are not paired with any other persons. For example, Alice is paired with Bob, Cindy, and David. However, Bob, Cindy, and David are never paired with each other or anyone else. Like the other designs, this design can either be reciprocal (both x and x' are gathered) or not (only x or x' is gathered). However, with this design the data are typically not reciprocal. As an example of the one-with-many design, Kashy (1992) asked people to rate the physical attractiveness of each person that they had interacted with over a period of 2 weeks. A second example of the one-with-many design would be having patients rate their satisfaction with their physician (so that there are multiple patients each rating the same physician).

We illustrate the differences between the three designs in Figure 1.1. Each circle represents a person, and the line connecting two circles represents a dyadic linkage. We see for the standard design that each circle is

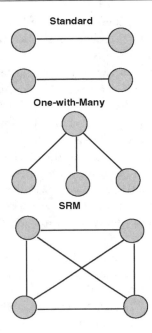

FIGURE 1.1. Diagramatic illustrations of the three design types.

linked to just one other. In the one-with-many design, three circles are linked to one, and in the SRM design, all possible links are formed.

Although the standard design, the one-with-many design, and the SRM design account for the majority of designs used in dyadic research, other designs are possible. For instance, as discussed in Chapter 11, in studies of social networks, the pairing of persons in a group can be relatively haphazard. Other designs are also considered in the final chapter of the book.

DATA ORGANIZATION

Standard Design

It is very important to consider the different ways that dyadic data sets can be structured. If the data have the wrong structure, then they cannot be analyzed by the appropriate statistical technique. There are three fundamentally different ways that dyadic data from the standard design (the design in which each person is a member of one and only one dyad) can be organized. We refer to these as *individual*, *dyad*, and *pairwise* structures. We show that the individual structure is not advisable. The other two structures have their own particular advantages and disadvantages. Because some statistical methods require a particular type of data organization and other methods require another organizational scheme, researchers should be aware that it may be necessary to create multiple data sets, each appropriate for a different statistical method.

In describing the three ways dyadic data sets can be structured, it helps to think of two types of variables. A dyad-level variable is one for which both dyad members have the same score. That is, a dyad-level variable is equivalent to what we previously termed a between-dyads variable. Marital status in a study of dating and married couples would be a dyad-level variable. An individual-level variable is one for which the dyad members each may have different scores (for some dyads, members may have the same score, but this would not be true for all dyads). Both mixed and within-dyads variables are individual-level variables. The highest educational degree obtained would be an example of an individual-level variable. Table 1.3 illustrates the three different data structures using a simple data set with three dyads (six persons) and three variables measured for each person. Variables X and Y are individual-level variables (both are mixed), and variable Z is a dyad-level variable (i.e., between dyads).

Before beginning our description of the three types of structures, we want to urge the reader to document the data carefully. Even for individual data, data management is a difficult problem, and dyadic data are much more complicated. It is essential to document the decisions that are made during the data management process. For example, researchers need to keep a careful record of how categorical variables are coded. Particular care should be given to the decisions concerning what units are excluded, how missing data are coded, and how variables are transformed.

Individual Structure

In this case, each member of the dyad is treated as a single unit. If there were n dyads, there would be $2n$ units in the individual file. In Table 1.3, we see that for the individual structure, there are six records of data, each one corresponding to one of the six persons in the data set. It is imperative that researchers include an identification variable (denoted *Dyad* in Table 1.3) that codes for dyad membership so that linked scores can be identified. Note that in this individual structure the dyad-level variables would have to be entered twice, once for each individual. For instance, a variable

TABLE 1.3. Illustration of Data Structures for a Data Set with Three Dyads, Six Persons, and Three Variables (X, Y, and Z)

Individual

Dyad	Person	X	Y	Z
1	1	5	9	3
1	2	2	8	3
2	1	6	3	7
2	2	4	6	7
3	1	3	6	5
3	2	9	7	5

Dyad

Dyad	X_1	Y_1	Z_1	X_2	Y_2	$Z_2{}^a$
1	5	9	3	2	8	3
2	6	3	7	4	6	7
3	3	6	5	9	7	5

Pairwise

Dyad	Person	X_1	Y_1	Z_1	X_2	Y_2	$Z_2{}^a$
1	1	5	9	3	2	8	3
1	2	2	8	3	5	9	3
2	1	6	3	7	4	6	7
2	2	4	6	7	6	3	7
3	1	3	6	5	9	7	5
3	2	9	7	5	3	6	5

^{a}This variable is redundant with Z_1 and need not be included.

Z is entered for both persons 1 and 2. As we later explain, an individual structure is not useful for many dyadic analyses. Nonetheless, it is the typical way that dyadic data are entered, and thus we later discuss how this structure can be transformed into the other structures.

The variable *Person* in the data set designates which member of the data the person is. One person is denoted as 1 and the other as 2. Having such a variable in the data file can be very helpful for some analyses—especially in studies that contain a categorical within-dyads variable (e.g., in married couples, husbands and wives; in sibling dyads, older and younger).

It is advisable to arrange the individual data set so that the data from each member of the dyad are adjacent: Units 1 and 2 represent data from the two members of dyad 1, units 3 and 4 are from dyad 2, and so on. Having the data ordered in this way facilitates certain analyses and is required for others. In addition, if dyad members are distinguishable, ordering the two members systematically using that distinguishing variable can also be useful. For example, if the dyads are married couples, the husband data would be entered consistently before (or after) the wife data, resulting in a data file in which odd-numbered units would be the husband (wife) data and even-numbered units would be the wife (husband) data. Such an ordering may not be required, but it is still advisable.

Using the individual structure has major disadvantages. The first is that the structure encourages researchers to analyze the data with person as the unit of analysis. Such a data analysis strategy ignores nonindependence, and so is ill advised. The second is that it fails to allow for the influence that partner characteristics can have on the person. The next two structures do allow for that possibility.

Dyad Structure

In this case there is a single unit for each dyad. If there were n dyads and $2n$ individuals, there would be n records in the dyad file. So the example in Table 1.3 shows three records, one for each dyad. Each unit would have only a single score for dyad-level variables (e.g., Z, which might be length of relationship), but there would be two variables, X_1 and X_2, for each individual-level variable. The variable X_1 refers to person 1's score on X (e.g., attachment avoidance), and X_2 refers to person 2's score on X. For example, in a study of roommates, each unit would have one score measuring the total cost of renting an apartment, two scores measuring percentage of housework done by each individual, and two scores measuring general satisfaction with the living arrangements.

Note that an individual file can be read as a dyad structure as long as it is arranged so that dyad members are adjacent. That is, the individual file would be sorted by dyad, and so persons 1 and 2 would be members of the same dyad, persons 3 and 4 the same, 5 and 6, and so on. If this were done, it would be unnecessary to read the dyad-level variables twice, and they would need to be read only on either the odd or even records.

We can create a dyad-structure data set from an individual-structure data set by merging records. The following SPSS syntax would be used to convert the structure of the individual data file depicted in the top panel of Table 1.3 to the dyadic data structure depicted in the middle panel of this table. To use this transformation procedure, it is crucial that there be a variable that identifies the dyad, such as *Dyad* in the example data set. The SPSS syntax for creating a dyad structure from an individual structure is

```
DELETE VARIABLES Person.
CASESTOVARS
      /ID = Dyad
      /GROUPBY = INDEX .
```

We first delete the variable Person. Then the following variables are created: Dyad, Z, X.1, Y.1, X.2, and Y.2. Note that SPSS creates a single variable Z because it is a between-dyads variable.

Pairwise Structure

The pairwise structure is a combination of the individual and dyad structures in the sense that there is one record for each individual but both partners' scores occur on each record as well. More specifically, in this file structure (sometimes called a *double-entry* structure), each record includes the person's scores on each of the variables, as well as the person's partner's scores on each of the individual-level variables. So, in a study of married partners, on the wife's data record the wife's scores would be entered as one set of variables, and the husband's scores would be entered as "partner" variables. For example, there might be two variables: SATISFACTION (which on the wife's record would be the wife's score on satisfaction) and a variable PARTNER SATISFACTION (which on the wife's record would be the husband's score on satisfaction).

As seen in Table 1.3, the pairwise structure is similar to the dyad structure in that it has two sets of X, Y, and Z variables. There are two key differences. First, the pairwise structure has a variable that designates the *Person*. Second, the meanings of the two variables, for example, X_1 and X_2, are very different for the two structures. For a pairwise structure, X_1 refers to the person whose record it is, and X_2 refers to that person's partner. For a dyad structure, X_1 refers to person 1, and X_2 refers to person 2.

One can create a pairwise structure by cutting and pasting the data from either an individual or a dyad structure. One would first sort the dyad structure by member such that the first n records would be for person 1 of the dyad and the last n for person 2. One would then copy the data for person 1 and paste it for person 2, and vice versa. For this strategy to work, there can be no missing records, and if a person is missing, a dummy record has to be created.

Other Designs

Although the standard design is by far the most common design in dyadic research, one-with-many and SRM designs also occur (about 28% of the time; see the next section). Recall that in the one-with-many design each person is linked to multiple others, but these others are linked only to that one person. As an example, consider a design in which each research participant interacts with a confederate who either acts interested or uninterested in getting to know the participant. To strengthen the generalizability of the research, 8 confederates participate in the study, and 10 participants interact dyadically with each confederate, making the total sample size 80. The data can be organized either by the persons (i.e., participants) or by the focal person (i.e., confederate) who has links to the other persons. If the data were organized by person, each record should include an identification variable for the focal person who has links to the other persons (i.e., the confederate in the example). In this way the data can be sorted so that they are linked together. This strategy is particularly useful when there are an unequal number of persons paired to each focal person.

Alternatively, the unit can be the focal person (i.e., the confederate in the previous example) and all of the data about partners (i.e., participants) can be on a single record. A common research design that might call for such an organization scheme occurs when participants are asked to report on their own dyadic relationships with multiple partners. For instance, if a person rates his or her closeness to each member of his or her social network, those ratings might all be placed in a single record. If there are multiple variables, as there usually are, researchers must decide whether partner or variable is "fastest moving." If there are three variables and five partners, the data would have "variable fastest moving" if the three variables for the first partner come before the three variables for the second partner, and so on. "Partner fastest moving" would occur if the five partners' scores on the first variable come before the five partners' scores on the second variable, and so on. Many computer programs require the user to specify whether partner or variable is faster moving.

SRM designs can be viewed as an extension of the one-with-many design with one major difference: Not only does each person interact with or rate multiple partners, but each partner also interacts with or is rated by multiple persons. For example, as in the one-with-many design, in a round-robin SRM design, person A is paired with persons B, C, and D. In an SRM design, however, person B is also paired with A, C, and D, C is paired with A, B, and D, and D is paired with A, B, and C. Thus, in this design, each individual serves as both an actor (rater) and a partner (target). Basically, there are two ways to order the data from an SRM design. For "dyad input," each unit or record refers to a particular dyadic combination. Thus, in the example, there would be separate records for A's outcomes with B, A's outcomes with C, A's outcomes with D, B's outcomes with A, B's outcomes with C, and so on. If this data structure is used, it is helpful to include identification codes on each record indicating who the actor and partner are for that record.

An alternative strategy with SRM data is to use "person or actor input." In this format each unit contains all of the data from one actor. Thus person A would be treated as a unit that would contain all of A's outcomes with B, C, and D. The issue of whether variable or partner is fastest moving (discussed previously) must be considered with this type of data structure.

A DATABASE OF DYADIC STUDIES

We conducted a survey of five major journals that often publish research involving dyads (*Child Development, Journal of Marriage and the Family, Journal of Personality and Social Psychology, Journal of Social and Personal Relationships*, and *Personal Relationships*). For each of the five journals, we started with the last paper in the last issue of the year 2000 and worked backward in time until we found 15 dyadic studies per journal—yielding a set of 75 studies in all. We eliminated the following studies:

- Studies that used the same data as another study previously included in the database.
- Meta-analyses.
- Methodological studies.
- Qualitative studies.
- Simulation studies.
- Studies with artificial data.
- Studies that focused on groups and not dyads.
- Studies that used confederates or phantom others.
- Studies that had people rate persons in general, not particular others.

When the article included two or more studies or samples, we chose the first study or the study that was the primary study in the paper. In this book, we sometimes refer to specific studies from the database, and at other times we characterize the general tenor of these studies.

The database is quite varied. The number of dyads included in the studies ranges from 16 to 4,066. The investigators are various types of psychologists (e.g., social, personality, developmental, and clinical), sociologists, family scientists, and communication scientists. Although most of the researchers were from North America, investigators also came from the Netherlands, Germany, Israel, Korea, and England.

We categorized the 75 studies into different design types. The results of the survey and in parentheses the results for the average study are as follows:

- Standard dyadic design: 54 studies
  - Reciprocal: 25 studies (101 dyads, 202 persons, both measured)
  - Nonreciprocal: 29 studies (200 dyads, 200 persons, one person measured)
- One-with-many design: 11 studies
  - Reciprocal: 1 study (121 persons paired with 2 partners)
  - Nonreciprocal: 10 studies (200 persons paired with 4 partners)
- SRM design: 10 studies
  - Reciprocal: 5 studies (254 persons with 4 partners)
  - Nonreciprocal: 5 studies (68 persons with 2 partners)

OVERVIEW OF THE BOOK

When is a book that discusses data-analytic issues for dyads not needed? Some dyadic data can easily be handled by methods developed for individual data. There are three cases in which "dyadic" data can be treated as individual data.

First, 39% of "dyadic" studies (the 29 nonreciprocal standard design studies) were really just studies of single persons. An example of these nonreciprocal studies might be one in which women who are involved in heterosexual dating relationships rate their commitment to the relationship.

Second, consider a study of father–child relationships in which both child and father are measured, but in which one set of variables is measured for the father and another set is measured for the child. For example, fathers might be asked about child-rearing style, and the child's self-esteem might be measured. Although such data are clearly dyadic, the dyad can be treated as an "individual."

Third, a dyad might be studied, but the outcome variable might be a between-dyads variable. For example, dyads are asked to solve anagrams, and the outcome is number of anagrams solved. For such a study, we can use individual methods of data analysis, but we treat the dyad as an "individual."

For those who need to read the book, we urge everyone to read Chapter 2. It defines the concept of nonindependence and considers its measurement. Because nonindependence is the fundamental concept of dyadic analysis, it needs to be thoroughly understood. We refer to nonindependence in every other chapter of the book.

Both multilevel modeling (MLM) and structural equation modeling (SEM) are valuable tools in the estimation of dyadic models. In Chapter 4, we show how MLM can be used to estimate models for dyadic data, and Chapter 5 presents models that are estimated by using SEM.

Much of what we discuss depends on the design of the research. Most readers will be interested in the standard design in which each person is linked or tied to just one other person in the study. If this is the case, then Chapters 3, 6, and 7 should be read. If means or regression coefficients are of primary interest, then Chapters 3 and 7 should be read, though reading Chapters 4 and 5 may be necessary before reading Chapter 7. Chapters 12, 13, and 14 may be relevant if the study has multiple outcome variables and the researcher is interested in conducting an analysis on each dyad, an idiographic analysis. In Chapter 12, we discuss dyadic indices of agreement and similarity, and in Chapters 13 and 14, we discuss over-time methods, and all of these chapters are useful for the analysis of data from the standard design.

Although most of the book presumes a standard design in which each person is a member of one and only one dyad, sometimes a person is a member of more than one dyad. Earlier we made a distinction between SRM and one-with-many designs. If the researcher's design is an SRM design, then Chapters 8 and 9 are important. If the one-with-many design is used, then it is still advisable to read about the SRM design in Chapters 8 and 9, because some concepts discussed in these chapters are presumed in the discussion of the one-with-many design in Chapter 10. Chapter 11 considers an SRM design, but the level of measurement is categorical.

The reader might be tempted to read selectively; however, we urge the reading of the entire book. Although books necessarily have a sequential or linear structure of one topic following another, dyadic data analysis is a complex topic that is not necessarily well characterized by a linear progression. Many topics could have been placed in several different chapters. Moreover, we were very surprised to discover that many topics that appeared to be fairly simple were much more complex than we thought. Thus a chapter that might have no intrinsic interest to the reader may provide a useful tool in another context. For instance, in Chapter 12, we discuss the use of pseudo-couple analysis in the study of profile similarity. This strategy represents the random pairing of couples to create a baseline measure. The strategy of pseudo-couple analysis can be very useful for other topics besides profile similarity.

The book emphasizes computer applications. We even sometimes give specific syntax for SPSS and SAS. That syntax is sure to change, and the reader is urged to consult the website *http://davidakenny.net/kkc.htm* for updates, changes, and elaborations. We also invite the reader to send us suggestions and corrections for the software updates.

SUMMARY AND CONCLUSIONS

In this chapter we provided definitions that are crucial in dyadic research. We defined nonindependence and discussed processes that can generate it, including compositional effects, partner effects, mutual-influence effects, and common-fate effects. We also defined distinguishability of dyad members and types of independent variables that are used in dyadic research. We noted that between-dyads variables vary from dyad to dyad, but within a dyad both individuals have the same score on that variable. Within-dyads variables, on the other hand, vary across the two dyad members but do not vary on average from dyad to dyad. Variables that vary both between and within dyads were defined as mixed variables.

We also introduced three basic dyadic designs: the standard design, the SRM design, and the one-with-many design. The analysis of data that arise from these designs is the central topic of this book. Perhaps one of the most important and pragmatic sections of this chapter was our discussion of data organization. Finally, we presented a database of dyadic studies that informs our discussion of dyadic data analysis in the remainder of this book.

As a final note of introduction, in this book we presume that the members of the dyad are two people. This need not be the case. The dyad might be two ears or two eyes from the same person or even two personalities. Alternatively, the members of the dyad might be groups of people or countries. The key idea is that the pair of scores are nonindependent—the topic of the next chapter.

NOTES

1. In some presentations, *indistinguishable* is called *exchangeable*.
2. Fraley and Waller (1998) have empirically determined that adult attachment is an interval, not a nominal, measurement.

2

The Measurement
of Nonindependence

In this chapter, we consider the topic that is at the core of dyadic data analysis: the nonindependence of observations from the two dyad members. This is the most important chapter in this book because dyadic data analysis begins with an analysis of the degree of nonindependence.

In the previous chapter, we gave the following definition for nonindependence: If the two scores from the two members of the dyad are nonindependent, then those two scores are more similar to (or different from) one another than are two scores from two people who are not members of the same dyad. We presume that the nonindependence is linear. Although nonlinear nonindependence is possible,[1] it is rarely investigated.

The standard statistical methods that most behavioral and social scientists currently use, analysis of variance (ANOVA) and multiple regression, were developed for agricultural researchers. Those researchers knew that two ears of corn from the same stalk were similar to one another and even that two ears from the same row were similar due to cross-fertilization. They created separate plots of land and computed the crop yields in the different plots. These plots served as "participants." It could then be safely assumed that the yields from different plots were independent of one another. The key assumption of ANOVA and multiple regression is that once variation due to the independent variables is controlled, the scores of different units are independent.

Why is the independence assumption so important for valid statistical inference? The answer concerns the fundamental logic of statistical analysis. Inference in data analysis is a form of induction and is based on repeatedly replicating a phenomenon. The exact number of replications of a phenomenon must be known in order to conduct a statistical analysis.

Consider a study of the effect of two different methods of conflict resolution on dyad members' attitudes toward one another after a discussion. If a sample of 80 individuals was divided into 40 dyads, and 20 dyads were then randomly assigned to each of the two conflict-resolution conditions, there would be 20 dyads (a total of 40 individuals) within each condition. One way to approach such a study would be to treat individual as the unit of analysis and analyze the data as if there were simply 80 individuals, 40 within each level of conflict style. In this approach there would be a total of 80 data points contributing to estimates of differences in attitudes between the two conflict-resolution methods. However, because the dyad members interact, they likely influence one another, and within a dyad the two members may share the same attitude. In this case, there are really only 20 unique or independent pieces of data within each condition, one from each dyad. Thus dyad, not individual, should be the unit of analysis. If the nonindependence is ignored and individual is treated as the unit, the conclusion from the study will be based upon 40 more pieces of evidence than it should be. The key idea in statistical analysis is independent replication, and nonindependence undermines independent replication.

In this chapter, we focus on measuring nonindependence, that is, developing a quantitative index of the degree of nonindependence. We consider variables measured at either the nominal or the interval level of measurement (see Chapter 1 for definitions). So, if we asked members of couples "Are you satisfied, yes or no?" the level of measurement would be nominal. Alternatively, if we asked them to complete a scale of marital satisfaction such as the Locke–Wallace (1959) marital satisfaction scale, the level of measurement would be interval.

We also assume that the design of the study is a reciprocal standard dyadic design (see Chapter 1). We found in our survey that 33% of the studies involving dyads used this design. Measuring nonindependence in the SRM and one-with-many designs is more complicated and is discussed in Chapters 8, 9, and 10. Chapter 15 also discusses the measurement and interpretation of nonindependence.

In this chapter, we describe how to measure nonindependence, taking into consideration both the interval and nominal levels of measurement, as well as the cases of distinguishable and indistinguishable dyad members.

We then discuss the consequences of ignoring nonindependence and then consider strategies for handling nonindependence that we see as less than optimal. Finally, we consider the power of the test of nonindependence. There are many formulas in this chapter, and the reader might be advised to ignore them when initially reading the chapter. On a subsequent reading, the reader could concentrate on the necessary formulas. One thing to remember is that, throughout the chapter, n stands for the number of dyads, not the number of persons.

INTERVAL LEVEL OF MEASUREMENT

Distinguishable Members

Recall from the previous chapter that distinguishable members of a dyad are those for whom there is some variable that can be used to differentiate between the two persons. For example, parent–child dyad members would be distinguished by their roles, heterosexual romantic couples by gender, and siblings by their relative age.

Bivariate

Measuring nonindependence with interval-level scores and distinguishable dyad members is straightforward: We correlate the dyad members' scores using a Pearson product–moment correlation coefficient. The distinguishing variable supplies a systematic way of assigning scores as either the x score or the x' score, so that the Pearson correlation can be computed. For example, with a measure of marital satisfaction gathered from both husbands and wives, the men's satisfaction scores could be the x scores, and the women's could be the x' scores. The unit of analysis in computing the correlation is the dyad, not the individual, and the data file would have to be organized with dyad as the unit of analysis (see Chapter 1). A Pearson correlation coefficient can vary from −1 to +1, and a value of 0 indicates no linear relationship between the two variables (i.e., independence).

It is important to realize that the correlation between dyad members' scores might be negative, as well as positive. For instance, if the measure is how much housework each member does, it might well be the case that the correlation is negative: The more work one person does, the less work the other does. Thus the test of the correlation coefficient usually should be two-tailed, not one-tailed. If it made no sense at all for the correlation to be negative, the test would be one-tailed.

The statistical test of the null hypothesis that the correlation coefficient equals 0 is

$$t(n-2) = \frac{r\sqrt{n-2}}{\sqrt{1-r^2}}$$

(r being the Pearson correlation and n being the number of dyads), which under the null hypothesis that the population correlation is zero has a t distribution with $n - 2$ degrees of freedom. This formula is the standard method for testing the statistical significance of Pearson correlation coefficients. For example, if n is 45 and r is .34, the result is $t(43) = 2.37$, which has a $p = .022$.

The usual assumptions for statistical significance testing apply to the test of the correlation coefficient, including the assumption of a bivariate normal distribution and the assumption of independence of the observations. In this case, however, independence refers to independence from dyad to dyad. If there are concerns about violation of the bivariate normality assumption, then other measures of association (e.g., Spearman's rho) might be computed, although inferential tests of correlation coefficients are relatively robust against violations of the normality assumption (Havlicek & Peterson, 1977).

Note that the correlation between the two members of a dyad can be very large, yet the two persons might have very different scores. For instance, consider the correlation between parents' and children's ratings of how bossy the parent is. That correlation might be large, and parents and children appear to agree, but it might be that children on average think that parents are much bossier than parents think they are on average. That is, once we control for the mean difference, children and parents agree in their assessments of parental bossiness. A correlation coefficient measures the correspondence between relative rank orderings, not absolute scores. When measuring nonindependence, the mean difference between the two dyad members should be controlled, as it is when the correlation coefficient is used.

Just how much nonindependence might we expect? Cohen (1988) defines .5 as a large correlation, .3 as medium, and .1 as small. We examined the 25 studies from our survey of 75 studies that used a reciprocal standard design. Of the 25 studies, only 2 reported the degree of nonindependence. We were both surprised and disappointed by the rareness of reporting this statistic. The degree of nonindependence is a fundamental datum of a dyadic study and should be reported. The average degree of nonindependence from these two studies was .4, but with so few studies this value is not very informative. Presumably the size of the correlation largely depends on the type of dyad studied (correlations being larger for intact vs. experimental pairs) and the variable being measured (correlations being larger for more relational variables).

As we have noted, the measure of nonindependence can be positive such that the two members are relatively similar to one another, or it can be negative such that the two members are relatively different from one another. Negative nonindependence can occur when there is:

- *Compensation:* If one person has a large score, the other person lowers his or her score. For example, if one person acts very friendly, the partner may distance him or herself (Argyle & Dean, 1965).
- *Social comparison:* The members of the dyad use the relative difference on some measure to determine some other variable. For instance, satisfaction after a tennis match is determined by who won or lost that match.
- *Zero sum:* The sum of two scores is the same for each dyad. For instance, the two members divide a reward that is the same for all dyads. Similarly, the percentage of time that the two persons talk in an interaction is measured such that the total time sums to 100.
- *Division of labor:* Dyad members assign one member to do one task and the other member to do another. For instance, the amount of housework done in the household may be negatively correlated.

Although nonindependence in dyads is usually positive, it can be negative, and researchers should not presume that it is positive.

Confidence Interval for r

Besides knowing whether a correlation is statistically significant, it is also useful to know its confidence interval. The confidence interval provides a way of determining the stability of a correlation; that is, the range of possibilities for the correlation if it were reestimated in a follow-up study. Additionally, by seeing whether 0 is in the confidence interval, we can perform a significance test. The formula for the confidence interval for the correlation requires first transforming r to Fisher's z or z_r, which uses the following formula:

$$z_r = \tfrac{1}{2}\ln\left(\frac{1+r}{1-r}\right),$$

where "ln" is the natural logarithm. The 95% confidence interval for this Fisher's z value is $z_r \pm 1.96/\sqrt{n-3}$. If a different width were desired, a value different from 1.96 would be substituted. Typically, we would report the confidence interval for r by transforming the Fisher's z value confidence interval endpoints back to r's by the following formula:

$$r = \frac{e^{2z_r} - 1}{e^{2z_r} + 1},$$

where e is the transcendental number that approximately equals 2.718. For example, with a correlation of .44 and n of 51, the Fisher's z value is z_r = .472, and the 95% confidence interval in terms of z_r is .472 ± .283, or 0.189 to 0.755. Transforming the endpoints of the interval back to r yields a 95% confidence interval for r of .187 to .638. Because 0 is not in the confidence interval, the correlation is statistically significant. Note that because the upper limit for a correlation coefficient is 1, the confidence interval for r (but not z_r) is asymmetric.

Multiple Distinguishing Variables

Sometimes there is more than one distinguishing variable. For instance, Badr (2003) studied heterosexual married couples in which one of the two members had a serious illness. There are then two factors that can be used to distinguish dyad members: gender (male or female) and disease status (present or absent). In this situation it is not obvious which distinguishing variable should be treated as the critical variable in the analysis of nonindependence, and as far as we know, there is no simple way to answer this question. We propose the following strategy. First, determine which variable has larger differences in both means and variances on the key outcome variables (e.g., marital satisfaction). Note that differences in variances are especially critical. Then use the variable with the larger differences as the distinguishing variable. In this situation, the other distinguishing variable should be used as a control variable in the analysis of nonindependence, a topic that we now discuss.

Controlling for Independent Variables

If there are independent variables (or additional distinguishing variables) in the study, we should control for these variables when measuring nonindependence. Failing to control for these variables may lead us to mistakenly conclude that there is nonindependence when, in fact, there is none. Less likely, though still possible, we might fail to find nonindependence when there is some. Either of these errors could occur if the independent variables have a large effect on the variable of interest.

We can control for these independent variables by computing a partial correlation between the two dyad members' scores, partialing out the effects of the independent variables. For instance, in correlating the degree of marital satisfaction between husband and wife, we may need to control for the length of marriage (or disease status, as in Badr, 2003).

The formula for a partial correlation, correlating variables 1 and 2 and partialing out variable 3, is

$$r_{12.3} = \frac{r_{12} - r_{13}r_{23}}{\sqrt{(1-r_{13}^2)(1-r_{23}^2)}}.$$

The correlation is tested like any correlation coefficient (see the preceding formula), but the degrees of freedom are $n - 3$, not $n - 2$. (Recall that n is the number of dyads in the study, not the number of persons.)

For example, if the correlation of husband's and wife's marital satisfaction is $r_{12} = .50$, $n = 100$, and husband's satisfaction correlates with length of marriage, $r_{13} = -.31$, and wife's satisfaction correlates with length of marriage, $r_{23} = -.33$, then the partial correlation of marital satisfaction between husbands and wives, controlling for length of marriage, is .443. The test of statistical significance is $t(97) = 4.87$, $p < .001$. Computing a partial correlation often, but not always, lowers the correlation.

Although it is not obvious, if the variable to be controlled is a second distinguishing variable, the same computations would be used, but the second distinguishing variable would need to be recoded. Consider the variable of disease status in the Badr (2003) study. A new variable, such as "disease status of the husband," could be created such that a 1 would indicate that the husband was the ill partner and a 0 would indicate that the husband was not the ill partner (rather, the wife was ill). The correlation r_{13} would then be the correlation between husband's satisfaction and husband's disease status, and, similarly, the correlation r_{23} would be the correlation between the wife's satisfaction and the husband's disease status.

The partial correlation can be viewed as a correlation between scores that have been "residualized." By residualized, we mean that a separate regression analysis for each type of dyad member (recall that we are discussing distinguishable dyads) has been run in which the independent variables (i.e., the variables to be controlled) are the predictors and in which the errors, or residuals, for each equation have been computed. The partial correlation can be viewed as the Pearson correlation between the errors across the dyad members. Note that one additional degree of freedom is lost for every variable that is controlled. Note also that if the value on the independent variable is not the same for the two dyad members (i.e., if it is mixed), then there are two variables that must be controlled, and so two degrees of freedom are lost.

Multivariate Tests

In this case, we have a series of measures, and we wish to evaluate whether the set of variables is independent across the dyad members. We can use a canonical correlation (Tabachnick & Fidell, 2001) to perform such a test. We treat one member's scores as the predictor variables and the other member's scores as the criterion variables. For example, say that we have a study in which 10 measures are assessed for husbands and 10 measures are assessed for wives. We can compute the canonical correlation by having the husbands' data predict the wives' data, or we can equivalently have the wives' data predict the husbands' data. It makes no difference which person is used to predict the other, as the results would be identical. The test that the canonical correlation is 0 evaluates whether there is a correlation in observations (i.e., nonindependence).

It is possible, although rather unlikely, to obtain a statistically significant canonical correlation even when none of the bivariate correlations between the two dyad members is statistically significant. There are two ways that this could happen. First, it might be that all the correlations are small but that they are consistently positive or negative. Second, several of the correlations between different variables (e.g., between husband's satisfaction and wife's commitment) might be large, but the correlations of the same two variables might be small.

Indistinguishable Members

As is shown throughout this book, dyadic data from distinguishable dyads can often be analyzed using conventional methods. However, when the dyad members are indistinguishable (e.g., coworkers), new methods need to be developed. As is shown, we cannot use the ordinary correlation coefficient to measure nonindependence; rather, we use the intraclass correlation.

Consider as an example the data in Table 2.1 from a fictitious study of liking between same-gender roommates. In this dyad-structured data set there are 10 pairs of roommates, and individuals are asked to rate how much they like their roommates on a 9-point scale. The following demonstration illustrates why a Pearson correlation would be the wrong approach for estimating the correspondence between liking scores when

TABLE 2.1. Intraclass Correlation Example Using Data from a Fictitious Study of Roommates

Dyad	x_i	x_i'	m_i	d_i
		Scores		
1	8	6	7.0	2
2	5	3	4.0	2
3	7	2	4.5	5
4	8	5	6.5	3
5	8	7	7.5	1
6	5	6	5.5	−1
7	3	4	3.5	−1
8	8	9	8.5	−1
9	6	7	6.5	−1
10	2	3	2.5	−1

$M = 5.60$; $MS_B = 7.42$; $MS_W = 2.40$; $r_I = .51$;
$F(9,10) = 7.42/2.40 = 3.09$, $p = .093$

dyad members are indistinguishable. Because there is no meaningful way to assign one set of scores as the x scores and the other set as the x' scores, we arbitrarily decide that the 10 scores in the left column (those entered on the data records first) are to be treated as the x scores and the 10 scores in the right column are to be treated as the x' scores. The Pearson correlation between x and x' is $r(8) = .53$, $p = .12$. Now, because the assignment to x and x' was totally arbitrary, we might reverse the scores for the last five roommate pairs (e.g., now the x score for the last dyad is 3, and the x' score is 2). The Pearson correlation now is $r(8) = .79$, $p = .006$. Clearly, the fact that the size and the statistical significance of the Pearson correlation can change substantially depending upon such an arbitrary rearrangement of the data implies that this particular statistic is not well suited for assessing the relatedness of scores from dyads with indistinguishable members.

The *intraclass correlation*, symbolized in this book as r_I, provides a unique estimate of the relationship between scores from indistinguishable dyad members. Intraclass correlations for dyads are interpreted in the same fashion as Pearson correlations. Thus, if a dyad member has a high score on a measure and the intraclass correlation is positive, then the other dyad member also has a relatively high score; if the intraclass correlation is negative, then the other dyad member has a relatively low score. A common alternative interpretation of a positive intraclass correlation is the proportion of variation in the outcome measure that is accounted for by dyad. That is, if the intraclass correlation equals .40, then 40% of the variation in the scores is accounted for by the particular dyad to which individuals belong. The shared-variance explanation of the nonindependence becomes problematic when the correlation is negative.

ANOVA Methods: Univariate

The intraclass correlation can be computed via several approaches, the first of which is based on ANOVA techniques. We denote the scores from two members of dyad i as X_{1i} and X_{2i}. There are a total of n dyads, and the average of all $2n$ scores is denoted as M. Let

$$d_i = X_{1i} - X_{2i}$$

and

$$m_i = \frac{X_{1i} + X_{2i}}{2}.$$

Thus d represents the difference between the dyad members' scores, and m represents the average of the scores. We define the mean square between dyads as

$$MS_B = \frac{2\sum (m_i - M)^2}{n-1},$$

and we define the mean square within dyads as

$$MS_W = \frac{\sum d_i^2}{2n}.$$

The intraclass correlation for dyads, or r_I (see Chapter 10 for a more general formula), is then defined as

$$r_I = \frac{MS_B - MS_W}{MS_B + MS_W}. \tag{2.1}$$

Tests of the statistical significance of the intraclass correlation depend on the sign of r_I. If the correlation is positive, the expression MS_B/MS_W (or, equivalently, $[1 + r_I]/[1 - r_I]$) has an F distribution with $n - 1$ degrees of freedom on the numerator and n on the denominator. If the correlation is negative (i.e., dyad members are less similar than two persons in different dyads are), the term MS_W/MS_B (or, equivalently, $[1 - r_I]/[1 + r_I]$) has an F distribution with n degrees of freedom on the numerator and $n - 1$ on the denominator. Because the test is two-tailed (unlike the usual F-test), the tabled p value must be doubled. For the example data in Table 2.1, $MS_B = 7.42$, $MS_W = 2.40$, and the intraclass correlation equals .51. Thus, in this example, the test of the intraclass correlation is $F(9,10) = 3.09$, $p = .093$, two-tailed.

The values of MS_B and MS_W can also be computed directly from an ANOVA. The data would need to be organized as either a pairwise or an individual structure (see Chapter 1). The independent variable is dyad, which has n levels. The MS_B measures the variance in the dyad means times 2, and equals 0 when all the dyad means are equal. The MS_W measures the variance in the two scores in the dyad divided by 2, and it is 0 when the two members of each dyad both have the same score. The intraclass correlation itself equals 0 not when MS_W is 0, but rather when $MS_B = MS_W$. In such a case, the variability in the dyad means can be explained by differences within the dyads: Two members of the same dyad are as similar as two members of different dyads.

One interesting historical fact is that the famous statistician R. A. Fisher invented the intraclass correlation. Not so well known is that Fisher developed the ANOVA from the intraclass correlation. The intraclass correlation is a measure of effect size in a one-way ANOVA.

The ANOVA intraclass correlation is a biased measure. As seen in Table 2.2, when the true correlation is zero, the estimated intraclass correlation tends to be negative. This bias declines as the number of dyads, n, increases and is trivial as long as n is greater than 30. For example, when the true correlation is .500 and the sample size is 50, the average estimate of the correlation

TABLE 2.2. Bias in the Estimation of the ANOVA Intraclass Correlation (r_I)

n^a			True intraclass correlation				
	−.5	−.3	−.1	0	.1	.3	.5
5	−.434	−.261	−.102	−.025	.053	.216	.397
10	−.465	−.276	−.095	−.006	.084	.266	.456
15	−.476	−.283	−.096	−.002	.091	.279	.472
20	−.482	−.287	−.096	−.001	.094	.285	.480
25	−.485	−.290	−.097	−.001	.095	.288	.484
30	−.488	−.291	−.097	−.001	.096	.290	.487
40	−.491	−.293	−.098	−.000	.097	.293	.490
50	−.492	−.295	−.098	−.000	.098	.294	.492
60	−.494	−.296	−.098	−.000	.098	.295	.494

[a]Number of dyads.

is .492, a bias of only .008. We also note that the Pearson product–moment correlation is biased when nonzero, but this bias is usually ignored. The bias is mainly an attenuation bias in that the estimated correlation is somewhat smaller in absolute value than the true correlation.

The formula for the confidence interval for the intraclass correlation (Shrout & Fleiss, 1979) is relatively complicated. First, determine the upper and lower critical values for the F-test of the intraclass and denote them as F_U and F_L, and denote F as the computed value of the F-test of the actual intraclass correlation. Then the upper limit of the confidence interval is given by

$$\frac{(F_U)(F) - 1}{(F_U)(F) + 1}$$

and the lower limit by

$$\frac{(F_L)(F) - 1}{(F_L)(F) + 1}.$$

For example, consider an intraclass correlation of .44 with 51 dyads. The test of statistical significance is $F(50, 51) = 2.571$. The value for F_U (the value that F would have to be significant for a *positive* r_I with 50 and 51 degrees of freedom, respectively) is 1.746 (note that the area under the curve for this F distribution from 0 to 1.746 is .975); and the value for F_L (the value that F would have to be significant for a *negative* r_I with 50 and 51 degrees of freedom, respectively) is 0.572 (note that the area under the curve for this F distribution from 0 to 0.572 is .025). The 95% confidence interval extends from .190 $[((0.572)(2.571) - 1)/((0.572)(2.571) + 1)]$ to .636 $[((1.746)(2.571) - 1)/((1.746)(2.571) + 1)]$. Because 0 is not in the confidence interval, the correlation would be statistically significant. It is interesting that this confidence interval is virtually identical in size to the confidence interval for the Pearson r. It seems reasonable to use the confidence interval for the Pearson correlation as an approximation of that for r_I.

The reader might wonder what would happen if an intraclass correlation were computed with distinguishable members of the dyad: How similar would the intraclass correlation be to the ordinary correlation? Typically, the two values are quite similar. They are nearly identical when the means and variances for the two types of members (e.g., husbands and wives) are similar.[2] However, if the means and variances are quite different, the intraclass correlation is usually smaller than the ordinary correlation coefficient. Gonzalez and Griffin (1999) recommend testing whether the means and variances are equal across the distinguishing variable for distinguishable dyad members. If they are not statistically different, the dyad can be treated as if the members were indistinguishable. In the next chapter, we review how to test the equality of means when dyad members are distinguishable, and in Chapter 6 we present methods for testing equality of variance.

ANOVA Methods: Partial Correlations

As seen earlier, the intraclass correlation can be defined in terms of mean squares, MS_B and MS_W. Most dyadic studies contain causal variables, experimental variables, couple-level variables (such as length of the relationship), and individual differences (such as personality variables). If there are variables to control for, we need to adjust these two mean squares and their degrees of freedom. One strategy for making the necessary adjustments is to compute a set of two regressions using a dyad-structured data set and combine their results. In the first regression, the sum of the two persons' outcome scores are regressed on any between-dyad variables, as well as the sum of any mixed variables. The sum of squared residuals from this regression equation equals SS_B. Because the degrees of freedom equal $n - k - 1$, where k is the number of predictor variables in the regression equation, the MS_B equals $SS_B/(n - k - 1)$. In the second regression equation, the dependent variable is the difference in the dyad outcome scores, and predictor variables include the dyad difference scores for any mixed variables and any within-dyad independent variables. Note that the intercept should not be included in this second equation. The intercept is not included because the direction of the difference is arbitrary. (We discuss this extensively in Chapter 3.) The sum of squared residuals from this second regression equals SS_W, with degrees of freedom equal to $n - k$, where k is the number of predictors in the regression equation. The ratio of this sum of squares to its degrees of freedom yields the MS_W. The intraclass correlation would then be estimated and tested as before with the new degrees of freedom.

Pairwise Correlational Methods

There is an alternative way of computing the intraclass correlation—the double-entry method. This method, which is as old as the ANOVA method, has been introduced by Griffin and Gonzalez (1995; Gonzalez & Griffin, 1999) into the psychological literature. They refer to the correlation as the *pairwise correlation*, and we symbolize this correlation as r_P. In this method, one of the persons is designated as X, and the other Y. Then the data are doubled, but the two persons' scores are flip-flopped, making each X a Y and each Y an X. Thus the sample size is $2n$, not n. The correlation is computed for the "double-entered" data set using the standard Pearson correlation formula. An equivalent formula for the pairwise correlation is

$$r_P = \frac{SS_B - SS_W}{SS_B + SS_W},$$

where $SS_B = df_B MS_B$ and $SS_W = df_W MS_W$ (Gonzalez & Griffin, 2001a). As with the ANOVA intraclass correlation, the formula changes if groups, not dyads, are studied.[3]

A pairwise correlation cannot be tested in the usual way. Griffin and Gonzalez (1995) recommend using $1/\sqrt{n}$ as the standard error for the test of r_P. The resulting test statistic is treated as a Z statistic. Such a test is asymptotic, and under the null hypothesis it approximates the Z distribution as the sample size increases. With a small number of dyads ($n < 30$), the test is somewhat liberal. The 95% confidence interval for r_P would be $r_P \pm 1.96/\sqrt{n}$.

We have reorganized the data in Table 2.1 to compute r_P and re-present it in Table 2.3. The resulting correlation is .47, a value slightly lower than the ANOVA intraclass correlation value. The Z test of the null hypothesis is 1.49, $p = .137$. The 95% confidence interval for r_P is .47 ± .620, or −.150 to 1.090. However, because the largest value that r_P can have is 1.00, the interval extends from −.150 to 1.000.

The difference between the two measures of the intraclass correlation, ANOVA minus pairwise, is

$$r_I - r_P = \frac{2SS_B SS_W (q-1)}{(SS_B + SS_W)(qSS_B + SS_W)}, \tag{2.2}$$

where $q = df_W/df_B$. Typically, r_P is a bit smaller than r_I. Both measures are negatively biased, but the pairwise measure is more biased. The amount of bias lessens as the sample size increases, becoming essentially trivial when n is 50 or more. Note, too, that the standard error is larger and the confidence interval is wider for r_P than for r_I. The reason is that the pairwise standard error is asymptotic. The pairwise correlation can be shown to be a maximum likelihood estimate of the correlation between the two persons' scores, and the ANOVA approach is the restricted maximum likelihood estimate (Gonzalez & Griffin, 2001a).

TABLE 2.3. Pairwise Correlation
Example Using Data from a Fictitious
Study of Roommates (see Table 2.1)

Dyad	Scores	
	x_i	x_i
1	8	6
2	5	3
3	7	2
4	8	5
5	8	7
6	5	6
7	3	4
8	8	9
9	6	7
10	2	3
1	6	8
2	3	5
3	2	7
4	5	8
5	7	8
6	6	5
7	4	3
8	9	8
9	7	6
10	3	2

$r_p = .47$, $Z = 1.49$, $p = .136$

Multilevel Modeling

The intraclass correlation can also be computed using a statistical technique called *multilevel modeling* (MLM). We describe this method in detail
for the standard dyadic design in Chapter 4, but for our purposes here we
assume that the reader is familiar with this technique. The intraclass correlation would be equal to the dyad variance (the variance of the dyad intercepts) divided by the sum of the residual variance plus the dyad variance.
A major problem with using the multilevel approach occurs if the intraclass correlation is negative, because the dyad variance is estimated as zero
in this case, and therefore the intraclass correlation is estimated to be zero.
We discuss the use of MLM to estimate the intraclass correlation in more
detail in Chapter 4.

Using the Intraclass When Members Are Distinguishable

In some instances it is appropriate to compute the intraclass correlation even when members are distinguishable. Consider the study by Sneeuw, Albertsen, and Aaronson (2001), who studied 72 patients with prostate cancer and their spouses. Patients and spouses independently completed several questionnaires. Because the purpose of the study was to investigate using spouse's reports as a proxy for patient reports, the intraclass correlation is the appropriate measure of nonindependence in that it measures exact agreement in responding.

CATEGORICAL MEASURES

We have thus far assumed that the level of measurement is interval, but sometimes the level of measurement may be nominal, and therefore dyad members' responses are categorical. In this section we consider the measurement of nonindependence for such variables.

Distinguishable Members

With a nominal variable, each member of the n dyads responds to a question that has two or more categories; they may be asked their ethnicity or which of several political candidates they prefer. As an example, consider the case in which we have both husbands and wives each state their religion. The religions might be Catholic, Protestant, Jewish, Muslim, Other, and None. We would then have a resulting 6-by-6 table with husband's choice on one side and wife's choice on the other. We can use Cohen's kappa (Cohen, 1960), or κ to determine whether the scores are independent or not. If κ were different from zero, then there would be evidence of nonindependence. In this case nonindependence would indicate that husbands and wives are more likely to be members of the same religion than members of two different religions.

Table 2.4 presents hypothetical data from 200 dyads in which each member of a distinguishable dyad makes a categorical response of either A, B, or C. To estimate kappa, we compute n_o, the number of times the two members of the dyad have the same response, that is, the number of agreements. In Table 2.4, $n_o = 106 + 28 + 6 = 140$. We also compute n_e, the expected or chance number of agreements. For any given category the expected number of agreements is the product of the number of times each judge chose the category divided by the total sample size. That is, the expected number of agreements is the row marginal frequency times the column marginal frequency divided by the number of dyads. (This is the same way expected frequencies are obtained in a standard chi-square test of independence.) The term n_e is the sum across categories of the expected number of agreements. In the example, $n_e = (130)(120)/200 + (50)(60)/200 + (20)(20)/200 = 95$. Cohen's kappa equals

$$\kappa = \frac{n_o - n_e}{n - n_e},$$

where n is the number of dyads. For the example, $\kappa = (140 - 95)/(200 - 95) = .429$. If we define p_o as n_o/n and p_e as n_e/n, kappa can be alternatively written as

$$\kappa = \frac{p_o - p_e}{1 - p_e}.$$

As another example, Christensen, Sullaway, and King (1983) asked 50 heterosexual couples to report on their interactions over the preceding 24 hours. Each member decided, for instance, whether he or she had had an argument in the past 24 hours. The average value of kappa across the behaviors in the study was about .50.

A kappa of zero implies that $p_o = p_e$ and that agreement is at chance levels. A kappa of 1 implies that $p_o = 1$ and there is complete agreement. Kappa is affected by margin differences. If, for instance, the wives are less likely to designate their religion as "None" than their husbands are, this would lower the value of kappa. Kappa can potentially equal 1 only when the margins are exactly equal. The upper limit of p_o is $\Sigma \, \text{Min}(p_{i.}, p_{.i})$ where "Min" means the smaller of the two values. The term $p_{i.}$ is the number of times the first judge chose category i divided by n, and $p_{.i}$ is the number of times the second judge chose category i divided by n. (Note for this example that $p_{1.}$ is $120/200 = .60$ and $p_{.1}$ is $130/200 = .65$.) For the example in

TABLE 2.4. Kappa Example with Two Members and Three Categories (A, B, and C)

		Member 2			
	Category	A	B	C	Total
	A	106	10	4	120
Member 1	B	22	28	10	60
	C	2	12	6	20
	Total	130	50	20	200

Table 2.4, given the margins, the maximum value of kappa is not 1 but .905. If kappa is negative, then agreement is less than expected by chance. Note that the lower limit of kappa can be less than −1.

The standard error of kappa, assuming that kappa is zero, which we designate as $s_{\kappa n}$ (the standard error for κ given the null hypothesis that kappa is zero) equals

$$s_{\kappa n} = \sqrt{\frac{p_e + p_e^2 - \sum[p_{i.}p_{.i}(p_{i.} + p_{.i})]}{n(1-p_e)^2}},$$

where the summation is across categories (Fleiss, 1981). To test whether kappa is statistically greater than zero, it is divided by its standard error. The resulting value is a one-tailed Z test.

The computation of a confidence interval for kappa is fairly complex. We cannot use the previous standard error, or $s_{\kappa n}$, as it presumes, under the null hypothesis, that kappa is zero. The proper standard error for a confidence interval, which we denote as s_κ, is

$$s_\kappa = \sqrt{\frac{\sum p_{ii}[1-(p_{.i}+p_{i.})(1-\kappa)]^2 + (1-\kappa)^2\sum\sum p_{ij}(p_{.i}+p_{j.})^2 - [\kappa - p_e(1-\kappa)]^2}{n[1-p_e]^2}}.$$

The 95% confidence interval for kappa is $\kappa \pm 1.96 s_\kappa$.

For the example data in Table 2.4, the estimated standard error of kappa is $s_{\kappa n}$, which is 0.0555, and the test of the null hypothesis yields $Z = 7.72$, which is statistically significant, $p < .001$. The other standard error, or s_κ, is 0.0537, and so its confidence interval is .429 ± .105, or between .323 and .534.

Kappa can be modified to weight various types of discrepancies more than others, and the resulting measure is called *weighted kappa* (Cohen, 1968). For the religion example, it might be that a Catholic–Protestant (a Catholic married to a Protestant) marriage is less discrepant than a None–Muslim marriage. As discussed by Krippendorff (1970), if the weights are chosen in a certain fashion (categories are given a numeric score and the weights are the squared difference between scores), the value of kappa is identical to an ANOVA intraclass correlation coefficient. Thus the intraclass correlation can be viewed as a special case of kappa.

Indistinguishable Members

We know of no previous work that presents methods for assessing and testing nonindependence on a categorical variable when dyad members are indistinguishable. Such a situation might occur in a study investigating similarity in marital status (e.g., single-never married, married, divorced, and so on) for same-sex best friends.

We suggest the following strategy. Arbitrarily designate the two dyad members as persons 1 and 2 and create a two-way table of association. Next, combine corresponding off-diagonal cells and average them. Considering the data in Table 2.4, the average of the two AB cells is 16, the average of the AC cells is 3, and the average of the BC cells is 11. This average may not be an integer (e.g., 12.5), but this is not problematic. We place this average in each of the two corresponding off-diagonal cells. Thus the AB (i.e., the cell in which member 1 says "A" and member 2 says "B") and BA cells (i.e., the cell in which member 1 says "B" and member 2 says "A") are both 16. We then recompute the row and column margins, which now should be equal. The A margin is now 125, the B margin is 55, and the C margin is 20. Using frequencies in the resulting new symmetric table, we compute Cohen's kappa. For the data in Table 2.4, we obtain a value of .427.

This measure of kappa can be interpreted in the same fashion as the standard measure of kappa. One thing to note is that one source of disagreement, marginal disagreement, is impossible. Additionally, the standard error presented previously is likely biased, and so using it in a test of statistical significance would be problematic. However, we know of no alternative.

CONSEQUENCES OF IGNORING NONINDEPENDENCE

In this section we consider the effect of treating person as the unit of analysis and ignoring the nonindependence in dyad members' scores on standard significance testing. As we show, sometimes tests of statistical significance are too liberal, and at other times the tests are too conservative. If a test is too liberal, the inferential test statistic (t or F statistic) is too large in absolute value, and the p value is smaller (i.e., more "significant") than its nominal value (e.g., .05). A liberal test results in too many Type I errors, concluding that the null hypothesis is false when it is not. If a test is too conservative, the inferential test statistic (t and F statistic) is too small in absolute value, and the p value is larger (i.e., less "significant") than it truly is. With a conservative test, the likelihood of rejecting a true null hypothesis (i.e., a Type I error) is lower than the nominal value of .05; therefore, such a test has less power than it should and results in an increase in the probability of a Type II error.

We should note that nonindependence does not bias the effect estimates themselves. So *unstandardized* regression coefficients and mean differences are not affected by nonindependence. What are biased are the variances, and the biased variances then likely affect the standard errors of test statistics (e.g., t and F), making tests of statistical significance, and their associated p values, biased. Because variances are biased, standardized measures (e.g., r, β, and d) are also biased.

In addition to the bias in the variance, there is also a bias in the degrees of freedom in tests of significance. Nonindependence always results in fewer degrees of freedom than there would be if the data were independent. This loss in degrees of freedom is easy to see when there is perfect nonindependence. With perfect nonindependence, the information supplied by one dyad member is completely redundant with that supplied by the other person, and although there are $2n$ data points, there are only n unique pieces of information. When nonindependence is weaker, fewer degrees of freedom are lost. The exact quantitative formulas for degrees of freedom loss are presented in Kenny, Kashy, and Bolger (1998). However, if the nonindependence is less than .5, the loss in degrees of freedom has relatively little effect on significance testing results. For instance, if the number of dyads is 50 and the intraclass correlation is .5, the effective degrees of freedom are 78.08, not 98. However, the critical t (alpha of .05) is increased to only 1.9845 from 1.9908, a trivial increase.

As we stated earlier, the typical effect of nonindependence is to bias variances. If the correlation between dyad members' scores were positive, then the variance of the observations would be smaller than it should be; and if the correlation were negative, then the variance would be larger than it should be. As we have mentioned, the bias in p values can either be too conservative or too liberal. A key factor in determining the direction of the p value bias is the nature of the independent variable—that is, whether it is a within- or between-dyads independent variable. This bias also depends on the direction of the correlation between the two members on the outcome variable. So we have two factors—the type of independent variable and the direction of the correlation on the outcome variable. Together they form four possible combinations.

As shown in Table 2.5, the test is too liberal when the independent variable is between dyads and the correlation is positive. This is perhaps the most prototypical case for the study of nonindependence. In this situation, the inferential statistic is too large, the p value too small, and too many Type I errors are made. The test is also too liberal when the independent variable is within dyads and the correlation is negative. There are two cases in which the test of statistical significance is too conservative: when the independent variable is within dyads and the correlation is positive, and when the independent variable is between dyads and the correlation is negative.

Consider an example of heterosexual couples, half of whom are distressed and half of whom are not distressed. Two outcome variables are measured: One variable, marital satisfaction, likely has a positive correlation, and the other, how much housework each person does, likely has a negative correlation. If we test whether distress (a between-dyads variable) has an impact on these two outcome variables and treat individual as the unit of analysis, the test of whether distress affects marital satisfaction is likely to be overly liberal, and the test of whether distress affects housework is likely to be overly conservative.

Table 2.5 is very useful when the independent variable is between or within dyads. However, if it is mixed, the direction of bias is less certain. To determine the direction of bias, we need to compute the intraclass correlation for the independent variable. Consider gender as the independent variable. If gender were a between-dyads independent variable, in some of the dyads both members would be men, and in others both would be women. The intraclass correlation for a dummy-coded gender variable would be 1. If gender were a within-dyads independent variable, each of the dyads would consist of one man and one woman, and the intraclass correlation for gender would be −1. If gender were a mixed independent variable, some of the dyads would be same sex and others would be opposite sex. If most of the dyads were same sex, gender would be very much like a between-dyads variable and would have a positive intraclass correla-

TABLE 2.5. Effects of Nonindependence on Significance Testing

Independent variable	Correlation for the outcome variable	
	Positive	Negative
Between dyad	Too high[a]	Too low[b]
Within dyad	Too low[c]	Too high[d]

[a]Married couples assigned to conditions, with satisfaction the outcome variable.
[b]Married couples assigned to conditions, with amount of housework the outcome variable.
[c]Gender of person in married couples is the independent variable, and satisfaction is the outcome variable.
[d]Gender of person in married couples is the independent variable, and amount of housework is the outcome variable.

tion. If most of the dyads were opposite sex, then the intraclass correlation would be negative. However, if there were approximately the same number of male–male, female–female, and male–female dyads, the intraclass correlation would be near zero. When the intraclass correlation for the independent variable is near zero and the individual is the unit of analysis, tests of significance are generally neither very conservative nor very liberal.

Kenny and colleagues (1998) present the formulas for computing the degree of bias in p values created by nonindependence. For example, in dyadic research with a between-dyads predictor variable, if there were 50 dyads, or 100 individuals, in two treatment conditions and the intraclass correlation for the dependent variable were .45, then test statistics that normally would be associated with an alpha of .05 would actually indicate an alpha of .10 (Kenny et al., 1998, p. 238). Thus, in this case, mistakenly treating individual as the unit of analysis when there is nonindependence can result in substantial increases in Type I errors.

When the intraclass correlation is negative and the independent variable is between dyads, inferential tests are overly conservative. For example, again consider dyadic research with 100 individuals and two treatment conditions; given an intraclass correlation equal to −.50, the actual alpha would be only .006, not .05. There would also be a corresponding increase in the probability of Type II errors and a drop in power.

WHAT NOT TO DO

If the data are determined to be nonindependent, what should a researcher do? We want to emphasize that the determination of whether there is nonindependence is in part an empirical question and in part a theoretical one. The theoretical aspects of the decision refer to the type of dyad being studied, the type of variable being studied, the research context, and whether previous researchers doing similar studies have found nonindependence. For example, if unacquainted people are randomly assigned to dyads and are asked to discuss an issue, their prior attitudes are likely independent, but their postdiscussion attitudes are probably nonindependent. An empirical analysis, as described in this chapter, would reveal whether there was any dependence.

The rest of this book considers how to handle nonindependence. However, we discuss in this section some strategies of data analysis and design that we see as less than optimal for dyadic data but that are nonetheless commonly used.

The first flawed strategy is just to ignore the nonindependence. As we discussed in the previous section, this strategy often results in biased significance tests. Sometimes the test is too liberal, and other times, too conservative. As long as the nonindependence is nontrivial, it is generally a mistake to ignore it.[4]

The second less-than-optimal strategy is to discard the data from one dyad member and analyze only one member's data. If there are no dyads and only individuals, then there is no nonindependence, and this is a "solution." Obviously, this strategy results in a loss of precision. Additionally, one would obtain different results if different data were discarded. Moreover, dyadic effects could not be measured.

The third less-than-optimal strategy is very much like the previous one. However, instead of discarding one person's data, data are collected from only one member of the dyad when they could have easily been collected from both. This strategy has the same drawbacks as the previous strategy.

The fourth flawed strategy is to treat the data as if they were two samples. This approach is often used when dyad members are distinguishable. For example, in a study of heterosexual couples, the data from men and women would be separately analyzed.[5] Although there are some advantages to this approach, it also has several key disadvantages. Most important, it presumes differences between genders (or whatever the distinguishing variable is) when in fact there may be no such differences. Additionally, power is likely lost by not combining results.

A fifth suboptimal strategy is not statistical but experimental. It is possible to prevent the nonindependence from occurring by ensuring that there is no social interaction between participants. There are two different ways in which this can be achieved. Participants interact not with another person but with a computer program that mimics a person, or they interact with an accomplice of the researcher. In some sense, this strategy takes the "social" out of social science. Duncan and Fiske (1977) discuss the difficulties of using accomplices in dyadic research.

Sometimes an alternative to using accomplices is to ask the participants themselves to alter their behavior. One participant may be asked to smile frequently during the interaction to determine the effect of smiling on how much a partner likes them. Alternatively, a variable can be manipulated (e.g., tell one participant that the other participant does not like him or her) in order to avoid the use of an experimental accomplice.

In essence, each of these strategies treats dyadic data as if they were individual data, not dyadic. Researchers need to confront the reality of dyadic data and reject these individualistic strategies. Although dyadic data create complications in the analysis, such data also create opportunities. Moreover, in many cases, if there were independence of observations, we would be distressed because, as researchers in the area of relationships, we expect and even require nonindependence; when we do not find it, we are very disappointed. Rather than avoiding dyadic data, researchers need to embrace it and apply the methods that are presented in this book.

POWER CONSIDERATIONS

Power, an important consideration in data analysis, refers to the probability of rejecting the null hypothesis when, in fact, it is false. Because the null hypothesis is virtually always false, power should be an important concern in the analysis. In dyadic analysis, there are two fundamentally different questions about power. The first question concerns the power of the test of nonindependence: If the data are nonindependent, will we be able to detect this nonindependence? The second question concerns the reduction or increase in power of the test of the independent variable that occurs when we change the unit of analysis from individual to dyad. That is, how much power in our key tests of independent variables is lost or gained when we use dyad as the unit of analysis rather than individual? In this chapter we consider the first topic. We consider the second topic in Chapters 3 and 7.

Power of the Test of r

Discussing the interval level of measurement first, in Table 2.6, we present the power for the test of a Pearson correlation coefficient for various correlations and for different sample sizes. (The power of the tests of the intraclass correlation, either ANOVA or pairwise, is slightly less than that of the Pearson correlation.) We used Cohen (1988) to determine the power. We might note that Cohen considered .1 a small correlation, .3 a medium one, and .5 a large one. For instance, if we conduct a study with 80 pairs of siblings, and we think the population correlation is .3, then the power of such a test would be .78. Importantly, there is relatively little power in the tests of nonindependence when that nonindependence is small in size, even when we have as many as 200 dyads.

How many dyads are there in the typical study? From our survey of 75 studies, we examined the subset of those 25 that measured both mem-

TABLE 2.6. Power of the Test of Nonindependence
(Pearson r) given Alpha of .05 for a Two-Tailed Test

n^a	Absolute value of the population correlation					
	.1	.2	.3	.4	.5	.6
10	.06	.08	.13	.21	.33	.49
20	.07	.14	.25	.43	.64	.83
40	.09	.24	.48	.74	.92	.99
80	.14	.43	.78	.96	*	*
120	.19	.59	.92	*	*	*
160	.24	.72	.97	*	*	*
200	.29	.81	.99	*	*	*
300	.46	.97	*	*	*	*
500	.61	*	*	*	*	*
800	.81	*	*	*	*	*

*Power greater than .995.
^{a}Number of dyads.

bers of the dyad and used the standard design. For studies of this type, the number of dyads ranged from 25 to 411, with the median number across the 25 studies being 101. Because this value was obtained from publications in major journals, it is likely that the number of dyads in a typical research study would be somewhat smaller. Therefore, we would estimate the typical sample size as being 80 dyads. Using this number, we determined the power of the test for a small, medium, and large correlation. Cohen recommended setting power at .80, or an 80% chance of ruling out the null hypothesis. As shown in Table 2.6, there is typically not very much power in tests of correlations when the effect size is small and n equals 80. When the correlation is large, there does appear to be sufficient power. The minimal n for sufficient (80%) power to detect a small effect size is 783 dyads. We need to realize that enrolling large numbers of dyads into a study can be difficult; therefore, other strategies for increasing power besides increasing the sample size should be explored (McClelland, 2000).

Kenny and colleagues (1998) have defined *consequential nonindependence* as the level of nonindependence that would have to be present to result in the probability of committing a Type I error (i.e., alpha) being .10 when it should equal .05. The value for consequential nonindependence for dyads and a between-dyads independent variable is about .45. A correlation of about .45 between dyad members' scores would result in the probability of making a Type I error of .10, if individual were the unit of analysis. The key question, then, is how many dyads are needed to have enough power (i.e., power of at least .80) to detect consequential non-independence? If we assume a two-tailed test of nonindependence,[6] an alpha of .05, and a between-dyads independent variable, we would need to have at least 44 dyads. However, it is conventionally recommended (e.g., Myers, 1979) that the test for nonindependence be quite liberal and that a two-tailed alpha be .20. Using this value, the number of dyads needed to be able to test for consequential nonindependence is 28. We recommend having a minimum of 25 dyads before testing for nonindependence and adopting a liberal test value for alpha (.20) in the test of nonindependence. If there are fewer than 25 dyads (fortunately, a rare occurrence according to our survey of the literature), it becomes necessary to assume that there is nonindependence, even if the test of statistical significance of non-independence is not statistically significant.

Power of Kappa

Turning now to the nominal level of measurement, we suggest the following strategy for determining the power of the test that kappa is greater than zero. We return to the example in Table 2.4, but imagine that the values in that table are theoretical, not empirical. That is, a researcher plans to have an n of 200 and has specified the expected numbers for each of the nine cells. From this table, the hypothetical value of kappa and the two standard errors of $s_{\kappa n}$ and s_{κ} can be determined. The test statistic is $\kappa \sqrt{n}/s_{\kappa n}$, or Z_{κ}. Power is the probability that Z_{κ} is greater than 1.645 (assuming the conventional .05 level of statistical significance and one tail). We treat Z_{κ} as a normally distributed variable with a mean of $\kappa \sqrt{n}/s_{\kappa n}$ and a variance of $s_{\kappa}^2/s_{\kappa n}^2$. With this information we can use the standard normal distribution or the Z distribution to determine power.

Again treating the values in Table 2.4 as theoretical, not empirical, the value of κ is .4286, $n = 200$, $s_{\kappa n} = 0.0555$, and $s_{\kappa} = 0.0537$. Then the mean of that Z_{κ} is 48.82, and its standard deviation is 0.967. The probability that that Z_{κ} would be greater than 1.645 is 1. That is, for a sample size of 200 and a kappa of .4286, it is a virtual certainly that kappa will be statistically significant. However, if n were 40, then $s_{\kappa n} = 0.7851$, and $s_{\kappa} = 0.7596$. The mean of that Z_{κ} is 3.452, and its standard deviation is 0.967. The probability that that Z_{κ} would be greater than 1.645 is .969.

SUMMARY AND CONCLUSIONS

The primary focus of this chapter has been to provide methods for estimating and testing the degree to which two dyad members' scores are nonindependent. For distinguishable dyads, we saw that nonindependence for variables measured at the interval level can be estimated using standard methods such as the Pearson correlation coefficient. We discussed the intraclass correlation as the measure of nonindependence for interval level outcomes when the dyad members are indistinguishable. We considered several data-analytic approaches to estimating the intraclass correlation, including ANOVA, pairwise, and MLM solutions. With categorical outcomes, we suggested kappa as the measure of nonindependence for distinguishable dyads, and we proposed a variant of kappa for indistinguishable dyads.

Our discussion turned to several important issues involved in measuring and testing the degree of nonindependence. We defined negative nonindependence and discussed processes that can generate it. We also described methods for estimating nonindependence that control for the effects of independent variables.

The latter part of the chapter considered the consequences of ignoring nonindependence when conducting tests of the effects of independent variables. We showed that ignoring nonindependence can bias hypothesis-testing results in either the overly liberal or overly conservative direction, depending on the direction of nonindependence and the type of independent variable (e.g., between dyads or within dyads). We also discussed several less-than-optimal strategies for "controlling" nonindependence. Finally, we described a range of issues concerning the power of the test of nonindependence.

All too often nonindependence is viewed as a problem in the analysis of dyadic data. However, very often the nonindependence is what is most interesting about dyadic data. Consider two examples. Niederhoffer and Pennebaker (2002) were interested in the degree to which interaction partners matched each other's linguistic style, for example, using big words and prepositions and speaking tentatively. They found a matching of linguistic styles on many variables. However, O'Rourke and Cappeliez (2003) examined whether marital aggrandizement, or an exceedingly positive portrayal, was similar in romantic couples. Contrary to what they predicted, they found no correlation of the two marital-aggrandizement measures once satisfaction was controlled.

In the next chapter, we consider hypotheses concerning means and regression coefficients when the independent variable is either between or within dyads. Later, in Chapter 7, we discuss mixed independent variables. We also return to the issue of measuring the similarity of responses of the two members of the dyad in Chapter 12. There, we develop a measure for each dyad, and we revisit the Pearson and intraclass correlation coefficients as measures of nonindependence. Finally, in Chapter 15, we review the conceptual meaning of nonindependence in dyadic research.

NOTES

1. The testing of nonlinear nonindependence is straightforward when dyad members are distinguishable. Nonlinear terms for both persons (e.g., squared terms) would be created and then correlated. We know of no way to measure nonlinear nonindependence when dyad members are indistinguishable, because nonlinearity implies an asymmetry.

2. Assuming equal variances, if the means of the two members are exactly equal, the intraclass and the ordinary correlation coefficients have the same value only when the correlation is exactly +1 or −1.

3. Some have suggested using eta squared, or η^2, as a measure of a dyadic or group effect: $SS_B/(SS_B + SS_W)$. We do not think that this measure should be used, because it is very positively biased. For instance, if the true correlation is zero, eta squared equals about .5.

4. When the independent variable is mixed and its intraclass correlation is near zero, there is relatively little bias in the p value. However, as will be seen in Chapter 7, there are still advantages in considering the dyadic nature of the data.

5. Some might wonder about adopting the following strategy: Analyze the data of men and women separately, and then combine the results using meta-analytic techniques. Although there is some merit in such a strategy, the two sets of results are themselves nonindependent, and traditional meta-analytic methods would improperly treat them as if they were independent.

6. The careful reader may note that the minimum number of dyads needed differs from the number given in Table 6 in Kenny and colleagues (1998). The difference is that they assume a one-tailed test of the intraclass correlation, whereas we assume a two-tailed test.

Analyzing Between-
and Within-Dyads
Independent Variables

In the previous chapter, we discussed how nonindependence biases significance test results (i.e., p values) when individual is treated as the unit of analysis. In this chapter, we turn our attention to methods of analyzing the effects of either between- or within-dyads independent variables for the standard dyadic design, treating dyad as the unit of analysis (Kashy & Kenny, 2000). That is, we consider the cases in which the scores on the independent variable are the same for both dyad members (i.e., a between-dyads variable) or in which the scores sum to the same value for every dyad (i.e., a within-dyads variable). We also provide methods for assessing the degree of nonindependence in the outcome scores after partialing out the effects of the independent variables, as well as advice concerning the appropriate data-analytic strategy if the data appear to be independent. If there are missing data, then the methods presented in Chapter 7 should be used instead of the methods presented in this chapter.

In the first two sections of this chapter, we consider outcome or dependent variables that are measured at the interval level of measurement. The first section considers categorical independent or predictor variables, and the second section discusses predictor variables measured at the interval level of measurement. In the third section of this chapter, we consider outcome variables that are dichotomous. We assume throughout that there are a total of n dyads and $2n$ persons measured, and we denote the intraclass correlation as r_i.

INTERVAL OUTCOME MEASURES
AND CATEGORICAL INDEPENDENT VARIABLES

We begin our discussion by considering the effects of categorical independent variables on interval outcome measures. We first examine the case of a single between-dyads independent variable and then extend that case to multiple between-dyads independent variables. We then turn to methods for analyzing a single within-dyads independent variable and then likewise extend that discussion to multiple within-dyads independent variables. Finally, we discuss data-analytic methods for models that include both types of independent variables.

One Between-Dyads Independent Variable

Recall that a between-dyads independent variable is one that varies from dyad to dyad but that within each dyad both dyad members have the same score. The number of levels of the categorical between-dyads independent variable can be two or greater, and examples include friendship status (e.g., best friends, casual friends, acquaintances) or experimental condition (e.g., high- versus low-stress manipulation). Note that in this section we assume that the dyad members are indistinguishable, because distinguishability would imply that there is a within-dyads variable in addition to our single between-dyads variable. Our discussion of analysis issues when there is a single between-dyads independent variable is quite extensive, as it is a prototypical case.

As an example, consider a study of age differences on eating attitudes and behaviors reported by Klump, McGue, and Iacono (2000). In this study researchers examined disordered eating attitudes and behaviors for identical and fraternal female twins in two age cohorts: 11-year-olds and 17-year-olds. The example data set described here is a random subsample of the data collected from the original 641 dyads included in the Klump and colleagues (2000) study. Our subsample includes a total of 200 dyads, 100 in the younger cohort and 100 in the older cohort. The mean score on the eating disorders inventory for our subsample of the 11-year-old cohort is $M = 5.29$, $SD = 4.64$, and for our subsample of the 17-year-old cohort, $M = 8.88$, $SD = 5.81$. The scale theoretically can range from 0 to 30, but the actual range of the subsample is from 0 to 23.

The structure of the data is what is called a *hierarchically nested design*. Persons are nested in dyads, and dyads are nested in conditions. Table 3.1 presents the ANOVA source table, which contains three sources

TABLE 3.1. Analysis of Variance Table for a Between-Dyads Factor: A Study of 200 Twin Dyads (D) and 400 Persons (S) (sampled from Klump et al., 2000)

11-year-olds (A_1)				17-year-olds (A_2)			
D_1	D_2	D_3 .... D_{100}		$D_{101}D_{102}D_{103}$.............. D_{200}			
S_1	S_3	S_5 .... S_{199}		S_{201} S_{203} S_{205}.............. S_{399}			
S_2	S_4	S_6 .... S_{200}		S_{202} S_{204} S_{206}.............. S_{400}			

Source	df	MS
Between dyads		
A	1	1285.22
D/A	198	42.52
Within dyads		
S/D/A	200	12.99
Total	399	

of variation. There is variation due to the independent variable—age in this example, which is denoted as Factor A in the table. Older girls may differ from younger girls in their levels of disordered eating behaviors and attitudes. Second, there may be variation from dyad to dyad within the same age group such that some dyads experience more disordered eating behaviors and attitudes than do other dyads. This factor is represented as D/A, or dyads nested within age. Finally, within a dyad one member may experience more disordered eating than the other member of the dyad, and this effect is $S/D/A$, or participants nested within dyads within age (where S stands for participants).

In Chapter 2 we discussed how the intraclass correlation can be estimated for dyadic data, and we gave an equation for the intraclass correlation where there are no independent variables (see Equation 2.1). That solution simply estimated the degree to which scores within dyads are especially similar (or dissimilar) to one another relative to the variation of scores between dyads. A partial intraclass correlation can be estimated such that it controls for the effect of the between-dyads independent variable. It is important to control for the effects of the independent variable when assessing nonindependence because, if the independent variable had a large effect, then scores would tend to be more variable between dyads than within dyads, regardless of whether there actually is interdependence within the dyads. The formula for estimating and testing the intraclass correlation that removes the effect of the between-dyads independent variable is

$$r_I = \frac{MS_{D/A} - MS_{S/D/A}}{MS_{D/A} + MS_{S/D/A}},$$

where $MS_{D/A}$ takes on the role of MS_B, and $MS_{S/D/A}$ takes on the role of MS_W (see Equation 2.1 in Chapter 2). Using the mean square values for the example, the value of the partial intraclass for the disordered eating measure across twins is $r_I = (42.52 - 12.99)/(42.52 + 12.99) = .53$. If one wishes to avoid the ANOVA approach, the two mean squares can be computed as follows. First d_i and m_i are computed as

$$d_i = X_{1i} - X_{2i}$$

and

$$m_i = \frac{X_{1i} + X_{2i}}{2}.$$

We compute $MS_{D/A}$ by

$$MS_{D/A} = \frac{2\sum(m_i - M_C)^2}{n-1},$$

where M_C is the mean of the outcome variable for the level of the between-dyads variable (i.e., for the 11-year-old condition, M_C would be 5.29, and for the 17-year-old condition, M_C would be 8.88). We compute $MS_{S/D/A}$ by

$$MS_{S/D/A} = \frac{\sum d_i^2}{2n}.$$

To test this partial intraclass correlation for statistical significance, we compute $MS_{D/A}/MS_{S/D/A}$, which, under the null hypothesis, has an F distribution with $n - a$ degrees of freedom on the numerator, where a is the number of levels of the between-dyads variable, and n degrees of freedom on the denominator, where n is the number of dyads. In the example, the partial intraclass correlation has an $F(198, 200) = 3.27$, which is statistically significant ($p < .001$). As explained in Chapter 2, the test is two-tailed, and so if $MS_{D/A} < MS_{S/D/A}$, then the F test is $MS_{S/D/A}/MS_{D/A}$ with n and $n - a$ degrees of freedom.

The most appropriate test of the effect of the between-dyads independent variable, A, depends on the results of the test of the partial intraclass correlation. Following the recommendation of Myers (1979), if there is any indication of nonindependence, as evidenced by a statistically significant intraclass correlation using an alpha of .20, then dyad must be treated as the unit of analysis. (The reason for the liberal test of the intraclass correlation was discussed in Chapter 2 and is reviewed later in this chapter.) The test of A, treating dyad as the unit, is accomplished by treating the $MS_{D/A}$ as the error term to test the A effect. For the example in Table 3.1, this would result in an $F(1, 198) = 1285.22/42.52 = 30.23$, $p < .001$.

The analysis that uses $MS_{D/A}$ as the error term is exactly equivalent to doing an analysis on the dyad means (or sums). That is, an equivalent strategy would be to average (or sum) the two dyad members' scores and then do an ANOVA treating the dyad averages as the outcome scores to see whether there is an effect of the between-dyads variable, A.

If an estimate of the effect size for the independent variable is desired, d can be computed. The formula to compute d from a t-statistic is $2t/\sqrt{n}$, where n is the sample size.[1] However, in the dyadic case with a between-dyads independent variable and dyad as the unit of analysis, this simple translation between the inferential statistic (t or F) and d is not appropriate. Using the ANOVA approach that we have taken for the test of the A effect, translating F to an effect-size measure actually results in what we call d_D because it is based on the dyad means. Thus

$$d_D = \frac{2\sqrt{F}}{\sqrt{n}},$$

where n is the number of dyads. Because the standard effect size measure, d, typically refers to independent units, the value d_D needs to be adjusted for the fact that the F or t value was based on dyad means rather than individual scores. The adjustment to compute d from d_D is

$$d = d_D \sqrt{\frac{1+r_I}{2}},$$

where r_I is the intraclass correlation between dyad members' outcome scores (Barcikowski, 1981). For the example, we obtain an $F(1, 198) = 30.23$, so the $d_D = 0.778$ and the corrected d is 0.680. Typically, the value of d is smaller than d_D. The exception to this case occurs when the intraclass correlation is negative.

To determine power before conducting a study, we ordinarily start with d or r for individuals. Because analyses are done at the level of the dyad, we must then multiply[2] that value by $\sqrt{2/(1+r_I)}$ and use n, the number of dyads, as the sample size. Thus, in doing a power analysis, the researcher must specify an effect size (d or r) and the degree of nonindependence (r_I).

Consider now the case in which there is no evidence of nonindependence (i.e., the test of the partial intraclass correlation is not statistically significant, $p > .20$). In this context dyad can be ignored, and person can be treated as the unit of analysis. To treat person as the unit, the *D/A* and *S/D/A* sums of squares and degrees of freedom can be combined to obtain a pooled error term that is denoted as the $MS_{S/A}$:

$$MS_{S/A} = \frac{SS_{D/A} + SS_{S/D/A}}{df_{D/A} + df_{S/D/A}},$$

for which the degrees of freedom are $df_{D/A}$ + $df_{S/D/A}$. Pooling these two sources of error variation into a $MS_{S/A}$ is equivalent to reestimating the ANOVA and dropping dyad from the model altogether. This would leave the traditional one-way ANOVA model with only two sources of variation, *A* and *S/A*. Clearly this analysis would be entirely inappropriate for the example data set.

Thus we are faced with the alternatives of either using dyad as the unit of analysis or using person as the unit of analysis, and the choice hinges on the test of the intraclass correlation. However, for this strategy to be viable, the test of the intraclass correlation must have sufficient power. Therefore, a key issue that should be considered when adopting this approach is the level of power of the test for the intraclass correlation.

In Chapter 2 we defined the concept of consequential nonindependence (Kenny et al., 1998), which is a term that can be applied in situations in which there are potentially nonindependent data but in which individual is treated as the unit of analysis. *Consequential nonindependence* is the level of nonindependence that would have to be present to result in the probability of committing a Type I error (i.e., alpha) being .10 when it was thought to be .05. The value for consequential nonindependence for dyads and a between-dyads independent variable is about .45 (the exact value depends on the number of dyads in the study). So a correlation of about .45 between dyad members' scores would result in the probability of making a Type I error of .10 if individual were the unit of analysis.

The key question, then, is how many dyads are needed so that we have enough power (i.e., power of at least .80) to detect consequential nonindependence. If we assume a two-tailed test of nonindependence and an alpha of .05, we would need to have at least 44 dyads. However, it is conventionally recommended (e.g., Myers, 1979) that the test for nonindependence should be quite liberal, with an alpha of .20. Using this value, the number of dyads needed to test for consequential nonindependence with a power of .80 is 28. Thus we recommend having a minimum of 25 dyads and adopting a liberal test value for alpha in the test of nonindependence. If there are fewer than 25 dyads (fortunately, something that rarely happens according to our survey of the published literature), our analysis suggests that researchers should simply assume that there is nonindependence and make dyad the unit even if the statistical test of the degree of nonindependence is not statistically significant.

A second question concerning power must now be addressed: What are the ramifications for the power of the test of the independent variable when dyad rather than person is used as the unit of analysis? Kenny and colleagues (1998) have studied this question, and we report here their conclusions. To facilitate this discussion, we compare two different designs. In the first, we simply have a sample of 100 independent individuals (50 in each treatment group), and in the second, we have a sample of 50 dyads from which we obtain data from both dyad members, resulting in a reciprocal design with 100 individuals. The dyadic study contains 25 dyads in each treatment group (i.e., the treatment variable is between dyads), and dyad is treated as the unit of analysis.

Table 3.2 presents the power for these two different designs as a function of the effect size, d, and the intraclass correlation, r_I. Note that the effect size measure presented in Table 3.2 for the dyadic design (as well as the independent-individuals design) is d and not d_D. Thus we have already made the adjustment to d to account for the fact that dyad was the unit of analysis. The key comparisons in the table involve contrasting power values for the independent-units design and the power values for the dyadic design for differing values of nonindependence. For example, the power to detect an effect size of $d = .5$ is .70 for the independent-individuals design.

TABLE 3.2. The Power (Times 100) of Using Dyad, Not Person, as the Unit of Analysis with 100 Persons and Two Treatment Groups

| | Independent individuals (n = 100) | Reciprocal dyadic design (50 dyads) intraclass correlation | | | | | | | | | |
d	n/a	−.35	−.25	−.15	−.05	.00	.05	.15	.25	.35	.45
.1	7	9	8	8	7	7	7	7	6	6	6
.2	17	23	20	18	17	16	15	14	14	13	13
.3	32	44	40	36	32	31	30	28	26	24	23
.4	51	68	62	57	52	50	48	45	42	39	37
.5	70	86	81	76	71	69	66	62	59	56	53
.6	84	95	92	89	86	84	82	78	75	72	68
.7	93	99	98	96	94	93	92	89	87	84	81
.8	98	99	99	99	98	97	97	96	94	92	90
.9	99	99	99	99	99	99	99	98	98	97	96

For the same effect size, and an intraclass correlation of $r_I = .25$, treating dyad as the unit of analysis in the dyadic design results in power of .59.

There are two striking results in the table. First, we see that when the intraclass correlation is zero or very small, there is relatively little loss of power in making dyad the unit of analysis. Despite the fact that the degrees of freedom are cut in half for the dyadic design ($df = 48$) relative to the individual design ($df = 98$), the power declines only slightly. The smaller number of degrees of freedom is almost entirely compensated for by the increase in the effect size that occurs when dyad means are studied (i.e., d_D rather than d). Second, as the intraclass correlation increases, the loss of power becomes more marked. The reason for this becomes fairly obvious when we consider what would happen if r_I were 1. An intraclass of 1 implies that there is nothing gained by sampling both members of the dyad, because the two scores are totally redundant with one another.

In summary, we suggest that researchers begin their analyses by assessing the degree of nonindependence, controlling for the effects of the independent variable. If the sample size permits ($n > 25$), the measure of nonindependence should also be tested for statistical significance; if it is significant, using a liberal alpha of .20, then dyad should be treated as the unit of analysis in subsequent analyses that examine the effects of the independent variable. If the sample size is too small to provide adequate power in the test of nonindependence, we again recommend treating dyad as the unit of analysis in subsequent analyses. In our view, person should be treated as the unit of analysis only in those instances in which a powerful test shows no evidence of nonindependence.

Multiple Between-Dyads Independent Variables

The general data-analysis strategy for multiple between-dyads independent variables is essentially the same as that for a single between-dyads independent variable. All of the between-dyads variables and their interactions are included as predictor variables in the model. For example, say that in our study of twins we have two between-dyads independent variables: age and zygosity. Our ANOVA model would include the effect of age, or the A effect; the effect of zygosity, or the B effect; the interaction between age and zygosity, or the $A \times B$ interaction; the effect of dyads nested within the interaction, or D/AB; and the effect of persons nested within dyads within the interaction, or $S/D/AB$.

We begin the analysis by estimating and testing the partial intraclass correlation. The partial intraclass can be computed from the ANOVA mean squares ($MS_{D/AB}$ substitutes for $MS_{D/A}$, and $MS_{S/D/AB}$ substitutes for $MS_{S/D/A}$) or from the formulas that we gave in the prior section (M_C would then refer to the cell means). Assuming that we have at least 25 dyads, we test the intraclass using the liberal alpha of .20. If it were not significant, we would use person as the unit of analysis. This is accomplished either by dropping dyad from the model and reestimating the ANOVA or by pooling the dyad and person components of the model. If the intraclass were statistically significant, we would use dyad as the unit of analysis. This could be done by treating the $MS_{D/AB}$ as the error term when testing the effects of A, B, and A × B. Alternatively, the sum or average of the two dyad members' outcome scores could be computed to form a dyad-level score, and this score could be treated as the outcome variable in an ANOVA in which the sample size is the number of dyads.

One Within-Dyads Independent Variable

Before we begin with the specifics of the case in which there is one within-dyads independent variable, it is useful to introduce a second example data set. Simpson, Rholes, and Nelligan (1992) conducted a study involving 83 heterosexual dating couples. At the beginning of the experimental session, both members of each couple independently completed a series of personality and relationship questionnaires (e.g., extroversion, attachment, love, commitment, self-disclosure). After completing the questionnaires, the female partner was confronted with an anxiety-provoking situation. The dating couples were then unobtrusively videotaped while waiting for the anxiety-provoking activity to begin, and the videotapes were coded on several behavioral dimensions. Some behaviors were coded separately for the men and women (e.g., criticism, hostility, support giving), and others were coded for the couple as a whole (e.g., synchrony).

A within-dyads independent variable is one that varies from person to person within a dyad, but the dyad average is the same across all dyads. The number of levels of a categorical within-dyads independent variable is limited to two by necessity, and examples include gender in heterosexual couples, relative age of child in nontwin sibling dyads, or relative proximity to the nest in a pair of fighting blackbirds (Roberts & Searcy, 1988). Note that when there is a dichotomous within-dyads variable, dyad members are distinguishable by definition because they can be distinguished by the levels of that variable. As our first example in this section, we consider the effect of gender on the degree of love felt by participants in the Simpson and colleagues (1992) study.

Dyadic data involving within-dyads independent variables fit well within the framework of traditional repeated-measures designs. Whereas in a traditional repeated-measures design the same person is measured at two (or more) times, with dyads the same dyad is measured twice, once for each member. Thus statistics developed to analyze repeated-measures data can be used for dyads.

Recall first that a one-way repeated-measures ANOVA design is really a two-way ANOVA in that participants (S) are crossed with the levels of the independent variable (A) such that every person participates in every level of A. This gives rise to three sources of variance: the A effect, the S effect, and the $A \times S$ interaction. The A effect measures the average effect of the independent variable, the S effect measures the variation in individual differences, and the $A \times S$ interaction measures the degree to which the A effect differs from person to person and is generally treated as the error term when testing the A effect.

Now consider the application of this design to dyads. As shown in Table 3.3, there are three sources of variation in a design involving a within-dyads independent variable. The first source of variation is the dyad main effect (D), which measures whether there are average differences between dyads on the outcome variable, amount of love reported by couples. The next source of variation is the effect of the within-dyads independent variable (A), which is typically the effect of most interest in the study. In this example the independent variable is gender, and so the A effect measures the difference between men's and women's reports of feeling love in their present dating relationship. In addition, there is an interaction between gender and dyad ($A \times D$). This interaction assesses the degree to which the gender effect varies from dyad to dyad.

TABLE 3.3. Analysis of Variance Table for a Within-Dyads Factor (A) from Simpson et al. (1992) with 83 Dyads (D) and 166 Persons (S)

D_1		D_2		D_3		. . . .	D_{83}	
A_1	A_2	A_1	A_2	A_1	A_2	. . . .	A_1	A_2
S_1	S_2	S_3	S_4	S_5	S_6	. . . .	S_{165}	S_{166}

Source	df	SS	MS
A	1	2.41	2.41
D	82	245.49	2.99
$A \times D$	82	59.29	0.72
Total	165	307.19	

Note: A, gender; D, dyad; S, participant.

Assessing nonindependence in dyadic designs that contain a within-dyads independent variable while controlling for the effect of this independent variable can be accomplished in one of two ways. The simplest way is to compute the simple Pearson product–moment correlation coefficient. So one would correlate the man's score with the woman's score. For the example data, the correlation between the man's score on the measure of love and the woman's score on the same measure is $r(81) = .61$, $t(81) = 6.95$, $p < .001$. Note that this approach does not assume equal variance in outcome scores for men and women.

Alternatively, if one is willing to assume that the variance for the two levels of the within-dyads variable is the same (the test for which is described in Chapter 6), a partial intraclass correlation can be computed as

$$r_I = \frac{MS_D - MS_{A \times D}}{MS_D + MS_{A \times D}}.$$

For the example, this value would be $r_I = (2.993 - 0.723)/(2.993 + 0.723) = .61$. So if the man is in love, so is the woman. (In this example the intraclass and the Pearson r's happen to have the same value, .61, but this equivalence does not always hold.) To test this partial intraclass correlation for statistical significance, we compute $MS_D/MS_{A \times D}$, which under the null hypothesis has an F distribution with $n - 1$ degrees of freedom on the numerator and $n - 1$ degrees of freedom on the denominator, where n is the number of dyads. For the example, the partial intraclass correlation is statistically significant, $F(82, 82) = 2.993/0.723 = 4.14$, $p < .001$. As explained in Chapter 2, the test is two-tailed, and so if $MS_D < MS_{A \times D}$, then the F-test would be $MS_{A \times D}/MS_D$, again with $n - 1$ and $n - 1$ degrees of freedom.

As with the between-dyads design, in the within-dyads design we can use either person or dyad as the unit of analysis when testing the effects of the independent variable. For the example, the mean score on the measure of love for men is $M = 7.03$, $SD = 1.36$, and for women the mean is $M = 7.27$, $SD = 1.37$, and the question at hand is whether these two means are statistically different. If the data were nonindependent, we would use dyad as the unit of analysis in answering this question, and there are several strategies that can be taken to accomplish this.

One way of treating dyad as the unit is the earlier described repeated-measures ANOVA that treats the dyad member as the repeated factor. Using the ANOVA summary results from Table 3.3, this would result in an $F(1, 82) = 2.41/0.72 = 3.33$, $p = .07$, indicating a marginally significant difference between the means for men and women. Women report higher levels of love than do men. Alternatively, we could conduct a paired t-test with dyad as the unit and find $t(82) = 1.83$, $p = .07$. Finally, and equivalently, we could create a difference score, for example, subtracting the man's score from the woman's score, and then use a t-test to evaluate the null hypothesis that mean of the difference scores is zero. The t value that results is $t(82) = 1.83$, $p = .07$. Each of these analyses would require that the data set be structured such that dyad is the unit (see Chapter 1). Whether we conduct a repeated-measures ANOVA, a paired t-test, or the analysis of difference scores, we get the same result and the same p value.

As was the case for between-dyads independent variables, when computing the effect size from an analysis of a within-dyads variable with dyad as the unit of analysis, the standard effect size formula must be adjusted. As before, this adjustment is a function of the intraclass correlation. Following Cohen (1988), we can compute the unadjusted value, or d_D, as

$$d_D = \frac{2t}{\sqrt{n}},$$

where n is the number of dyads. The adjustment to compute d from d_D is

$$d = d_D \sqrt{1 - r_I}.$$

So for the example, we would obtain an uncorrected effect size of 0.284, which, when adjusted, yields the value of 0.177.

An alternative procedure is to compute the effect size directly. For d, we compute $(M_1 - M_2)/s$, where s is the pooled standard deviation for the two members. That is,

$$s = \sqrt{\frac{(s_1^2 + s_2^2)}{2}},$$

where 1 and 2 refer to the two levels of the within-dyads independent variable. So for the example, s equals $\sqrt{(1.36^2 + 1.37^2)/2}$, or 1.365, and the value of d equals $(7.27 - 7.03)/1.365$, or 0.176. Note that the two procedures yield slightly different answers. Dunlop, Cortina, Vaslow, and Burke (1996) suggest that although both strategies are reasonable, the approach that makes an adjustment based on the intraclass correlation is slightly more accurate than the direct estimation approach.

To determine power for a within-dyads variable, we usually start with an effect size measure for individuals, what we have called d. Because the analysis is of dyads, we must adjust d to determine what we have called d_D

by dividing that measure by $\sqrt{1-r_1}$. We then compute power, where the sample size refers to the number of dyads in the study.

If there is independence between the dyad members' outcome scores after controlling for the independent variable, person can be used as the unit of analysis. Each individual would have a unique score on the independent variable, and each individual would have a score on the dependent variable, and t-tests, F-tests, or regressions could be computed across the individuals.

If nonindependence is at all plausible (i.e., even when the test of nonindependence is nonsignificant but theory suggests that the dyad members' scores could be related), we think using dyad as the unit of analysis provides the best test of within-dyads independent variables, because with positive nonindependence power is almost always increased by using dyad as the unit of analysis. For example, had we (mistakenly) used individual as the unit of analysis in our example and employed an independent-groups t-test to compare men's and women's love scores, the t-test results would have been $t(164) = 1.14$, $p = .26$. That is, unlike the between-dyads case, typically a gain in power results from using dyad as the unit of analysis because average variation from dyad to dyad (i.e., variation due to the D effect) is removed from the error term used to test the effect of the independent variable. However, in those relatively rare instances in which the nonindependence is negative, treating person as the unit of analysis and ignoring the nonindependence would result in an overly liberal test, as was shown in Table 2.5. So typically, by making dyad the unit of analysis for within-dyad variables, we decrease Type II errors for positive nonindependence, and we decrease Type I errors for negative nonindependence.

Multiple Within-Dyads Variables

Consider the study conducted by Badr (2003) in which she had two different within-dyads independent variables: gender (the participants were heterosexual couples) and illness (one member of the couple had a serious illness and the other did not). One outcome variable Badr examined was the mental health of each of the members of the couple. Although it is simple to examine whether men or women are mentally healthier or, in a separate analysis, whether the ill partner or the physically healthy partner is mentally healthier, an analysis that can simultaneously examine the two variables is less obvious. That is, an interesting question might be whether gender and illness interact such that the effect of illness differs depending on whether it is the man or the woman who is ill.

To examine simultaneously the effects of two within-dyads independent variables, one of the two variables is treated as a within-dyads or repeated-measure independent variable, but the other variable is not. Instead, a new variable, which we call Z, is created that represents the interaction between the two within-dyads variables, and this new variable varies between dyads rather than within dyads. For the Badr (2003) example, Z has two levels, one in which the ill member of the couple is the woman and the other in which the ill member is the man. Once the Z variable has been created, a mixed-model ANOVA can be conducted with dyad as the unit of analysis. The within-dyads variable, gender in the example, is treated as a repeated measure, and the Z variable is treated as a between-dyads factor. This analysis produces three effects: the gender effect, the Z effect, and the gender-by-Z interaction. Obviously, the gender effect measures whether men or women are mentally healthier in general. Less apparently, the gender-by-Z interaction measures the main effect of illness, or whether the ill person or the healthy person is mentally healthier in general. Finally, as mentioned, the Z effect measures the interaction between gender and illness, or whether people are mentally healthier in couples in which the male partner is ill versus those in which the female partner is ill.[3]

The strategy can be generalized to a third within-dyads variable, but it is somewhat awkward. Say that we add a third within-dyads variable to Badr's (2003) study—breadwinner (assuming that only one of the two dyad members is employed in each couple). So we now have gender, illness, and breadwinner all as within-dyads independent variables. Again we designate gender as the repeated measure. We then create two new variables, Z_1 and Z_2. The variable Z_1 differentiates between couples in which the ill member is the man and those in which the ill member is the woman. The variable Z_2 differentiates between couples for whom the breadwinner is the man and couples for whom the breadwinner is the woman.

The analysis would again be a mixed-model ANOVA, with dyad as the unit of analysis and treating gender as a repeated measure. This time, however, there would be two between-dyads variables in the analysis, Z_1 and Z_2. The main effect of gender would obviously be readily available from this analysis. The main effect of illness would be tested by the gender-by-Z_1 interaction, and the main effect of breadwinner would be tested by the gender-by-Z_2 interaction. The gender-by-illness interaction would be the

Z_1 effect, the gender-by-breadwinner interaction would be the Z_2 effect, and the illness-by-breadwinner interaction would be the Z_1 by Z_2 interaction. Finally, the three-way interaction, gender-by-illness by breadwinner, would be the interaction between gender, Z_1, and Z_2, or the effect of Z_1 times Z_2 on the difference in outcome scores.

One Between-Dyads and One Within-Dyads Variable

To illustrate this data-analytic situation, we return to the Simpson and colleagues (1992) study. Recall that in this study heterosexual dating couples were videotaped while interacting after the woman had experienced a stressful situation. Although no categorical between-dyads variables were included in this study, we can create one based on the length of time the couples had been dating. We define our between-dyads variable, length, to equal 1 if the couple has dated longer than 12 months ($n = 48$) and -1 if the couple has dated less than 12 months ($n = 35$). (Although it would be better statistically to treat length as a continuous variable, for pedagogical reasons, we make it categorical.) As before, we consider gender as our within-dyads independent variable. The outcome variable that we examine is the amount of negative behavior expressed during the videotaped interactions.

The degree of nonindependence can be assessed using a partial correlation, partialing out the effects of the between-dyads variable. So for the example we would correlate the man's amount of negative behavior with the woman's amount of negative behavior and partial out the length variable. In our example, this partial correlation is $r(80) = .52, p < .001$. As was the case in the analysis of a single within-dyads variable, for reasons of power we recommend that nonindependence be presumed to exist if it is plausible, even if it is not statistically significant in a specific instance.

The tests of the effects of gender, length, and their interaction can be conducted within the context of a mixed-model ANOVA treating dyad as the unit of analysis. Gender is treated as a repeated-measures factor, whereas length is treated as a between-dyads factor. The means, standard deviations, and ANOVA summary table for the example are shown in Table 3.4. As can be seen in this table, although there is no main effect of length, there is a gender main effect, as well as an interaction between length and gender. The gender main effect indicates that men exhibited more negative behavior overall than did women. The interaction indicates that although there was not much difference in negativity between men and women for

TABLE 3.4. Analysis of One Within-Dyads and One Between-Dyads Independent Variable: The Effects of Gender and Length of Relationship on Negative Behavior (Simpson et al., 1992)

	Length of relationship			
	Less than 1 year		More than 1 year	
	Men	Women	Men	Women
M	3.16	3.07	3.52	2.95
SD	0.77	0.73	1.00	0.64

ANOVA summary

Source	df	MS	F
Length	1	0.60	0.62
Dyads/Length	81	0.97	
Gender	1	4.51	13.97
Gender × Length	1	2.34	7.23
Gender × Dyad/Length	81	0.32	

partners who had not been dating for a long time (i.e., less than a year), for those who had been dating longer than a year, the men's behavior tended to be substantially more negative than the women's.

These tests could be also be conducted by treating the sum and the difference of the dyad members' outcome scores as dependent variables in two separate regression analyses. The difference would be computed by subtracting one level of the within-dyads factor from the other level. That is, the man's negative behavior score could be subtracted from the woman's negative behavior score. The sum would be computed by simply adding the two negative behavior scores together. The between-dyads variable, effect coded, would be used to predict the sum and the difference. Thus the variable of length would first be used to predict the difference, and the test of the grand mean from this analysis (i.e., the intercept, assuming effect coding of the between-dyads variable) evaluates the main effect of the within-dyads variable, gender in this example. The effect of length on the difference score (i.e., the regression coefficient) evaluates the interaction of the between- and within-dyads variables—whether the difference in the amount of negative behavior for men and women differs depending on how long they have dated. When length is used to predict the sum of the negative behavior scores, the effect of length on the sum evaluates the main effect of length.

General Case

In this section we assume that at least one within-dyads independent variable and one between-dyads independent variable are to be included in the analysis. The analysis can be conducted either by mixed-model ANOVA or by predicting the dyad sum and difference.

For the ANOVA approach, one of the within-dyads independent variables is chosen as the repeated-measures factor. A Z variable is then created to represent the interaction between the repeated-measures factor and each additional within-dyads variable to be included. Recall that these Z variables would be between-dyads variables. Additionally, the between-dyads independent variables and their interactions would be added to the model. All of the relevant effects and their interactions can be estimated and tested.

Alternatively, the sum and the difference of the two dyad members' outcome scores can be computed for each dyad, and these can be treated as the dependent variables in two regression analyses. As we have discussed, one of the within-dyads variables is used to determine the direction of the differences (e.g., if the within variable is gender, the difference might be male minus female). Both regression analyses would have as potential predictors:

> Between-dyads variables
> Interactions of between-dyads variables
> Z variables
> Interactions of Z variables with each other
> Interactions of the between-dyads and Z variables

The results of the regression predicting the dyad sum are interpreted directly, whereas the results of the regressions predicting the dyad difference are interpreted as interactions between the within-dyads factor used to create the differences and the effects in the regression model. The grand mean of the difference score (i.e., the intercept, assuming effect coding of the within-dyads factor) is used to index the main effect of that within-dyads factor.

There are some general rules for understanding whether an interaction is either between- or within-dyads. First, if both variables in the interaction are between dyads, then their interaction is also between dyads. Second, if both variables are within dyads, their interaction is between dyads. Finally, if one is between and the other is within, their interaction is within dyads. These rules can be used for complex interactions. For a three-way interaction of two between effects and one within, the interaction would be within dyads, because at least one of the variables is between dyads and one is within dyads.

In the next chapter, we discuss multilevel analysis of dyadic data for the standard dyadic design. Although a multilevel analysis could be conducted for the data described in this chapter, we do not present a multilevel analysis in this chapter because such an analysis yields essentially the same results as those that would be obtained had we done the analysis as we suggested. So very often nothing is gained by conducting a multilevel analysis in these cases. In fact, the significance tests that we discuss in this chapter are exact, whereas in a multilevel analysis some tests of significance are approximate. So in some sense the ANOVA and regression analyses are better than multilevel analyses.

There is, however, one particular case in which multilevel analysis is more advantageous than ANOVA and regression analyses. If there were randomly missing data from some dyads such that we have data from only one of the two members of the dyad, then a multilevel analysis can analyze all the data, not just the data from dyads in which both members are measured. Moreover, those familiar with multilevel analysis might find that analysis to be somewhat simpler than some of the strategies presented in this chapter. The details of multilevel analysis of dyadic data are presented in the next chapter and in Chapter 7.

INTERVAL OUTCOME MEASURES AND INTERVAL INDEPENDENT VARIABLES

In the previous section, all of the independent variables were categorical. In this section, we consider independent variables that are measured at the interval level of measurement. As before, we first describe the analysis of a single between-dyads independent variable, then turn to the analysis of a within-dyads independent variable, and conclude with the general case in which both types of variables are included. A discussion of the analysis of mixed independent variables is deferred until Chapter 7.

Between-Dyads Independent Variable

Returning to the Klump and colleagues (2000) twin study investigating eating disorders, these researchers also collected information concerning the twins' mothers' eating behavior. Thus we can treat the mothers' eating behavior, specifically the amount of binge eating that they report, as an interval-level between-dyads predictor variable. The question under consideration is the degree to which the mothers' bingeing behavior predicts the total level of disordered eating on the part of their twin daughters.

A regression analysis predicting the sum of the twins' total disordered eating scores with the mothers' binge score can be used to address this question. Thus we first compute the average (or sum) of the twins' total disordered eating scores. We then regress the average (or sum) on the independent variable using dyad as the unit of analysis. As is generally the case, we should make sure that zero is a meaningful value for the independent variable, and, if it is not, we should center the variable by subtracting the mean of the variable from every score. The effective n in such an analysis is the number of dyads. For the Klump and colleagues (2000) example, this regression results in an intercept of $b_0 = 6.55$, indicating that a mother who reports no binging herself would be predicted to have daughters who have disordered eating scores of 6.55. The regression slope from the regression equation is $b = 0.34$, $t(198) = 1.72$, $p = .09$, indicating a marginally significant tendency for girls whose mothers binge more to have more disordered eating patterns (or, for each 1-point increase on the part of the mother, the girls' predicted disordered eating score increases by 0.34 points).

We can determine the power of this test by first determining the theoretical value of r_D, the correlation of the independent variable with the average of the two dyad members' scores. An estimate of that correlation can be obtained from the t-test of the regression coefficient

$$r_D = \sqrt{t^2 / (t^2 + n - 2)},$$

where n is the number of dyads. This correlation needs to be adjusted by a function of the intraclass correlation to obtain the proper value of the effect size for individuals:

$$r = r_D \sqrt{\frac{1 + r_I}{2}}.$$

Thus the effect of mother's bingeing on child's disordered eating is estimated by an unadjusted correlation of .121. Correction of that value yields an r of .106, given an intraclass correlation of .53.

Within-Dyads Independent Variable

In this case, we have a single within-dyads independent variable that is measured at the interval level of measurement. For instance, we might be interested in the effect of the proportion of housework done by each roommate on the amount of conflict that occurs on a weekly basis. Our measure of the proportion of housework done by each roommate would sum to 1 for all dyads and so is a within-dyads variable (i.e., the mean for each dyad is .50).

To conduct the analysis, the difference between the two roommates' outcome scores (weekly conflict) would be regressed on the difference between the two roommates' scores on the independent variable (proportion of housework). The direction of differencing should be consistent for the predictor and outcome scores such that if Bob's housework score is subtracted from Jim's housework score, then Bob's conflict score should also be subtracted from Jim's conflict score.

The direction of differencing is arbitrary in the sense that we can either subtract Jim's score from Bob's or vice versa. Because of this arbitrariness of direction, the intercept should not be estimated in the regression. It is likely that most readers have never estimated a regression equation in which the intercept is not included, but it is a simple matter to do so. Most computer packages have a "no-intercept" option for multiple-regression analyses. For example, in SPSS, within "Linear Regression," the "Options" box is clicked, and then one deletes the check from the box "Include the constant in the equation." For SPSS univariate analysis of variance, one clicks "Model" and then deletes the check from "Include intercept in the model." SAS has the NOINT option in PROC GLM or PROC REG. Forcing the intercept to be zero ensures that the regression solution is the same even if the direction of differencing were switched for some dyads.

To understand better the use of "no-intercept" regression, consider the simple example in Table 3.5 with just five dyads. To simplify matters, we have a dichotomous within-dyads independent variable, gender, in married couples. Say that the outcome variable is a measure of satisfaction. In the table, we first compute the difference in the satisfaction scores by taking the husband's score minus the wife's score (Rule 1 in Table 3.5), and we run a t-test to see whether the mean difference is greater than zero. The mean difference score is -0.60, and the obtained t value equals -1.50 with 4 degrees of freedom. We now create a difference score for the predictor variable, gender, and use that difference score as a predictor variable in a

TABLE 3.5. Illustration of the Arbitrariness of the Direction of Differencing

| | Raw data | | | | Differences | | | |
| | Satisfaction | | Gender | | Rule 1: $S_1 - S_2$ for all | | Rule 2: $S_1 - S_2$ odd; $S_2 - S_1$ even | |
Dyad	S_1	S_2	S_1	S_2	Satisfaction	Gender	Satisfaction	Gender
1	2	3	1	−1	−1	2	−1	2
2	3	4	1	−1	−1	2	1	−2
3	4	5	1	−1	−1	2	−1	2
4	4	3	1	−1	1	2	−1	−2
5	3	4	1	−1	−1	2	−1	2

regression equation without an intercept, predicting the difference in satisfaction. Note that the difference score of the gender variable always equals 2.00. This regression results in a regression coefficient of $b = -0.30$, $t(4) = -1.50$. Note that the regression coefficient is half the size of the mean difference score because effect coding was used.

Now if we take husband minus wife for the odd-numbered dyads and wife minus husband for the even-numbered dyads (Rule 2 in Table 3.5), we obtain the same solution using a no-intercept model, but if we include the intercept in the model, the solution changes. That is, if we (wrongly) allow the intercept to be estimated, we get a model with an intercept of −0.50 and a regression slope of −0.25 when predicting the effects of gender on satisfaction. If, instead, we suppress the intercept, we again get the regression coefficient $b = -0.30$, $t(4) = -1.50$. Thus how the difference score is computed does not really matter, as long as the within-dyads independent variable is differenced in the same way and the intercept is not included in the equation. We invite readers to experiment with their own data to see that, by dropping the intercept from the model, we can difference in whatever direction and get the very same results.

To determine the effect size, we can compute r_D, which is $t/\sqrt{t^2 + df}$. We then need to use the intraclass correlation to adjust r_D to get an estimate of the effect size, r:

$$r = r_D \sqrt{1 - r_I}.$$

So for the simple example in Table 3.5, given that r_I equals .33, r_D would be .60, and the adjusted value of r would be .49.

General Case

At this point we have discussed the analysis of only a single interval-level between-dyads or within-dyads independent variable. The extension to the general case for interval-level predictor variables becomes rather complex, and, in the interest of clarity, we defer a complete discussion of this topic until Chapter 7.

CATEGORICAL OUTCOME VARIABLES

Throughout this chapter, our discussion has focused on the analysis of outcome variables measured at the interval level of measurement. In this section, we consider ways to analyze categorical outcome variables, but we limit ourselves to dichotomous outcomes.

Within-Dyads Independent Variable

When we have a dichotomous within-dyads independent variable and a dichotomous outcome variable, a McNemar test can be used to test the effects of the independent variable. Returning to the Simpson and colleagues (1992) data, we can examine the effects of gender on happiness with the relationship. Specifically, we can test whether men or women are more likely to express being "extremely happy" with their relationships. Note that for the purposes of this example we refer to happiness scores that are lower than *extremely happy* as simply *unhappy*, so that happiness becomes a dichotomy.

In this test, we examine only couples in which the two individuals disagree on their level of happiness. Thus couples who agree in their happiness ($n = 26$ in the Simpson et al. data) or unhappiness ($n = 38$) are dropped from the analysis. Disagreement has two different types in some couples, the man is happy but the woman is not; in others, the woman is happy, but the man is not. We denote the number of couples in which the man is happy and the woman is not as a, and in the example $a = 6$. The number of couples in which the woman is happy and the man is not is referred to as b, and $b = 13$. If there were no gender differences in happiness, then the size of these two groups should be the same, and so $a = b$. For the McNemar test, we compute $(a - b)^2/(a + b)$, which under the null hypothesis of no difference is distributed as χ^2 with 1 degree of freedom. For the example, we find $\chi^2(1) = (6 - 13)^2/(6 + 13) = 2.58$, $p = .11$. We thus conclude that there is no gender difference in happiness.

Although it is not so obvious, the McNemar test treats dyad as the unit of analysis. Both *a* and *b* are dyad-level variables in that both persons are considered. The extension of the test to three or more categories is discussed in Chapter 6.

Between-Dyads Independent Variable

In this situation, we have a between-dyads independent variable and a dichotomous outcome variable. Returning to the Klump and colleagues (2000) eating disorder example data, we can examine the effects of cohort (11- vs. 17-year-olds) on whether or not the girls have ever binged. Thus, for the purposes of this example, the binge variable is simply 0 if the girl has never binged or 1 if she has binged at all. We then sum the two outcome scores across the dyad members to obtain a single variable for each dyad. In the example, this measure equals 0 if neither girl has ever binged; it would be 2 if they have both binged, and it would be 1 if one girl has binged but the other has not. Of the 11-year-olds, in 27 sets of twins neither girl had binged; in 44, only one girl had binged; and in 29, both had binged. For the 17-year-olds, these values were 11, 30, and 59, respectively.

We perform a Mann–Whitney U-test on this outcome measure. The Mann–Whitney U-test is a nonparametric alternative to an independent-groups t-test. It is nonparametric in the sense that it does not make the traditional homogeneity of variance or normality assumptions concerning the nature of the outcome scores. Moreover, the null hypothesis is that the medians, not the means, of the two groups are equal. The test simply rank orders the scores in the entire sample and then tests whether the average rank differs between two independent samples. For the example data, the mean rank for the 11-year-old cohort is 83.87, and for the 17-year-old cohort, this mean is 117.13. The value of U is 3337.0, $p < .001$. Thus, as would be expected, bingeing is more likely to have occurred in the older cohort.

SUMMARY AND CONCLUSIONS

In this chapter we examined the analysis of between- and within-dyads independent variables. We have seen that a variety of data-analytic techniques can be used to test the effects of these two types of independent variables. Generally speaking, the tests we have considered involve treating the dyad average on the outcome variable as the dependent variable for the analysis of between-dyads independent variables. When the independent variable is within dyads, however, the difference between dyad members' outcome scores serves as the dependent variable. We have emphasized the importance of measuring the degree of nonindependence in the outcome scores, and we have suggested that, when in doubt, researchers should assume that dyadic data are nonindependent. We have provided several data-analytic strategies that treat dyad as the unit of analysis to adjust for that nonindependence. For example, if the outcome is measured at the interval level of measurement, we can use standard ANOVA and regression methods. We also considered complications when there are multiple between- and within-dyads independent variables. Various nonparametric methods were discussed as tools to analyze outcomes that are measured at the nominal level of measurement. We have also provided methods to determine the effect size that can be used to interpret the results and plan for new studies through the computation of power.

Because dyadic researchers are often most interested in testing the effects of between- or within-dyads independent variables, this is perhaps the most useful chapter of the book. For instance, researchers are often interested in the difference between husbands and wives in heterosexual couples. This question, and questions like it, can be answered by the methods described in this chapter.

In Chapter 7, we consider data-analytic approaches for mixed independent variables. We shall see that such approaches are much more complicated than those described in this chapter, but again dyad is the unit of analysis. In Chapter 7 we present the general case that is able to simultaneously analyze between-dyads, within-dyads, and mixed predictor variables. We also consider strategies that allow for missing data. However, before we discuss these topics, we need to introduce two important data-analytic strategies. In Chapter 4, we discuss how multilevel modeling (MLM) can be used to study dyads, and in Chapter 5, we discuss how structural equation modeling (SEM) can be used.

NOTES

1. In some presentations, df or $n - 2$ is used instead of n. We prefer to use n, but using df instead is a reasonable alternative.

2. Note that the adjusted value of r could be greater than 1 in absolute value after multiplying by $\sqrt{2 / (1 + r_l)}$. If such were the case, the investigator has chosen much too optimistic a value of r and should lower that value.

3. The repeated-measures analysis can be conducted by using difference scores based on one of the two within-dyads independent variables. We feel that this difference-score approach is more awkward than the repeated-measures approach. For the example, we could base our difference scores on gender by always subtracting the wife's outcome score from the husband's outcome score. We again create our Z variable representing the interaction between the two within-dyads variables, making sure that we code the Z variable using effect coding, 1 and −1 for the two levels. Then we compute a regression analysis examining the effect of the Z variable on the difference score. The test of the grand mean of the difference scores (i.e., the intercept from the regression assuming that Z has been effect coded) gives the gender effect, and the test of the effect of Z on the difference (i.e., the test of the regression coefficient for Z) gives the illness-status effect. This analysis does not provide a direct test of the interaction between the two variables, however. To determine whether there is an interaction, the sum of rather than the difference between the two dyad members' outcome variable scores must be created, and that sum is then treated as the outcome variable in a regression analysis, with the Z variable serving as the predictor. The effect of Z on the sum of the outcome scores (i.e., the regression coefficient for Z) represents the interaction between the two within-dyads variables.

4

Using Multilevel Modeling to Study Dyads

Multilevel modeling (MLM), also commonly referred to as hierarchical linear modeling,[1] is a relatively new statistical technique that is particularly useful for the analysis of dyadic data. In fact, many of the analyses discussed in this book can be accomplished only by using MLM, and almost every chapter in the remainder of this book includes sections detailing such analyses. This chapter is intended to provide an introduction to multilevel models in general and then to describe specifically how they can be applied to dyadic data. There are many issues involved in MLM that we do not venture into in this brief chapter, and we urge the reader to consult more detailed treatments of this topic (Bryk & Raudenbush, 1992; Hox, 2002; Raudenbush & Bryk, 2002; Snijders & Bosker, 1999). Some of those more advanced issues are discussed in Chapters 10 and 13.

As the name suggests, in a multilevel data structure, there are multiple levels within the data. That is, there is a hierarchy of units, with one set of units nested[2] within another. There are two classic cases that generate multilevel data. In one case, persons are nested in groups; examples might be students nested within classrooms or workers nested within work groups. In the other case, known as a *repeated-measures study*, each person is observed several times, and observations are nested within persons. Experience sampling or daily diary studies generate this second type of multilevel data. In this chapter, we focus our attention on the multilevel case in which persons are nested within groups, because it has a direct application to the dyadic context: A dyad can be viewed as a group with two members.

Turning to the specifics of the multilevel data structure, a basic multilevel model contains two levels. First, there is the lower level, or level 1; for the case of persons nested within groups, the lower-level unit is person. Second, there is the upper level, or level 2, and for persons in groups, the upper-level unit is group. (In a repeated-measures context, the lower level is observation and the upper level is person.)

Variables can also be characterized by level. A level-1 variable is a variable for which a score is obtained for each lower-level unit; some examples are student achievement scores in a classroom study and momentary stress in a repeated-measures experience sampling study. The outcome measure is always a level-1 variable in MLM. Variables can also be measured for the upper-level units. In a classroom study, a measure of the teacher's experience or ability is an example of a level-2 variable. Another level-2 variable would be class size. In a repeated-measures study, a level-2 variable might be a score on a personality scale or the person's ethnicity. Note that the score on the level-2 variable is the same for all of the level-1 units nested within the level-2 unit.

In illustrating the basic model, it is helpful to consider a hypothetical study of the effectiveness of two teaching methods. This study involves 60 classrooms, each with 10 children, 5 boys and 5 girls. Thirty of the classrooms have teachers who use a new experimental teaching method; teachers in the other 30 classrooms use the standard teaching method. At the conclusion of the academic marking period, the amount learned is measured for each student. Thus the level-1 unit is student, and the level-2 unit is classroom. Two level-1 variables are measured: student learning, which is the outcome, and gender of the student. The level-2 variable is teaching method (experimental vs. standard). We denote the outcome (learning) as Y, the level-1 predictor variable (gender) as X, and the level-2 predictor variable (teaching method) as Z.

We first consider a conventional ANOVA of the classroom data set. We then explain how that same data set can be analyzed using MLM. Finally, we adapt MLM to the analysis of dyadic data.

MIXED-MODEL ANOVA

Using conventional ANOVA to analyze the data from the classroom study would result in a source table, as presented in Table 4.1. In the table, par-

TABLE 4.1. ANOVA Source Table and Corresponding Multilevel Parameters for the Group Data Example: The Effects of Gender and Teaching Method on Learning in Classrooms

Source	df	Error term	Multilevel parameter
Between groups	60		
Mean	1	G/Z	a_0
Condition (Z)	1	G/Z	a_1
Classroom (G/Z)	58	S/G/Z	σ_d^2
Children within groups	540		
Gender (X)	1	XG/Z	c_0
Gender by condition (XZ)	1	XG/Z	c_1
Gender by classroom (XG/Z)	58	S/XG/Z	σ_f^2
Error (S/XG/Z)	480		σ_e^2
Total	600		

Note. There are 600 children (300 boys and 300 girls), who are members of 60 classrooms.

ticipant gender is symbolized as X and experimental condition as Z; G represents classrooms or groups, and S represents participants. Presented in the table are the sources of variance, their degrees of freedom, and the error terms for the F-tests (the denominator of the F-ratio) that evaluate whether each effect differs significantly from zero. The MLM terms that correspond to each effect are presented in the last column of the table; these terms are introduced later in the chapter.

It is helpful to have an understanding of the different sources of variance. The between-group variation in Table 4.1 refers to the variation in the 60 classroom means, derived by averaging the students' learning scores over the 10 students within each classroom. This between-group variation can be partitioned into three sources: the grand mean, condition (Z), and classroom within condition (G/Z). The mean term represents how different the grand mean is from zero, which is a question not typically estimated or tested in traditional ANOVA. The condition variation measures the effect of the intervention—that is, the condition effect estimates the degree to which average learning scores are higher in classes that use the experimental teaching method relative to those that use the standard method. The third source of variation results from differences between classrooms that were in the same level of the treatment condition: Within the classrooms in which the teaching method was the same (either experimental or standard), were average learning scores higher in some classrooms than in others?

The children-within-groups variation refers to differences among children in each class: Do children within the same classroom differ in how much they learn? The gender effect (X) refers to whether boys or girls learn more on average, controlling for condition and classroom. The gender-by-condition interaction (XZ) refers to whether the effectiveness of the two teaching methods differs for boys or girls. The gender-by-classroom interaction (XG/Z) estimates the degree to which gender differences vary from classroom to classroom when controlling for condition. That is, the gender-by-classroom interaction assesses the degree to which the gender difference (i.e., the difference between the mean of the girls' scores minus the mean of the boys' scores) varies from group to group within the same treatment condition. Finally, there is variation due to child ($S/XG/Z$), and this source of variance measures variation in learning from child to child after controlling for gender, classroom, and condition.

Within this ANOVA model, there are three random effects: classroom (G/Z), gender × classroom (XG/Z), and error ($S/XG/Z$). The classroom variance, symbolized as σ_d^2, for reasons that will become clear, measures the variation in average learning from classroom to classroom after controlling for condition. The gender × classroom variance, symbolized as σ_f^2, measures the degree to which the gender difference in learning varies from classroom to classroom after controlling for condition. Denoting a as the number of levels of X ($a = 2$ in this example) and b as the number of students within one level of X ($b = 5$ in this example), the standard ANOVA estimates of these variances are given by

$$\text{classroom:} \quad \sigma_d^2 = \frac{MS_{G/Z} - MS_{S/XG/Z}}{ab}, \quad\quad (4.1)$$

$$\text{gender} \times \text{classroom:} \quad \sigma_f^2 = \frac{MS_{XG/Z} - MS_{S/XG/Z}}{b}. \quad\quad (4.2)$$

An exact estimate of the student variance cannot be obtained because it is confounded with error variance, and thus we represent the combination of student variance and error variance as σ_e^2. Finally, although it is not usually estimated, we can compute the covariance between classroom and gender × classroom by computing the covariance between the mean amount learned by the group minus the amount learned for condition and the mean difference in the amount learned by boys and girls in each classroom. Such a covariance would represent the tendency for groups that learn more to have larger (or smaller) gender differences. Although this covariance is rarely estimated within ANOVA, the method does permit such a covariance.

Table 4.1 also presents the usual mixed-model error terms for each of the sources of variance. Tests of the fixed between-groups sources of variance, both the grand mean and the condition main effects, are conducted treating the $MS_{G/Z}$ as the error term. To test whether there are classroom differences, $MS_{G/Z}$ is divided by $MS_{S/XG/Z}$. The error term for the fixed within-classroom effects, including the gender main effect and the gender-by-condition interaction, is $MS_{XG/Z}$. Finally, the error term for $MS_{XG/Z}$ is $MS_{S/XG/Z}$, which itself cannot be tested.

MULTILEVEL-MODEL EQUATIONS

Estimation in multilevel models can be thought of as a two-step procedure. In the first step, a separate regression equation, in which Y is treated as the criterion variable that is predicted by the set of X variables, is estimated for each upper-level unit. In our classroom example, this involves computing a separate regression equation for each classroom. In the formulas that follow, the term i represents the upper-level unit (classroom or group), and j represents the lower-level unit (student). In the example, the first-step regression equation for student j in classroom i is

$$Y_{ij} = b_{0i} + b_{1i}X_{ij} + e_{ij}, \tag{4.3}$$

where b_{0i} represents the average learning for classroom i, and b_{1i} represents the coefficient for the relationship between learning and gender in group i. Assuming that we have used effect coding for gender (i.e., one gender is coded as 1 and the other as -1), the slope and the intercept are interpreted as follows:

- b_{0i}: The average learning in classroom i across boys and girls.
- b_{1i}: The difference between girls' and boys' mean learning, divided by 2, for classroom i.

The second step of the analysis involves treating the slopes and intercepts from the first-step analyses as outcome variables in two regressions. For these second-step analyses, the regression coefficients from the first step (see equation 4.3) are assumed to be a function of a group-level predictor variable Z:

$$b_{0i} = a_0 + a_1 Z_i + d_i, \tag{4.4}$$

$$b_{1i} = c_0 + c_1 Z_i + f_i. \qquad (4.5)$$

There are two second-step regression equations, the first of which treats the first-step intercepts as a function of the Z variable and the second of which treats the first-step regression coefficients as a function of Z. So, in our example, the criterion variable in equation 4.4 is the average classroom learning, and it is modeled to be a function of the teaching method condition. The outcome variable in equation 4.5 is the gender difference in learning, and it is also modeled to be a function of the teaching method condition. In general, if there are p level-1 predictor variables (i.e., X variables) and q level-2 predictor variables (i.e., Z variables), and all possible fixed effects were estimated, there would be $p + 1$ second-step regressions, each with q predictors and an intercept. There are then a maximum total of $(p + 1)(q + 1)$ fixed-effect parameters in the set of second-step regressions.

Assuming that we have used effect coding for the teaching method condition variable (i.e., 1 = treated, -1 = control) and gender (1 = girl, -1 = boy), the parameters in equations 4.4 and 4.5 estimate the following effects:

- a_0: Grand mean for learning across all students and classrooms.
- a_1: Degree to which students in the experimental classrooms learned more than those in the control classrooms.
- c_0: Degree to which girls learned more than boys.
- c_1: Degree to which the effect of teaching method differs for boys and girls.

Table 4.2 presents a more general interpretation of these four parameters. For the intercepts (b_{0i}, a_0, and c_0) to be interpretable, both X and Z must be scaled so that either zero is meaningful or the grand mean of the variable is subtracted from each score (i.e., the X and Z variables are centered). As mentioned, in the example used here, X and Z (gender and experimental condition, respectively) are both effect-coded (-1, 1) categorical variables, and therefore zero can be thought of as an "average" across boys and girls and teaching method conditions.

In introducing MLM, we have thus far taken the sequential, two-step approach using two sets of equations, one set for level 1 and the other for level 2. An alternative approach is to combine all of the equations into a single equation. That combined equation can be obtained by substituting equations 4.4 and 4.5 directly into 4.3 to obtain

TABLE 4.2. Definition of Fixed Effects and Variance Components in the Multilevel Context

Effect estimate	Parameter	Definition of effect
Fixed effect		
Constant	a_0	Average response on Y for persons scoring 0 on both X and Z
Level-2 predictor (Z)	a_1	Effect of Z on the average response on Y
Level-1 predictor (X)	c_0	Effect of X on Y for groups scoring 0 on Z
Interaction (X by Z)	c_1	Effect of Z on the effect of X on Y
Variance		
Group	σ_d^2	Group variation in average Y, controlling for X and Z
X by Group	σ_f^2	Group variation in the effects of X on Y, controlling for Z
Error	σ_e^2	Within-group variation, controlling for X (includes error variance)

$$Y_{ij} = a_0 + a_1 Z_i + d_i + (c_0 + c_1 Z_i + f_i)X_{ij} + e_{ij},$$

and rearranging terms yields

$$Y_{ij} = (a_0 + d_i) + a_1 Z_i + (c_0 + f_i)X_{ij} + c_1 Z_i X_{ij} + e_{ij}. \qquad (4.6)$$

The combined equation is not as complex as it might first appear to be. The intercept in this equation involves two components—a_0, which is the fixed-effect piece that estimates the grand mean, and d_i, which is the random-effects piece that indicates that the intercept also varies from classroom to classroom. We then have the main effect of Z, teaching method, which is straightforward. Next we have the main effect of X, gender, which has an overall fixed-effect component, c_0, as well as a random effect, f_i, that varies from classroom to classroom. The last fixed effect is the gender-by-teaching-method interaction, or XZ. Finally, the last term in the model is error.

As was the case in the ANOVA discussion for balanced data, there are three random effects in multilevel models. First, there is the error component, e_{ij}, in the lower-level or first-step regressions (see equation 4.3 or 4.6). This error component represents variation in responses across the lower-level units after controlling for the effects of both the lower-level and upper-level predictor variables; its variance can be represented as σ_e^2.

In the example, this component represents variation in learning from student to student within classroom, controlling for both teaching method and gender.

There are also random effects in each of the two second-step regression equations. In equations 4.4 and 4.6, the random effect d_i represents variation in the intercepts that is not explained by Z. For the example, d_i represents variation in the classroom mean learning scores that is not explained by the teaching method variable. Note that d_i, in this context, is parallel to $MS_{G/Z}$ within the balanced repeated-measures ANOVA context, as shown in equation 4.1. The variance in d_i is a combination of σ_d^2, which was previously referred to as classroom variance, and σ_e^2. Finally, in equations 4.5 and 4.6, the random effect f_i represents the degree to which the size of the gender difference in learning varies from classroom to classroom. Note that f_i here is parallel to $MS_{XG/Z}$ within the ANOVA context, as shown in equation 4.2. The variance in f_i is a combination of σ_f^2, which was previously referred to as the gender-by-classroom variance, and σ_e^2. A more general description of these variances is given in Table 4.2.

The multilevel model, with its multistep regression approach, seems radically different from the ANOVA model. However, as we have pointed out, the seven parameters of this multilevel model correspond directly to the seven mean squares of the ANOVA model for balanced data. The multilevel approach has numerous advantages over ANOVA, including its ability to handle continuous, as well as categorical, predictor variables and its ability to handle unbalanced designs. Thus the multilevel model provides a more general and more flexible approach to analyzing multilevel data than that given by ANOVA.

MULTILEVEL MODELING WITH MAXIMUM LIKELIHOOD

The two-step regression approach to MLM involves the repeated estimation of regression equations for each upper-level unit. That is, for the example, we would compute 60 regression equations, one for each classroom. The estimates derived from these regression analyses are then pooled at the second stage of estimation via a regression analysis across the level-2 units. In the example, this involves aggregating the results across the classrooms by predicting the step-1 results as a function of the teaching method condition variable.

Although it is possible to do a simple (and perhaps simplistic) analysis in which the first-step coefficients (b_{0i} and b_{1i}) are literally the outcomes in an ordinary regression at level 2—a solution known as ordinary least squares, or OLS—there are reasons why this may not be the optimal solution. An OLS approach treats all of the first-step regression coefficients as if they were of equal quality without consideration of such important factors as the sample size for each group and the amount of variation in X for each group. The issue is that the regression coefficients for larger groups or groups for which there is greater variance in X are estimated with greater precision than are those estimated for smaller groups or groups with lower variance in X.

Our example was rather basic in the sense that neither of these factors varied across classrooms: Every classroom had 10 children, and the distribution of X, or gender, was identical for each group (i.e., there were 5 boys and 5 girls in each classroom). In this special case of a balanced design, there is no variation in the precision of the first-step regression coefficients from group to group. If the first-step coefficients do vary in precision, however, factoring the quality or precision of those estimates into the second-step regressions (i.e., equations 4.4 and 4.5) is an important element of MLM (Kenny et al., 1998).

One common estimation strategy used for MLM is maximum likelihood estimation. With maximum likelihood, the two stages of estimation are done simultaneously in one step, and the solution is weighted so that the precision of the coefficients (e.g., b_{0i}, b_{1i}) is taken into account. The maximum likelihood weights are a function of the standard errors and the variance of the term being estimated. For example, the weight given to a particular b_{0i} is a function of its standard error and the variance of d_i. Specialized stand-alone computer programs, such as HLM6 (Raudenbush, Bryk, Cheong, & Congdon, 2004), have been written that use maximum likelihood to derive estimates for multilevel data. Within major statistical packages, SAS's PROC MIXED and SPSS's Mixed Model can be used to estimate multilevel models.

It turns out that maximum likelihood estimation provides biased estimates of variances. For instance, the maximum likelihood estimate of an ordinary variance divides the sums of squares by N. We are more familiar with the unbiased estimator of the variance that uses $N-1$ in the denominator; such an estimate is called a restricted maximum likelihood estimate, or REML. Generally REML estimation is preferred over maximum likelihood, and REML is the default estimation method in most computer programs and packages.

With both maximum likelihood and REML, the log likelihood, denoted as L, is minimized. For a given model we can compute the model's deviance, or $-2L$. Although the deviance of a particular model cannot be readily interpreted, the deviances of two nested models can be compared. This comparison is different depending on whether maximum likelihood or REML is used. Consider, first, maximum likelihood and the example that we have been discussing, with eight parameters, four fixed effects, three variances, and one covariance (between slope and intercept). If we removed one of the parameters from the model (i.e., set it to zero), we can difference the deviances of the two models to obtain a value that is distributed as a χ^2 with 1 degree of freedom. For REML, the χ^2 difference can be used only if the fixed parameters in the two models are the same. For example, the deviance of a model that has two fixed parameters (e.g., intercept and gender of student) and a random component (e.g., the effect of gender is random and varies by classroom) can be compared with the deviance of a model without the random component only if the same fixed effects (intercept and gender) are in the reduced model. Thus, with REML, the χ^2 difference test can be used to compare changes in only the random portion of the model, whereas maximum likelihood can be used for changes in the fixed, random, or combinations of both.

Additionally, the computer program MLwiN uses generalized least squares (GLS) estimation and not maximum likelihood. However, the results using GLS and restricted GLS, or RGLS, closely parallel the results using maximum likelihood and REML. Also, if RGLS is chosen for estimation, the GLS value is given for the deviance value. So, for the program MLwiN, the deviances can be subtracted regardless of which estimation method is chosen.

For both maximum likelihood and REML, t-tests are given for the fixed effects. To obtain the proper degrees of freedom, the Satterthwaite approximation should be used (Kenny, Bolger, & Kashy, 2002). We explain this complex approximation in more detail in Chapter 7. We note here that both SAS and SPSS use the approximation; the computer program HLM gives approximate degrees of freedom. Finally, the program MLwiN does not provide any degrees of freedom, and tests of the coefficients must be computed by dividing each estimate by its standard error and using a Z table to obtain an approximate p value.

ADAPTATION OF MULTILEVEL MODELS TO DYADIC DATA

The adaptation from the person-within-group perspective to dyadic data is straightforward: Statistically, dyads can be viewed as groups composed of two persons. As with group data, with dyadic data the outcome variable, Y, is measured once for each person within the dyad, and so each dyad has two scores on *Y*. Similarly, there can be level-1 predictor variables, the *X* variables, as well as level-2 predictor variables, the *Z* variables.

As an example, consider the data from a hypothetical study of 10 cohabiting heterosexual couples in Table 4.3. We realize that the example does not include enough dyads for meaningful estimates and significance tests, but by using a small data set the reader can easily replicate our results. In this study, researchers wanted to examine whether the contribution a person made to the household (a composite score based on financial contributions, as well as household labor) was associated with that person's predictions for the relationship's future—specifically, the likelihood of marriage within the next 5 years, measured as a percentage. The researchers were also interested in the degree to which there is cultural variation in this association, and so some of the cohabiting couples were Asian and others were American. Note that both the sex and culture vari-

TABLE 4.3. Hypothetical Dyadic Data Set for a Study Predicting Likelihood of Marriage

Dyad	Person	Future	Gender	Contribution	Culture
1	1	75	−1	−10	1
1	2	90	1	−5	1
2	1	55	−1	0	1
2	2	75	1	10	1
3	1	45	−1	−10	1
3	2	33	1	−15	1
4	1	70	−1	5	1
4	2	75	1	15	1
5	1	50	−1	0	1
5	2	40	1	−5	1
6	1	85	−1	−10	−1
6	2	90	1	20	−1
7	1	75	−1	−5	−1
7	2	80	1	0	−1
8	1	90	−1	5	−1
8	2	68	1	0	−1
9	1	65	−1	0	−1
9	2	78	1	15	−1
10	1	88	−1	−15	−1
10	2	95	1	5	−1

Note. For gender, women = −1 and men = 1; and for culture, American = 1 and Asian = −1. Contribution is a composite score and has been centered about the sample mean. The variable Future is a prediction of the likelihood of marriage in the next 5 years.

ables have been effect coded $(1, -1)$ and that contribution has already been centered around its grand mean value for the entire sample so that interactions among the predictors can be readily interpreted.

With these data, we can specify a model that estimates several effects. We can estimate the grand mean for future predictions (a_0). If we restrict ourselves to a single X variable—contribution—then we can examine whether individuals who make greater contributions to their relationships have more positive predictions for the future (c_0). If we also include a Z variable—culture—we can test a main effect of whether predictions are more optimistic in one culture or the other (a_1). Finally, we can also estimate the interaction between X and Z to test whether the relationship between household contribution and predictions for the future differs across cultures (c_1). Thus we can estimate the same four fixed effects as in the more general multilevel model with groups.

Application of MLM to dyadic data requires one major restriction that need not be made for groups with more than two members. In the most general multilevel model, the coefficients from the first-stage analyses (intercepts and slopes) are allowed to vary from group to group, but with dyadic data the slopes (i.e., the effect of X on Y for each dyad) must be constrained to be equal across all dyads. In other words, we must constrain the model to include only a fixed effect with respect to the effect of X on Y—the random component, f_i, is omitted from the model. The reason is that dyads do not have enough lower-level units (i.e., dyad members) to allow the slopes to vary from dyad to dyad. However, the intercepts for the dyads can vary, and it is through the variation of intercepts that the nonindependence in the members' scores within dyads is modeled. Thus a dyadic model with one X variable and one Z variable has four fixed effects and two random effects (variation in the intercepts and error variance).

One might assume that being unable to estimate a model with different slopes for each dyad biases the estimates of the multilevel model for dyads. It does not. Rather, what it does is confound the variance of the slopes with error variance. Tests of the null hypothesis are not biased by having differential slopes.

As mentioned, PROC MIXED in SAS can be used to estimate multilevel models. Singer (1998) gives an excellent overview of how various multilevel models can be specified using this procedure. In this chapter, we focus solely on the problem posed by dyadic data. We initially provide the statements used by SAS. Later, we discuss the use of SPSS, HLM, and MLwiN. All multilevel programs presume that data set is an individual or pairwise data set. The SAS code to estimate the model in which CON-TRIBUTION and CULTURE predict likelihood of marriage or FUTURE is

```
PROC MIXED COVTEST;
CLASS DYAD;
MODEL FUTURE = CONTRIB CULTURE CONTRIB*CULTURE
    /SOLUTION DDFM=SATTERTH;
RANDOM INTERCEPT / SUBJECT = DYAD;
```

(Note that SAS requires a semicolon at the end of each statement and that the variable DYAD is a dyad identification number for which both partners have the same value.)

The default estimation method used by PROC MIXED is REML. If maximum likelihood estimation is desired, the optional statement METHOD = ML is added to the PROC MIXED line. The COVTEST option requests that Z tests of the random effects (e.g., the variance of the intercepts) be included in the output. The CLASS statement specifies the variable that identifies dyad membership (i.e., DYAD). FUTURE is the individual's outcome, or Y score; CONTRIB is the person's contribution score, or X; CULTURE is the person's Z score. Note that we have included the X-by-Z interaction in this model. The SOLUTION option in the MODEL statement requests that SAS print the estimates for the fixed effects: a_0, the intercept or grand mean; a_1, the effect of culture on future predictions; c_0, the effect of contribution on future predictions; and c_1, the interaction between culture and contribution. The DDFM = SATTERTH option requests the Satterthwaite (1946) approximation to determine the degrees of freedom for the intercept and slopes.

The final line of SAS code can take one of two forms. The first, as presented previously, is the RANDOM statement, which identifies the random-effect components of the model. In the dyadic model, only the INTERCEPT is random. The SUBJECT option identifies the level at which there is independence. Thus having SUBJECT = DYAD instructs the program that there is independence from dyad to dyad. This method of specifying the random effects has a significant disadvantage in dyadic research because it assumes that the nonindependence in the outcome scores is positive. That is, nonindependence is specified as a variance rather than as a correlation. Fortunately, there is an alternative:

```
PROC MIXED COVTEST;
CLASS DYAD;
MODEL FUTURE = CONTRIB CULTURE CONTRIB*CULTURE
    /SOLUTION DDFM=SATTERTH;
REPEATED / TYPE=CS SUBJECT=DYAD;
```

The REPEATED statement treats the individual scores as repeated measures in the dyad, and CS implies what is called *compound symmetry*, which forces the degree of unexplained variance for the dyad members to be equal. Nonindependence is estimated as a correlation (more technically a covariance) and not as a variance.

Because the nonindependence in Y scores from Table 4.3 is positive, both methods of specifying the model yield the same results. The intercept (analogous to the grand mean in this example) for future predictions is a_0 = 71.83, indicating that across the 20 participants, the average estimate of likelihood of future marriage was slightly under 72%. The main effect of contribution was statistically significant, with c_0 = 0.84, $t(13.9)$ = 3.30, $p <$ .01, indicating that individuals who made greater financial/household-labor contributions to their relationships had more positive predictions for the future. More exactly, this coefficient estimates that with each 1-unit increase in contribution, the likelihood of future marriage increased by .84. The effect of culture, as well as the interaction between culture and contribution, were both marginally significant, with a_1 = −9.03, $t(7.66)$ = 2.02, $p <$ .08, and c_1 = 0.49, $t(13.9)$ = 1.91, $p <$ .08. Given the coding scheme used, the culture main effect indicates that Asian participants were generally more positive in their forecasts of the future than American participants. The interaction suggests that the relationship between contribution and future predictions is especially pronounced for American couples. The random-effect parameter for the model is the variance in the intercepts; it is estimated as 176.42 and is statistically significant, $\chi^2(1)$ = 8.44, $p <$ .001. The deviance of the model is 142.93.

An alternative estimation strategy is to use SPSS. One needs version 11 or later of SPSS; we recommend using at least version 12.0. The SPSS syntax statements are as follows:

```
MIXED
    FUTURE WITH CONTRIB CULTURE
    /FIXED = CONTRIB CULTURE CONTRIB*CULTURE
    /PRINT = SOLUTION TESTCOV
    /RANDOM INTERCEPT | SUBJECT(DYAD) COVTYPE(VC).
```

(Note that SPSS requires a period after the last statement and "VC" stands for variance component.) The SPSS output is identical to the SAS output, with one exception. The p values for variances are two-tailed when they should be one-tailed. After dividing the p values in SPSS by 2, we obtain the same value as SAS. To allow for compound symmetry in SPSS, we remove the RANDOM statement and add the following statement:

```
/REPEATED = SEX | SUBJECT(DYAD) COVTYPE(CS).
```

Note that SPSS requires a repeated-measures variable (such as SEX in the example) in the REPEATED statement even if that variable is never used in analyses.

The code for HLM equations is entered as follows:

```
LEVEL 1 MODEL
  FUTURE = β₀ + β₁(CONTRIB) + r
LEVEL 2 MODEL
  β₀ = γ₀₀ + γ₀₁(CULTURE) + u₀
  β₁ = γ₁₀ + γ₁₁(CULTURE) + u₁
```

Observe that the "+ u_1" in the last line is lighter than the rest of the text to signify that the effect of CONTRIB is fixed; that is, it does not vary across dyads. In the output, the same model is expressed as

```
Level-1 Model
   Y = B0 + B1*(CONTRIB) + R
Level-2 Model
   B0 = G00 + G01*(CULTURE) + U0
   B1 = G10 + G11*(CULTURE)
```

Finally, the estimates given by HLM6 are as follows:

Fixed Effect	Coefficient	Standard Error	Approx. T-ratio	d.f.	P-value
For INTRCPT1, B0					
INTRCPT2, G00	71.830862	4.469434	16.072	8	0.000
CULTURE, G01	-9.032863	4.469434	-2.021	8	0.077
For CONTRIB slope, B1					
INTRCPT2, G10	0.844758	0.255669	3.304	16	0.005
CULTURE, G11	0.487241	0.255669	1.906	16	0.074

If we compare the HLM estimates to the SAS and SPSS estimates, they are identical within the limits of rounding error. The estimates of the two variances and the deviance are also identical. The only difference is the degrees of freedom and their corresponding p values. As we discuss in Chapter 7, the degrees of freedom and p values given in SAS and SPSS are more appropriate.

Finally, we used MLwiN to estimate the parameters of the model. The equations for the model, including the estimated parameter values, are as follows:

```
FUTUREᵢⱼ~N(XB,Ω)
FUTUREᵢⱼ = β₀ᵢⱼINTERCPT + 0.845(0.256) CONTRIBUTEᵢⱼ +
    -9.033(4.470)CULTURⱼ + 0.487(0.256)CONTRIBxCULᵢⱼ
β₀ᵢⱼ = 71.831(4.470) + u₀ⱼ + e₀ᵢⱼ
[u₀ⱼ]~N(0, Ωᵤ): Ωᵤ = [176.430(89.223)]
[e₀ᵢⱼ]~N(0, Ωₑ): Ωₑ = [43.753(19.567)]
-2*loglikelihood(IGLS) = 150.373(20 of 20 cases
    in use)
```

The first line indicates that the outcome has a normal distribution. In parentheses next to each estimate is the standard error of the parameter. Notice that no degrees of freedom are given for the estimates. Notice also that the deviance, called IGLS by MLwiN, of –2*loglikelihood is comparable to the maximum likelihood deviance, not the REML deviance. The estimates are RIGLS.

Computing the Intraclass Correlation and Variance Explained with Multilevel Models

We begin by assuming the simplest possible multilevel model—one with no X or Z variables. The only fixed factor in this model is the intercept, a_0, which is equal to the grand mean of the observations. There are two random factors in this model, the first of which is the dyad covariance s_{dd}. Note that the dyad covariance is the same thing as the variance of the intercepts if the nonindependence in the outcome is positive. The second random factor is the error variance, or s_e^2. The estimate of the intraclass correlation can be computed by $s_{dd}/(s_{dd} + s_e^2)$. The SAS code to estimate this model is

```
PROC MIXED COVTEST;
CLASS DYAD;
MODEL FUTURE = /SOLUTION DDFM=SATTERTH;
REPEATED / TYPE=CS SUBJECT=DYAD;
```

Using the data in Table 4.3, the results of this analysis are s_{dd} = 255.45 and s_e^2 = 82.30. The intraclass correlation is then 255.45/(255.45 + 82.30), which equals .76. Note that, with no missing data, this REML estimate is identical to the ANOVA intraclass correlation described in Chapter 2, and the maximum likelihood estimate is identical to the pairwise estimate of the intraclass correlation (Gonzalez & Griffin, 2001a). A key advantage that the MLM estimate has over the ANOVA approach is that ANOVA requires complete data (i.e., both dyad members must supply scores to be included in the analysis), whereas with MLM we can use all the obtained data, even if scores from some dyad members are missing at random.

The comparable code for SPSS is

```
MIXED
    FUTURE
    /FIXED =
    /PRINT = SOLUTION TESTCOV
    /REPEATED = SEX | SUBJECT(DYAD) COVTYPE(CS).
```

(The statement "/FIXED =" looks wrong but it is not.)

More typically, there are predictor variables at both the upper and lower levels, as in our initial example with the data from Table 4.3. One can again compute the ratio of the dyad covariance (i.e., the variance in the intercepts) to the sum of the dyad covariance and the error variance. This ratio represents the proportion of variance due to dyads and is a partial intraclass correlation from which the effects of the predictor variables are partialed. For our model, we find $s_{dd} = 176.42$ and $s_e^2 = 43.76$. The partial intraclass correlation is .80.

The units of measurement of the predictor variables are always an important consideration, but this is especially true in MLM. Normally, it is advisable to center all X and Z variables; that is, subtract the grand means from the variables.

Two types of centering are not advisable. The first type is called *group centering*: Here, a mean is computed for the dyad, and then it is subtracted from each member's score. Such a strategy removes all the variance due to dyad. The second type of inadvisable centering occurs with distinguishable dyads when the mean for each type of dyad member is subtracted from that type of individuals' scores. For instance, if the dyads were heterosexual couples, researchers might subtract the women's mean from each of the women's scores, and likewise for men. The problem with this type of centering is that it prevents researchers from examining the effects of the distinguishing variable on the outcome. Although grand mean centering affects the values of the coefficients, for dyads it has no effect[3] on s_{dd} and s_e^2.

One method of determining variance explained in a multilevel model is to compute s_{dd} and s_e^2 for the model with the fixed variables included and then again with them excluded. The latter is sometimes called the unrestricted model. The degree of variance explained, sometimes called a *pseudo R^2*, is defined as

$$R^2 = 1 - \frac{s_{dd} + s_e^2}{s_{dd}' + s_e^{2'}}$$

where the prime signifies the estimates of variance and covariance from the unrestricted model (i.e., the model without any predictors). There is a chance that this R^2 value might be estimated as a negative value. This would occur if the predictor variables were essentially unrelated to the outcome, so the values of s_{dd} and/or s_e^2 might actually be larger than s_{dd}' and $s_e^{2'}$. If the R^2 value were estimated to be negative, it would be reported as zero. For the example, the proportion of variance explained by the two predictor variables and their interaction is $1 - (176.42 + 43.76)/(255.45 + 82.30)$, or .348.

Random Effects with Dyads

Typically any level-1 or X variable can be treated as a random variable in a multilevel model. That is, the effect of that variable can vary across level 2. Returning to the earlier classroom example, we can allow the gender effect to vary across classrooms such that in some classrooms girls perform better than boys, whereas in other classrooms boys perform better than girls. Normally, we can have as many random variables as we want, with the restriction that there must be more level-1 units within each level-2 unit than there are random variables. With dyadic data, there are only two level-1 units within each level-2 unit (i.e., two people in each dyad). Thus we can allow for only one random variable. Almost without exception, that one random effect is the intercept or constant. We cannot allow for any other variation. However, this does not bias our results, because that variation is properly included in the error variance. Although only one random effect can be estimated, models with dyads can still include the fixed effects from multiple X variables and multiple Z variables.

Distinguishable Dyads

The preceding method of using multilevel models is particularly useful when members of the dyads are indistinguishable. It is not as useful when dyad members are distinguishable. There are several strategies for handling dyadic data within MLM when members are distinguishable. We discuss three different strategies, starting with the simplest. We want to mention that structural equation modeling (SEM), discussed in the next chapter, tends to handle dyadic data with distinguishable dyads more simply.

The first strategy is identical to the one presented previously for handling indistinguishable dyads, but a dummy variable is added to code for the distinguishing variable. For the example data set, the dyad members are distinguishable by their gender. When we include gender in the model, we find that its effect is not statistically significant, $b = -1.26$, $t(7.77) = -0.70$, $p = .50$.

Additionally, we might wish to allow for interactions between the other variables in the model and the distinguishing variable. Ordinarily, we can accomplish this by multiplying the dummy variable for the distinguishing variable by each other level-1 variable in the model. (Remember that we cannot multiply the distinguishing variable by a level-2 variable because that variable is the same for both members of the dyad.) For the example, CONTRIBUTE is a level-1 variable, and we can examine its interaction with gender. We find that there is no effect of this interaction, $b = -0.087$, $t(7.56) = -0.33$, $p = .75$. This first strategy presumes that the variances are the same for both types of members, that is, homogeneity of variance.

The second strategy is an extension of the previous strategy but allows for heterogeneity of variance across levels of the distinguishing variable. For the example data set, that would mean allowing for different variances for men and women. If we were to use SAS, the data within dyad must be sorted by the distinguishable variable. Thus, for the example, the dyads would either all be sorted as "man then woman" or sorted as "woman then man." If there are missing cases, these cases would be added into the data set with the outcome variable coded as missing. Additionally, within SAS we would change the "REPEATED" statement to

```
REPEATED / TYPE=CSH SUBJECT=DYAD;
```

For SPSS, the comparable statement is

```
/REPEATED = GENDER | SUBJECT(DYAD) COVTYPE(CSH).
```

The term CSH refers to *heterogeneous compound symmetry*. Note that "gender" is added to the statement in SPSS even though it need not be a variable in the model. It is included just to code for a repeated-measures variable, that is, to designate the two members as "1" and "2." Both HLM and MLwiN have a repeated-measures option that we do not illustrate.

We estimated such a model for the example data set using both SPSS and SAS, and we find that the error variance for women is 180.00 and for men is 253.77. Because the fixed variables are the same, we can use the difference between the REML deviance values from models with and without heterogeneous compound symmetry to evaluate whether in fact the variances are different. We find that they are not statistically different, $\chi^2(1) = 0.68$, $p = .59$.

The third strategy for handling distinguishable dyad members, originally suggested by Raudenbush, Brennan, and Barnett (1995), is the most complicated. We call this model the *two-intercept model*. We estimate the following equation, for member j of dyad i:

$$Y_{ij} = a_i X_{1i} + b_i X_{2i},$$

where X_1 is 1 for member 1 and 0 for member 2, whereas X_2 is 0 for member 1 and 1 for member 2. (The correlation between X_1 and X_2 is −1.) Within the model, the effect of X_1 and X_2 are random variables (both a and b have an i subscript). Be aware also that in this model there is no intercept, at least not in the usual sense. In addition, there is no error term in the model, making this a very unusual model. The model does have a variance–covariance matrix of a_i and b_i with three elements: the variance of a_i or s_a^2 (the error variance for the 1's), the variance of b_i or s_b^2 (the error variance for the 2's), and the covariance between the two, or s_{ab} (the degree of nonindependence). We can test whether the two variances are equal and whether the covariance is statistically different from zero.

If there are any X or Z variables, they are added to the model, but any X variables need to be multiplied by each of the two X dummies. In that way, we can test whether the effect of the X variable is the same for the two types of members.

Because there is currently no way to force the error variance to zero within SAS or SPSS, the two-intercept model cannot be estimated using these programs. (We shall see in Chapter 7 that for both SAS and SPSS, there is a way to mimic the two-intercept model.) These models can, however, be estimated using MLwiN. Also, HLM6 can be used by setting the error variance to a very small value (e.g., 0.00001) or by using the multivariate option.

The results using MLwiN with RIGLS to estimate the two-intercept model for the example data are as follows:

```
FUTURE_ij  ~  N(XB,Ω)
FUTURE_ij  =  β_0ij X1  +  β_1ij X2  +  0.885(0.311)  CONTRIBUTE_ij
         +-9.667(4.418)CULTUR_j  +  0.459(0.275)CONTRIBxCUL_ij
β_0ij  =  72.882(4.498)  +  u_0j
β_1ij  =  70.695(5.248)  +  u_1j
```

$$\begin{bmatrix} u_{0j} \\ u_{1j} \end{bmatrix} \sim N(0, \ \Omega_u) : \ \Omega_u = \begin{bmatrix} 189.886(84.916) \\ 180.181(90.805) \ \ 263.265(117.735) \end{bmatrix}$$

```
-2*loglikelihood(IGLS)  =  149.638(20  of  20  cases
     in use)
```

These results are identical to the results obtained using the second strategy for handling distinguishing variables by allowing for heterogeneous variances.

SUMMARY AND CONCLUSIONS

This chapter provides a brief introduction to MLM in general and MLM specifically in the dyadic context. We saw that this data-analytic approach can be used when data are hierarchically nested, with observations at a lower level (e.g., persons) being nested within an upper level (e.g., groups). We noted that this method is used when the outcome variable is measured for each lower-level unit but that independent or predictor variables can occur at either the lower level or the upper level.

Our introduction to MLM began with the balanced case, and we considered conventional mixed-model ANOVA as a data-analytic method. We then described the multilevel equations using the two-step procedure as a means for outlining the MLM technique. We defined the fixed and random effects that are generally estimated in MLM, and we discussed the restrictions required for applications of this method to dyadic data. Two estimation methods, maximum likelihood and REML, were briefly described, and implementation of MLM analyses using the data-analytic programs SAS, SPSS, HLM, and MLwiN was provided. Finally, we discussed the case of distinguishable dyads and described three estimation models that can accommodate such data. Thus, although MLM is particularly useful for studying dyad members that are indistinguishable, it can also be used when members are distinguishable.

Given the brevity of our discussion, we urge the interested reader to consult the books that we have mentioned. We also urge the reader to use the sample data to reproduce the parameter estimates we reported in this chapter.

Many of the following chapters employ MLM. Chapter 7 is especially important because we recommend MLM as the best method for estimating the Actor–Partner Interdependence Model (APIM) when dyad members are indistinguishable. MLM is also useful for testing hypotheses about variances and covariances, as is discussed in Chapter 6. Chapter 10 uses MLM extensively in the analysis of the one-on-many design when partners (the many) are indistinguishable. For Social Relations Model (SRM) designs, MLM has been proposed as an estimation technique (Snijders & Kenny, 1999), but at the moment, this method is far too complicated to recommend for general use. As we stated in the introduction to this chapter, there are two types of multilevel data: persons within groups and repeated measures. In this chapter we focused on the within-groups (i.e., dyads) application. It is possible to combine the two types when dyads are measured over time, and this complex three-level model (dyads, persons, and times) is discussed in Chapters 13 and 14.

MLM is a very important tool for the estimation of dyadic models and will likely become increasingly popular. If one is serious about analyzing dyadic data, one should learn how to use it.

NOTES

1. Sometimes models are called HLM for hierarchical linear modeling. Because HLM is also a computer program for multilevel modeling, the term "HLM" for multilevel modeling is not desirable.

2. Recent treatment of multilevel models (e.g., Raudenbush & Bryk, 2002) allows for crossing, as well as nesting, of units.

3. As seen in Chapters 10, 13, and 14, for models in which X variables are random, the units of measurement affect estimates of the variances and covariances. However, dyadic models discussed in Chapter 7 almost never contain random X variables.

5

Using Structural Equation Modeling to Study Dyads

Structural equation modeling, or SEM, is one of the most commonly used data-analytic techniques in the social and behavioral sciences, and it is particularly useful in the analysis of dyadic data. A variety of SEM applications to dyadic data are presented in Chapters 6, 7, 9, 10, 13, and 15. In this chapter we discuss several nuances that occur with SEM applications to dyadic data. Because we cannot present a complete description of the technique in a single chapter, we presume that the reader has some background knowledge on this topic. For those readers who are learning about SEM, we recommend Kline's (2005) book for novices and Bollen's (1989) book for more advanced users.

Making an appropriate choice of the unit of analysis is a key issue when applying SEM to dyadic data. For example, in the standard design (in which each person is paired with only one partner), the unit of analysis should usually be the dyad, not the person. The data may need to be reconfigured in order for dyad to be the unit of analysis (see Chapter 1). Recall that, in the dyad-as-unit data format, each variable is contained twice in the data set, once for each dyad member. Person is rarely (if ever) the unit of analysis for other dyadic designs, such as Social Relations Model designs in Chapter 9 and the one-with-many designs in Chapter 10. A general rule is that dyad or group is the unit of analysis for SEM, not person.

In the first section of this chapter, we review the four steps in conducting SEM. The second section discusses confirmatory factor analysis of dyadic data. A discussion of the estimation of path models for dyadic data follows, and in the final section we discuss SEM analysis of indistinguishable dyads. We limit our discussion to the standard design in this chapter. Chapter 9 introduces the use of SEM for Social Relations Model designs, and Chapter 10 describes the use of SEM for the one-with-many design.

STEPS IN SEM

SEM is a complicated and elaborate procedure. It helps to think of the procedure (and most other model-testing procedures) as having four principal steps: specification, identification, estimation, and testing. Each can be viewed as asking a simple question.

- Specification: What is the model?
- Identification: Can the model be uniquely estimated?
- Estimation: What statistical technique can be used to yield reasonable guesses of the model's parameters?
- Testing: Is the model a good model?

In the remainder of this section, we detail these steps.

Specification

Specification concerns the nature of the links between variables in the model, or more simply: What causes what? There are two possible links between two variables. One is a causal path, which is represented by a single-headed arrow from cause to effect. In some models, the two variables may cause each other, and this would be indicated by two single-headed arrows, one pointing each way. The other type of link is a correlation between variables, which would be represented by a single line (usually curved) between variables with an arrowhead at each end.

How do we know what causes what? Ideally, theory tells the researcher the causal direction. Research design, measurement theory, and common sense also guide the specification of the model.

Variables that are not caused by any other variables in the model are called *exogenous variables*. Normally, curved lines are drawn between all pairs of exogenous variables, allowing for possible correlations among them. Variables that are caused by the exogenous variables are called *endogenous variables*. Models often contain a series of causal variables such that the exogenous variables cause a set of other variables, and these other variables then act as causes for the endogenous variables. These middle variables that serve as both causes and effects are called mediating variables and are referred to as *partially endogenous variables* in SEM lingo.

Each variable that is caused by another variable has a disturbance, which represents the total set of unspecified causes of the variable. The disturbance takes on the role of an error term. Normally, the path from the disturbance to the variable is set to 1. Setting this path to 1 forces the disturbance variable to be in the same units as the endogenous variable that it causes. The disturbance can also be correlated with exogenous variables and with other disturbances in the model.

Sometimes a variable in SEM is called a *latent variable*. A latent variable is a theoretical variable that is not perfectly measured by the observed variables. For instance, marital satisfaction can be conceptualized as a latent variable. There are usually multiple indicators of each latent variable, for example, multiple observed measures of marital satisfaction. The disturbance for an indicator variable represents errors of measurement. Measurement errors of two different indicators may be correlated, and a curved line would represent that correlation.

A path diagram can conveniently summarize the entire set of paths and correlations. The causes are placed on the left, and the arrows point from left to right. Latent variables are placed in circles, and measured variables are placed in rectangles. The figures in this chapter represent examples of path models. For large models—models with 15 or more variables—a path diagram may be too cluttered to be interpretable, and in these cases the results may be best presented in a table. Alternatively, with complex models sometimes only parts of the model are drawn.

Identification

It may seem that model specification is an easy task: We simply draw paths between all pairs of variables, and we correlate all possible pairs. That is, we make the model as complicated as we can. However, this strategy is not feasible, because such models have so many parameters that they cannot be uniquely estimated. These models are said to be *underidentified*.

A given model may have some paths or parameters fixed at particular values (e.g., some paths may be fixed to equal zero) and others that are free to be estimated. A model's degrees of freedom, or *df*, equals the number of variances and covariances[1] among the measured variables minus the number of free parameters. The number of free parameters is the number of paths and curved lines for which path coefficients or correlations need to be estimated. If there are k variables in the model, there are a total of $k(k + 1)/2$ variances and covariances. If the number of the degrees of freedom is negative (i.e., the number of parameters to be estimated exceeds the number of variances and covariances), then the model is said to be *underidentified*. A model is said to be identified if there is sufficient information in the data to estimate uniquely the model's parameters. A model that has zero degrees of freedom, or just enough information to estimate each free parameter, and that is identified is called *saturated* or *just-identified*.

For models with latent variables, there must usually be at least two indicators of each latent variable for the model to be identified. However, to be safe, there need to be at least three indicators of each latent variable. Usually with any latent variable model the path coefficient from one of the measured variables (i.e., its loading) is fixed to 1; the variable with the fixed loading is called a *marker variable*. This variable sets the scale of measurement for the latent variable. Accordingly, if the marker variable is a 5-point Likert scale, the latent variable will be measured on a 5-point scale regardless of the scale of measurement for the other indicator variables (e.g., they might be measured on 7-point scales). Identification is a complex topic, and we have provided only a very elementary introduction. More comprehensive discussions can be found in Kline (2005), Kenny and colleagues (1998), and Bollen (1989).

Estimation

Many multivariate techniques (e.g., multiple regression, factor analysis, canonical correlation, and partial correlation) can be used to estimate an SEM model. For instance, most path-analysis models can be estimated using multiple regression. However, SEM models are usually estimated using a specialized SEM program such as LISREL, Mx, Amos, Mplus, CALIS, or EQS. Virtually all models with latent variables are estimated by one of these programs. The estimation method most often used is maximum likelihood. Maximum likelihood estimation solves the set of equations implied by the model using an iterative solution. That is, initial estimates are chosen for each free parameter and then improved upon iteratively to produce a better solution. Eventually, the program finds the statistically "best" or maximum likelihood model. For some models that are not identified, the solution does not converge (i.e., the program does not find a good solution). Maximum likelihood estimation presumes that the variables in the model have a multivariate normal distribution, which is best ensured if each of the individual observed variables has a normal distribution. Although other estimation criteria can be used (e.g., least squares and generalized least squares), they are not often applied in SEM.

The "data" for SEM can either be the raw data (e.g., an SPSS "sav" file or a text file) or it can be a variance–covariance matrix. The variance–covariance matrix can be read as a correlation matrix with standard deviations. For some models, the means are also read into the computer program.

Testing

As we just stated, most SEM models are estimated using maximum likelihood analysis. The parameter estimates, along with the values of the fixed parameters, are used to create an *implied* variance–covariance matrix among the observed variables. The fit of the model is tested by comparing this implied variance–covariance matrix with the actual observed variance–covariance matrix. A chi-square test based on these discrepancies can be used to evaluate the model fit. Thus a large difference between the observed and implied variance–covariance matrices indicates that the proposed model does not fit or correspond closely to the observed variance–covariance matrix. The estimation procedure tries to minimize these differences (and thus minimize the chi-square value) in a way similar to the way that multiple regression analysis minimizes the distance of the data points (X, Y coordinates) from the regression line. When the iteration procedure has reached the best possible solution, the final chi-square goodness-of-fit value is determined, along with the final estimates for all the parameters. The degrees of freedom of the chi-square test are the number of variances and covariances among the measured variables minus the number of free parameters. The null hypothesis that the specified model is correct implies a very small chi-square value. Thus a statistically significant chi-square indicates that the model is not properly specified.

Sometimes two models are said to be *nested*. Nested models are ones for which one model is a more complex version of the other. For instance, the more complex model might contain paths that are not included in the simpler model. The chi-square difference test, in which the chi-square from the more complex model is subtracted from the chi-square of the simpler model, is used to compare the two models. The degrees of freedom are similarly differenced. The resulting chi-square difference (with the corresponding degrees of freedom difference) is evaluated for statistical significance. If it is statistically significant, the simpler model (i.e., the one with fewer free parameters) should be rejected. In other words, a statistically significant chi-square difference test indicates that simplifying the model has significantly worsened the fit of the model to the observed data. In principle, the more complex model should have a nonsignificant chi-square before it is compared to a simpler model. The chi-square difference test is very useful both for making simpler models more complex and for making complex models simpler.

Unfortunately, the chi-square test and chi-square difference test can be misleading indicators of whether the model is a good- or bad-fitting model. If the sample size is very large (i.e., greater than 400), it is almost certain that the chi-square test will be statistically significant, indicating poor model fit. Conversely, if the sample size is small, it is difficult for the chi-square to be statistically significant. Additionally, the chi-square test is upwardly biased (i.e., too large) with non-normal distributions. Because of these problems with the chi-square test, alternative measures of model fit have been developed. There are nearly 100 different measures of fit, but we focus on two of the most useful. The first is the comparative fit index, or CFI (Hu & Bentler, 1998). To estimate the CFI, we need to first estimate an independence or null model. In such a model, all of the model's correlations are assumed to be zero, but the variances (and means) are allowed to vary. The formula for the CFI is

$$CFI = \frac{\chi_N^2 - df_N - \chi_M^2 + df_M}{\chi_N^2 - df_N},$$

where χ_N^2 and df_N refer to the null model and where χ_M^2 and df_M refer to the estimated model. If the χ_M^2 is less than df_M, then the CFI is set to 1. We strive for the CFI to be at least .95, and if the CFI is less than .90, the model is a poor fit to the data.

The second measure of fit is the root mean square error of approximation, or RMSEA (Steiger & Lind, 1980). The RMSEA is an absolute measure of fit, whereas the CFI is a relative measure of fit (i.e., the model is compared with or relative to the null model). The formula for the RMSEA is

$$RMSEA = \sqrt{\frac{\frac{\chi^2}{df} - 1}{N - 1}},$$

where χ^2 and df refer to the estimated model and N refers to the sample size. If χ^2 is less than the degrees of freedom, the measure is set to 0. Ideally the RMSEA is 0, and an RMSEA greater than .10 indicates that the model does not fit the data well. Again, there are many measures of fit besides the two that we have discussed, and new measures of fit are being developed as well.

Parameters estimated from SEM are tested for statistical significance using a Wald test, which is called a t-test in some programs and a critical ratio in others. The Wald test evaluates the effect of fixing the value of a free parameter to 0. It is a substitute for doing a separate chi-square difference test for the contribution of each parameter on the overall model fit. These tests are very useful in determining what parameters to keep in the model.

If the model has poor fit, we can return to the first step and respecify the model. Such post hoc respecifications are based on a combination of empirical analyses (e.g., standardized residuals and modification indices) and theoretical analyses. Sometimes we recycle through the four steps repeatedly until a good-fitting or at least a reasonably good-fitting model is found. However, the conclusions reached through post hoc model fitting are not as strong as those from an a priori model.

CONFIRMATORY FACTOR ANALYSIS

Most social and behavioral scientists are familiar with factor analysis. We often use factor analysis when faced with a large number of variables that we wish to reduce to a much smaller number of variables. This is generally done somewhat mindlessly, letting software determine how many factors (i.e., underlying latent variables) are in the data and which items load on these factors. Naming of the factors is usually based on the content of the items with the largest loadings on the factor. Such an analysis is called *exploratory factor analysis*, or EFA. In confirmatory factor analysis, or CFA, the researcher specifies a priori which items load on which factor, thus creating a theory-driven measurement model. The remaining loadings are fixed to zero, and if enough zero constraints are made, the CFA model is identified. In contrast, the standard EFA model is not identified if there is more than one factor. Because of the lack of identification, an EFA solution can be rotated, whereas a CFA solution is unique and cannot be rotated. Having a unique solution is advantageous because many seemingly arbitrary decisions are made in model rotation. In CFA, unlike EFA, the factors are usually correlated. Also, unlike EFA, the covariance matrix rather than the correlation matrix is factored in CFA. Finally, in CFA, the factors are not necessarily standardized (i.e., their variances are not fixed at 1.0) as they are in traditional factor analysis.

One key concern in CFA is the issue of the *discriminant validity* between two constructs. Very strong correlations between factors indicate a failure of discriminant validity. One reasonable strategy is to make sure that the correlations between factors are no greater than .85 in absolute value. If a correlation is larger than this, the two correlated factors should be combined into a single factor.

One thing that can be done with CFA, but not with EFA, is to correlate the errors of the indicators. If it is believed that two indicators share variance, their errors can be correlated. Normally, the source of correlated measurement error is some type of method variance. For example, consider a study of life satisfaction for husbands and wives. Life satisfaction may have three indicators, including satisfaction with the marriage, satisfaction with job, and satisfaction with children. With CFA it is possible to correlate the errors between the domains or indicators of life satisfaction, such that there is a correlation between the two partners' marital satisfaction, the two partners' job satisfaction, and their satisfaction with their children.

In Figure 5.1, we present a path diagram of a small CFA depicting the life satisfaction example with distinguishable dyads (husbands and wives). As described, we have the same three indicators for each dyad member: satisfaction with marriage, job, and children. We have also correlated the life satisfaction factors of the two persons, and that correlation represents a latent variable correlation that measures nonindependence between the two partners' life satisfaction. We usually want to correlate errors across the same indicators for the two members of the dyad, as shown in Figure 5.1.

One advisable revision of this model is to set the loadings on each measure to be equal for the two members. In the example, we set the factor loadings to be the same for husbands and wives. If the model fits, then the life satisfaction construct comprises the same combination of variables for both members. In other words, the construct of life satisfaction has the same meaning for both members of the dyad. Additionally, we could fix the latent variable variances and the error variances of the observed variables to be equal across dyad members. This would indicate, for instance, that women differ from each other to the same degree that men differ from each other. Finally, the intercepts can be set equal. This would indicate that the average wife has the same score on the latent variable as the average husband. According to Gonzalez and Griffin (1999), if the husband and wife are alike in all these ways, then the distinction between the two roles is meaningless.

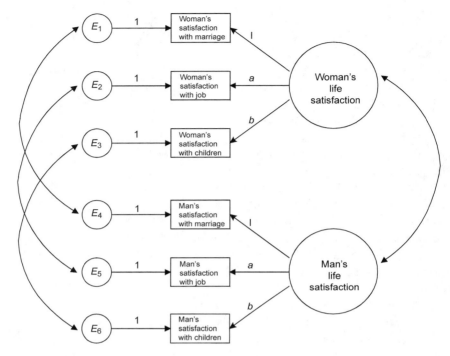

FIGURE 5.1. Confirmatory factor analysis of dyadic data.

One fact not well known is that Wald tests of loadings and correlations depend on the choice of the marker variable (in Figure 5.1, the marker variable is satisfaction with the marriage). That is, when the marker variable changes, the significance tests are likely to change (Gonzalez & Griffin, 2001b). If a path or correlation is of central interest, it should be tested not by a Wald test but by the chi-square difference test.

We use the method of CFA in Chapters 6, 9, 10, and 13. The fundamental idea is that we make dyad or group, not person, the unit of analysis. We allow the latent variables for partners to correlate, thus measuring nonindependence. Later in the chapter, we present a CFA example using indistinguishable dyads.

PATH ANALYSES WITH DYADIC DATA

Consider what is perhaps the simplest possible causal model: Variable X causes Y, or $X \rightarrow Y$. For such a model we would regress Y on X. How is this done with dyadic data? We presume in this section that dyad members are distinguishable. For instance, we may have a study investigating the degree to which stress causes perceptions of conflict in family relationships for parents and their adult children. In this example, X_P represents the parent's stress level, X_C represents the adult child's stress level, Y_P represents the parent's perceptions of conflict, and Y_C represents the child's perceptions of conflict. Before discussing how to analyze the data, we need to discuss how *not* to analyze the data. We could treat the data set with n dyads as if we had a data set with $2n$ persons. We could then simply run an analysis in which Y is regressed on X. However, such an analysis would violate the independence assumption, because it is likely that X_P and X_C are correlated, as would be Y_P and Y_C.

Because we want to use dyad as the unit of analysis, we need our raw data organized as a dyad data file. For each record in the file, there would be four variables: X_P, X_C, Y_P, and Y_C. A simple model in which Stress (X) causes Conflict (Y) for these variables is depicted in Figure 5.2. Note that the path from Stress to Conflict is estimated separately for parent and child and that the paths are unstandardized.

To estimate the model, we would input into an SEM program either the raw data or the variance–covariance matrix computed from them. When we estimate this model, the χ^2 test has 2 degrees of freedom, because there are 10 knowns (4 variances and 6 covariances) and 8 parameters to be estimated (2 paths, 2 covariances—the curved lines—and 4 variances). We can view the 2 degrees of freedom as being due to the missing cross-paths from Parent Stress to Child Conflict and from Child Stress to Parent Conflict. These missing paths are called *partner paths* and are discussed in Chapter 7. We can test having the two Stress → Conflict paths equal to each other. One degree of freedom is gained by forcing the two paths to be equal. We rerun the SEM and determine the χ^2 that now has 3

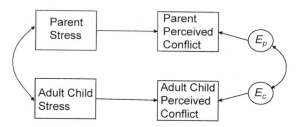

FIGURE 5.2. Simple path model for a distinguishable dyad, parent and child, in which stress causes perceived conflict.

degrees of freedom. We can subtract this χ^2 from the one that did not force the equality constraint. If the difference between the χ^2 values is statistically significant (or if a fit index worsens), then the assumption of equal paths is not supported. If the fit does not worsen, the two paths can remain equal to each other. Such a strategy normally increases the power in the test to determine whether the combined paths are significantly different from zero.

The general strategy in specifying path models with dyadic data is that the model is drawn twice, once for each member of the dyad. We correlate all exogenous variables (X_P with X_C) across dyad members, and we also correlate the disturbances across dyad members (E_P and E_C in the figure). The correlated disturbances allow for the nonindependence in the data. They can be viewed as partial correlations between the Y variables, controlling for both partners' X variables.

Generally, we want to allow for differences in the means of Y_P and Y_C, and this is modeled by allowing them to have nonzero intercepts. If means or intercepts are included in an SEM, then either the raw data must be read by the program or the means must be included with the variance–covariance matrix. Additionally, we should make sure that zero is a meaningful value for X_P and X_C. If not, we ordinarily should center X_P and X_C. Centering refers to the subtraction of the grand mean from the scores so that the transformed scores would have a mean of zero. However, we should center them all using the same value. For example, if the mean stress score for the parents is 10.2 and the mean for the adult children 8.0, we should center both stress variables by subtracting the mean of the two means, or (10.2 + 8.0)/2 = 9.1, from each. We use the same mean to keep the unit of the measurement the same for the two dyad members. The test of the difference between the intercepts is similar to a matched-pairs t-test (see Chapter 3) after covarying out the variable X. The intercepts for E_P and E_C are set to zero.

As an example of a dyadic path analysis, Bui, Peplau, and Hill (1996) tested Rusbult's (1983) social exchange model on a sample of 167 heterosexual couples who had been in a relationship for at least 15 years. As part of that model, relationship satisfaction, relationship investments, and relationship alternatives caused commitment to the relationship. The Rusbult model was estimated simultaneously for both members of the pair (i.e., the man and the woman). Differences in the paths for the men and women were also tested, but no gender differences were found. They did find evidence for a partner effect: Commitment to the relationship diminishes as the partner's alternatives increase. The chi-square test was statistically significant, $\chi^2(40) = 81.05$, $p < .001$, but the CFI was .95 and the RMSEA was .079, which indicates reasonably good fit.

SEM FOR DYADS WITH INDISTINGUISHABLE MEMBERS

When dyad members are distinguishable, we estimate the path model or CFA model for each of the two members combined in a single model. We might place constraints across the two solutions within that model. However, when members are indistinguishable, it is less clear exactly how to do the analysis. The use of SEM with indistinguishable or exchangeable dyad members has generally been viewed pessimistically:

- Note that the standard SEM approach is not easy to implement in the exchangeable case (Gonzalez & Griffin, 1999, p. 461).
- The dyadic SEM model is restricted to data with nonexchangeable partners (Newsom, 2002, p. 445).

If the researcher seeks to run a path analysis, it is often possible to use multilevel modeling (MLM), which was discussed in the previous chapter. However, multilevel models cannot be used for the estimation of most CFA and other latent variable models.

Recently, several approaches for estimation of SEM models with indistinguishable members have been proposed. Woody and Sadler (2005) were the first to develop a coherent method for this type of analysis. Their method involves creating two different covariance matrices, one within dyads and the other between dyads. Also, the method usually requires the use of phantom variables and hand computation of various parameters.

Fortunately, Olsen and Kenny (2006) have developed an alternate, and much simpler, strategy for using SEM with indistinguishable dyads. In this approach, we analyze a dyadic data set in which the designation of persons 1 and 2 is totally arbitrary. Moreover, we estimate a model of the variance–covariance matrix with the means. We then place equality constraints on all parameters—means, variances, covariances, and paths—that are "indistinguishable." Finally, we make adjustments to the model chi-square and degrees of freedom to take into account the arbitrary nature of the assignment of persons to 1 and 2. Additional adjustments must be made to the estimation of the null model, which is used to measure various fit indices, for example, the CFI. The method proposed by Olsen and Kenny, although straightforward, is not easy to implement. Consequently, it requires careful attention to detail. The interested reader should consult the article in addition to reading the following.

We illustrate this approach using an example described in Olsen and Kenny (2006) of a simple CFA for indistinguishable dyads. The path model, presented in Figure 5.3, involves a single factor with four indicators. We denote the variables as X_{ij}, where i refers to variable and j to dyad member. So X_{32} refers to variable 3 for member 2. The latent variable F causes each of the measures, but we use two F variables, one for member 1 and one for member 2. The F variables are correlated, and this correlation can be viewed as a latent variable intraclass correlation. We treat variable 4 for both members as the marker variable, so the paths from each F variable to variable 4 are set to 1. Finally, we correlate the residuals (i.e., the E variables) across dyad members. These correlations can be viewed as residual intraclass correlations for the indicators, partialing out the effect of the latent factor.

Note that we have set the corresponding intercepts (a, b, c, and d) and factor loadings (e, f, and g) equal for the two members. Moreover, we have set the parallel error variances (j, k, l, and m) equal. Additionally, we have set the means of the latent variables and the errors to 0. As seen in Figure 5.3, this model has 17 unique parameters: a factor variance (h) and factor intraclass covariance (i), along with the four intercepts, three factor loadings, four error variances, and four residual intraclass covariances (n, o, p, and q) for the indicators.

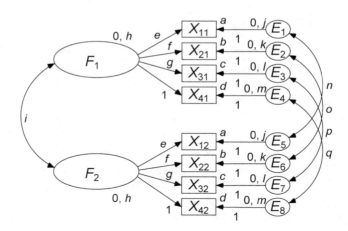

FIGURE 5.3. One-factor, four-indicator CFA for indistinguishable dyads.

Model Fit and Model Comparisons

For the model in Figure 5.3, there are two different reasons why the chi-square is bigger than zero. The first reason is specification error, which is what we are most interested in: Does a single-factor model explain the covariation in scores? The second is due to the arbitrary assignment of persons as either person "1" or "2." This latter source of lack of fit is not important and is irrelevant assuming that the designation of 1 and 2 is totally arbitrary. When computing the chi-square and degrees of freedom, we must remove from the chi-square the effect of this second type of lack of fit. To do so, we must compute how much the lack of fit is directly due to arbitrary assignment of persons. We need to estimate an additional model, a model called I-SAT, or the "saturated model for indistinguishable dyads."

To estimate the I-SAT model, we input the variance–covariance matrix and the means using a dyad data file. The model has no latent variables. Rather, we estimate a model consisting of variances and covariances among the observed variables, but with certain constraints on the means, variances, and covariances. Specifically, we constrain the means and variances of the same variable for the two members to be equal. Additionally, we set the covariances between two variables, X_i and X_j, to be equal when they are from the same member, or $s_{i1j1} = s_{i2j2}$, and when they are from different members, or $s_{i1j2} = s_{i2j1}$. (In Chapter 6, we refer to the former covariances as the *intrapersonal* covariances, and the latter as the *interpersonal* covariances.) In general, the saturated model has a total of $k(k + 1)$ constraints, k means, k variances, and $k(k - 1)$ covariances, and its degrees of freedom are $k(k + 1)$. However, the χ^2 from this saturated model should not be interpreted,[2] as it reflects only the arbitrary assignment of persons to "1" and "2." Instead, we should treat the I-SAT model as the baseline and compare any estimated dyad model with this saturated model. We refer to the adjusted chi-square, the one in which the I-SAT chi-square is subtracted, as $\chi^{2\prime}$ and to the adjusted degrees of freedom as df'. Recall that the adjustment to the degrees of freedom is $k(k + 1)$. Interestingly and importantly, the value of chi-square from the I-SAT changes depending on who is assigned a 1 or a 2. However, as long as the designation of dyad members to 1 or 2 is made consistently in the data used to estimate both of the models, the value of $\chi^{2\prime}$ is the same regardless of how the assignment is made. When using the Olsen and Kenny (2006) method, the chi-square and degrees of freedom are always adjusted to take the I-SAT model into account.

There is one further complication. Recall that a null model of no correlation between variables is estimated to compute the CFI and several other measures of fit. We cannot use the ordinary null model when we have indistinguishable dyads. The proper null model must constrain the covariances to be equal to zero and the variances and means to be parameters to be estimated, with the additional requirement that means and variances from the same measure for both members are set equal.

With $k = 4$ (the example data set), the I-SAT model has $k(k + 2) = 24$ parameters: the $k = 4$ unique means, the $k(k + 1)/2 = 10$ unique intrapartner variances and covariances, and the $k(k + 1)/2 = 10$ unique cross-partner intraclass and cross-intraclass covariances. For $k = 4$, the null model has $2k = 8$ parameters, estimating only the unique means and intrapartner variances, setting all the covariances to zero. To repeat, the chi-square for any model (i.e., the null model, as well as other SEM models) is corrected by the chi-square for the I-SAT model, as are the degrees of freedom.

Example

Same-sex twins are used as an example of indistinguishable pairs. We use the same example as that from Olsen and Kenny (2006), adult male identical twin pairs from the Midlife Development Study, to illustrate appropriate analysis of data from indistinguishable dyads. We restricted our analysis to 137 male monozygotic (MZ) twin pairs, providing complete data on four 4-item personality variables: reappraisal (e.g., "I find I usually learn something meaningful from a difficult situation"), foresight (e.g., "I am good at figuring out how things will turn out"), insight (e.g., "I try to make sense of things that have happened to me"), and self-directedness (e.g., "I like to make plans for the future"). The correlations, means, and standard deviations for the dyad-level data are reproduced in Table 5.1 (Olsen & Kenny, 2006).

The fit of the CFA model is tested using the chi-square difference between the model as depicted in Figure 5.3 and the I-SAT models. These results are presented in Table 5.2. Again, the chi-square values are adjusted by the I-SAT model because they depend on the arbitrary assignment of persons to "1" and "2." The result of the correction yields a $\chi^{2\prime}(7) = 12.701, p = .080$. The RMSEA equals 0.077 and the CFI is .977, making the model fit quite acceptable. The estimates and standard errors are presented in Table 5.3. All parameters are statistically significant except the residual

TABLE 5.1. Correlations, Means, and Standard Deviations (SD) for Male MZ Twins (n = 137)

	X_{11}	X_{21}	X_{31}	X_{41}	X_{12}	X_{22}	X_{32}	X_{42}
X_{11}	1.000							
X_{21}	.380	1.000						
X_{31}	.351	.483	1.000					
X_{41}	.531	.386	.385	1.000				
X_{12}	.411	.161	.142	.228	1.000			
X_{22}	.313	.453	.266	.245	.348	1.000		
X_{32}	.118	.080	.092	.099	.323	.381	1.000	
X_{42}	.214	.148	.129	.357	.403	.431	.256	1.000
Mean	3.042	2.571	2.903	3.095	3.074	2.474	2.913	3.144
SD	0.579	0.626	0.607	0.653	0.662	0.605	0.615	0.694

Note. X_1 = reappraisal, X_2 = foresight, X_3 = insight, X_4 = self-directedness. The second subscript refers to dyad member, 1 and 2.
Source: Olsen and Kenny (2006).

TABLE 5.2. Chi-Square Tests for Male MZ Twins

	df	χ^2	df'	$\chi^{2'}$	RMSEA	CFI
Null	36	283.210	16	261.519	0.336	.000
CFA	27	34.392	7	12.701	0.077	.977
I-SAT	20	21.691				

TABLE 5.3. CFA Estimates (Standard Errors in Parentheses) for 137 Male MZ Twins

	Loading	Mean	Variance	Covariance	Correlation
Factor			.194 (.042)	.093 (.030)	.479
Measures					
Reappraisal	.864 (.128)	3.058 (.044)	.236 (.028)	.077 (.026)	.326
Foresight	.880 (.129)	2.523 (.044)	.223 (.028)	.082 (.026)	.368
Insight	.775 (.119)	2.908 (.039)	.254 (.027)	−.005 (.025)	−.020
Self-directedness	1.000	3.119 (.048)	.261 (.034)	.079 (.030)	.303

intraclass correlation for insight. Notice that the estimate of the latent variable intraclass correlation of the latent factor across the twins is .479 and that the residual correlations are smaller, ranging from −.020 to .368. The standardized loadings, not contained in the table, are all approximately .65.

Double-Entry Method

Olsen and Kenny (2006) present a second method for SEM of indistinguishable members that is quite different from the previous method but that, interestingly, yields the same results. We only briefly discuss this second method and refer the reader to the original article for more details. We emphasize the dyad method because that method more closely parallels the analysis for data with distinguishable members. That is, sometimes a researcher may be uncertain as to whether the distinguishing variable is really meaningful. If he or she decides to treat members as indistinguishable, that transition is much easier with the method that we have described.

In the double-entry method, we begin with a double-entry or pairwise data set, which we have described in Chapters 1 and 2. We weight each case by 0.5, which makes intuitive sense in that each data point is entered twice. We then estimate the model without any equality constraints. Next, we adjust the degrees of freedom of the model by $k(k + 1)/2$. (There is no need to adjust χ^2 because the χ^2 for the I-SAT is 0.) This adjustment to the degrees of freedom must also be made to the null model. Again, after the adjustments are made, this second method yields the same results as the method that we have detailed in this chapter.

SUMMARY AND CONCLUSIONS

The goal of this chapter was to give a brief overview of SEM techniques. Our discussion assumed that the reader has some background in this area, and so we focused primarily on applications of SEM in the dyadic case. We noted that, in almost every case, dyad needs to be treated as the unit of analysis with SEM. We then turned our attention to the four distinct steps involved in SEM: specification, identification, estimation, and testing. In the specification step, the nature of the links between variables (i.e., correlational vs. causal) is detailed. Our discussion of identification described the interplay between model complexity and the degree to which the available data provide sufficient information to estimate the model's parameters. We next briefly discussed estimation methods, noting that specialized programs that use maximum likelihood estimation are typically employed with this data-analytic approach. Finally we described several ways of testing the overall quality of the model, as well as ways to test specific restrictions to the model.

We focused on one key application of SEM techniques: confirmatory factor analysis. Many SEM models employ latent variables (i.e., theoretical constructs that are imperfectly indicated). A CFA estimates a latent variable model in which the latent variables are correlated. We discussed how this confirmatory method differs from more commonly used exploratory factor analysis methods, and we noted that in CFA the factor structure is specified by the researcher, not the data. We discussed how with dyadic data separate latent variables are estimated for each member and the errors of the same measure are correlated across dyad members.

We also saw that applying SEM models to dyadic data is relatively straightforward when dyad members are distinguishable. Basically, parallel SEM models are created for each member, and correlations across members are added to model nonindependence.

Finally, we discussed SEM with indistinguishable dyads. We saw that although methods are much more complicated, it is still possible to estimate such models. The method we described requires equality constraints across dyad members and adjustments to the chi-square test and its degrees of freedom.

SEM is a complex method about which entire books have been written (e.g., Bollen, 1989; Kline, 2005). Adding dyads to the mix increases that complexity, especially for the case of indistinguishable dyads. However, it is a complexity that is worth adding because of the useful information that it yields. Moreover, many types of models (CFA and path analysis with latent variables) require SEM. Although some models, such as the Actor–Partner Interdependence Model (APIM) with distinguishable dyads (see Chapter 7), may be analyzed by other techniques (e.g., multilevel modeling), they are more easily analyzed by SEM. SEM is a valuable tool that dyadic researchers need to understand.

We use SEM to test models of equivalence of variances and correlations in Chapter 6. We use confirmatory factor analysis in Chapter 9 for Social Relations Model designs, and in Chapter 11 for one-with-many designs. Finally, in Chapter 13, we discuss applications of SEM for the study of over-time processes. SEM is a very important technique for the analysis of dyadic data (Wendorf, 2002). It is the method of choice for analyzing data in which members are distinguishable, and as we have described, it can also be used with members who are indistinguishable. In the next chapter, we consider estimating and testing variances and correlations in dyadic research, and, as noted, SEM is one of the methods we apply.

NOTES

1. We are not considering here models that have means (e.g., growth-curve models; see Chapter 13).

2. In essence, the chi-square is treated like a deviance, a relative measure of fit used in multilevel models (see Chapter 4). However, as is shown in Chapter 6, the I-SAT model is the very same model used to test whether members that are presumed to be distinguishable are in fact distinguishable.

6

Tests of Correlational Structure and Differential Variance

Dyadic researchers frequently search for differences either within or between dyads. Most often studies focus on either means or regression coefficients. For example, researchers might want to test whether husbands or wives are more committed to their marriages, and so they measure and compare mean differences in commitment for husbands and wives. In this chapter, we consider a very different set of questions. Rather than focusing on means and regression coefficients, this chapter examines ways of estimating and testing differences between correlations and variances.

Consider examples of differences between correlation and variance.

- Do husbands or wives vary more in how satisfied they are in their marriages?
- Is the correlation between work satisfaction and job commitment greater for supervisors than for supervisees?
- Is the correlational structure in the ratings of attachment the same for children and parents?
- Is the intraclass correlation for relationship satisfaction greater for gay men than it is for lesbian couples?
- What is the variance in relationship satisfaction for roommates?
- Do husbands and wives differ in their leisure choices?

The last question examines variation in a categorical variable.

All too often, researchers fail to address questions concerning the differences between correlations and variances, focusing instead on differences in the means. However, these questions are important and deserve attention. (In fact, some readers may be tempted to skip ahead to the next chapter, but we advise against such a strategy.) Questions of a difference in correlations concern the issue of moderation: Does an association between variables change across dyad types or across a distinguishing variable within dyads? Questions of a difference in variances concern the issue of the range of response: Do some types of relationships place a greater constraint on the range of possibilities than others?

In this chapter we assume that both members of n dyads are measured, each on k measures. We are therefore assuming that we have a reciprocal standard design, the most common design in dyadic research (see Chapter 1). We also assume that there is, to some degree, nonindependence in the dyad members' scores (see Chapter 2).

As an example data set, we use the 148 married couples from Acitelli (1997). For both the husband and the wife, we have measures of closeness, commitment, and satisfaction, all of which are assessed on 4-point scales. We also have the length of the marriage in years, a between-dyads variable. Although the members are distinguishable by gender, for illustration purposes we sometimes treat them as if they were indistinguishable. Table 6.1 presents the means and standard deviations for the seven variables. We also present the basic statistics for the pairwise data (see Chapter 1). Note

TABLE 6.1. Means and Standard Deviations for 148 Married Couples from the Acitelli (1997) Data Set

Variable	Mean	SD
Length of Marriage	11.21	7.720
Wife		
Closeness	3.43	0.730
Commitment	3.70	0.579
Satisfaction	3.61	0.656
Husband		
Closeness	3.43	0.640
Commitment	3.74	0.523
Satisfaction	3.59	0.638
Double-Entered Variables		
Closeness	3.43	0.685
Commitment	3.72	0.552
Satisfaction	3.60	0.646

that for some example analyses that require a categorical between-dyads factor, we also include data from the 90 dating couples from Acitelli.

The first section of this chapter discusses the analysis of distinguishable dyads. The second section discusses indistinguishable dyads. For some of the statistical tests presented in this chapter, we use structural equation modeling (SEM), multilevel modeling (MLM), and log-linear modeling. Readers should familiarize themselves with MLM in Chapter 4 and SEM in Chapter 5 prior to working through this chapter. We provide a brief introduction to log-linear modeling in this chapter.

DISTINGUISHABLE DYADS

Equality of Variances

To begin, we assume that there is a within-dyads variable that distinguishes the two dyad members (e.g., boss–employee or parent–child), and the question is whether the variances differ for the two types. For instance, researchers might assess marital satisfaction to determine whether there is more or less variance in the husbands' satisfaction than in the wives'. If the data were independent (husbands and wives were not married to each other, but instead represented two different samples), the test would be straightforward. We would compute a ratio of the two variances, s_1^2/s_2^2, putting the larger variance, s_1^2, on the top and the smaller variance, s_2^2, on the bottom. Under the null hypothesis of equal variances, the quantity has an F distribution with $n_1 - 1$ degrees of freedom in the numerator and $n_2 - 1$ in the denominator. If a standard one-tailed F table were used, the p value would need to be doubled. This doubling is required because the larger variance is always placed on the numerator, and so the F-ratio is always greater than or equal to 1. As a fictitious example, say that the variance for 95 men who are married is 1.37, and the variance for 83 women who are married (but not to any of the 95 men) is 1.86. The F-ratio would be $F(82, 94) = 1.36$. The standard one-tailed p value would be .076, but it should be doubled in this case, and so $p = .152$.

Although this test is useful for unrelated individuals, it can rarely be used for dyadic data from a reciprocal design because both members of the dyad are measured and scores are nonindependent. When a reciprocal standard dyad design is used, the test of equal variance needs to be modified as follows: We designate the two scores as X_1 and X_2, where X_1 refers to the scores for husbands and X_2 to those for wives. We compute $X_1 - X_2$ (e.g., husband's score minus wife's score) and $X_1 + X_2$ (e.g., the sum of the husband's and wife's scores). Then the sum and the difference are correlated. Although it is not obvious, the test of whether this correlation coefficient equals zero evaluates a difference in the variances for X_1 and X_2. (See Kenny, 1979, p. 21, for a proof.)

As an example using the Acitelli (1997) data, we tested whether husbands and wives differed in the variance of their marital satisfaction. As seen in Table 6.1, wives have a slightly greater standard deviation than do husbands (0.656 vs. 0.638). When we correlate the sum with the difference, we obtain a correlation of $-.033$, $t(146) = 0.402$, $p = .688$, which is not statistically significant. We thus conclude that there is no statistically meaningful difference between the two variances.

A more general hypothesis is that the variances of k measures are equal for the two members of the dyad. To perform this more general test, we use SEM (see Chapter 5). Each measure is correlated with each other. The variances of the same measure are set to be equal for the two members. The total number of constraints on the model is k, the number of variances.

Consider the Acitelli example that we introduced earlier. Figure 6.1 presents this model with the six variables as a path diagram. In the model, we simultaneously test whether the variances for the three measures (closeness, commitment, and satisfaction) are the same for husbands and wives. Note that the variances are placed next to the variables—the terms in the boxes—and that the corresponding measures for husbands and wives are set equal. For instance, the variance for closeness measure is 0.469 for both husbands and wives. We obtain a $\chi^2(3) = 4.51$, $p = .211$. Thus we conclude that the variances are not statistically different for husbands and wives for these three variables.

Equality of Correlations

Before detailing how to test whether correlations vary, we need to discuss whether researchers should even test for differences between correlations at all. In many cases, the variables measured have a causal ordering. In other words, researchers often think of particular variables as causes and others as effects. If there is a causal ordering of the variables, it makes more sense to compare regression coefficients (see Chapter 7) than to compare correlation coefficients. Correlations are affected by differences in the variances of the causal variable and, therefore, comparing them can be problematic if such differences exist. However, if the variances do not differ, comparing correlation coefficients may be justifiable.

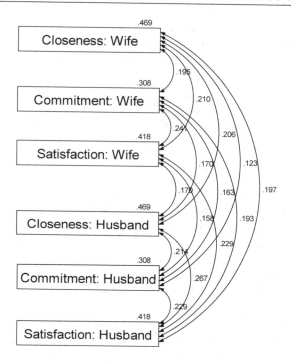

FIGURE 6.1. Model to test invariance for husbands and wives across variables.

Suppose that we do decide to compare correlations. There are two types of dyadic correlations that can be tested for equality: correlations that share one variable in common and correlations that have no common variables. For example, we might have a study of marital dyads in which length of marriage, satisfaction, and commitment are all measured. Both satisfaction and commitment are mixed variables (i.e., they vary both between and within dyads), and length of marriage is a between-dyads variable (i.e., both partners have the same score, and variation occurs from dyad to dyad). One question that could be addressed with these data might be whether the relationship between length of marriage and the husband's satisfaction differs from the relationship between length of marriage and the wife's satisfaction. This is the common-variable case in which the null hypothesis is $\rho_{12} = \rho_{13}$, where variable 1 is length of marriage, variable 2 is husband's satisfaction, and variable 3 is wife's satisfaction. Note that ρ symbolizes the population, not the sample, correlation coefficient.

For the null hypothesis with one variable shared in common, the generally recommended test is the Williams modification of the Hotelling test (Kenny, 1987). The formula for this t-test of the equality of ρ_{12} and ρ_{13} with $n - 3$ degrees of freedom is

$$t(n-3) = \frac{(r_{12} - r_{13})\sqrt{(n-1)(1+r_{23})}}{\sqrt{2K\dfrac{(n-1)}{(n-3)} + 2(1-r_{23})^3 \dfrac{(r_{12}+r_{13})^2}{4}}},$$

where $K = 1 - r_{12}^2 - r_{13}^2 - r_{23}^2 + 2r_{12}r_{13}r_{23}$.

As an example using the Acitelli (1997) data, we correlated length of marriage with marital satisfaction for husbands and wives. The correlation for husbands is $r_{12} = -.032$ and for wives is $r_{13} = -.113$. Thus, for both, the longer people were married, the less satisfied they were, although the size of the relationship is weak. Using the Williams test (the correlation of the two satisfaction measures is $r_{23} = .554$), there is no statistically significant difference in the correlations between husbands and wives, $t(145) = 1.040$, $p = .300$. Thus we would conclude that the correlation between satisfaction and length of marriage does not differ for husbands and wives.

If none of the variables is shared in common (e.g., the correlations between commitment and satisfaction, separately computed for both husbands and wives), we would have a null hypothesis of the type $\rho_{12} = \rho_{34}$, where X_1 might be the husband's commitment, X_2 might be the husband's satisfaction, X_3 might be the wife's commitment, and X_4 might be the wife's satisfaction. We refer to these correlations as *intrapersonal correlations* because each is a correlation between two measures from one member of the dyad. We can also measure the cross-dyad correlation between the husband's commitment and the wife's satisfaction (r_{14}) and the cross-dyad correlation of the wife's commitment and the husband's satisfaction (r_{23}). We refer to these cross-dyad correlations as *interpersonal correlations* because one variable is measured from one member and the other variable is measured from the second member. We not only refer to intrapersonal and interpersonal correlations in this chapter, but we also consider them in subsequent chapters.

The example data set helps clarify these distinctions. In Table 6.2, we have the correlations between wives' and husbands' satisfaction and commitment. The two intrapersonal correlations concern the correlation between one member's satisfaction and that same member's commitment. Those correlations are .687 and .618 for wife and husband, respectively. The interpersonal correlations are .438 for the wife's satisfaction and the

TABLE 6.2. Intrapersonal and Interpersonal Correlations for 148 Couples

	1	2	3	4	5	6
Wife						
Closeness (1)	1.000					
Commitment (2)	.538	1.000				
Satisfaction (3)	.498	.687	1.000			
Husband						
Closeness (4)	.448	.443	.384	1.000		
Commitment (5)	.328	.526	.438	.532	1.000	
Satisfaction (6)	.458	.542	.554	.583	.618	1.000

Note. See Table 6.1 for means and variances.

husband's commitment and .542 for the wife's commitment and the husband's satisfaction.

For the null hypothesis of equality of two correlations with no variables in common, there are several tests that can be used. An older test is the Pearson and Filon test (1898), which was modified by Steiger (1980). (See also an approximation given by Raghunathan, Rosenthal, & Rubin, 1996.) That test of the null hypothesis that $\rho_{12} = \rho_{34}$ is as follows:

$$Z = \frac{(z_{12} - z_{34})\sqrt{n-3}}{\sqrt{2 - K(1-r^2)^2}},$$

where

$$K = (r_{13} - r_{23}r)(r_{24} - r_{23}r) + (r_{14} - r_{13}r)(r_{23} - r_{13}r) + (r_{13} - r_{14}r)(r_{24} - r_{14}r) + (r_{14} - r_{24}r)(r_{23} - r_{24}r),$$

z_{12} and z_{34} are the Fisher's z transformations of the correlations (see Chapter 2), and r equals $(r_{12} + r_{34})/2$. The power of this test can be very low. One may need hundreds of cases to have reasonable power. Applying this test to the example data, the test that the two intrapersonal correlations are equal was $Z = 1.04$, $p = .30$, and the test that the two interpersonal correlations are equal was $Z = 1.24$, $p = .22$. Thus there is no indication that the correlations differed significantly.

Sometimes we need a multivariate test of equality of correlational structure. We can use SEM (see Chapter 5) for this general test. The model for testing such a hypothesis, which is not very obvious, is depicted in Figure 6.2. Each measure is "caused" by a latent variable whose variance is

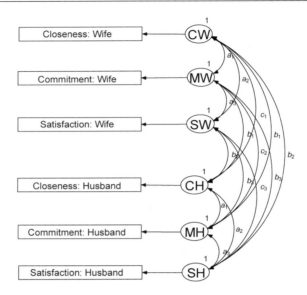

FIGURE 6.2. Model to test equality of relationships across distinguishable members.

fixed to 1, that is, the latent variable is standardized. (Note that there are no errors or disturbances for the measures.) We then place constraints on the correlations, indicated by the curved lines with the same letter. Note that there are two types of constraints. First, we set the intrapersonal correlations, that is, the husband and wife correlations, equal. Second, we set the interpersonal correlations equal to each other. The paths from the latent variables to the measures are free and estimate the standard deviations of the measures.

We tested whether the correlations were equal using the Acitelli data. Recall that we have measures of closeness, commitment, and satisfaction from both husbands and wives. The test of equality of correlational structure across husbands and wives results in $\chi^2(6) = 7.95$, $p = .242$, and thus we conclude that both the intrapersonal and interpersonal correlations for wives and husbands do not differ.

We can also test whether the standard deviations are equal for the two members by forcing the corresponding paths from the latent variable to the measured variable to be equal. Note that this test presumes that correlations are also equal, unlike the earlier described multivariate test of equal variances that made no such assumption. For the example, we find that the test of equal variances, given equal correlations, is $\chi^2(9) = 12.88$, $p =$

.168. If we use a χ^2 difference test, we find $\chi^2(3) = 4.93$, $p = .177$, and thus conclude that the three variances do not statistically differ.

We might also want to allow for differences in reliability of the measures. Generally, greater reliability implies larger correlations. For instance, for some measures the data from husbands might be more reliable than the data from wives, whereas for other variables, the data from wives might be more reliable. If corrections for differential reliability were made in this case, the correlations would be equal. We begin with the model in Figure 6.2, in which each measure has its own latent variable, and we force the equality constraints in the correlations. To allow differential reliability for the two members, we free the factor variances of one of the members. For instance, the three variances for husbands were set to 1 in Figure 6.2, but now the variances of the husband latent variables (CH, MH, and SH) would be set free. If the estimated variance for a given variable were greater than 1, that member would have more correlatable variance on that variable (i.e., greater reliability) than the other member. If the estimated variance were less than 1, that member would have less correlatable variance (i.e., lower reliability) on that measure.

For the Acitelli (1997) study, we tested whether the reliability of measurement varied for the wives and husbands. The model fit is $\chi^2(3) = 2.57$, $p = .462$, which indicates a good-fitting model. Using the chi-square difference test, we find $\chi^2(3) = 5.38$, $p = .146$, and, therefore, there is no evidence that the reliabilities vary by gender. There was more correlatable variance for wives with the closeness and satisfaction measures but more correlatable variance for husbands with the commitment measure; but again, these differences were not statistically significant.

Latent-Variable Correlations

Sometimes there is a set of measures that are all thought to be caused by the same construct for each member. We can estimate and test such a model using CFA (see Chapter 5). The model illustrated in Figure 6.3 has the same three measures for each member. Again using the Acitelli (1997) example, we have three measures for the wife and three for the husband. There are two latent variables, wife and husband, which are designated by circles in Figure 6.3. We have made the closeness measures the marker variables by forcing the paths from the factor to the measures (i.e., factor loadings) to 1. We have also forced the loadings to be the same for the variables for husbands and wives. Finally, we have correlated the errors of the same measures across dyad members. The correlation of the factors across

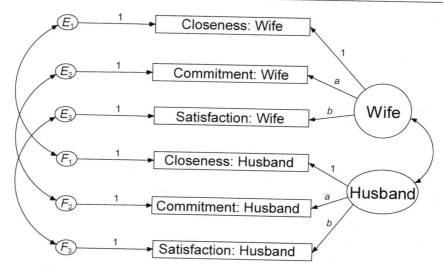

FIGURE 6.3. Latent-variable model for distinguishable members.

the two members can be viewed as a measure of latent nonindependence. In addition, the test of the equality of loadings evaluates whether the constructs have the same meaning for both members. That is, we test whether the factor is the "same" for the two members.

For this model to be identified, there must be at least three indicators per latent variable per member. Normally, only two indicators per latent variable are needed, but the presence of correlated errors requires one additional indicator per factor. There can be just two indicators if we fix all the loadings equal (i.e., set them all to 1) or if we have a between-dyads variable (e.g., length of the relationship) that is correlated with the factors.

We can test the equality of the variance of the two factors by forcing the factor variances to be equal. This should be done only if the loadings are also set equal. We compare the fit of two models, one with the factor variances set equal and one without.

The model can be extended by having multiple latent variables for each member of the dyad. In essence, the model is a parallel CFA across the two members. With two or more latent variables, we can compute intrapersonal and interpersonal latent correlations and covariances that can be tested for equality. When testing for equality of correlations and covariance, the factor loadings must be the same for both members. Thus equality of loadings must be tested first.

The model fit is $\chi^2(7) = 7.08$, $p = .421$, CFI = 1.000, RMSEA = 0.009, which indicates that the latent variable model is consistent with the data. Constraining the wife and husband factor loadings to be equal does not worsen the fit of the model, $\chi^2(2) = 4.04$, $p = .133$, and we so can assume that the loadings do not differ. The loadings for the commitment measures are 0.97 and for the satisfaction measures are 1.15. The correlation between the wife and husband latent variables is .754, $Z = 4.607$, $p < .001$, and it can be viewed as a latent variable measure of nonindependence.

When we examine the factor variances, we note that the variance for husbands is 0.189 and the variance for wives is 0.227. Note that the variances would change if the marker variable were changed, but the ratio of the husband and wife variances would be the same. Note also that the variances should be compared only if the loadings are set equal and the model fits. To test whether the variances are different, we reran the model, setting the two factor variances equal. Using the chi-square difference test, we find that the husband and wife variances are not statistically different, $\chi^2(1) = 1.398$, $p = .237$.

Raudenbush, Brennan, and Barnett (1995) have developed a method for the estimation of latent variable models using MLM. However, the method greatly restricts the measurement model. The loadings across indicators must be set equal, and the error variances must also be set equal. Moreover, these restrictions cannot be tested. Currently, SEM, not MLM, is generally the more appropriate estimation method of most latent variable models.

Omnibus Test of Distinguishability

We might think that the dyad members are distinguishable, but empirically this may not be the case. If dyad members were actually indistinguishable, then all of the following would necessarily hold:

- For each variable, the means for the two members would be the same.
- For each variable, the variances for the two members would be the same.
- For each pair of variables, both the intrapersonal and the interpersonal correlations would be the same.

Thus, if all three of these conditions were to hold, then the dyad members would be indistinguishable for those variables. Following Gonzalez and

Griffin (1999), we can simultaneously test all three conditions by using SEM. If there were k measured variables per member, there would be a total of $k(k + 1)$ constraints on the data. To test the equality of the means, we need to include both the means and the covariance matrix (or the raw data) in the statistical analysis. Note that this model is identical to the saturated, or I-SAT, model described for the analysis of dyadic data using SEM (Olsen & Kenny, 2006) in Chapter 5. The model is illustrated in Figure 6.4.

When we apply this test to the Acitelli (1997) data set to determine whether gender should be used as a distinguishing variable, we obtain $\chi^2(12) = 14.80$, $p = .252$. Thus we conclude that it is not statistically necessary to treat the dyad members as if they were distinguishable by their gender. That is, gender does not make a meaningful difference, at least not as far as these three variables are concerned.

We could also treat dyad members as indistinguishable if the only difference between them is in the means. To ascertain whether this is the

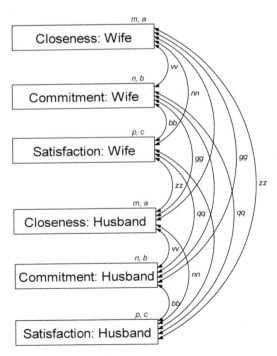

FIGURE 6.4. Model of an omnibus test of distinguishability.

case, we test the conditions of equal correlations and equal variances but do not force the means to be equal. If these assumptions hold (i.e., the model fits the data well), then we can treat the dyad as indistinguishable, but we must control for the mean differences across the distinguishing variables in subsequent statistical analyses. When we apply this test to the Acitelli (1997) data set, we obtain $\chi^2(9) = 12.88$, $p = .168$. We conclude, as before, that it is not statistically necessary to treat the dyad members as if they were distinguishable.

The dyad members may be indistinguishable on one set of variables but not on another. We recommend that when working with distinguishable dyads, standard practice should be to begin with a test that demonstrates empirically that the members are in fact distinguishable. If there is no statistical evidence that the members are distinguishable, they should be treated as if they were indistinguishable. We return to this topic in the final chapter of the book.

Categorical Variables[1]

Until this point we have presumed that the variables under consideration are measured at the interval level. In this section, we assume that the variables are categorical, or nominal (see Chapter 1). We consider three different types of questions for categorical variables: marginal agreement, quasi-independence, and symmetry. We presume that the categorical variable of interest has three or more levels,[2] the number of which is symbolized by m. Much of the material in this section is somewhat difficult and likely requires careful study for most readers, even those familiar with log-linear analysis.

Log-Linear Analysis

When the data are counts (i.e., the number of observations that fit into a particular category), log-linear analysis can be used. Most readers are more familiar with traditional χ^2 tests of independence for count or frequency data. For instance, consider a two-way table of Ethnicity and Religion. The χ^2 test of independence evaluates a bivariate relationship between ethnicity and religion. However, a log-linear analysis can test much more complicated models. Similar to a multiple regression model, a log-linear model is one in which an observation is a function of parameters. However, in log-linear analysis, the observation is a cell count, and the parameters refer to variables. If we have two-way table counts, we can model a cell in that two-way table in terms of the average count (similar to a grand mean), a row effect, a column effect, and a row-by-column interaction effect. In log-linear analysis, there is no designation of independent and dependent variable. The effect of Ethnicity (E) on Religion (R) would be measured by the ER association.

Log-linear analysis estimation requires the fitting of tables. If we have a three-way table of Ethnicity, Gender, and Religion, or an EGR table, we might fit a model of all two-way tables (EG, ER, and GR), or fit a model of just the "main effects" (E, G, and R). The model that fits the full three-way table, or EGR, is called the *saturated model*, and it exactly reproduces the cell counts.

Once the tables are fitted for the model, we can compare observed to expected values as in an ordinary Pearson χ^2 test. However, in log-linear analysis it is more common to use a maximum likelihood ratio test. That test, commonly symbolized as G^2, is

$$-2\sum_i f_i \ln(f_i/e_i),$$

where f_i is the observed number of cases in cell i, e_i is the value expected in cell i given the model, and "ln" is the natural logarithm. The summation is across all cells in the full table. The likelihood ratio chi-square is used because, when two models are estimated, one of which is nested within the other, the difference between the chi-squares is itself a chi-square under the null hypothesis. The same is not true of the Pearson chi-square. Note that f_i must not be zero for G^2 to be defined, and if there are zeros in the table, it can be helpful in log-linear analysis to add 0.5 to each cell.

Again, this is a very brief description of log-linear analysis. If the reader plans to use this method, he or she would be well advised to consult a text on the topic (e.g., Bishop, Feinberg, & Holland, 1975). Moreover, the tests that we describe in this chapter are much more complicated than those done in an "ordinary" log-linear analysis. We do return to the topic in Chapters 11 and 14.

Illustrative Data

To illustrate the analysis, we use the data in Table 6.3 with five categories. The data are taken from Acitelli (1997) and are religion preferences of the husband and the wife. The categories are Protestant (mainstream), Evangelical (fundamentalist Protestant), Catholic, Other, and None (or atheist).

TABLE 6.3. 5 × 5 Table of Number of Agreements (Descending Diagonal) and Disagreements (Off Diagonal) on Religion

	Husband's Religion				
Wife's Religion	Protestant	Evangelical	Catholic	Other	None
Protestant	31	2	9	0	8
Evangelical	3	16	1	0	1
Catholic	3	3	38	0	6
Other	1	0	3	2	1
None	1	3	4	3	5

There are 144 cases in this two-way table of husband religion and wife religion. When husbands and wives have a different religion (e.g., he is Catholic and she is Protestant), we say there is a *disagreement*. As is customary in log-linear analysis, we have added 0.5 to each of the cells. (If there were zero values in one or more cells, the saturated model, and possibly other models, could not be estimated.) Also, unless otherwise stated, all reported χ^2 tests use the likelihood ratio and not the more familiar Pearson goodness-of-fit test.

Marginal Agreement

In this case we wish to test whether the probability of each of m categories is the same for both members of the dyad. Such a test is the categorical analogue to a test of equal variance. Recall that marginal agreement is important in measuring kappa (see Chapter 2), which is a measure of categorical nonindependence.

To measure and test marginal agreement, we estimate a log-linear model in which the row and column parameters are forced to equal each other. We first create $m - 1$ dummy variables for each row and $m - 1$ dummy variables for each column. Thus, if we denote a_i as the effect for religion i for member 1 and b_i as the effect for religion i for member 2, then marginal agreement implies $a_i = b_i$. We also fit the row and column interaction; that is, we allow for agreement between dyad members on the variable of interest.[3] The degrees of freedom of the model are $m - 1$.

For the religion data in Table 6.3, the null hypothesis is that the same percentage of husbands and wives are members of the five different religious categories. For example, wives are as likely to be Catholic as husbands. If we apply the model to the sample data, we obtain a likelihood ratio chi-square of 1.72, $p = .79$, with 4 degrees of freedom. Because this value is not statistically significant, we conclude that the margins are not different for husbands and wives.

Quasi-Independence

If a scale were truly categorical and not ordered, then all disagreements would be random. If, however, the scale were ordinal, then there would be more disagreements between categories that are adjacent than between categories that are nonadjacent. The model of random disagreement is called *quasi-independence* because, if the diagonal cells (cases in which the two members agree) were excluded, then the responses would be independent. Thus the disagreements would be random.

To estimate the quasi-independence model, we begin by setting the diagonal values to zero, which are called *a priori* or *structural zeros*. That is, the cells are not zero empirically, but rather these cells are ignored in the analysis. In the estimation of the log-linear model, the cells with the a priori zeros are not fitted in the iterative estimation process. In the test of quasi-independence, the row and column effects are fitted but not the interaction. The degrees of freedom for the quasi-independence model are $m^2 - 3m + 1$, where again m is the number of levels of the categorical variable.

To use SPSS to test for quasi-independence, we first create a data set in which each case is a cell in a two-way table. The cell frequencies must be in a variable called COUNT. The syntax is

```
GENLOG
    WIFE HUSBAND /CSTRUCTURE = WT
    /MODEL = MULTINOMIAL
    /PRINT = FREQ RESID DEV ESTIM
    /CRITERIA = DELTA(.5)
    /DESIGN WIFE HUSBAND.
```

where WIFE and HUSBAND are variables that denote the wife's and the husband's religion, respectively, and WT is a variable that is 0 for the cells in which wife and husband have the same religion, and 1 otherwise. If we apply the sample data to this model, we obtain $\chi^2(11) = 12.58$, $p = .321$. Thus we conclude that the disagreements are random. Although the overall result is not significant, for illustration purposes we examined the residuals to determine where there is more disagreement than expected. The largest residual is from the wife–none with husband–other cell.

Symmetry

Related to the analysis of marginal agreement is the analysis of the symmetry of disagreement. In this case we assume $f_{ij} = f_{ji}$, where f_{ij} is the frequency for a cell from row i and column j. In Chapter 3, we discussed the McNemar test of proportions. That test considers a dichotomy and evaluates whether $f_{12} = f_{21}$. For a dichotomy, symmetry and marginal agreement are the very same question, but with more than two levels, they become different questions.

Given symmetry, the expected value for cell ij is $(f_{ij} + f_{ji})/2$. The generalization of the McNemar test can be obtained by computing the goodness-of-fit chi-square $\Sigma \Sigma[(f_{ij} - f_{ji})^2/(f_{ij} + f_{ji})]$ for the $m(m - 1)/2$ pairs of cells in which i is not equal to j (i.e., $i < j$). We can also compute the likelihood ratio chi-square. The quantity has a chi-square distribution with $m(m - 1)/2$ degrees of freedom. Because the test is a generalization of the McNemar test when m is greater than 2, we can view it as a more detailed examination of differences in the distribution of categorical variables between the two members.

For the religion data, the null hypothesis is that, when couples have different religions, the disagreements are symmetric. Using the goodness-of-fit test, we find $\chi^2(10) = 13.35$, $p = .205$, and using the maximum likelihood test, we find $\chi^2(10) = 14.34$, $p = .158$. Regardless of the test used, we find that there is no statistically significant difference. We thus conclude that differences in religion are parallel.

The test for symmetry is more complicated if we allow for marginal disagreement. We test for quasi-independence, which allows for different margins, but we constrain the interaction effects to be symmetric. So if we denote the interaction effects as p_{ij}, then the assumption is that $p_{ij} = p_{ji}$.[4] The degrees of freedom of such a model are $(m - 1)(m - 2)$. If we apply the example data to this model, we find that $\chi^2(6) = 9.69$, $p = .138$. Again we conclude that the disagreements are random and parallel once the margins are corrected.

INDISTINGUISHABLE DYADS

Not all dyads are distinguishable. For example, friends and roommates are usually treated as indistinguishable. Indeed, as we discussed earlier in this chapter, it is sometimes the case that "distinguishable" dyads are in fact indistinguishable. When members are indistinguishable, different analyses must be undertaken, and usually these analyses are more complex. In this section, we discuss tests of correlations and variances when members are indistinguishable.

Correlations

When dyad members are indistinguishable, we might seek to measure the correlation between two variables, for example, relationship satisfaction and stability. As was the case with distinguishable dyads, such a correlation can be viewed from two perspectives: an intrapersonal perspective and an interpersonal perspective (Griffin & Gonzalez, 1995). The intrapersonal correlation is the correlation between a dyad member's satisfaction and his or her own stability and is denoted as r_{xy}. The interpersonal correlation is between one member's satisfaction and the other member's stability and is denoted as $r_{xy'}$. Thus the intrapersonal correlation is within a single individual, and the interpersonal correlation crosses the two dyad members. There is only a single correlation of each type when dyad members are indistinguishable.

Computation of these two correlations is not obvious. The problem that we face is analogous to the difficulty that we encountered in Chapter 2 when we attempted to compute the correlation between members of an indistinguishable dyad. To solve this problem, we used the intraclass correlation. Thus we seek a bivariate extension to the intraclass correlation. Much as we did in estimating the intraclass correlation in Chapter 2, we can adopt three different strategies to estimate a statistic that can be called a *bivariate intraclass correlation*: ANOVA, pairwise methods, and MLM.

ANOVA

To compute r_{xy} and $r_{xy'}$ by ANOVA methods, the researcher needs to compute the MCP_{BXY}, or the mean cross-products between variables X and Y, and MCP_{WXY}, or the mean cross-products within X and Y. These mean cross-products are the bivariate analogues of MS_W and MS_B, introduced in Chapter 2. The MCP_{BXY} equals

$$\frac{2\Sigma_j[(M_{Xj} - M_X)(M_{Yj} - M_Y)]}{n-1},$$

and MCP_{WXY} equals

$$\frac{\Sigma_i \Sigma_j [(X - M_{Xj})(Y - M_{Yj})]}{n},$$

where M_X and M_Y are the grand means for variables X and Y, respectively, and where M_{Xj} and M_{Yj} are the means for variables X and Y, respectively, for dyad j. The subscript i refers to members 1 and 2. Note that $MCP_{BXX} = MS_B$ and that $MCP_{WXX} = MS_W$.

The intrapersonal correlation, r_{xy}, is defined by

$$\frac{MCP_{BXY} + MCP_{WXY}}{\sqrt{(MS_{BX} + MS_{WX})(MS_{BY} + MS_{WY})}},$$

and the interpersonal correlation, $r_{xy'}$, is defined by

$$\frac{MCP_{BXY} - MCP_{WXY}}{\sqrt{(MS_{BX} + MS_{WX})(MS_{BY} + MS_{WY})}}.$$

Note that when X and Y are the very same variable, then $r_{xy} = 1$ and $r_{xy'}$ is the intraclass correlation.

There is no standard test of statistical significance for these two ANOVA-based correlations. One possibility is to use the SEM method that was developed by Olsen and Kenny (2006). As discussed in Chapter 5, pairwise data are used to estimate an SEM model analogous to the model in Figure 6.1, but we set parallel parameters (the two intercepts, the two variances, the two interpersonal and intrapersonal correlations) equal.

For the example data, the estimate of the intrapersonal correlation between satisfaction and stability is .653, and the interpersonal correlation is .491. Both of these correlations are statistically significant ($Z = 8.00$ and 6.02, respectively) using the Olsen and Kenny (2006) procedure. The reader might wish to compare these values with the correlations obtained presuming that the members are distinguishable (see Table 6.2). We can see that the ANOVA-based estimate of the intrapersonal correlation is very close to an average of the husbands' and wives' intrapersonal correlations. Similarly, the ANOVA estimate of the interpersonal correlation is virtually the same as the average of the two interpersonal correlations for husbands and wives.

Pairwise Method

We can also estimate r_{xy} and $r_{xy'}$ by the pairwise method that we described in Chapter 2. We first create $2n$ scores for variable X, where the first n scores are for member 1 and the second n are for member 2. For variable Y, the first n scores are for member 2 and the second n are for member 1. We then compute the ordinary Pearson product–moment correlation for these scores using these $2n$ scores. The approximate standard error for both correlations is the square root of $1/n$, where n is the number of dyads.

Using the Acitelli (1997) data, the estimate of the intrapersonal correlation between satisfaction and stability is .653, $Z = 7.944$, $p < .001$, and the interpersonal correlation is .491, $Z = 5.973$, $p < .001$. Not surprisingly, the ANOVA and pairwise estimates have the same value, something that we would expect given the reasonably large sample sizes.

Multilevel Modeling

The use of MLM (see Chapter 4) to estimate the correlations with indistinguishable members is relatively complex. The strategy involves adapting the two-intercept approach that was presented in Chapter 4. Even a sophisticated user of MLM may have some difficulties implementing such an analysis. It requires a computer program that allows for both no intercept and no error variance and for equality constraints on the parameters. Although we briefly describe the technique, we recommend the simpler ANOVA and pairwise methods.

Following the usual practice with MLM, there are two levels in the data: Individuals are the lower-level unit, and dyad is the upper level. As is typical for MLM, we use a pairwise data set so that each individual's X score is associated with both that person's Y and the partner's Y. For each case, we create four dummy variables:

Z_1: 1 if the case is from member 1 for variable X, and 0 otherwise.
Z_2: 1 if the case is from member 2 for variable X, and 0 otherwise.
Z_3: 1 if the case is from member 1 for variable Y, and 0 otherwise.
Z_4: 1 if the case is from member 2 for variable Y, and 0 otherwise.

We then estimate a model with no intercept and no error variance, and we treat the four dummy variables as random variables at the level of the dyad. Thus the model in equation form is

$$Y_{ijk} = b_{1j}Z_{1ijk} + b_{2j}Z_{2ijk} + b_{3j}Z_{3ijk} + b_{4j}Z_{4ijk},$$

where the subscript i refers to person (from 1 to 2), j refers to dyad (from 1 to n), and k refers to variable (from 1 to 2). In addition to specifying no intercept and no error term, we also make the following constraints on the variances of the 4×4 variance–covariance matrix for the model: The variances of b_1 and b_2 are equal to each other, and the variances of b_3 and b_4 are equal to each other. The intraclass correlation for X is $C(b_1, b_2)/V(b_1)$ and for Y is $C(b_3, b_4)/V(b_3)$. Additionally, we set the following pairs of covariances to be equal: $C(b_1, b_3) = C(b_2, b_4)$ and $C(b_1, b_4) = C(b_2, b_3)$. These covariances correspond to the numerators of r_{xy} and $r_{xy'}$, respectively.

Although not a simple analysis to execute, this method of analysis has some distinct advantages over more conventional methods. First, MLM can handle missing data, as long as it can be assumed that the observations are missing at random. Second, it can handle fixed variables that need to be controlled in the analysis. Third, we could easily adapt the analysis to the case of distinguishable dyads. The model would be the same except that we would not force the equality constraints of variances and covariances of the dummy variables. We again discuss this strategy in Chapter 10.

For the example data set, we used the computer program MLwiN to estimate intrapersonal and interpersonal correlations between satisfaction and stability. The intrapersonal correlation is estimated as .653, $Z = 8.00$, $p < .001$, and the interpersonal correlation between the two variables is .490, $Z = 6.00$, $p < .001$. Note that both of the correlations are nearly identical to the ANOVA and pairwise correlations.

Latent Variable Correlations

Estimation of latent variable models with indistinguishable dyad members by MLM is not simple. Moreover, if we use MLM, we must assume that the loadings on the latent variable are equal. With a latent variable that has k indicators, there would be $2k$ measured variables, and we would need to create $2k$ dummy variables.

A more realistic strategy is to use the SEM approach developed by Olsen and Kenny (2006) for indistinguishable dyad members, which we discussed in Chapter 5. As an example, we applied the technique to the Acitelli (1997) data, treating dyad members as if they were indistinguishable. We found $\chi^2(14) = 15.58$, $p = .339$, but we need to subtract the χ^2 for the I-SAT model, or the model in which we test for indistinguishability, which was $\chi^2(12) = 14.80$. The resulting adjusted value is $\chi^{2'}(2) = 0.78$, $p = .64$. The latent variable intraclass correlation was estimated to be .753.

Comparing Intraclass Correlations

We next address the question of whether intraclass correlations differ for different types of dyads. For instance, McBride and Field (1997) studied emotional states of adolescent friends. They found that intraclass correlations were larger when friends were of opposite genders than when they were of the same gender. As in other cases, there are three different ways to test such a hypothesis: ANOVA, pairwise methods, and MLM.

ANOVA

For the ANOVA intraclass correlations, a procedure suggested by Haggard (1958) can be used. We first transform the intraclass correlations using Fisher's z transformation (see Chapter 2). The standard error of the difference between the two transformed correlations is simply the square root of $1/(n_1 - 2) + 1/(n_2 - 2)$, where n_1 and n_2 refer to the number of dyads in each of the two subgroups. We then compute Z as the difference between the two intraclass correlations divided by the standard error of the difference.

As an example we compare the intraclass correlations for relationship satisfaction for married and dating couples. Using the Acitelli (1997) data, we find that the correlation is .338 for the 90 dating couples and .553 for the 148 married couples. The standard error of the difference between the two correlations is the square root of $1/146 + 1/88$, or 0.135. The test of the difference is $Z = 2.007$, $p = .045$, and we conclude that there is a difference between the intraclass correlations for dating and married couples: The correlation is stronger for married couples.

An alternative strategy to testing for differences in the intraclass correlations (but one that is very complicated) is to use the multiple-groups SEM with indistinguishable dyad members. We estimate the intraclass correlations for each of the groups, and we force an equality constraint across groups to make the correlations equal. We can then use a chi-square difference test to evaluate the reasonableness of that constraint. If such a strategy were adopted, we should first test whether the variances are equal across groups before we test for differences between correlations.

Pairwise Method

A very complicated iterative method for testing the difference between two pairwise intraclass correlations is presented by Donner and Bull (1983). The procedure by Haggard (1958) that we discussed in the previous section can be used as a much simpler procedure. We transform the intraclass correlations using the Fisher's z transformation (see Chapter 2). Then the standard error of the difference between the two transformed correlations is simply the square root of $1/(n_1 - 2) + 1/(n_2 - 2)$, where 1 and 2 refer to the two subgroups.[5]

We find that the pairwise intraclass correlation on relationship satisfaction is .553 for married couples and .334 for dating couples. The test that the difference is statistically significant is $Z = 2.040$, $p = .041$. We conclude that there is a difference in the intraclass correlations between dating and married couples.

Variances

What is the variance when dyad members are indistinguishable? For instance, we may have a set of roommates, and we might want to determine the variance in their responses. It is not at all obvious how to compute this variance, and the naive idea of simply taking all the scores and computing a variance turns out not to be very useful.

Within the ANOVA approach and MLM (without missing data and any fixed variables), the estimate of the variance is simply $(MS_B + MS_W)/2$, where the two mean squares were defined in Chapter 2. This estimate of variance is a restricted maximum likelihood estimate (see Chapter 4). Returning to our example (and treating the married couples as indistinguishable), the estimate of the variance is 0.416.

Alternatively, if we used the pairwise method, the estimate of the variance would be $(SS_B + SS_W)/(2n)$. This estimate of the variance is a maximum likelihood estimate (see Chapter 4), and we used this estimate for double-entry values in Table 6.1. For the satisfaction variable, the variance is .417, a value slightly different from the ANOVA and multilevel estimates.

SUMMARY AND CONCLUSIONS

This chapter focused on estimating and testing differences in variance and correlational structure both within dyads (e.g., for husbands and wives) and across dyads (e.g., for male roommate dyads vs. female roommate dyads). We first considered the simpler case, that of distinguishable dyads. With distinguishable dyads, correlations and variances are computed in the usual way, but significance tests are modified to allow for the non-independence in the data. In addition, when variables have a causal order-

142 DYADIC DATA ANALYSIS

ing, we suggested that researchers examine regression coefficients rather than correlations. Our discussion of correlational structure introduced intrapersonal versus interpersonal correlations, and we presented two ways of testing the difference between these correlated correlations. We then suggested that if there are many variables, SEM can be used.

Perhaps the most useful part of this chapter is the omnibus test of distinguishability. This test examines whether the distinguishing variable really distinguishes between two different "types" of dyad partner. For example, if husbands and wives do not differ in their means, variances, or correlations, then empirically they are actually indistinguishable.

This chapter also proposed methods for estimating and testing differences in categorical variables. We presented a brief introduction to log-linear modeling and then applied this method to examine marginal agreement, quasi-independence, and symmetry of responses.

Finally, we discussed the indistinguishable dyad case, and we noted that with such dyads, there is only one intrapersonal correlation and one interpersonal correlation. We described three ways of estimating these correlations, including the ANOVA approach, the pairwise approach, and MLM. We noted that MLM is quite complex, and we recommended the other two methods instead. Finally, we discussed ways of testing whether two intraclass correlations differ.

Researchers rarely test for differences between correlations and variances. We hope that dyadic researchers will use the methods that we have presented in this chapter more often. Although some of the methods can be a bit cumbersome, we have presented a great deal of detail on the computational steps in order to facilitate their use.

In the next chapter, we return to the problem of testing for mean differences in dyadic research. We began answering this question in Chapter 3 for cases in which the independent variable is either within or between dyads. In Chapter 7, we consider estimating and testing the effects of mixed independent variables. We introduce the Actor–Partner Interdependence Model (APIM), an important tool in dyadic analysis. In Chapter 8, we return to the important distinction between intrapersonal and interpersonal correlations.

NOTES

1. We do not discuss in this section how to test the difference between two kappas. The interested reader should consult Donner and Zou (2002).

2. If there are two levels, then the McNemar test described in Chapter 3 can be used.

3. We could not find a way to set parameters equal within SPSS log-linear analysis, so we included the sum of the two margins (e.g., $a_i + b_i$) as predictors in the analysis.

4. As in Note 1, we summed the two interaction effects to force the equality constraint.

5. In Chapter 4, we discuss how MLM can be used to estimate models of dyadic data. That method can be used to evaluate differences in the intraclass correlations. However, so far as we know, currently only the program MLwiN can perform such a test.

Analyzing Mixed
Independent Variables

*The Actor–Partner
Interdependence Model*

People involved in dyadic relationships (or even brief dyadic interactions) can, and often do, influence each other's thoughts, emotions, and behaviors. This certainly occurs in romantic relationships, where the potential for mutual influence may be the quintessential feature of closeness in relationships (Kelley et al., 1983). Indeed, virtually all major theories of romantic relationships, including theories of equity (Messick & Crook, 1983; Walster, Walster, & Berscheid, 1978), commitment (Rusbult, 1980), trust (Rempel, Holmes, & Zanna, 1985), interdependence (Kelley & Thibaut, 1978; Thibaut & Kelley, 1959), and attachment (Bowlby, 1969, 1973, 1980) acknowledge the idea that one partner's attributes and behaviors can affect the other partner's outcomes. Mutual influence is also present in other types of dyadic relationships, such as friendships and work relationships.

In Chapter 3, we described analyses appropriate for independent or predictor variables that vary either only between dyads or only within dyads. This chapter focuses on the analysis of independent variables that are mixed in nature (see Chapter 1). Mixed independent variables vary both between and within dyads; they can vary on average from dyad to dyad, and they can vary from person to person within each dyad. Thus two sources of variation contribute to variation in mixed variables: The between-dyad source is characterized by variation in the dyad means, M_j, and the within-dyads source is characterized by variation in the deviations of each individual's score from the dyad mean, $X_{ij} - M_j$. The analysis of mixed independent variables allows researchers to investigate issues of mutual influence and is, therefore, a very important part of dyadic data analysis.

This chapter first introduces the model that we use to estimate the effects of a mixed independent variable. We focus on the two key components of that model, actor and partner, and consider their conceptual interpretation. Next, we present the statistical estimation of the model, first describing the analysis for indistinguishable dyads and second describing the analysis for distinguishable dyads. We consider three different estimation techniques: pooled regression, MLM, and SEM. For MLM we discuss four computer programs: SAS, SPSS, HLM, and MLwiN. We also present several extensive examples. Then we discuss the measurement of effect sizes for mixed independent variables. Finally, we discuss specification error in the model.

THE MODEL

As an example, consider the effects of depression on marital satisfaction. It may be that a wife's depression influences both her own and her husband's marital satisfaction. The effect of a wife's depression on her own marital satisfaction is called an *actor effect*, and the effect of her depression on her husband's satisfaction is called a *partner effect* (Kenny, 1996b). That is, an actor effect occurs when a person's score on a predictor variable affects that same person's score on an outcome variable; a partner effect occurs when a person's score on a predictor variable affects his or her partner's score on an outcome variable.

Figure 7.1 depicts the model that we call the *Actor–Partner Interdependence Model* (APIM). There are two dyad members and two variables, X and Y, for each. We denote the two X scores as X_1 and X_2 and the two Y scores as Y_1 and Y_2. We assume that X causes, or is antecedent to, Y. A per-

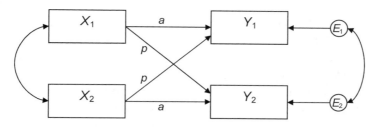

FIGURE 7.1. APIM model where a is the actor effect and p is the partner effect.

son's own X affects his or her own Y, and the effects of X_1 on Y_1 and of X_2 on Y_2 are called *actor effects*. Actor effects are symbolized by a in our discussion and in Figure 7.1. In addition, a person's X affects his or her partner's Y, and the effects of X_1 on Y_2 and of X_2 on Y_1 are called *partner effects*. Partner effects are symbolized by p. If dyad members are distinguishable, there are potentially two actor effects—one for person 1, or a_1, and one for person 2, or a_2. There are also potentially two partner effects, one from person 1 to person 2, or p_{21}, and one from person 2 to person 1, or p_{12}. Because partner effects are interpersonal, they are given double subscripts, and we follow the usual convention for regression coefficients of listing the effect first and then the cause. Note that an actor effect is like an intrapersonal effect (see Chapter 6) in that it refers to one person and a partner effect is like an interpersonal effect in that it refers to two persons.

There are two correlations in the model. The two X's might be correlated, represented by the curved line on the left. Such a correlation might be due to a compositional effect (see Chapter 1). The second correlation is the residual nonindependence in the outcome scores (Y's), which is represented by the correlation between E_1 and E_2. This represents the nonindependence not explained by the APIM. If we denote the correlation between X_1 and X_2 as r, then that part of the correlation between Y_1 and Y_2 that can be explained by actor and partner effects can be shown to equal

$$a_1 p_{21} + a_2 p_{12} + r(a_1 a_2 + p_{12} p_{21}).$$

[In the case in which actor and partner effects are equal, with $a_1 = a_2 = a$ and $p_{12} = p_{21} = p$, the formula becomes $2ap + r(a^2 + p^2)$.] Note that there are four sources of correlation. The first two involve the combination of actor and partner effects. The effect of X_1 on Y_1 and Y_2 is represented by $a_1 p_{21}$, and the effect of X_2 on Y_1 and Y_2 is represented by $a_2 p_{12}$. These are two sources of nonindependence. The impact of the next two sources depends on the size of the correlation between X_1 and X_2, or r.

The analysis implied by the APIM can be used to estimate actor and partner effects for both dyadic and group data (see Kenny, Mannetti, Pierro, Livi, & Kashy, 2002, for a discussion of the application of the APIM to groups) when the independent variable is mixed, and it allows either categorical or continuous independent variables. It can also incorporate independent variables that are not mixed (i.e., those that vary only within dyads or only between dyads); however, separation of actor and partner effects can occur only with mixed predictor variables. Notice that when X is a between-dyads variable, the correlation between X_1 and X_2 is +1, and when X is a within-dyads variable, the correlation between X_1 and X_2 is -1. In either case, there is perfect multicollinearity, and only one effect, not two, can be estimated.

The APIM is increasingly being used in the social sciences. For example, investigators have used it in researching such varied topics as emotion (Butler et al., 2003), health (Butterfield & Lewis, 2002; Franks, Wendorf, Gonzalez, & Ketterer, 2004), leisure activities (Berg, Trost, Schneider, & Allison, 2001), communication competence (Lakey & Canary, 2002), personality (Robins, Caspi, & Moffitt, 2000), commitment (Kurdek, 1997a, 1997b, 2000), interpersonal perception (Kenny & Acitelli, 2001), relationship violence (Landolt & Dutton, 1997; Moffitt, Robins, & Caspi, 2001), social influence (Oriña, Wood, & Simpson, 2002), and attachment style (Campbell, Simpson, Kashy, & Rholes, 2001). The model has also been recommended for use in the study of families (Rayens & Svavardottir, 2003) and small groups (Bonito, 2002).

CONCEPTUAL INTERPRETATION OF ACTOR AND PARTNER EFFECTS

Many researchers are most comfortable with intraindividual or psychological explanations of behavior. This may partially account for the fact that actor effects are routinely estimated, whereas partner effects are often ignored. By studying only actor effects, researchers focus on the individual level of analysis. However, when partner effects are included, identifying truly relational phenomena becomes a possibility. In fact, the presence of partner effects implies that something relational has occurred, because a person's response depends on some characteristic of his or her partner.

The Relative Size of Actor and Partner Effects

Although the sizes of actor and partner effects are independent in principle, specific combinations of these effects are particularly relevant to the study of couples. Following Kenny and Cook (1999), four models have important implications in relationships research:

- Actor-oriented: $a \neq 0$, $p = 0$
- Partner-oriented: $a = 0$, $p \neq 0$
- Couple-oriented: $a = p$
- Social comparison: $a + p = 0$

(The reader should consult Kelley & Thibaut, 1978, for a parallel formulation.)

In the actor-oriented model, a person's outcomes are a function of that person's characteristics only; the partner's characteristics have no impact. Most researchers who adopt the actor-oriented perspective assume that there are actor effects but no partner effects. They rarely bother to test that assumption. This approach to dyadic data occurs frequently with studies of heterosexual dating or married couples in which separate analyses are conducted for men and women (Kashy, Campbell, & Harris, 2006). We suggest that even if a researcher believes that a process is individualistic, it is still necessary to estimate partner effects to show that they are zero. For instance, Rusbult's (1983) social exchange model is individualistic, and when Bui, Peplau, and Hill (1996) looked for partner effects, they found very few. Thus the individualistic perspective of the Rusbult model was validated. Moreover, if there were unestimated partner effects, the estimated actor effects would be biased.

In the partner-oriented model, a person is affected by his or her partner's score on X but is not affected by his or her own X score. One plausible example for which there could be partner effects and not actor effects is the effects of physical attractiveness on relationship satisfaction. It could very well be the case that a person's own attractiveness has little association with his or her own relationship satisfaction, but the person's partner's attractiveness could be strongly related to the person's satisfaction. Although such a partner-effect-only model is plausible, it is still helpful to include actor effects. The physical attractiveness of two members of a couple tends to be correlated (Feingold, 1988), and the curved line between X_1 and X_2 in Figure 7.1 represents this correlation. If there are actor effects that are ignored, then partner effects would be overestimated. Accordingly, even if partner effects are of primary interest, controlling for actor effects in the analysis is still necessary.

In the couple-oriented model, the actor and partner effects are equal such that the person is affected as much by his or her own X as by his or her partner's X. This pattern would occur if the person were as concerned with the partner's outcomes as with his or her own outcomes. For example, playing one's best in a tennis match may make one satisfied with the outcome of the game, and knowing that one's spouse played his or her best could also lead to satisfaction. When one's spouse has a bad game, one's own satisfaction may be less, independent of how one played. Such an orientation would be characteristic of communal relationships (Clark & Mills, 1979).

It is helpful to examine the equation when actor and partner effects are equal. Consider the model:

$$Y_1 = aX_1 + pX_2 + E_1.$$

If actor and partner effects are equal ($a = p$), then we can rewrite the equation as

$$Y_1 = 2a(X_1 + X_2)/2 + E_1.$$

Thus the sum or average of the X variables—that is, $(X_1 + X_2)/2$—can be used to predict Y_1 instead of both X_1 and X_2. This analysis then implies that researchers who use the dyad sum or average of the independent variable to predict a person's outcomes are implicitly assuming a couple orientation. The APIM permits an empirical test of the validity of using a dyad sum: equal actor and partner effects.

It may happen that one member of the couple is couple oriented and the other is not. For example, in a tennis match between a parent and a child, the parent may be couple oriented, feeling satisfaction with either his or her own game and with the child's game. In other words, both the actor and the partner effect are positive for the parent. However, the child may not be couple oriented, feeling less satisfied the better the parent plays. Thus, for the child, the actor effect (i.e., playing well) would be a positive predictor of satisfaction, and the partner effect (i.e., the parent's playing well) would be a negative predictor of satisfaction. A competitive orientation such as this leads to the next pattern.

In the social comparison model, the actor and partner effects are relatively equal in absolute magnitude and have opposite signs. Usually, the actor effect is positive, and the partner effect is negative. Here the person implicitly or explicitly compares him- or herself with the partner. In contrast to the couple-oriented case, in which the partner's success is valued as much as one's own outcome, the social comparison orientation typically involves dissatisfaction with the partner's success. Both imply couple effects, but their conceptual meanings are totally opposite.

Partner-Oriented Interaction Effects

If there were partner effects, then there would be evidence that the two persons are part of an interdependent system. Conversely, if there were no interdependence, there would be no partner effect. It follows logically that the greater the interdependence, the greater the partner effect—or, in other words, that the degree of interdependence moderates the size of partner effects. Therefore, the more important the partner is to someone (consciously or unconsciously), the more he or she would be affected by the partner's characteristics. Hence, researchers can validate a measure of relationship closeness by demonstrating that it interacts with a partner score in producing a particular outcome.

Such an analysis suggests that a relationship scale's "neutral point" or "zero point" can be empirically defined. This neutral point is the predicted score on the relationship scale for individuals who are not interdependent on one another. Imagine a dyadic study of the effects of two partners' happiness on their own and their partner's health. Imagine further that a measure of relationship closeness interacts with the partner effect for feelings of happiness. We can compute at what value of closeness the partner effect for happiness is zero, and that value would be the neutral point of the closeness measure. Those scoring at the neutral point on the measure of relationship closeness would tend to be actor oriented (i.e., the partner's happiness is irrelevant in determining the actor's health); those scoring above the neutral point on the measure of relationship closeness would tend to be couple oriented (i.e., the partner's happiness increases the actor's health); and those scoring below the neutral point would be guided by social comparison (i.e., the partner's happiness decreases the actor's health, or "I do best when you are miserable").

Actor–Partner Interactions

The major research question in dyadic research often involves actor–partner interactions. Interaction variables are typically operationalized as the product of two independent variables. Thus, for couples, the actor-by-partner interaction term would be the product of X_1 and X_2. However, multiplying is just one of an infinite number of ways to specify an interaction between two *continuous* variables. For instance, consider a study of the effect of personality similarity on relationship outcomes. Personality similarity is typically operationalized as the absolute difference between the person's own personality (X_1) and the partner's personality (X_2). It can be viewed as an interaction of actor and partner effects. If X is a dichotomy, then the absolute difference and the product are statistically the same (i.e., the absolute difference and the product correlate perfectly with each other).

Still other specifications of actor–partner interactions are possible and often reasonable. For example, a researcher may speculate that relationships need only one member with a certain skill or attribute in order for an outcome to occur; similarly, a deficit (e.g., substance abuse) on the part of only one member can precipitate some negative consequence. In such cases, it makes sense to use only the higher or lower of the two members' X scores as the interaction term. Consider the effects of interpersonal competence on relationship outcomes. If the more competent member of the couple is able to compensate for the deficits of the less competent member, then relationships may only need one interpersonally competent member in order for both members to be satisfied. In this case, the interaction variable should be operationalized as the score of the member with the higher score. In some couples, this will be the X_1 score, and in other couples, the X_2 score, and so it is not simply a main effect (unless X_1 is always greater or less than X_2). If dyad members are distinguishable, then the maximum or minimum measure of interaction should not be used if one member's value of X is always greater than the other member's (e.g., if the woman's X is always greater than the man's X).

Although there are many ways to operationalize actor–partner interactions, empirically it is very difficult to distinguish among them. For instance, the multiplicative operationalization of interaction and the discrepancy measure are usually highly correlated. Generally, theory, and not statistical analysis, must be used to choose the appropriate operationalization. In addition, one should always interpret the actor–partner interaction using the measure that was operationalized. That is, if a product is used, one should not interpret it as a similarity measure.

Whenever interactive effects are estimated, the main effects should usually be controlled. (For a contrasting view, see Brauer & Judd, 2000.) For instance, if a discrepancy score is computed to form a similarity score, the components that make up that discrepancy should also be included in the analysis. All too often, interaction scores are computed, but the main effects of actor and partner are not controlled. Frequently, "interactions" (e.g., similarity) are statistically significant because the confounding effects of actor and partner have not been removed. For example, suppose a study indicates that couples with similar levels of depression are more satisfied, but the main effects are not controlled. The similarity effect may actually be due to actor and partner effects of depression. That is, most people are not depressed, and so if two people are "similar," then it is likely that they are *both not* depressed. However, if one member is depressed, it is likely that the absolute difference in the two depression scores would be large and that the dyad members would be "dissimilar." Thus couple similarity is confounded with individual levels of depression, and these effects should be controlled.

ESTIMATION OF THE APIM: INDISTINGUISHABLE DYAD MEMBERS

We present three different methods to estimate the APIM: the pooled regression method, MLM, and SEM. We do not discuss the pioneering estimation method presented by Kraemer and Jacklin (1979). Theirs was the first explicit attempt to estimate the model that came to be known as APIM. However, their technique is limited to the case in which there is a single dichotomous independent variable (X) and tests of statistical significance are approximate. Also, we do not discuss pairwise estimation of the model, and we refer the reader to Gonzalez and Griffin (2001a).

Although not required, it advisable to make zero a meaningful value for the predictor variables. This is often done by centering the X variable (i.e., subtracting the mean). In our first example, the key predictor variable is the number of hours per week each of two roommates spend doing housework. Because zero is a meaningful value (i.e., the person does no housework), we do not center this variable. In our second example, however, the key predictor variable is a measure of neuroticism, which does not have a meaningful zero value. Thus, for the second example data set, we computed the grand mean of X_1 and X_2 combined and subtracted it from all of the X scores.

Pooled-Regression Method

The pooled-regression approach to the APIM involves estimating two regression equations and then pooling the results together to estimate the APIM parameters (Kashy & Kenny, 2000). One of the regression equations focuses on the within-dyads effects of the mixed independent variable (referred to as the *within-dyads regression*), and the other regression equation focuses on the between-dyads effects of the mixed independent variable (referred to as the *between-dyads regression*).

Analysis with a Single Predictor Variable

As a very simple example, consider a fictitious study of housing satisfaction involving 20 pairs of same-sex roommates. Say that one predictor variable under consideration is a measure of the number of hours each individual spends per week cleaning and maintaining the residence. The fictitious data for this example are presented in Table 7.1. As can be seen in this table, for the first pair of roommates, the first roommate spends a little over 1 hour per week on housework and has a satisfaction score of 6 (on a 9-point scale). The other roommate works about half as much (0.6 of an hour) and has a satisfaction score of 7. Note that this is a dyad-level data set in which each record is one dyad (see Chapter 1).

To estimate actor and partner effects, two regression equations are computed. The within-dyads regression involves predicting the difference between the dyad members' scores on the outcome variable $(Y_1 - Y_2)$ with the difference between the dyad members' scores on the mixed predictor variable $(X_1 - X_2)$. The between-dyads regression involves predicting the dyad mean on outcome variable $[(Y_1 + Y_2)/2]$ with the dyad mean on the mixed predictor variable $[(X_1 + X_2)/2]$. The difference in X predicts the difference in Y, and the mean of X predicts the mean of Y.

Thus, in the within-dyads regression, the data would be derived by subtracting one roommate's score on satisfaction from the other roommate's score on satisfaction. This difference between the two partners' scores on satisfaction (roommate 1's satisfaction score minus roommate 2's satisfaction score) serves as the outcome score in a regression in which the predictor score is the difference (subtracting in the same direction across the two dyad members: person 1 minus person 2) between the two partners' housework scores. Using the data in Table 7.1, for the first three dyads, the outcome and predictor scores, respectively, would be, for Dyad 1, 0.6, –1; for Dyad 2, 2.0, –4; and for Dyad 3, –0.2, –1.

It is important to note that the intercept should not be estimated in the within-dyads regression. We discussed this in Chapter 3 when we

TABLE 7.1. Data for Fictitious Study of Roommates

Dyad	H R_1	R_2	S R_1	R_2	G R_1	R_2	Dyad	H R_1	R_2	S R_1	R_2	G R_1	R_2
1	1.2	0.6	6	7	1	1	11	0.8	2.1	8	5	–1	–1
2	4.3	2.3	5	9	–1	–1	12	2.3	2.5	5	7	–1	–1
3	0.4	0.6	3	4	1	1	13	1.0	2.0	4	6	1	1
4	0.3	0.5	6	8	1	1	14	2.5	1.5	6	7	1	1
5	3.2	1.0	2	6	–1	–1	15	2.0	.5	5	6	1	1
6	1.1	0.8	3	8	1	1	16	1.8	2.6	7	4	–1	–1
7	2.0	1.5	5	7	1	1	17	4.3	2.0	2	4	–1	–1
8	0.4	1.6	7	4	–1	–1	18	1.0	2.0	4	4	–1	–1
9	0.3	0.5	3	3	1	1	19	2.5	2.5	6	5	–1	–1
10	3.2	2.0	5	8	1	1	20	1.0	0.5	3	4	–1	–1

Note. H, housework; S, satisfaction; G, gender; R_1, respondent 1; R_2, respondent 2. For gender, men = 1 and women = –1.

described the analysis of within-dyads independent variables. The issue is that when we compute the difference between the dyad members' scores, the direction of differencing is arbitrary in the sense that we can either subtract Joan's score from Sue's or vice versa. Because of this arbitrariness of direction, the intercept should not be estimated in the within-dyads regression. As we described in Chapter 3, most computer packages have a no-intercept option for regression analyses. For example, in SPSS, within "Linear Regression," the "Options" box is checked, and then the check is deleted from the box "Include the constant in the equation." For SAS, this is the NOINT option in PROC GLM or PROC REG. Forcing the intercept to be zero ensures that the regression solution is the same even if the direction of differencing was switched for some dyads. Accordingly, the within-dyads equation for dyad i is

$$Y_{1i} - Y_{2i} = b_w(X_{1i} - X_{2i}) + E_{wi}.$$

Note that there is no intercept in the equation.

In the between-dyads regression, the average of the two satisfaction scores is computed for each dyad, as is the average of the two housework scores. The mean housework score for the dyad is then used to predict the mean satisfaction score for the dyad. Again, using the data in Table 7.1, for the first three dyads the outcome and predictor scores, respectively, for the between-dyads regression would be, for Dyad 1, 0.9, 6.5; for Dyad 2, 3.3, 7.0; and for Dyad 3, 0.5, 3.5. The no-intercept option is not used in this part of the analysis, and the intercept is estimated. The equation for dyad i would be as follows:

$$(Y_{1i} + Y_{2i})/2 = b_0 + b_b(X_{1i} + X_{2i})/2 + E_{bi}.$$

The unstandardized regression coefficients derived from these two regressions, b_b from the between regression and b_w from the within regression, are then used to estimate actor and partner effects as follows (Kenny, 1996b):

Actor: $(b_b + b_w)/2$
Partner: $(b_b - b_w)/2$

For the housework and satisfaction data in Table 7.1, the between regression equation yields a b_b of 0.297, and the within regression yields a b_w of -1.479, and thus the actor effect is estimated to be -0.591 and the partner effect, 0.888. Both the actor and partner effect estimates can be interpreted as unstandardized regression coefficients. The actor effect in this example indicates that each 1-hour increase in housework done by an individual yields a drop in housing satisfaction of 0.591 points—people who do more housework are less satisfied. The partner effect estimate indicates that each 1-hour increase in housework done by a person's roommate corresponds to a 0.888 increase in the person's satisfaction—so people whose roommates do more housework are more satisfied.

To test whether the actor and partner effects differ significantly from zero, the standard errors associated with the between and within regression coefficients (s_b = 0.347 and s_w = 0.359, respectively) must be pooled. (The standard error for each of these regression coefficients can be derived by taking the t value associated with the regression coefficient and dividing it by the regression coefficient.) The formula for calculating the pooled standard error is

$$\text{Pooled standard error} = \sqrt{\frac{s_b^2 + s_w^2}{4}}.$$

For the example of roommate housing satisfaction, the pooled standard error is estimated as 0.250. The estimate of the actor effect is divided by this pooled standard error to yield a t-test indicating whether the actor effect differs significantly from zero. In the example, the t value for the actor effect is $-0.591/0.250 = -2.36$. Similarly, the partner-effect t value is $0.888/0.250 = 3.55$. The degrees of freedom (Satterthwaite, 1946) for both of these tests are estimated as

$$df = \frac{(s_b^2 + s_w^2)^2}{\dfrac{s_b^4}{df_b} + \dfrac{s_w^4}{df_w}}.$$

Surprisingly, the degrees of freedom can be fractional. For the t distribution, critical values and exact p values can be determined for fractional values of degrees of freedom. If a fractional answer is obtained and a critical value is to be sought from a t table, to be conservative, one rounds down. For the example, the degrees of freedom are estimated to be 37.07, and so both the actor and partner effects are statistically significant.

An additional relevant statistic in this analysis is the amount of variance explained by the actor and partner effects combined. To compute this statistic, the total variance that can potentially be explained by the actor and partner effects must be computed. To compute this total variance, two additional regressions are conducted: a between-dyads regression without the averaged mixed predictor variable and a within-dyads regression without the differenced mixed predictor variable. As before, the within-dyads regression should be estimated without the intercept. For the data in Table 7.1 from our fictitious roommate study, this involves computing a between-dyads regression in which average satisfaction is predicted only by an intercept and a within-dyads regression in which the difference in satisfaction is the criterion and in which there are no predictors (again suppressing the intercept).[1]

The between regression without the mixed predictor yields a sum of squares error, SSE_b', and a mean square error, MSE_b'; for the example, these values are 119.00 and 5.95, respectively. The within-dyads regression without the mixed predictor also yields a sum of squares error, SSE_w', and a mean square error, MSE_w', 33.24 and 1.75, respectively. The total variance that can be explained is then $(MSE_b' + MSE_w')/2$, or 3.85. The total variance left unexplained by the mixed independent variable is computed from the regressions that include the mixed variable as a predictor and equals $(MSE_b + MSE_w)/2$, where MSE_b is the mean square error from the between regression that included the averaged mixed independent variable as a predictor and MSE_w is the mean square error from the within-dyads regression that included the differenced mixed independent variable as the predictor. The variance left unexplained by housework is $(1.77 + 3.31)/2 = 2.54$. To compute the proportion of variance explained by the actor and partner effects combined, the value of R^2 is

$$R^2 = 1 - \frac{SSE_b + SSE_w}{SSE_b' + SSE_w'}$$

where SSE_b is the sum of squares error from the between regression that included the averaged mixed independent variable and SSE_w is the sum of squares error from the within regression that included the differenced mixed independent variable. (Recall that a mean square is defined as a sum of squares divided by its degrees of freedom.) For the example, $R^2 = .378$, and so the actor and partner effects for housework combined account for almost 38% of the variance in satisfaction scores.

Analysis with Multiple Predictor Variables

The pooled-regression approach to analyzing the APIM has a natural extension in which multiple predictor variables can be examined simultaneously. In the multiple predictor variable extension, the two regressions (within and between dyads) are conducted as multiple regressions. For the within-dyads regression, each of the mixed predictor variables, as well as the outcome variable, are differenced (always in the same direction across partners). For the between-dyads regression, each of the mixed predictor variables and the outcome variable are averaged across partners. Actor and partner effects for each mixed predictor can then be estimated using the formulas presented previously.

Some analyses may contain purely between-dyads or purely within-dyads predictor variables. In our example study with roommates, some of the roommate dyads are both men, and others are both women, and so gender is a between-dyads variable. (Although not included in this fictitious example, a within-dyads variable might be a categorical variable denoting which of the two roommates has greater financial resources.) For both purely within- or purely between-dyads variables, separate actor and partner effects cannot be estimated; however, such variables can be included in the model when estimating actor and partner effects for mixed variables, and their effects can be controlled. Purely between-dyads variables would be included only in the between-dyads regression. Thus, in the example, the gender variable (coded 1 for men and −1 for women) would be included in the between-dyads regression. If a within-dyads variable were to be included as a predictor variable, the difference between the dyad members' scores (always differencing in a way consistent with how the outcome variable was differenced) would be included as a predictor only in the within-dyads regression. Such analyses would provide estimates of the general effects of the purely between-dyads and purely within-dyads variables, as well as estimates of both actor and partner effects for all mixed variables.

In addition to including the main effects of purely between- or within-dyads variables, this approach can also accommodate interactions between mixed variables and between- or within-dyads variables. Such interactions allow researchers to test whether actor and partner effects for the mixed variables vary significantly across the levels of a between-dyads or a within-dyads variable. In our example study of roommates, we could estimate and test the interaction between the hours of housework done (the mixed variable) and gender (the between-dyads variable). The actor component of this interaction tests whether the relation between a person's time spent on housework and his or her own satisfaction differs for men and women. The partner component tests whether the relation between a person's time spent on housework and his or her partner's satisfaction (the partner effect) differs for men and women. Similar effects can be computed for the interactions between within-dyads variables and mixed variables. A detailed multivariate example using the pooled regression approach can be found in Kashy and Kenny (2000).

Although the pooled regression method provides estimates of the APIM, it has three serious drawbacks. First, it is awkward and cumbersome, because it requires piecing together several analyses. This awkwardness can easily lead to computational errors. Second, unsaturated models (e.g., models in which some variables may have only actor effects, and other variables may have only partner effects) cannot be estimated. Third, the pooled regression method does not allow for missing data, whereas both MLM and SEM allow for missing data for one member of the dyad (although if Y_1 is missing, X_1 should not be missing, because X_1 is in the Y_2 equation.) For these reasons, MLM and SEM are now the preferred methods for estimating the APIM.

Estimating the APIM with Multilevel Analysis

In this section we discuss estimating the APIM effects using four multilevel programs, SAS, SPSS, HLM, and MLwiN. We do not discuss the use of some SEM programs (e.g., LISREL and Mplus) that directly estimate multilevel models.

SAS and SPSS

To estimate the APIM using a multilevel approach, the data set needs to be arranged as a pairwise data set (see Chapter 1). For such a data set, each individual is an observation (i.e., each individual has his or her own data record), and each individual's outcome score is associated with both his or her own predictor scores and his or her partner's predictor scores. Thus each person's predictor score is entered twice, once as an actor predictor score associated with that person's outcome and once as a partner predictor score associated with the partner's outcome. For the data in Table 7.1, the first two dyads' data would be entered as:

Dyad	Person	Gender	Satisfaction	Actor Housework	Partner Housework
1	1	1	6	1.2	0.6
1	2	1	7	0.6	1.2
2	1	−1	5	4.3	2.3
2	2	−1	9	2.3	4.3

The data are input for each individual independently, such that each individual is treated as one case and there are two cases for each couple. Therefore, with 20 couples in the example, the input statement would read in 40 individual cases. It is advisable, though not always necessary, to sort the data set by dyad and to create a dummy record if a case is missing.

The SAS code for a multilevel analysis that estimates the basic APIM parameters (i.e., actor and partner effects for housework predicting satisfaction) is

```
PROC MIXED COVTEST;
CLASS DYADID;
MODEL SATISFACTION = ACT_HOUSE PART_HOUSE / SOLUTION
    DDFM=SATTERTH;
REPEATED / TYPE=CS SUBJECT=DYADID;
```

Alternatively, instead of the "REPEATED" statement, we could have the following record:

```
RANDOM INTERCEPT / SUBJECT = DYADID;
```

As explained in Chapter 4, the latter approach treats the nonindependence as a variance and not as a correlation, and so it cannot handle negative nonindependence. The "REPEATED" statement, which we prefer, allows for negative nonindependence.

As we discussed in Chapter 4, the default estimation method used by SAS's PROC MIXED is REML, and the estimates derived from this default exactly replicate those given using the pooled-regression approach. The COVTEST option requests that SAS provide tests of the variance components. The CLASS statement indicates the variable that identifies dyad membership (DYADID). SATISFACTION is the individual's outcome score, ACT_HOUSE is the number of hours per week that the person does housework, and PART_HOUSE is the number of hours per week that the person's partner does housework. The SOLUTION option in the MODEL statement requests that SAS print the estimates for the intercept and the actor and partner effects for housework. The DDFM = SATTERTH option requests the Satterthwaite (1946) approximation to determine the degrees of freedom for the intercept and slopes (Kashy & Kenny, 2000). The degrees of freedom for mixed predictor variables using the Satterthwaite approximation is some value between the number of dyads less 1 and the number of individuals in the study less 2. The REPEATED statement treats the individual scores as repeated measures in the dyad, and CS implies *compound symmetry*, which means that the variances of the intercepts for the two dyad members are equal. As we said earlier, nonindependence is estimated as a correlation and not as a variance.

A subset of the results from the SAS's PROC MIXED analysis is presented in Table 7.2. Turning to these results, in the solution for the fixed effects, the effect estimate for ACT_HOUSE is the actor effect for housework, $b = -0.59$, $t(37) = 2.37$, and the effect estimate for PART_HOUSE is the partner effect for housework, $b = 0.89$, $t(37) = 3.56$. The value of the intraclass correlation in satisfaction scores, controlling for the effects of housework, can be computed by taking the ratio of the CS covariance parameter estimate (0.95) to the sum of the CS parameter and the residual variance estimate (0.95 + 1.65). Thus the partial intraclass correlation is .36, indicating that after controlling for the effects of housework, satisfaction levels for the two roommates were somewhat similar.

TABLE 7.2. APIM Results from SAS's PROC MIXED for the Artificial Roommate Data in Table 7.1

Covariance Parameter Estimates

Cov Parm	Subject	Estimate	Standard Error	Z Value	Pr Z
CS	DYADID	0.9477	0.6493	1.46	0.1444
Residual		1.6530	0.5363	3.08	0.0010

Fit Statistics

-2 Res Log Likelihood	148.4
AIC (smaller is better)	152.4
AICC (smaller is better)	152.7
BIC (smaller is better)	154.4

Null Model Likelihood Ratio Test

DF	Chi-Square	Pr > ChiSq
1	2.65	0.1035

Solution for Fixed Effects

Effect	Estimate	Standard Error	DF	t Value	Pr > |t|
Intercept	4.7910	0.6387	18	7.50	<.0001
ACT_HOUSE	-0.5908	0.2494	37	-2.37	0.0232
PART_HOUSE	0.8878	0.2494	37	3.56	0.0010

We have requested the Satterthwaithe degrees of freedom that represent a complicated weighted average of the between and within degrees of freedom (see the earlier formula). Fortunately, SAS and SPSS do provide them. However, some multilevel programs do not give degrees of freedom (e.g., MLwiN), and others give either the between or the within (HLM6) degrees of freedom. We believe that the Satterthwaithe estimate of degrees of freedom is more appropriate because it takes into account the mixture of the between and within parts of the estimate. However, when there is a reasonable number of cases, the differences in the t-test and p values due to differences in degrees of freedom are trivial.

The estimate of the pseudo R^2 can be obtained by computing

$$R^2 = 1 - \frac{CS + RES}{CS' + RES'},$$

where CS is the compound symmetry term and RES is the residual error variance. The prime refers to the unrestricted model, that is, a model without ACT_HOUSE or PART_HOUSE in the equation. For the example, the estimate of pseudo R^2 is $1 - (0.948 + 1.653)/(.262 + 2.975) = .196$. Note that this value differs from the pooled regression value because variance and covariance components are used, not sums of squares. If the coefficients are small, it is possible that the estimated value for R^2 would be negative. In such a case, it would be reported as zero.

The SPSS specification for the APIM is quite similar to that of SAS. One needs version 11 of SPSS or later; we recommend having at least version 12.0. Again, the data set needs to be structured such that each individual's outcome is associated with both that person's predictor score and the person's partner's predictor score (i.e., a pairwise data set; see Chapter 1). The SPSS code for the analysis that includes both actor and partner effects of housework predicting satisfaction is

```
MIXED
    SATISFAC WITH ACT_HOU PART_HOU
    /FIXED = ACT_HOU PART_HOU
    /PRINT = SOLUTION TESTCOV
    /REPEATED = PERSONID | SUBJECT(DYADID) COVTYPE(CS).
```

The estimates from SPSS are contained in Table 7.3. Note that the values are essentially the same as those from SAS. The only difference is that the p value for the error variance is twice as large as that from SAS. Because tests of variance should be one-sided, the p value for the variances from SPSS should be divided by 2.

TABLE 7.3. APIM Results from SPSS for the Artificial Roommate Data in Table 7.1

Estimates of Fixed Effects[a]

Parameter	Estimate	Std. Error	df	t	Sig.	95% Confidence Interval	
						Lower Bound	Upper Bound
Intercept	4.7909782	.6386893	18	7.501	.000	3.4491418	6.1328145
ACT_HOU	−.5908267	.2493903	36.998	−2.369	.023	−1.0961402	−.0855131
PART_HOU	.8877726	.2493903	36.998	3.560	.001	.3824590	1.3930861

[a]Dependent Variable: SATISFAC.

Estimates of Covariance Parameters[a]

Parameter		Estimate	Std. Error	Wald Z	Sig.	95% Confidence Interval	
						Lower Bound	Upper Bound
Repeated Measures	CS diagonal offset	1.6529797	.5362974	3.082	.002	.8751878	3.1220063
	CS covariance	.9476986	.6493482	1.459	.144	−.3250006	2.2203978

[a]Dependent Variable: SATISFAC.

HLM

Currently the most commonly used stand-alone computer program for estimating multilevel models is the HLM program (Raudenbush, Bryk, Cheong, & Congdon, 2004). To use this program, two separate data files need to be created. The first data set is very similar to the data set described earlier for use with PROC MIXED. This *level-1* data set is composed of one record for each individual, and each record must include a variable identifying dyad membership, the individual's outcome scores, and actor and partner values for any mixed predictor variables. In our example, each record in the level-1 data set would include the DYADID variable for the person, as well as the person's score on the outcome measure (SATISFAC), the person's score on the mixed predictor variable (ACT_HOU), and the person's partner's score on the mixed predictor variable (PART_HOU). There would be 40 observations or records in this data set.

The second data set, referred to as the *level-2* data set in HLM, has one record for each dyad and includes the variable that identifies dyad membership (identical to the identification variable in the level-1 data set), as well as any variables that vary only between dyads. In our roommate example, gender is a between-dyads variable, and so it would be included in the level-2 data set, along with the DYADID variable. This level-2 data set would have 20 observations or records. HLM6 can run using data files imported from commercial software programs such as SPSS, as well as data files that are text files.

To estimate the basic APIM effects for our fictitious data set, SATISFAC needs to be identified as the outcome variable. Then ACT_HOU and PART_HOU each need to be selected as predictors. This should result in the following level-1 model within HLM notation:

$$SATISFAC = \beta_0 + \beta_1(ACT\_HOU) + \beta_2(PART\_HOU) + r.$$

This model suggests that each individual's satisfaction is a function of his or her time spent on housework and his or her partner's time spent on housework. The level-2 models within HLM6 are

$$\beta_0 = \gamma_{00} + u_0$$
$$\beta_1 = \gamma_{10}$$
$$\beta_2 = \gamma_{20}$$

In the first of these models, the intercept for the dyad is a function of both a fixed component, γ_{00}, and a random component, u_0. The fixed component provides an estimate of satisfaction for roommates in which both partner's housework is zero. The random component estimates the degree to which satisfaction scores vary from dyad to dyad after controlling for the effects of housework. That is, the random component provides a measure of the partial intraclass correlation on the outcome variable between dyad members. The second and third models suggest that the effects of actor and partner are constant across dyads. In other words, there is no random component for the actor and partner effects in the APIM for dyads because of restrictions in the data structure (see Chapter 4).

Table 7.4 presents a subset of the output for these models from HLM6. An examination of the fixed effects shows that HLM and SAS estimated identical coefficients and standard errors for each effect in the model. One major difference between HLM and SAS is the calculation of degrees of freedom used to test the significance of the model parameters. As we have discussed, SAS and SPSS use the Satterthwaite (1946) approximation to determine the degrees of freedom for the intercept and slopes, resulting in degrees of freedom that are between the number of couples and individuals in the sample. In contrast, HLM bases the degrees of freedom for the

TABLE 7.4. APIM Results from HLM6 Analysis of Artificial Roommate Data in Table 7.1

Summary of the model specified (in equation format)

Level-1 Model

Y = B0 + B1*(ACT_HOU) + B2*(PART_HOU) + R

Level-2 Model
B0 = G00 + U0
    B1 = G10
    B2 = G20

Sigma_squared =   1.65301

Tau
INTRCPT1,B0   0.94763

Random level-1 coefficient	Reliability estimate
INTRCPT1, B0	0.534

The outcome variable is   SATISFAC

Final estimation of fixed effects:

Fixed Effect	Coefficient	Standard Error	T-ratio	d.f.	Approx. P-value
For INTRCPT1, B0					
INTRCPT2, G00	4.790978	0.638676	7.501	19	0.000
For ACT_HOU slope, B1					
INTRCPT2, G10	-0.590827	0.249389	-2.369	37	0.023
For PART_HOU slope, B2					
INTRCPT2, G20	0.887773	0.249389	3.560	37	0.001

actor and partner effects on the number of individuals in the sample. Therefore, the significance tests are very slightly more liberal in HLM than in SAS and SPSS.

MLwiN

Finally, we have used the computer program MLwiN to estimate the APIM. As explained in Chapter 4, MLwiN requires an individual data file, and for the APIM the data file would need to be a pairwise data file in which each person's outcome score is associated with that person's predictor score and the partner's predictor score. As was the case with HLM, there are two levels in the analysis, level 1 being individual and level 2 being dyad. In Table 7.5, we have the output from the analysis using MLwiN. We see that the estimates are identical to those of the other programs. However, the deviance is somewhat different, because MLwiN uses generalized least squares as its estimation method rather than the REML method used by the other programs. As mentioned in Chapter 4, MLwiN does not provide degrees of freedom or statistical tests of the parameter estimates. However, the parameter estimates may be divided by their standard errors of the estimate (the term in parentheses after the estimate), which are provided, to obtain a Z score.

Comparing the Size of Actor and Partner Effects

Recall our earlier discussion of the relative sizes of actor and partner effects. In this discussion, we suggested that in the couple-oriented model, actor and partner effects are equal such that a person's outcome is equally

TABLE 7.5. APIM Results from MLwiN Analysis of Artificial Roommate Data in Table 7.1

```
satisf_ij ~N(XB,  Ω)
satisf_ij = β_0i intercept + -0.591(0.258)act_house_ij +
    0.888(0.258)part_house_ij
β_0i = 4.791(0.523) + e_0ij

[e_0ij] ~ N(0, Ω_e): Ω_e = [2.382(0.533)]

-2*loglikelihood(IGLS Deviance) = 148.232(40 of 40 cases
in use)
```

determined by his or her own and his or her partner's predictors. We can conduct a statistical test that determines whether or not the actor and partner effects differ significantly. To do such a test, we would estimate a multilevel model in which two predictors, $(X_1 + X_2)/2$ and $X_1 - X_2$, are used to predict each person's score on Y. That is, we predict each person's outcome with the dyad average and the dyad difference of the predictor. Note that the difference refers to the person's score minus the partner's score. If the average has an effect and the difference does not (i.e., it is not statistically significant), then we would conclude that actor and partner effects were not significantly different from each other.[2]

We can also conduct a similar test for social comparison effects. Recall that social comparison effects are seen when the actor and partner effects are of similar size but opposite sign. Again, we would enter the dyad average and difference, $(X_1 + X_2)/2$ and $X_1 - X_2$, as predictors of Y in a multilevel analysis. In this case, if the average had no effect and the difference did, then we would conclude that actor and partner effects were equal but have opposite signs.

Analyses with Interactions and Multiple Predictor Variables

Inclusion of actor and partner effects for more than one mixed predictor variable, purely within- or between-dyads variables, interactions between actor and partner effects, or interactions between actor and partner effects and within- or between-dyads variables is quite straightforward with MLM using SAS or SPSS. In either program, new variables (such as multiplicative interactions or the absolute value of actor and partner differences) can be created that are functions of existing variables. Such variables or interactions between variables are simply added to the MODEL statement in SAS or the statement that specifies the outcome and the predictor variables in SPSS. However, as we noted in Chapter 4, it is important that any variables included in interactions should: (1) have a meaningful zero and, if they do not, should be grand-mean centered; and (2) have their main effects included in the model statement, in addition to the interaction. Moreover, as we discussed earlier in the chapter, the interaction should be created in a manner that is theoretically relevant. For instance, if the interest is similarity, then the absolute difference, not the product, should be formed.

In SAS's PROC MIXED, multiplicative interactions can be formed directly in the model statement itself. For example, the following SAS

MODEL statement could be used to estimate the actor and partner effects of housework, as well as the multiplicative interaction between actor and partner effects:

```
PROC MIXED COVTEST;
    CLASS DYADID;
    MODEL SATISFACTION = ACT_HOUSE PART_HOUSE
    ACT_HOUSE*PART_HOUSE / SOLUTION
        DDFM=SATTERTH;
    REPEATED / TYPE=CS SUBJECT=DYADID;
```

In the example, the interaction estimates the degree to which the impact that the partner's housework contribution has on a person's satisfaction is moderated by the amount of housework the person does. For the example data, the interaction coefficient is only −0.05 and is not statistically significant.

Similarly, the more recent version of SPSS also allows users to specify multiplicative interactions directly in the statement of the model:

```
/FIXED = ACT_HOU PART_HOU ACT_HOU*PART_HOU
```

In older versions of SPSS, interaction variables must first be created via a "compute" statement. For example, if we wanted to test a model that allowed for interactions between gender and actor or partner effects, we would first compute the interaction variables:

```
COMPUTE ACTGEND = ACT_HOU*GENDER
COMPUTE PARTGEND = PART_HOU*GENDER
```

We would then include the main effect variables, as well as the interaction variables, with gender in our model:

```
SATISFAC WITH ACT_HOU PART_HOU GENDER ACTGEND PARTGEND
    /FIXED = ACT_HOU PART_HOU GENDER ACTGEND PARTGEND
```

This model allows us to estimate the degree to which actor and partner effects for housework on satisfaction vary for men and women.

Specifying interactions with HLM6 and MLwiN requires some forethought. Interactions between actor and partner effects, or between within-dyads variables and actor (or partner) effects, cannot be created while running HLM6 or MLwiN. Instead, they must exist as already computed values within the appropriate data set. For example, to create an actor–partner interaction for housework, a variable that represents the interaction between the two partners' housework scores would need to be created prior to the analysis. Note that interactions between actor and partner effects are dyad-level effects and would need to be included in the level-2 data set. Interactions between a level-1 variable (i.e., a mixed variable such as ACT_HOU or a within-dyads variable) and a between-dyads variable, which is a level-2 variable, such as GENDER in the example, can be estimated within the HLM or MLwiN program itself and need not be included in the data sets.

Summary

MLM is perhaps the most flexible estimation approach for the APIM. Unlike the pooled-regression solution, MLM provides direct estimates of actor and partner effects, as well as tests of these effects. It also allows researchers to specify constrained models in which some mixed predictor variables have only actor effects, whereas others may have only partner effects. A third approach offers some advantages under certain situations: SEM.

Estimating the APIM with SEM

SEM with indistinguishable dyads is not easy to do, and we recommend that its use be restricted to two situations. It is the approach of choice for researchers who are interested in estimating latent variable models or models in which the X variables have measurement error. We should also note that one advantage of SEM is that the entire model is estimated. Thus the correlation between X_1 and X_2 is estimated within the same model and does not have to be estimated separately.

The model depicted in Figure 7.1 is used to estimate the actor and partner effects. Dyad is the unit of analysis, and we treat the dyad as if members were distinguishable. In Chapter 5, we presented the method developed by Olsen and Kenny (2006) using equality constraints. To estimate the APIM parameters for indistinguishable dyads, we estimate means and intercepts forcing the following constraints—$a_1 = a_2$, $p_{12} = p_{21}$, $V(X_1) = V(X_2)$, $V(E_1) = V(E_2)$, $M_{X1} = M_{X2}$—and also forcing the intercepts of E_1 and E_2 to be equal. Thus a total of six equality constraints are made. The resulting model is invariant under different assignment of person to 1 and 2.

However, the chi-square value varies. This model is the baseline model with 6 degrees of freedom.

We used the housework example in Table 7.1, and we present the estimates in a path diagram in Figure 7.2. Note that paths, means, intercepts, and variances have been set equal. We obtained essentially the same estimates as we obtained using multilevel programs. (They would be exactly the same if we use the maximum likelihood option within MLM.) We find a $\chi^2(6) = 10.83$. If we reversed assignments of person 1 and person 2 for some of the dyads, the chi-square would change, but the parameter estimates would remain the same. As explained in Chapter 5, the chi-square test for the base model should not be interpreted. Rather, this model serves as the I-SAT model and is used to adjust models' chi-squares and degrees of freedom.

Consider a model that forces the actor and partner effects to be equal. We obtain a $\chi^2(7) = 22.97$. We take this chi-square and adjust it by the I-SAT one to obtain $\chi^2(1) = 12.06$, $p < .001$. Thus we conclude that actor and partner effects are statistically significantly different.

Clearly, the SEM solution for indistinguishable dyads is awkward and may be difficult for researchers to implement. As we have noted earlier, we strongly recommend that most researchers with indistinguishable dyads use the MLM approach described earlier in this chapter. However, SEM is relatively easy to implement for estimating the APIM when dyad members are distinguishable, the topic that we now consider.

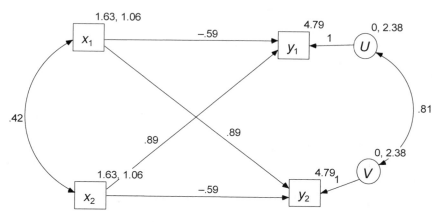

FIGURE 7.2. Estimation of the APIM parameters using structural equation modeling.

ESTIMATION OF THE APIM: DISTINGUISHABLE DYADS

Distinguishable dyad members, by definition, vary on a within-dyads variable. For example, heterosexual couples are distinguishable by their gender: Each couple has one man and one woman. Other distinguishable dyads might be mother–daughter dyads or supervisor–subordinate dyads. When dyad members are distinguishable on a nonarbitrary variable, the APIM can again be estimated using either pooled regression, MLM, or SEM. Relatively minor changes are required for the pooled-regression and MLM approaches to accommodate distinguishable dyads. The SEM approach, however, changes substantially, and as a result of the changes, this approach becomes dramatically easier to implement.

In describing the APIM for distinguishable dyads, we use data gathered from 98 heterosexual dating couples (Campbell, Simpson, Boldry, & Kashy, 2005). In this example, both members of each couple completed a measure of neuroticism at the beginning of the study. Then, following a 2-week-long diary study, in which individuals reported on the daily conflicts and supportive interactions that occurred with their partners, the couples returned to the laboratory. During a videotaped interaction, they were to try to resolve one of the most serious conflicts that had occurred during the diary data collection period. The videotapes were then coded for a range of behaviors, including five indicators of distress: appearing upset, disappointed, unhappy, satisfied (reversed), and positive (reversed). Our example examines the degree to which a person's own neuroticism predicts that person's distress (an actor effect) and the degree to which a person's partner's neuroticism predicts that person's distress (a partner effect). Because the dyads are distinguishable with respect to gender, we also examine whether the actor and partner effects differ for men and women. An APIM diagram with these variables is presented in Figure 7.3.

Pooled-Regression Method

In the pooled-regression approach, the data are organized with dyad as the unit of analysis (see Chapter 1). With this data organization, each record contains two measurements of the outcome variable, one for the man and one for the woman. Similarly, each record also contains two measurements of the mixed predictor variable. Thus there are the scores X_M and X_F for each predictor variable and Y_M and Y_F for the outcome variable. Recall that in the pooled-regression solution, two regressions are computed: a between-dyads regression in which the dyad averages on the outcome are

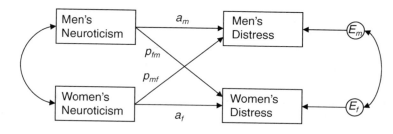

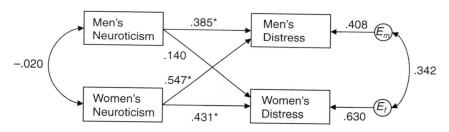

FIGURE 7.3. APIM for Simpson et al. example.

predicted by the dyad averages on the predictor and a within-dyads regression in which the dyad differences on the outcome are predicted by the dyad differences on the predictor. Recall, too, that the intercept is suppressed (i.e., fixed to zero) in the within-dyads regression. To compute the APIM using the pooled-regression solution for distinguishable dyads, several additional variables need to be formed and added to the within- and between-dyads regressions.

First, two variables denoting the gender of the men and women (or whatever the distinguishing variable is) need to be created. Be aware that these are actually constants, because each dyad contains one man and one woman, and for each dyad there is a variable M_GENDER that equals 1.0 for every dyad and a variable F_GENDER that equals −1.0 for every dyad. These two variables are then used to create a gender-difference variable (e.g., in SAS GENDDIFF = M_GENDER − F_GENDER; GENDDIFF is a constant that always equals 2.0). In the example, the mixed predictor variable is neuroticism, and there is a score for men (M_NEURO) and a score for women (F_NEURO). A difference score of this variable must be created: NEURODIFF = M_NEURO − F_NEURO. Finally, the interaction between gender and the mixed predictor variable is also a mixed variable for which actor and partner effects can be estimated. These values are formed by multiplying the men's neuroticism score by the men's gender and the women's neuroticism score by the women's gender: M_INTER = M_NEURO*M_GENDER; and F_INTER = F_NEURO*F_GENDER. A difference score for the interaction is then created: INTERDIFF = M_INTER − F_INTER. The within-dyads regression has three variables predicting the dyad difference in distress (DISTRESSDIFF), including the difference in neuroticism scores, the gender difference variable, and the difference in the interaction scores (i.e., NEURODIFF, GENDERDIFF, and INTERDIFF). The resulting difference score equation is

$$\text{DISTRESSDIFF} = .065(\text{NEURODIFF}) - .035(\text{GENDERDIFF}) + 0.180(\text{INTERDIFF}) + E_w$$

For each of the mixed predictor variables (neuroticism and the neuroticism-by-gender interaction), a dyad-average variable must be created [e.g., NEUROAVG = (M_NEURO + F_NEURO)/2; INTERAVG = (M_INTER + F_INTER)/2]. The between-dyads regression involves predicting the dyad average on distress (DISTRESSAVG) as a function of the two-dyad average variables. Note that gender is not included in the between equation because it does not vary between dyads (i.e., all dyads have one man and one woman). The resulting "average" equation is

$$\text{DISTRESSAVG} = 3.647 + .751(\text{NEUROAVG}) - 0.227(\text{INTERAVG}) + E_b$$

The results of the between- and within-dyads regressions are then pooled using the formulas provided earlier. For the example data, the neuroticism actor effect is $(0.751 + 0.065)/2 = 0.408$; the neuroticism partner effect is $(0.751 - 0.065)/2 = 0.343$. The standard error for these two effects, again using the formula presented earlier, is $\sqrt{(0.139^2 + 0.061^2)/4} = 0.076$. The degrees of freedom are estimated to be 130.00. Thus, both the actor effect, $t(130) = 5.39$, $p < .001$, and the partner effect, $t(130) = 4.54$, $p < .001$, are statistically significant, indicating that individuals higher in neuroticism appeared to be more distressed during the discussion and that individuals whose partners were higher in neuroticism also appeared to be more distressed.

The gender difference for distress was not statistically significant, $b = -0.035$, $t(95) = 0.90$. However, examination of the actor and partner effects (again using the earlier formulas) shows some interesting interactions between neuroticism and gender. The actor effect for the interaction was small, $(-0.227 + 0.180)/2 = -0.023$, but the partner effect was relatively large, $(-0.227 - 0.180)/2 = -0.204$, and statistically significant, $t(135) = -2.76$. This partner effect indicates that the neuroticism partner effect described earlier is qualified by gender such that men with highly neurotic female partners showed a great deal of distress (the partner effect for women's neuroticism on men's distress, given how gender is coded, is $0.343 + 0.204 = 0.547$), but women with highly neurotic male partners were not as affected by their partner's neuroticism (the partner effect for men's neuroticism on women's distress is $0.343 - 0.204 = 0.139$).

As was the case with indistinguishable dyads, the pooled-regression solution for distinguishable dyads is awkward. It has one additional drawback in the distinguishable case: We must assume homogeneity of variance for the two levels of the distinguishing variable. That is, we must assume that the men and women in our example have the same variance in their distress scores. The MLM and SEM approaches for the APIM do not necessarily require such an assumption, and these methods are preferred over the pooled-regression approach.

Multilevel Modeling

We discuss two different approaches to estimation of the APIM with distinguishable dyads using MLM. The first is an extension of the approach with indistinguishable dyads and uses interaction terms to factor in the effects of the distinguishing variable. The second is the two-intercept approach that was introduced in Chapter 4.

Interaction Model

Recall that for MLM the data set needs to be structured so that each individual has his or her own data record on which that person's outcome score is recorded (e.g., DISTRESS). In addition to the person's outcome score, the person's own score on the mixed predictor variable is also recorded (e.g., ACT_NEURO), as is his or her partner's score on the mixed predictor variable (e.g., PART_NEURO). Three additional variables need to be included in the distinguishable case: a variable denoting the actor's score on the distinguishing variable (e.g., GENDER) and interactions between the distinguishing variable and the actor and partner scores on the predictor. In this example, GENDER, our distinguishing variable, is coded as 1 for men and −1 for women. The two interaction variables are ACT_INTER = ACT_NEURO*GENDER and PART_INTER = PART_NEURO*GENDER. Researchers using HLM6 or MLwiN are advised to form these interaction scores within the level-1 data set itself, whereas researchers using SAS or SPSS can use the statistical program to form the interaction variables.

Only two alterations need to be made to the general MLM approach we described earlier to apply it to the case of distinguishable dyads. The first change is that the distinguishing variable and its interactions with the mixed predictor variable need to be added to the model. For example, using PROC MIXED in SAS, the syntax would be

```
PROC MIXED COVTEST;
CLASS DYADID;
MODEL DISTRESS = ACT_NEURO PART_NEURO GENDER
    ACT_NEURO*GENDER PART_NEURO* GENDER/
    SOLUTION DDFM=SATTERTH;
```

Notice that in this model, in addition to including the actor and partner effects for the mixed variable and the interactions between the distinguishing variable and the mixed variable, we have included the main effect of the distinguishing variable (i.e., the person's GENDER). This main effect simply estimates and tests whether there are mean-level differences in DISTRESS for men and women.

The second change that can be made to the analysis to accommodate the distinguishability factor is that the specification of compound symmetry can be changed to *heterogeneous compound symmetry*. In SAS this is done in the REPEATED statement, with the TYPE being set to CSH rather than CS:

```
REPEATED / TYPE=CSH SUBJECT=DYADID;
```

This change to heterogeneous compound symmetry removes the homogeneity-of-variance assumption and allows the error variances to differ for the two types of dyad members. A partial section of the results from PROC MIXED using the example data are presented in Table 7.6. The actor and partner effect estimates exactly replicate those from the pooled-regression approach. The significance tests differ slightly, however, because the MLM solution allows for heterogeneous variances.

The parallel statements for SPSS are as follows:

```
MIXED
    DISTRESS WITH ACT_NEURO PART_NEURO GENDER
    /FIXED = ACT_NEURO PART_NEURO GENDER
        ACT_NEURO*GENDER PART_NEURO*GENDER
    /PRINT = SOLUTION TESTCOV
    /REPEATED = GENDER | SUBJECT(DYADID) COVTYPE(CSH).
```

Recall that tests of variances within SPSS are two-tailed when they should be one-tailed, and so *p* values should be divided by 2.

TABLE 7.6. Results from the Neuroticism Example Using PROC MIXED with Heterogeneous Compound Symmetry

Cov Parm	Subject	Estimate	Standard Error	Z Value	Pr Z
Var(1)	DYADID	0.6503	0.09436	6.89	<.0001
Var(2)	DYADID	0.4211	0.06110	6.89	<.0001
CSH	DYADID	0.6735	0.05606	12.01	<.0001

Covariance Parameter Estimates

Fit Statistics

-2 Res Log Likelihood	387.6
AIC (smaller is better)	393.6
AICC (smaller is better)	393.7
BIC (smaller is better)	401.5

Null Model Likelihood Ratio Test

DF	Chi-Square	Pr > ChiSq
2	61.87	<.0001

Solution for Fixed Effects

Effect	Estimate	Standard Error	DF	t Value	Pr > |t|
Intercept	3.6474	0.08625	95	42.29	<.0001
ACT_NEURO	0.4079	0.07438	128	5.48	<.0001
PART_NEURO	0.3432	0.07692	123	4.46	<.0001
GENDER	-0.03541	0.03918	95	-0.90	0.3684
ACT_NEURO*GENDER	-0.02340	0.07241	133	-0.32	0.7471
PART_NEURO*GENDER	0.2036	0.07502	127	2.71	0.0076

Note. GENDER is coded men = 1 and women = –1.

Two-Intercept Model

An alternative approach for MLM estimation with a distinguishable variable is to estimate the two-intercept model that we described in Chapter 4. Two dummy variables must be created. One might be called MALE (MALE = 1 if the person is male, 0 otherwise) and the other called FEMALE (FEMALE = 1 if the person is female, 0 otherwise). The correlation of these two variables is −1, and, ordinarily, they could not both be included in the same equation. However, they can both be included if we drop the intercept from the model.

We illustrated in Chapter 4 how such a model can be estimated using MLwiN, and we discussed how it can be estimated using HLM. Fortunately, a version of the model can also be estimated using SAS and SPSS. The basic code in SAS is:

```
PROC MIXED COVTEST;
CLASS DYADID;
MODEL DISTRESS = MALE FEMALE ACT_NEURO*MALE
    ACT_NEURO*FEMALE PART_NEURO*MALE PART_NEURO*FEMALE /
    NOINT SOLUTION DDFM=SATTERTH;
REPEATED / TYPE=CSH SUBJECT=DYADID;
```

An alternative, equivalent, and simpler[3] code is:

```
PROC MIXED COVTEST;
CLASS DYADID GENDER;
MODEL DISTRESS = GENDER ACT_NEURO*GENDER
    PART_NEURO*GENDER/   NOINT SOLUTION DDFM=SATTERTH;
    REPEATED / TYPE=CSH SUBJECT=DYADID;
```

Results from the first version of this SAS code are presented in Table 7.7. This table shows an advantage of the two-intercept model: The actor and partner effects for men and women can be read directly from the output, and no hand computations are required. There is, however, one substantial disadvantage to the two-intercept model—that is, that there is no direct test of whether the actor or partner effects differ significantly for men versus women. To perform that test, we need to use the earlier model that included gender interactions.

The parallel two-intercept code for SPSS is:

```
MIXED
    DISTRESS WITH MALE FEMALE ACT_NEURO PART_NEURO |
        NOINT
```

```
/FIXED = MALE FEMALE ACT_NEURO*MALE
    ACT_NEURO*FEMALE PART_NEURO*MALE
PART_NEURO*FEMALE
/PRINT = SOLUTION TESTCOV
/REPEATED = GENDER | SUBJECT(DYADID) COVTYPE(CSH).
```

The alternative specification is:

```
MIXED
    DISTRESS WITH GENDER ACT_NEURO PART_NEURO | NOINT
    /FIXED = GENDER ACT_NEURO*GENDER PART_NEURO*GENDER
    /PRINT = SOLUTION TESTCOV
    /REPEATED = GENDER | SUBJECT(DYADID) COVTYPE(CSH).
```

TABLE 7.7. Results from the Neuroticism Example Using PROC MIXED with the Two-Intercept Model and Heterogeneous Compound Symmetry

Covariance Parameter Estimates

Cov Parm	Subject	Estimate	Standard Error	Z Value	Pr Z
Var(1)	DYADID	0.6503	0.09436	6.89	<.0001
Var(2)	DYADID	0.4211	0.06110	6.89	<.0001
CSH	DYADID	0.6735	0.05606	12.01	<.0001

Fit Statistics

-2 Res Log Likelihood	383.4
AIC (smaller is better)	389.4
AICC (smaller is better)	389.6
BIC (smaller is better)	397.3

Null Model Likelihood Ratio Test

DF	Chi-Square	Pr > ChiSq
2	61.87	<.0001

Solution for Fixed Effects

Effect	Estimate	Standard Error	DF	t Value	Pr > |t|
MALE	1.1663	0.3581	95	3.26	0.0016
FEMALE	2.1838	0.4451	95	4.91	<.0001
MALE*ACT_NEURO	0.3845	0.1009	95	3.81	0.0002
FEMALE*ACT_NEURO	0.4313	0.1066	95	4.05	0.0001
MALE*PART_NEURO	0.5468	0.0858	95	6.38	<.0001
FEMALE*PART_NEURO	0.1396	0.1254	95	1.11	0.2687

Structural Equation Modeling

The SEM solution with distinguishable dyads is perhaps the simplest data-analytic method for estimating the APIM, in the sense that the model can be directly estimated using a standard application of a well-known data analytic method. (See Bui et al., 1996; Kenny & Acitelli, 2001; and Murray, Holmes, & Griffin, 1996, for illustrations of this approach.) Essentially, the SEM approach involves estimating the APIM parameters as they appear in the model presented in Figure 7.3. The data have a dyad-level structure. Written in the form of two linear equations, where Y_m is the man's distress, Y_f is the woman's distress, X_m is the man's neuroticism (centered around the grand mean across *both* men and women), and X_f is the woman's neuroticism (also centered around the grand mean across *both* men and women), this model can be summarized as:

$$Y_m = a_m X_m + p_{mf} X_f + E_m,$$

$$Y_f = p_{fm} X_m + a_f X_f + E_f.$$

Note that the couple is the unit of analysis, and thus the sample size for this analysis is the number of couples (which is 98 in the example). The model in Figure 7.3 is identical to that in Figure 7.1, but now separate actor and partner effects are estimated for both members of the dyad.

Interpretation of the actor and partner effects is straightforward. For this example, a_m refers to the effect of the man's neuroticism on his own level of distress. The partner effect, p_{fm}, is the effect of the man's neuroticism on his partner's distress, and p_{mf} is the effect of the woman's neuroticism on her partner's distress. Recall that the usual convention is to have the effect first and the cause second.

The SEM solution allows model constraints to be placed and tested. For example, one can test whether the actor effects differ significantly for men and women by constraining the two actor parameters to be equal and then assessing the degree to which this constraint significantly worsens the model fit. When this constraint is placed for the example data, the actor effect is estimated to be .407 (for both men and women), and the chi-square test with 1 degree of freedom indicates that this constraint does not significantly worsen fit, $\chi^2(1) = 0.107$, $p = .744$. On the other hand, constraining the partner effects to be equal does significantly worsen the model fit, $\chi^2(1) = 7.311$, $p = .007$, indicating that there is a statistically significant difference between the two partner effects. The effect from the woman's neuroticism to the man's distress is larger than the effect from the man's neuroticism to the woman's distress.

Finally, we must add one note of caution. When using SEM, it is essential that the coefficients *not* be standardized separately for each dyad member type (e.g., for men and women separately), because such a procedure renders the coefficients incomparable across dyad member type. The safest course of action is not to standardize at all but, instead, to report the unstandardized coefficients (as we have done in Figure 7.3). Alternatively, one can standardize the variables before computing the model. Such an approach would involve standardizing the data using the mean computed across men and women, as well as the standard deviation computed across the entire sample (see Chapter 6).

POWER AND EFFECT SIZE COMPUTATION

As discussed in Chapter 3, determining effect sizes and power when predictor variables are either entirely between or within dyads is relatively straightforward. To determine power, the effect size measure based on the nonindependent data (either d or r, what we called d_D and r_D in Chapter 3) is determined, and then that value is adjusted by the degree of nonindependence in the data to create an adjusted d (or r). Recall that this adjusted value is the estimate of the effect size for independent units. With the adjusted d or r, the level of power is determined using the appropriate sample size.

We adopt the same strategy here, but it is quite a bit more complicated. In fact, it is so complex that we suggest the following approximation. We first compute the intraclass, or Pearson, correlation for the predictor variable, or X, and we denote that value as r_x. If r_x is > .5, treat the variable as if it were a between-dyads variable. If $r_x < -.5$, treat it as if it were a within-dyads variable. For all other values, ignore the nonindependence when estimating power (i.e., use the unadjusted effect size measure). This general strategy yields a good approximation of the power.

The more complicated and exact strategy is to combine the between- and within-dyads adjustments that we presented in Chapter 3, weighting by the intraclass correlation of the mixed variable. We first need to determine the adjustment factor that corrects for the nonindependence between dyad members' scores. This value is:

$$\sqrt{\frac{(r_x+1)^2}{2(1+r_y)}+\frac{(1-r_x)^2}{2(1-r_y)}},$$

where r_x is the intraclass, or Pearson, correlation for the mixed variable, and r_y is the residual intraclass, or Pearson, correlation for the outcome variable.

To determine power, we estimate d or r from the nonindependent data, and then we multiply that value[4] by the preceding adjustment factor to obtain a modified measure of effect size. However, there are two additional complications. First, note that in an APIM analysis we generally measure actor effects controlling for partner effects, and vice versa. To control for multicollinearity between the two effects, we further need to adjust the effect size by $\sqrt{1-r_x^2}$. The resulting modified formula that includes both adjustments is

$$\sqrt{\left[\frac{1-r_x^2}{2}\right]\left[\frac{(r_x+1)^2}{(1+r_y)}+\frac{(1-r_x)^2}{(1-r_y)}\right]}.$$

Of course, if the design is either between or within (r_x equals 1 or -1), this adjustment should not be made.

Finally, in determining power, we need to correct the sample size by the degree of nonindependence. If we denote the total sample size as $2n$ (where n is the number of dyads), the effective sample size in terms of a power computation can be shown to be approximately equal to $2n/(1 + r_x^2)$. This corrected value is less than or equal to $2n$, and this value is used as the sample size to determine power.

As an example, assume that the effect size based on nonindependent data, d (what we referred to as d_D in Chapter 3), is 0.5; the correlation between the dyad members' mixed predictor scores, r_x, is .3; and the correlation between the outcome scores, or r_y, is .5. These values result in a corrected d of 0.490 (the adjustment for nonindependence is 1.026 and the adjustment for multicollinearity is 0.954, and therefore the overall adjustment is 0.979). The effective sample size using 100 persons, or 50 dyads, is 91.7. The estimated power is .64. If, instead, we were to use the simple approximation of not adjusting the effect size, and using 100 as the sample size, the power, assuming independent data for a d of 0.5 and 100 cases, would be .697, not all that different from the value of .64.

Returning to the fictitious roommate data that we considered earlier in the chapter, we can use the adjustment factor to compute the effect size. We compute d or r using the standard formulas. Then we take that d or r and divide by the adjustment factor to determine the effect size. Specifically, consider the estimate of the partner effect for the roommate data in Table 7.1. We obtained $t(37)$ = 3.56, with r_x = .415 and r_y = .364. Using the t to r formula of $t/\sqrt{df+t^2}$, we obtain an estimated r for the non-independent data of 0.505. The adjustment for multicollinearity is .910, and the adjustment for nonindependence is 1.001, resulting in an overall adjustment of 0.910. Thus the estimated effect size is 0.460. Note that the adjustment factor results in a relatively small change in the effect size measure.

SPECIFICATION ERROR IN THE APIM

The basic APIM model in Figure 7.1 specifies a particular pattern of causation. If that model were not correctly specified, then the parameter estimates would be misleading. An important type of specification error occurs when the structure of the causal relationship is erroneous. Chapter 15 considers two models that are alternatives to the APIM: the mutual-feedback model and the common-fate model. In the mutual-feedback model, Y_1 causes Y_2, and vice versa. In the common-fate model, the causal effect from X to Y occurs between latent variables.

A fundamental assumption of the APIM is that X causes Y. We could treat the APIM as a prediction model (i.e., X is used to predict Y), but, typically, the assumption is that X causes Y. Thus, if there were actor and partner effects, a change in X would lead to a change in both Y_1 and Y_2. Rarely (in fact, we know of no case in which it has happened) is X a manipulated variable. If X were manipulated, then the direction of causality would be known: X causes Y, and not vice versa.

Measurement error is also an important issue with the APIM. Measurement error in a causal variable biases not only the coefficient of that causal variable but also the coefficients of the other variables in the equation (Kenny, 1979). Three approaches can be used to address the measurement error problem: disattenuation, latent variables, and instrumental variable estimation. We discuss each in turn. We note that each can relatively easily be accomplished using SEM and cannot be done within either pooled regression or MLM.

For the disattenuation strategy, the reliability of the X variable must be known. If X is a scale, its internal consistency estimate may be available. Following the strategy of Williams and Hazer (1986), an SEM program can be used, and we set the path from true X to measured X to 1 and fix the error variance to $s_x^2 (1 - \alpha)$, where α is the reliability of X and s_x^2 is the variance of the measure X. It is possible that X_1 and X_2 might have different values of reliability, and those different values should each be used.

A latent variable strategy is the most common approach to the estimation of models with measurement error. For example, for X_1, there would be multiple measures. Normally, just two measures per latent variable would be needed, but because of the likelihood of correlated error across dyad members (see Chapters 5 and 6), three measures per X variable would be needed to have an identified model. Also, one would want to test that the measurement model is the same for X_1 and X_2, so that their units of measurement would be comparable. Ferrer and Nesselroade (2003) illustrate a version of the APIM with latent variables in a study of emotions in heterosexual couples. They found effects from prior negative husband emotion to later wife emotion, but not vice versa.

The instrumental variable solution to estimating models with measurement error in the X variables is not commonly used. In instrumental variable estimation, the model must specify that the variable measured with measurement error, X_1, correlates with another variable, Z_1, which is the instrumental variable. However, Z_1 does not cause either Y_1 or Y_2, and it is the absence of the paths from Z_1 to Y_1 or Y_2 that allows estimation of the error variance in X_1.

Finally, if we allow for measurement error in X_1 and X_2, estimation of interaction effects becomes problematic. Kenny and Judd (1984) have provided a general strategy for the estimation of multiplicative interaction effects (i.e., $X_1 X_2$). In principle, the method they advocate could be adapted to test interactions that are specified as the absolute value of the difference between X_1 and X_2, as well as interactions that are specified as the maximum or minimum value of the two partners' scores. However, very large sample sizes are needed to estimate these models with any precision.

SUMMARY AND CONCLUSIONS

This chapter presents the Actor–Partner Interdependence Model (APIM), which can be used to analyze the effects of mixed predictor variables. This model of dyadic data suggests that a person's standing on a predictor variable affects his or her partner's outcomes (i.e., partner effects), as well as their own outcomes (i.e., actor effects). We noted that this general model can be applied to data from groups larger than dyads and that it can incorporate other types of independent variables and interactions among variables. Four different configurations or models of actor and partner effects were considered: actor-oriented (the partner's standing has little effect on the person's outcomes), partner-oriented (only the partner's standing predicts the person's outcomes), couple-oriented (both actor and partner effects occur and are similar in size and sign), and social comparison (actor and partner effects are similar in size but opposite in sign).

Our discussion then considered estimation of the APIM effects for both indistinguishable and distinguishable dyads. For each we discussed three different methods: pooled regression, MLM, and SEM. The pooled-regression method can be accomplished by pooling together results from regressions that use simple ordinary least squares. Note, however, that this method is now outdated, and researchers should consider MLM or SEM as better options. Although both MLM and SEM can be used for either indistinguishable or distinguishable dyads, MLM is clearly the estimation method of preference for indistinguishable dyads. However, for distinguishable dyads, SEM is the most straightforward method. We detailed methods for computing effect sizes and estimating power for the APIM. Finally, we presented a brief discussion of specification errors and their impact on APIM estimates.

The APIM is a simple yet compelling model of dyadic behavior. When two people interact or are involved in a relationship, each person's outcomes are affected by *both* his or her own inputs and his or her partner's inputs. In fact, the presence of partner effects can be used as an operational definition of a relationship. As we noted, actor and partner effects may also interact, and sometimes that interaction is the major research focus (e.g., when researchers are interested in the effects of the similarity between dyad members). Although we did not extensively discuss the estimation of interaction effects, they should be considered. We also limited our attention to outcome variables measured at the interval level of measurement (see Chapter 1), and we have not discussed outcomes measured at the nominal level of measurement. Such models can be estimated by several different programs (e.g., HLM6, MLwiN, and SAS's PROC NMIXED). Also, Thomson (1995) has developed a method that tests the effect of a mixed dichotomous variable on a dichotomous outcome. We do discuss multilevel models with a dichotomous outcome in Chapter 14.

In the next four chapters, we leave the standard dyad design (see Chapter 1), and we consider more complicated designs. In Chapters 8, 9, and 11, we consider SRM designs. In Chapter 10, we consider the one-with-many design.

NOTES

1. Note that in the difference equation there are no predictors or intercept. Some computer programs do not allow the estimation of an equation with no predictors or intercept.

2. The sum and difference approach can be used when there is a couple-level outcome variable (e.g., relationship breakup) and distinguishable dyad members. For such outcomes, we can examine the extent to which one member has more of an effect than the other (Attridge, Berscheid, & Simpson, 1995).

3. We thank Joseph Olsen, who suggested this method to us.

4. As we noted in Chapter 3, the <u>adjusted</u> value of r could be greater than 1 in absolute value after multiplying by $\sqrt{2/(1+r_i)}$. If such were the case, the investigator has chosen much too optimistic a value of r and should lower that value.

8

Social Relations Designs with Indistinguishable Members

Some research questions can be addressed only by designs in which persons participate in more than one dyad (Kashy & Kenny, 2000). For example, consider the question of whether affective evaluations are primarily determined by the unique relationship between two individuals. If individuals participate in only one dyad, then a measure of liking of the partner may not necessarily represent unique liking. A high liking score from one member of the dyad could be due to the fact that the individual is a "liker" and that he or she likes everyone. Similarly, it may be that the partner is simply "likable" and is liked by everyone. Finally, it may be the case that liking is, in fact, relationally determined and that ratings of liking within dyads are unique. To separate these three factors, each individual would have to participate in more than one dyad. With multiple interactions, the degree to which a person is a "liker" can be assessed by looking at whether that person generally likes everyone with whom he or she interacts. Similarly, the degree to which a person is "likable" can be assessed by observing whether everyone who interacts with that person likes him or her. Finally, if there is evidence that one person likes the other, over and above the person's tendency to be a "liker" and over and above the partner's tendency to be liked, then there is evidence that liking is uniquely determined by the specific relationship between the two individuals.

In the previous chapter we introduced the Actor–Partner Interdependence Model (APIM). In that model, each individual participates in a single dyad, and one person's outcomes are affected both by properties of that individual (actor effects) and by properties of the person's partner (partner effects). The approach taken by the APIM is to treat some variables as exogenous (i.e., causal or predictor variables), whereas others are endogenous (i.e., outcome variables). The researcher specifies that the exogenous variable can have both actor and partner effects on the outcome. For instance, in a study predicting disclosure levels in friendship dyads, the degree to which a person is extroverted can have both actor and partner effects, such that being extroverted may increase a person's own level of disclosure and may increase the partner's level of disclosure, as well. In this example, the person's degree of disclosure is treated as an outcome, and it is predicted specifically by the two friends' extroversion scores.

The model discussed in this chapter, known as the Social Relations Model, or the SRM, takes a different approach in that it seeks to estimate how much of the variation in disclosure scores is a function of the discloser or actor and how much of the variation is a function of the target of disclosure, or the partner. Thus the SRM does not require that a particular variable be treated as the predictor to estimate actor and partner effects; instead, it estimates generic actor and partner effects. Kenny and La Voie (1984) presented the first detailed description of the model. Kenny (1994) presents many of the statistical details of the model, which are not given here. Kashy and Kenny (2000) also present a detailed overview of the model for social and personality psychologists.

The SRM has been used in more than 150 published papers. Most applications have been analyses of interpersonal perception, and much of the focus has been on consensus: How much do two persons agree with each other in their ratings of a third person? A secondary focus in much of this work has been on questions of accuracy: Are perceptions of another person correct? Do people know what other people think of them?

Other applications besides interpersonal perceptions have been attempted. For instance, there have been studies of self-disclosure (Miller & Kenny, 1986), memory (Bond, Dorsky, & Kenny, 1992), and aggression (Hubbard, Dodge, Cillessen, Coie, & Schwartz, 2001). There have even been studies of children (Ross & Lollis, 1989), animal behavior (Capitanio, 1984; Dunlap, 2002), and behavior in 24 regional groups in three countries (Malloy & Albright, 2001).

An important and unique feature of the SRM is that it can address the fundamental question of how much of the total variance in dyadic behavior is due to individual-level effects (e.g., Person A behaved the way she did when with Person B because she always behaves that way, or Person A behaved the way she did when with Person B because everyone who is with B behaves that way), and how much of the variance is due to the specific relationship between the two persons (e.g., A's behavior when with B is unique). The SRM quantifies the degree to which a variable is fundamentally dyadic, and no other method described in this book allows for such a refined assessment. Furthermore, because the SRM can partition variation in dyadic scores into individual and dyadic components, it can also provide a detailed analysis of reciprocity or interdependence of dyadic measurements. We shall see that reciprocity can exist at either the individual level or the level of the relationship, or both.

Because SRM research generally involves intensive data collection, it occurs with only moderate frequency. Of the 75 studies that we surveyed for this book, 15% utilized an SRM design. However, SRM designs have been used to address several especially important issues in dyadic research. For instance, the judgments of attraction in the famous acquaintance studies of Newcomb (1961) used an SRM design. Moreover, research on empathic accuracy (Ickes et al., 2000) also used this design. Cook (2000) has examined the degree to which attachment orientation (e.g., security or avoidance) reflects the person, his or her partner, or the relationship between the two (see Chapter 9). Studies of reciprocity of verbal and nonverbal behavior also fit well into such a research paradigm (e.g., Miller & Kenny, 1986).

We present the details of the SRM in this and the next chapter. This chapter introduces the model and is limited to the case in which persons are indistinguishable, as is typically seen with groups formed in the laboratory and groups of friends or classmates. In Chapter 9, we discuss group members who can be distinguished by role, usually family role. This chapter provides a great deal of introductory information concerning the SRM and SRM research, and even readers primarily interested in the distinguishable case should first read this chapter. Additionally, we should warn the reader that this chapter contains many formulas, more than the other chapters. Because standard software cannot estimate SRM variances and correlations, we feel it is important to provide researchers with the specific formulas.

We often refer to research participants in an SRM design using names such as Allison and Beth. However, at times we use a shorthand of A and B or i and j. The reader should feel free to turn A and B into Allison and Beth and i and j into Ike and Jake.

THE BASIC DATA STRUCTURES

Round-Robin Design

There are several SRM data structures (see Kenny, 1990a), the most common of which is the round-robin design. As shown in Table 8.1, in round-robin data structures every member of the group interacts with or rates every other individual in the group; the key requirement is that each dyad provides two scores, one for each person. Consider a group composed of four members: Allison (A), Beth (B), Cathy (C), and Diane (D). Dyadic interactions can occur in the presence of the entire group (A, B, C, and D interact simultaneously); or they can occur one-on-one, such that Allison and Beth interact in one room while Cathy and Diane interact in another,

TABLE 8.1. Common Designs Used for the Social Relations Model

Round robin

	A	B	C	D
A	s	x	x	x
B	x	s	x	x
C	x	x	s	x
D	x	x	x	s

Block

	A	B	C	D	E	F	G	H
A	s				x	x	x	x
B		s			x	x	x	x
C			s		x	x	x	x
D				s	x	x	x	x
E	x	x	x	x	s			
F	x	x	x	x		s		
G	x	x	x	x			s	
H	x	x	x	x				s

Half block

	E	F	G	H
A	x	x	x	x
B	x	x	x	x
C	x	x	x	x
D	x	x	x	x

Note. "x" denotes a dyadic measurement and "s" a self-measurement.

then A and C interact while B and D interact, and so on. An example of the former type of round robin is a study of perceptions of and by lonely people, in which groups of four individuals scoring at differing levels of loneliness worked together on problem-solving tasks and then rated one another on measures of social skills and intelligence (Christensen & Kashy, 1998). An example of the latter can be found in Levesque and Kenny (1993). In their study of the accuracy of behavioral predictions, both behavioral and interpersonal perception measures were gathered from four-person groups in which the participants interacted in dyads.

Typically, round-robin data are directional, so that Allison's rating of or behavior with Beth differs from Beth's rating of or behavior with Allison. Sometimes the data are nondirectional, as in the case of the distance between two interacting persons, and so $X_{ij} = X_{ji}$. The diagonal of a round-robin design represents self-data (see Table 8.1). Self-data occur frequently in rating studies and generally involve having the research participants rate how they see themselves on the variables being measured. Self-data are uncommon in studies of behaviors such as self-disclosure or nonverbal behavior. To estimate all of the parameters of the SRM, the minimum size for a round-robin design is four. If some constraints are made—specifically, if dyadic reciprocity is constrained to be zero (i.e., constraining the correlation between A's unique perception of B with B's unique perception of A to zero)—round robins with three group members can be used.

Block Design

Dyad-level group data also occur in the form of block designs. The block design is actually a family of designs including the symmetric block, half block, and asymmetric block. In the symmetric-block design (see Table 8.1), a group is broken into two subgroups, and individuals interact with only those in the other subgroup. If the group includes eight individuals, A through H, persons A, B, C, and D interact with persons E, F, G, and H. Thus, as indicated in Table 8.1, the symmetric-block design results in two sets of observations: the upper-right section and the lower-left section. Self-data can be collected in the block design; these are represented along the diagonal.

Sometimes data are collected from only one half of the block design, such that A, B, C, and D rate E, F, G, and H, but not vice versa. Such a design is called the *half-block design*. An example of a half-block design is presented in Kenny, Horner, Kashy, and Chu (1992, Study 1). In that study 113 participants rated 32 videotaped targets on 10 personality traits. Studies that present participants with multiple stimuli are half-block designs.

Finally, the asymmetric-block design is similar to the symmetric-block design with the exception that, in this design, persons A through D can be distinguished from persons E through H on a meaningful variable. For example, in Kenny and DePaulo (1993), members of one subgroup were assigned to the role of interviewers, and members of the other subgroup were assigned to the role of applicants for a hypothetical resident associate position.

The minimum size for a block design is two persons in each subgroup. Usually power considerations require larger sized groups. The number of members within each subgroup need not be equal for either the symmetric-block design or the asymmetric-block design, but it often is.

Block–Round-Robin Designs

The block and round-robin designs can be combined into a single design. As in a block design, people are divided into two groups. They rate or interact with all other persons, both those who are members of their group and those who are members of the other group. This design has been used to study intergroup perceptions (Boldry & Kashy, 1999) and perceptions of boys and girls in schools (Card, Hodges, Little, & Hawley, 2005). Ratings of members of the same group are called *ingroup data*, and ratings of members of the other group are called *outgroup data*.

Other Designs

In principle, any design in which each person interacts with or rates at least two other persons and those persons also interact with or rate at least two others is an SRM design. In some cases one might begin by gathering round-robin data, but because of missing data, the design is no longer round robin. The statistical analysis of such designs can be difficult. Gill and Swartz (2001), Kenny and Judd (1986), and Snijders and Kenny (1999) discuss statistical methods for the analysis of such data. We suggest that such designs should be avoided by all but the statistically adept. The remainder of the chapter considers only the round-robin and block designs.

MODEL

To illustrate the SRM, consider a study in which the group consisting of Allison, Beth, Cathy, and Diane is one of 10 groups of unacquainted individuals who interact dyadically in a round-robin pattern. The dyadic interactions are videotaped, and the tapes are coded for the amount of self-disclosure on the part of each dyad member. In addition, after each interaction, the two dyad members rate one another on a measure of extroversion. Note that we include two measures (ratings of extroversion and amount of disclosure) in our example because the meanings of the SRM effects differ somewhat depending upon whether the outcome scores are interpersonal ratings or measures of behavior.

The SRM Components

In the SRM, each dyadic score is a function of four components. Consider, for example, Allison's rating of Beth's extroversion and the degree to which Allison self-discloses to Beth. Table 8.2 presents the SRM breakdown of these dyadic scores for both extroversion and self-disclosure.

At the group level, Allison and Beth's group might, on average, have scored high on extroversion relative to the other nine groups. That is, one component that contributes to Allison's rating of Beth's extroversion is the general level of extroversion in the group as a whole: Some groups are more extroverted than others. This first component is called the *group*

TABLE 8.2. Social Relations Model Components for a Rating of Extroversion and Self-Disclosure

Allison's rating of Beth's extroversion	=	Group mean for extroversion	+	Allison's tendency to see others as extroverted	+	Beth's tendency to be seen by others as extroverted	+	Allison's unique perception of Beth's extroversion
Allison's level of self-disclosure with Beth	=	Group mean for self-disclosure	+	Allison's tendency to self-disclose to others	+	Beth's tendency to elicit self-disclosure from others	+	Allison's unique amount of self-disclosure to Beth

mean and reflects the average level of the outcome score for the group. Similarly, the degree to which Allison self-discloses to Beth, in part, reflects the group mean for self-disclosure, because some groups may self-disclose more than others; that is, the norm of some groups may be to disclose to each other and that of other groups, not to disclose.

Next, at the individual level, Allison's ratings or behavior may be consistent across all of her interactions with the other group members (B, C, and D). For ratings of extroversion, Allison may tend to rate everyone as highly extroverted, and one reason for Allison's high rating of Beth's extroversion may be Allison's general tendency to view others as extroverted. In terms of self-disclosure, one factor that contributes to Allison's level of self-disclosure with Beth is Allison's general tendency to disclose to others. In the SRM, the tendency for a person to exhibit a consistent level of response across all interaction partners is called an *actor effect*. Persons differ in their actor effects. Some people may have very positive actor effects, and thus they tend to see others as extroverted, or they tend to disclose a lot to others. Other people may have negative actor effects, and so they see others as not very extroverted, or they do not disclose much to others.

The *partner effect* is also an individual-level effect, and it measures the tendency for others to be consistent with a particular partner. Thus, for Allison's rating of Beth's extroversion, the partner effect measures the tendency for Beth to be seen as extroverted by all of her interaction partners. When outcome measures are behavioral, the partner effect measures the degree to which certain individuals tend to elicit similar behavior from all of their interaction partners. In terms of self-disclosure, the partner effect measures the tendency for all group members to self-disclose a great deal to Beth. Like the actor effect, the partner effect can be positive or negative. For instance, for self-disclosure, a positive partner effect would mean that all group members tend to disclose a great deal to the person, and a negative partner effect would mean that the person does not receive much self-disclosure from others.

Although we use the terms *actor* and *partner*, other terms could be used. For instance, researchers of interpersonal perception typically use the terms *perceiver* and *target*. In studies of nonverbal communication, the terms *receiver* and *sender* are common, and the terms *source* and *target* may be employed in persuasion research.

The *relationship effect* is at the dyad level. For Allison's rating of Beth's extroversion, the relationship effect measures the degree to which Allison sees Beth as especially extroverted, over and above Allison's general tendency to see others as extroverted, as well as Beth's tendency to be seen by others as extroverted. Thus the relationship effect reflects the unique combination of two individuals after removing their individual-level tendencies. For the self-disclosure variable, the relationship effect measures the degree to which Allison discloses to Beth, after taking into account both Allison's actor effect for self-disclosure and Beth's partner effect for self-disclosure. The relationship effect is directional in the sense that Allison's unique level of disclosure to Beth need not necessarily equal Beth's unique level of disclosure to Allison.

The basic SRM equation then, is that a score equals the mean plus actor plus partner plus relationship. The SRM equation for actor i with partner j is

$$X_{ij} = m + a_i + b_j + g_{ij},$$

where X_{ij} is the score for person i rating (or behaving with) person j, m is the group mean, a_i is person i's actor effect, b_j is person j's partner effect, and g_{ij} is the relationship effect. The terms a, b, and g are random variables. That is, both persons and relationships are assumed to be sampled from a population. A major focus of an SRM analysis is the variance of these three random variables. One aspect of the SRM illustrated by this equation is that the relationship effect cannot be separated from error. Partitioning true relationship effects from error requires multiple measures of the same underlying variable for each dyad. In this case the equation would be expanded to

$$X_{ijl} = m + a_i + b_j + g_{ij} + e_{ijl},$$

where e_{ijl} refers to the error in measure l for actor i and partner j.

To obtain multiple measures of extroversion, Allison might rate Beth on two indicators of extroversion, such as sociability and talkativeness. These two measures would be treated as indicators of extroversion, and the extent to which Allison's unique ratings of Beth are consistent or stable across both indicators would be treated as the relationship effect; any inconsistency or instability across these two indicators would be treated as error. Replications over time also may be used to partition relationship effects from error. That is, if Allison and Beth interact twice and self-disclosure is measured each time, Allison's relationship effect for self-disclosure with Beth could be separated from noise due to chance fluctuations over time.

Estimation of SRM Effects

In this section we first use the block design to introduce how the SRM effects (i.e., mean, actor, partner, and relationship) are estimated. The block design is used initially because the formulas are simpler and easier to understand. We then consider the more complicated formulas for the round-robin design. There are many formulas in this section; some readers might want to initially skip to the next section.

Block Design

The SRM is a version of a two-way random-effects ANOVA model. Although it is possible to think of any SRM data structure in such a fashion, it is easiest to exemplify this connection with the half-block design in which one set of individuals (say persons A, B, C, and D) rate or judge a second set of individuals (say E, F, G, and H) on some variable, for example, laziness. Within the ANOVA framework, actor is the first factor, with the "levels" being the individuals A, B, C, and D. The second factor is partner, and its levels are persons E, F, G, and H. Using this framework, we can define the variance due to actor, the variance due to partner, and the variance due to relationship.

Panel A of Table 8.3 contains an example data set in which there is only variance due to the actor effect. As can be seen, the row marginal means vary, ranging from 3.0 to 6.0, but the column marginal means are constant, and all equal 4.5. Further, once the variance in the row marginal means has been taken into account, there is no variation in scores from cell to cell. The equation for estimating the actor effect for person i is

Actor effect for person i = row mean for person i − group mean.

It follows from this formula that the sum of all of the actor effects is necessarily zero.

Panel B of Table 8.3 contains an example data set in which there is only partner variance. Note that the column means vary from 3.0 to 6.0 and that the row means all equal 4.5. The equation for estimating the partner effect for person i is

Partner effect for person i = column mean for person i − group mean.

Like actor effects, the sum of the partner effects is necessarily zero.

TABLE 8.3. The Social Relations Effects for a Half-Block Design

A. Actor effects only

		Partner					
		E	F	G	H	Means	Effects
Actor	A	3	3	3	3	3.0	−1.5
	B	4	4	4	4	4.0	−0.5
	C	5	5	5	5	5.0	0.5
	D	6	6	6	6	6.0	1.5
	Means	4.5	4.5	4.5	4.5	4.5	
	Effects	0	0	0	0		

B. Partner effects only

		Partner					
		E	F	G	H	Means	Effects
Actor	A	3	4	5	6	4.5	0
	B	3	4	5	6	4.5	0
	C	3	4	5	6	4.5	0
	D	3	4	5	6	4.5	0
	Means	3.0	4.0	5.0	6.0	4.5	
	Effects	−1.5	−0.5	0.5	1.5		

C. Relationship effects only

		Partner					
		E	F	G	H	Means	Effects
Actor	A	3	4	5	6	4.5	0
	B	4	5	6	3	4.5	0
	C	5	6	3	4	4.5	0
	D	6	3	4	5	4.5	0
	Means	4.5	4.5	4.5	4.5	4.5	
	Effects	0	0	0	0		

D. Actor, partner, and relationship effects

		Partner					
		E	F	G	H	Means	Effects
Actor	A	0	2	4	6	3.0	−1.5
	B	2	4	6	4	4.0	−0.5
	C	4	6	4	6	5.0	0.5
	D	6	4	6	8	6.0	1.5
	Means	3.0	4.0	5.0	6.0	4.5	
	Effects	−1.5	−0.5	0.5	1.5		

Panel C shows a situation in which scores vary as a function of the relationship effect. The relationship effect can be viewed as the interaction of actor and partner. Note that the row and column means do not vary, but there still remains variance in the scores. The estimate of the relationship effect for a given cell is

Relationship effect for person i with partner j =
cell score ij − row mean i − column mean j + group mean.

An alternative, but mathematically equivalent, formula is

Relationship effect for person i with partner j =
cell score ij − actor effect i − partner effect j − group mean.

These estimates are the standard two-way ANOVA effect estimates (e.g., Maxwell & Delaney, 2004).

In Panel D in Table 8.3, we have the more typical data set in which all three effects—actor, partner, and relationship—are simultaneously present. We can use the preceding formulas to estimate the SRM effect estimates, and with them we can reproduce the score using the SRM equation. So, for instance, the score for Person A as actor with Person G as partner equals (ignore the terms in parentheses in computing the score)

4.0 = 4.5 (mean) − 1.5 (actor) + 0.5 (partner) + 0.5 (relationship).

As a second example, the score for Person C as actor with Person H as partner equals (ignore the terms in parentheses in computing the score)

6.0 = 4.5 (mean) + 0.5 (actor) + 1.5 (partner) − 0.5 (relationship).

Thus we can reproduce any score in terms of the mean, actor, partner, and relationship.

Round-Robin Design

When the design is round robin, estimating actor, partner, and relationship effects is more complicated. To facilitate this discussion, we created the round-robin data set that is presented in Table 8.4. The grand mean is 6.0, and the table presents the row and column means.

TABLE 8.4. Hypothetical Round-Robin Data Set

Raw data

		Partner				Means	Effects
		A	B	C	D		
	A	—	8	5	10	7.67	2
Actor	B	7	—	7	6	6.67	1
	C	8	7	—	5	6.67	0
	D	4	5	0	—	3.00	−3
	Means	6.33	6.67	4.00	7.00	6.00	
	Effects	1	1	−2	0		

Relationship effects

		Partner			
		A	B	C	D
	A	—	−1	−1	2
Actor	B	−1	—	2	−1
	C	1	0	—	−1
	D	0	1	−1	—

We denote the mean of scores for actor i as $M_{i.}$, the mean of scores for partner i as $M_{.i}$, and the mean of all of the observations as $M_{..}$. Following Warner, Kenny, and Stoto (1979), the estimate of the actor effect for person i equals

$$a_i = \frac{(n-1)^2}{n(n-2)} M_{i.} + \frac{n-1}{n(n-2)} M_{.i} - \frac{n-1}{n-2} M_{..},$$

and the estimate of the partner effect for person i is

$$b_i = \frac{(n-1)^2}{n(n-2)} M_{.i} + \frac{n-1}{n(n-2)} M_{i.} - \frac{n-1}{n-2} M_{..},$$

where n is the group size. The reader may note that the estimate of the actor effect contains the mean for the person as a partner and that the estimate of the partner effect contains the mean for the person as an actor. These terms are included because there are missing data in a round-robin data set—the diagonal of the round robin (i.e., the self-data). If such corrections were not made, actor and partner effects would be biased. For instance, if a person has a large actor effect, he or she would mistakenly appear to have a small partner effect, only because he or she does not interact with or rate him- or herself.

The formulas, although complicated, are simple to apply. For instance, the estimate of the actor effect for person A in Table 8.4 equals

$$7.67(9/8) + 6.33(3/8) - 6.00(3/2),$$

which equals 2.00. The estimate of the partner effect for person C equals

$$4.00(9/8) + 6.77(3/8) - 6.00(3/2),$$

which equals −2.00. As in the block design, the actor effects always sum to zero, and the partner effects always sum to zero. The estimate of the relationship effect is given by

$$g_{ij} = X_{ij} - a_i - b_j - M_{..},$$

or the score minus actor and partner effects minus the grand mean. So, for example, the estimate of the relationship effect for A as the actor and D as the partner equals

$$10.00 - 2.00 - 0.00 - 6.00,$$

or 2.00. Note that relationship effects sum to zero across both row and column.

The SRM Variances

The focus in an SRM study is not who has the larger actor effect but on the extent to which individuals differ in their actor effects. Consider a study of ratings of intelligence. The actor variance, measuring the degree to which some individuals see all partners as very intelligent and other individuals see all partners as not very intelligent, is essentially (but not exactly) the variance among the row marginal means. Thus the actor variance depends on the row main effect. The partner variance, measuring the degree to which some individuals are seen by all actors as high in intelligence and other individuals are seen by all actors as low in intelligence, is essentially (but again not exactly) the variance among the column marginal means; it is the column main effect. The relationship variance, measuring the degree to which ratings of intelligence are unique to particular pairings of actors and partners, reflects the variance due to the interaction between actor and partner. That is, the relationship variance is the variance in the cells after the actor and partner effects have been removed.

One common mistake in presentations of SRM analyses is to confuse effect estimates and variances. When referring to a particular score, the term *effect* should be used. A person might have a large actor effect but not a large actor variance. When referring across persons or the results from a study, one is not referring to actor effects but rather to actor variance. A given group might have a great deal of actor variance, not actor effects.

As we noted at the beginning of this chapter, the meaning of the actor effect in the SRM differs dramatically from that for the APIM. In the APIM, the actor effect is a causal effect: the impact of a person's predictor variable score on that person's outcome score. In the SRM, the actor effect is the degree to which an individual provides consistent scores on the outcome variable across multiple dyads, there being no predictor variable. The actor variance provided by the SRM can be viewed as an estimate of the overall amount of variation in dyadic scores that is potentially explainable by characteristics of the individuals who generated them. A parallel comparison can be made for the partner effects in the APIM relative to the partner effects in the SRM.

In this section we present the formulas for the estimation of actor, partner, and relationship variances. As we did in the previous section, we consider first the simpler block design and then the more complex round-robin design. We then discuss interpretations of those variances. Some readers may wish to skip ahead to the interpretation section.

Block Design

Using the formulas for a two-way random-effects ANOVA, we can estimate actor, partner, and relationship variances. The relationship variance, or s_g^2, is

$$ s_g^2 = \frac{\Sigma\Sigma g_{ij}^2}{(n-1)(m-1)}, $$

where the summations are across rows and columns, n is the number of actors, and m is the number of partners. Recall that g_{ij} is the estimated relationship effect for person i with partner j (defined earlier). For the example data in Panel D of Table 8.3, n and m both equal 4, and the relationship variance equals 20/9, or 2.22. The actor variance is given by the variance of the actor effect estimates minus the relationship variance divided by the number of partners. (The variance of actor effects equals the sum of squared actor effects divided by the number of actors less one.) Thus the actor variance is

$$s_a^2 = \frac{\Sigma a_i^2}{n-1} - \frac{s_g^2}{m}.$$

Therefore, for the example in Panel D in Table 8.3, the variance of the actor effect estimates is 5/3, or 1.67. The estimated actor variance is then 1.67 − 2.22/4, or 1.11.

The partner variance is given by the variance of the partner effect estimates minus the relationship variance divided by the number of actors. (The variance of partner effects equals the sum of squared partner effects divided by the number of partners less 1.) That is, the partner variance is:

$$s_b^2 = \frac{\Sigma b_j^2}{m-1} - \frac{s_g^2}{n}.$$

Readers might wonder why the actor variance does not simply equal the variance of the actor effect estimates, or, alternatively, why the relationship variance must be subtracted from that variance. This question becomes all the more pertinent when we realize that subtracting the relationship variance implies that the estimates of actor and partner variances might well be negative. To illustrate this, consider Panel C in Table 8.3. The variances of the actor and partner effects are zero, and so once relationship variances are subtracted, the resulting estimates would be negative.

The statistical answer to this question is that we have a random-effects model. Most readers are familiar with fixed-effects models, and in fixed-effects models, the means can be used to directly estimate effects. However, with random effects, the formula used to estimate the variance of effects is more complicated.

The "random effects" answer is not very satisfying to most of us. There is another way to understand why we use a random-effects model. For the data in Panel D of Table 8.3, the variance of the actor effect estimates is 1.67. We might ask the question, what would the variance be if we had just three partners and not four? If we compute the variance of the actor effects for the four combinations of three partners, the average of these four estimated variances of effects is 1.85. If there were just two partners, the average estimated actor variance of the six possibilities would increase to 2.22. Note that, as we have fewer partners, we would have "more" actor variance. However, see what happens when we subtract the relationship variance divided by the number of partners from the variances in the effect estimates:

Four partners: $1.67 - 2.22/4 = 1.11$
Three partners: $1.85 - 2.22/3 = 1.11$
Two partners: $2.22 - 2.22/2 = 1.11$

If we use the SRM formulas, the actor variance is always 1.11, regardless of the number of partners.

We now have a better understanding of what a variance means in a random-effects model: It is a forecast of what the actor variance would be if there were an infinite number of partners. Correspondingly, the partner variance is what the variance of the partner effects would be if there were an infinite number of actors. The variances of effect estimates depend on specific sample characteristics. By subtracting the relationship variance, we make the actor and partner variances independent of the specific number of actors and partners in the study.

To determine how reliable the estimates of the actor and partner effects are for the block design, we compute for the actor:

$$\frac{s_a^2}{s_a^2 + s_g^2 / m},$$

where s_a^2 is the actor variance, s_g^2 is the relationship variance, and m is the number of partners. The reliability of the partner effect is

$$\frac{s_b^2}{s_b^2 + s_g^2 / n},$$

where s_b^2 is the partner variance and n is the number of actors. For the example, the reliability of the actor and partner effects is $1.11/(1.11 + 2.22/4)$, or 0.67.

Round-Robin Design

Just as the effect estimates are much more complicated for the round-robin design than they are for the half-block design, the formulas for the variances for the round-robin design are also more complicated. We first consider a method for computing the relationship variance, focusing on the data in Table 8.5. In that table we have 12 estimates of relationship effects, which are denoted as g_{ij}. We can take those estimates and treat them as if they were from 6 different dyads. As was done in Chapter 2, we could compute a mean square between dyads, or MS_B, and a mean square within dyads, or MS_W (see Chapter 2 for formulas). The degrees of freedom for the MS_B are $(n-1)(n-2)/2 - 1$ and for the MS_W are $(n-1)(n-2)/2$. So, if n equals 4, as it does for the example, the degrees of freedom for these mean squares are 2 and 3, respectively. The estimate of the relationship variance is simply $(MS_B + MS_W)/2$. For this example, MS_B equals 4.0, MS_W equals 2.67, and the estimate of the relationship variance is 3.33.

The estimates of the actor and partner variances also use the MS_B and MS_W. We compute the variance of the effect estimates and then subtract

$$\frac{MS_B}{2(n-2)} + \frac{MS_W}{2n}.$$

For this example, the actor variance would be

$$4.67 - 1.00 - 0.33 = 3.33,$$

and the partner variance would be

$$2.00 - 1.00 - 0.33 = 0.67.$$

To determine how reliable the estimates of the actor and partner effects are, we need to know the dyadic covariance, and so we defer computation of these reliabilities until later.

TABLE 8.5. The 12 Relationship Effects in Table 8.4 Arranged as 6 Dyads

Dyad	Member	
	1	2
AB	-1	-1
AC	-1	1
AD	2	0
BC	2	0
BD	-1	1
CD	-1	-1

Interpretation

Typically, in an SRM study the proportion of total variance due to each of these components is computed. In Table 8.6, we present examples of the variance partitioning for four different types of variables that have been studied in previous SRM research.

The first variance partitioning is for the measure of how much one person likes another. About 17% of the total variance is due to actor, 13% to partner, 38% to relationship, and 32% to error. The actor effect reflects how much persons tend to like or dislike others in general, the partner effect reflects how much a person is liked or disliked by others, and the relationship effect reflects the unique liking of one person for another. Thus the dominant component is relationship, and therefore liking is fundamentally a dyadic phenomenon (Kenny, 1994).

The next variable that we consider is a person's rating of another person on a personality trait. The actor effect reflects how a person sees others in general on the trait, the partner effect reflects how others see the person, and the relationship effect reflects the unique perception that a person has of another. For these ratings of personality, the variance partitioning shows that about 20% of the variance is due to actor, 15% to partner, 20% to relationship, and 45% to error (Kenny, 1994).

Kenny (1988b, 1994) and Malloy and Albright (1990) have developed specific terms for actor, partner, and relationship variances in trait ratings. The actor variance measures the degree of *assimilation* (the degree to which some individuals tend to rate all others as high on a trait, whereas other individuals rate all others as low). The partner variance measures

TABLE 8.6. Summaries of Variance Partitioning for Four Types of Variables (Proportions of Total Variance)

	Relative variance partitioning			
	Actor	Partner	Relationship	Error
Liking[a]	.17	.13	.38	.32
Trait ratings[b]	.20	.15	.20	.45
Metaperceptions[c]	.55	.04	.10	.31
Behaviors[d]	.31	.02	.67[e]	—

[a]Kenny (1994, p. 86).
[b]Kenny (1994, pp. 203–204).
[c]Kenny (1994, p. 153).
[d]Kenny, Mohr, and Levesque (2001, p. 135).
[e]Error and relationship confounded.

consensus (the degree to which all individuals agree that some partners are high on a trait, whereas other partners are low on the trait). The relationship variance measures *uniqueness* (the degree to which ratings vary depending upon the specific individuals in the dyad, after partialing out variance due to those individuals' actor and partner effects).

Metaperception is the prediction of how a person thinks others see him or her. The actor effect reflects how a person thinks that others generally see him or her on the trait, the partner effect reflects how others think a person views them, and the relationship effect reflects the unique prediction that a person has of how a particular partner views him or her. Most of the variance in metaperception is due to actor variance. People generally think that all others see them the same way. There is some relationship variance and very little partner variance.

Kenny, Mohr, and Levesque (2001) surveyed the variance partitioning of behavioral measurements. The actor effect reflects how a person consistently behaves with others, the partner effect reflects how people behave in general with the person, and the relationship effect reflects the unique behavior that a person has with another. Kenny and colleagues. (2001) found that about 31% of the variance is due to actor, 2% to partner, and 67% to relationship and error. Thus liking, personality trait ratings, metaperceptions, and behavioral measurements have very different variance-partitioning patterns.

The SRM Reciprocity Correlations

The SRM also specifies two different correlations between the SRM components of a variable, both of which can be viewed as reciprocity correlations. At the individual level, a person's actor effect can be correlated with that person's partner effect to assess *generalized reciprocity*. In the self-disclosure example, a positive generalized reciprocity correlation would imply that individuals who disclose a great deal to all of their partners also receive a great deal of disclosure from all of their partners. At the dyadic level, the two members' relationship effects can be correlated to assess *dyadic reciprocity*. That is, if Allison self-discloses at a particularly high level when with Beth, does Beth also disclose to an unusually high degree when with Allison? For extroversion, positive generalized reciprocity would mean that extroverts see others as extroverted, and positive dyadic reciprocity would mean that members of the dyad see each other as extroverted to similar degree. These reciprocity correlations can be negative, in which case the correlation might indicate compensation. For instance, the amount of time each dyad member spends talking tends to show negative reciprocity: The more one person talks, the less his or her partner talks.

In this section we consider how to estimate these two reciprocity correlations. Our discussion begins with the simplest case: Estimating dyadic reciprocity in the asymmetric block design. Next we illustrate estimation of generalized reciprocity for symmetric block designs. Finally, we present similar discussions for the round-robin design.

Block Design

To illustrate reciprocity, we use an asymmetric block design, which is presented in Table 8.7. We assume that three adolescent boys and three adolescent girls rate one another. Persons A, B, and C are the boys, and persons D, E, and F are the girls. Note that there are two sets of ratings. In the upper block are the boys' ratings of the girls, and in the lower block are the girls' ratings of the boys. These two half blocks create the asymmetric block design. For each half block, we can compute actor, partner, and relationship variances. For boys rating girls, the actor variance is 2.17, the

TABLE 8.7. Hypothetical Asymmetric Block Data Set

Raw data

		Partner						Means	Effects
		A	B	C	D	E	F		
	A	—	—	—	11	7	6	8	2
	B	—	—	—	9	6	3	6	0
Actor	C	—	—	—	4	2	6	4	−2
	D	8	7	6	—	—	—	7	1
	E	7	9	8	—	—	—	8	2
	F	0	2	7	—	—	—	3	−3
Means		5	6	7	8	5	5	6	
Effects		−1	0	1	2	−1	−1		

Interaction effects

		Partner					
		A	B	C	D	E	F
	A	—	—	—	1	0	−1
	B	—	—	—	1	1	−2
Actor	C	—	—	—	−2	−1	3
	D	2	0	−2	—	—	—
	E	0	1	−1	—	—	—
	F	−2	−1	3	—	—	—

partner variance is 1.17, and the relationship variance is 5.50; for girls rating boys, the actor variance is 5.00, the partner variance is −1.00, and the relationship variance is 6.00. The negative variance for partner indicates that the variation in partner effects for boys is less than what would be expected, given the size of the relationship variance. Therefore, this partner variance for girls rating boys would be treated as zero.

Because the dyads consist of individuals who can be distinguished by their gender, we can treat each boy's rating of a girl as an X score, and each girl's rating of a boy as a Y score, and the dyadic reciprocity correlation is then an ordinary correlation coefficient. We simply correlate the two sets of interaction effects (e.g., for dyad AD, X would be 1 and Y would be 2). The degrees of freedom are $(n-1)(m-1)-1$, where n and m are the numbers of persons in each subgroup, or 3 and 3, respectively, for the example data in Table 8.7. For the example data, the correlation is .914. This correlation can be tested for statistical significance like any Pearson correlation (see Chapter 2), and the resulting value is $t(3) = 5.04$, $p = .015$. The data indicate that boys and girls uniquely view each other in similar ways.

The dyadic correlation is a little different if the design is a symmetric-block design (i.e., one in which the two subgroups cannot be distinguished). It equals the correlation we just described, multiplied by the square root of the product of the two relationship variances, and this value is then divided by the average of the two relationship variances. So for this example the dyadic correlation is $.914\sqrt{(5.50)(6.00)}/[(5.50 + 6.00)/2]$, or .913.

There are two generalized reciprocity covariances for the asymmetric block design, one for each subgroup. For the example, the generalized reciprocity covariance for boys measures the degree to which boys, who perceive girls in a generally consistent way, are consistently seen by girls in a similar (or dissimilar) way. The formulas for these two generalized reciprocity covariances are

$$\frac{\sum a_i b_i}{n-1} - \frac{\sum\sum g_{ij}g_{ji}}{m}$$

and

$$\frac{\sum a_j b_j}{m-1} - \frac{\sum\sum g_{ij}g_{ji}}{n},$$

where, again, a_i is the actor effect for person i, b_i is the partner effect for person i, g_{ij} is the relationship effect for person i with person j, g_{ji} is the relationship effect for person j with person i, and n and m are the group sizes. To obtain the generalized reciprocity correlation, each covariance is divided by the square root of the actor variance times the partner variance. For the data in Table 8.7, the generalized reciprocity covariance for A, B, and C is $-2.00 - 5.25/3$, or -3.75, and for D, E, and F is $1.50 - 5.25/3$, or -0.25. The correlation cannot be computed for boys because the partner variance is negative. The correlation for girls is -0.25 divided by the square root of 5.00 times 1.17, or $-.10$. Thus the correlation is slightly negative for girls, indicating only a small tendency for girls who see all boys in one way to be seen by all boys in the opposite way.

Round-Robin Design

Earlier we defined the MS_B and the MS_W for the round-robin design. Recall that each was computed by stringing out the data from the round robin by dyads, as we did in Table 8.5. The dyadic reciprocity covariance equals $(MS_B - MS_W)/2$. The dyadic reciprocity correlation can be viewed as an intraclass correlation and equals $(MS_B - MS_W)/(MS_B + MS_W)$. Given the example data in Table 8.5, the reciprocity correlation equals $0.67/3.33$, or $.20$. This correlation can be tested, like any intraclass correlation (see Chapter 2). The degrees of freedom for the MS_B are $(n - 1)(n - 2)/2 - 1$ and for the MS_W are $(n - 1)(n - 2)/2$. The resulting value for the example is $F(2,3) = 1.50$, $p = .354$.

The generalized reciprocity covariance equals

$$\frac{\sum a_i b_i}{n-1} - \frac{MS_B}{2(n-2)} + \frac{MS_W}{2n},$$

which can be divided by the square root of the actor variance times the partner variance to obtain the actor–partner correlation. The actor–partner correlation should usually not be computed unless both the actor and partner terms explain at least 10% of the total variance. For the example data in Table 8.4, the generalized reciprocity covariance is $1.00 - 1.00 + 0.33$, which equals 0.33. The resulting correlation equals 0.33 divided by the square root of 3.33 times 0.67, or $.224$.

Returning now to the question of how reliable the estimates of the actor and partner effects are in the round-robin design, for actor we compute

$$\frac{s_a^2}{s_a^2 + s_g^2 / (n-1) - s_{gg} / (n-1)^2},$$

where s_{gg} is the dyadic covariance, and for partner we compute

$$\frac{s_b^2}{s_b^2 + s_g^2 \, / \, (n-1) - s_{gg} \, / \, (n-1)^2} \, .$$

For the example data, the reliability of the actor effect is

$$3.33/(3.33 + 3.33/3 - 0.67/9) = .71,$$

and the reliability of the partner effect is

$$0.67/(0.67 + 3.33/3 - 0.67/9) = .33.$$

Thus the partner effect is not very reliably estimated, and correlations involving the partner effect (e.g., the generalized reciprocity correlation) should be interpreted with caution.

Note that in most SRM research, and in the computations given in this chapter, correlations involving the actor or partner effects are adjusted or disattenuated for unreliability; they are estimates of the population correlations assuming that the actor and partner effects are estimated with perfect reliability. To undo the disattenuation, the correlation is multiplied by the square root of the two variables' reliabilities. In this example, that would result in an uncorrected generalized reciprocity correlation of $.224\sqrt{(.71)(.33)} = .108$.

Self–Actor and Self–Partner Correlations

It is common for researchers to collect self-data when doing SRM research, especially when perceptions are measured. For example, in addition to having each group member rate every other group member on a variable such as extroversion, researchers may ask participants to rate themselves on that same variable. Although the self-ratings are not included when actor and partner effects are estimated, such ratings can be correlated with the individual-level SRM effects (actor and partner). The correlation between self-ratings of extroversion and actor effects for extroversion measures whether the way a person sees him- or herself corresponds to how he or she sees others (this is sometimes referred to as *assumed similarity*). The correlation between self-ratings and partner effects of trait ratings measures *self–other agreement*: Do others see a person as that person sees him- or herself?

Computationally, we estimate the actor and partner effects for each individual using the dyadic data and then correlate these effect estimates with self-data. The only complication is that we need to partial out the group effects. This can be accomplished by creating $g - 1$ dummy variables to code for the effects of the g groups and then partialing out the effects of the dummy variables from the correlation.

Kwan, John, Kenny, Bond, and Robins (2004) suggest computing a self-enhancement index by removing actor and partner effects, as well as the group mean, from self-ratings. Such an index provides an estimate of the degree to which individuals view themselves higher on the attribute than they see others and than others see them. Their index is computed as

$$X_{ii} - a_i - b_i - M_{..}.$$

An alternative strategy is to subtract actor and partner effects from self-ratings after weighting them by their influence on self-ratings:

$$X_{ii} - ka_i - qb_i - M_{..}.$$

The terms k and q are regression weights obtained by regression of the self-measure on a and b. They could be estimated empirically, by using estimated values for a and b, or theoretically, using a latent variable approach.

Actor and Partner Correlations with Individual-Difference Variables

It is also common in SRM research to collect information concerning individual-difference variables—variables that do not change across interaction partners. Such variables might be demographic characteristics such as age or gender, they might be personality measures such as internal–external control, or they might be an experimental condition to which the person is assigned. As was the case with self-data, individual difference measures can be correlated with the actor and partner effects of the SRM. For instance, Winquist, Mohr, and Kenny (1998) were interested in the correlation of gender with actor effects in rating data. They found a small but consistent correlation such that women tended to rate others more positively than did men.

As we described for self-data, to compute these correlations we first estimate the actor and partner effects and then correlate them with the individual difference. Again, we partial out the effect of group. Because the correlations are computed within groups, it is necessary for there to be variation in the individual-difference variable within groups. For instance, if all members of a group are in the same experimental condition, it is not possible to correlate that variable with actor and partner effects.

Dyadic Analysis of Relationship Effects

Earlier we showed how it is possible to estimate relationship effects by taking the score and subtracting the estimated actor, partner, and mean effects. For instance, a researcher might have round-robin measures of liking and trust from 10 people. Using the effect estimates, we can treat the data set as if it were from 45 dyads. We could create a pairwise data set in which we would have four scores: relational liking and trust of i toward j and relational liking and trust of j toward i. We could conduct an APIM analysis or any of the analyses that we have discussed in this book on this data set.

There is one complication. For a 10-person round robin, we lose 9 degrees of freedom for removing actor effects and 9 for partner effects. We could either create 18 dummy variables to account for these effects, or we could treat actor and partner as categorical variables and control for their effects in the analysis.

Multivariate Correlations

Generally, in an SRM analysis, more than one variable is measured. For example, each person may be asked to rate every other group member on both extroversion and likability. It then becomes possible to correlate SRM components in one variable with those in the other. Surprisingly, the correlation between two variables results in six SRM correlations, four of which are at the individual level and two at the dyadic level.

At the individual level, there are two SRM components, actor and partner. Both of these components for one variable can be correlated with the components for the other variable, resulting in four correlations. These correlations are actor–actor, partner–partner, actor–partner, and partner–actor. The actor–actor correlation would estimate the degree to which people who generally see others as extroverted also generally see others as likable. The partner–partner correlation measures whether people who are seen as extroverted are also seen as likable. The actor–partner correlation assesses whether people who see others as extroverted are seen as likable by others. Lastly, the partner–actor correlation measures whether people who are seen as extroverted tend to see others as likable.

At the relationship level, there are two SRM correlations, one of which is an intrapersonal correlation and the other an interpersonal correlation. Denote the relationship effect for one variable (e.g., extroversion) as g_{ij} and the second (e.g. likability) as h_{ij}. Then g_{ij} would estimate how extroverted person i thinks person j is, over and above i's actor effect and j's partner effect. Similarly, h_{ij} estimates how uniquely likable person i thinks person j is. The intrapersonal correlation would be the correlation of g_{ij} with h_{ij}, which would be the correlation between how uniquely extroverted person i thinks person j is with how uniquely likable i thinks j is. The interpersonal correlation would be between g_{ij} and $h_{ji,}$ which would be the correlation between how uniquely extroverted i sees j with how uniquely likable j sees i. For the intrapersonal correlation, the perceiver and the target are the same for both variables in the correlation, and it is computed across the two variables. For the interpersonal correlation, the perceiver and target for one variable are the target and perceiver, respectively, for the other variable.

Very often, these multivariate correlations are of central interest in SRM studies. For instance, in accuracy studies (Kenny & Albright, 1987), the key question is whether there is a correlation between partner effects in trait ratings (e.g., how the person is seen in general) and actor effects in behavior (e.g., what the person does in general). Studies of meta-accuracy also involve multivariate correlations. At the individual level, generalized meta-accuracy is measured by correlating actor effects in metaperceptions (i.e., how a person thinks others generally see him or her) with partner effects in perceptions (i.e., how others actually see that person). At the dyadic level, dyadic meta-accuracy is measured by correlating how a person uniquely sees a particular target with how that target thinks the person uniquely sees him or her. Kenny (1994, Appendix B) provides the details for the computation of these correlations.

DETAILS OF AN SRM ANALYSIS

The SRM model is rather complicated, and it is not very surprising that the technical details for implementing an SRM analysis are also comparatively complicated. This section discusses software, statistical issues, significance testing, and power considerations.

Software

The computational formulas for estimating the SRM parameters (the variances and covariances) are complex, and although this chapter provides a significant amount of the computational information, it is far from complete. For example, we have presented formulas for only the univariate case, omitting discussion of multivariate estimation. We also have not provided the formulas for separating error from relationship variance. These details are presented elsewhere (see Kenny, 1994, Appendix B).

Kenny has developed two computer programs that perform SRM analyses, SOREMO for round-robin data structures and BLOCKO for block data structures. The program WinSoReMo can be used to assist in the running of SOREMO, and the program WinBLOCKO can be used with BLOCKO (*http://davidakenny.net/srm/srmp.htm*). It is likely that in the future multilevel models (see Chapter 4) will be modified to estimate the SRM variances and correlations.[1] Snijders and Kenny (1999) present a beginning exposition of this topic. Also Gill and Swartz (2001), Li and Loken (2002), and Hoff (2005) have developed a Bayesian approach to estimating SRM parameters. Finally, we believe that the confirmatory factor analysis method discussed in the next chapter for estimating SRM models for distinguishable group members can be modified by using the Olsen and Kenny (2006) approach to estimate SRM models in the indistinguishable case.

Statistical Issues

Actor and partner variances are defined by computing the variance of the effect estimates and then subtracting the relationship variance. A problem sometimes arises when the relationship variance is larger than the variance from which it is subtracted, resulting in estimates of negative actor or partner variance. We explained earlier that the relationship variance is subtracted because the model is a random-effects model. Although an ordinary variance can never be negative, a random-effects variance computed in this way can indeed be negative. Note that if the variance were actually very small and near zero, then about half the time the estimated variance would be estimated as negative. Thus a negative variance is likely an indication of a very small variance. When a negative actor or partner variance is obtained, it is usually reported as zero.

There is another interpretation of a negative variance. The model may not be correctly specified. Consider what would happen to the actor variance in a half-block design if the members of the group were asked to rank order a set of targets on some variable. The mean for each actor would be identical and would equal the number of targets plus 1 divided by 2. Because there would be zero variance in the actor means, the actor variance would almost certainly be negative. In this case, the actor effect is not a random variable, but, rather, actor is a fixed variable, and all of the actor effects are set to zero. Treating actor as if it were a random variable creates the negative variance estimate for actor.

Even if the actor and partner variances are positive, another statistical anomaly can still occur: Correlations involving actor or partner effects can be out of range, that is, larger than 1 or less than −1. This situation arises because the denominators of the correlations include a function of the reliability of the actor or partner effects, and these reliabilities can be close to zero if there is little or no actor or partner variance. Out-of-range correlations can often be avoided by computing correlations involving actor or partner effects only if the actor or partner variances are statistically significant or if they explain a meaningful amount of variance (i.e., at least 5–10% of the total variance). Obviously, if either variance is negative, the correlation cannot be computed. Generally, we set these out-of-range correlations to +1 or −1.

One solution to negative variances and out-of-range estimates is to use a different estimation method. The formulas that we have presented use the method of moments. If maximum likelihood estimation were used, it would not yield such embarrassing estimates.

Significance Testing

Most SRM studies include multiple groups. For instance, Shechtman and Kenny (1994) had persons in 22 groups rate each other in a round-robin format. When multiple groups are studied, the standard approach to significance testing is to treat group as the unit of analysis for tests of the variances and for most of the correlations. That is, separate estimates are derived for each group, and then the mean of the estimates is computed. The standard error of the mean equals the standard deviation of the estimates divided by the square root of the number of groups. The mean of the estimates is divided by its standard error, and under the null hypothesis that the variance is zero, the distribution of this statistic is a t statistic, assuming normality. One-tailed tests are used to test variances, because variances are positive. Two-tailed tests are used to test correlations. More exactly, rather than testing the correlations directly, an SRM analysis tests the covariances to determine whether they differ significantly from zero. A covariance equals the correlation times the product of the standard deviations of the components.

Some presentations of the SRM (e.g., Warner et al., 1979) use the jackknife method of significance testing. However, this test is extremely conservative and should not be used. The sampling variances for the SRM parameters have been derived by Bond and Lashley (1996) for the round-robin design and by Lashley and Kenny (1998) for the various block designs. These estimates should be used if there is only one or very few groups. As a case in point, Jung (1999) used the Lashley and Kenny (1998b) values for the block design because he had just one group.

Tests of correlations between actor effects (or partner effects) and either self-measures or personality variables are ordinary tests of partial correlations with group effects partialed out. Essentially, these correlations are computed with the group means for the self-measures or personality variables subtracted (i.e., the variables are centered). The degrees of freedom for these correlations are the total number of persons minus the number of groups minus one. Although these are the correlations that are tested, the correlations presented in the output of the SRM programs are the disattenuated correlations, which take into account the reliability of actor and partner effects and forecast what the correlations would be if the actor or partner effects were measured without error.

Power

Building on the work of Bond and Lashley (1996) for the round-robin design and of Lashley and Kenny (1998b) for the block design, Lashley and Kenny (1998a) have developed a method to determine the power of SRM tests of variances and covariances.

Table 8.8 presents the number of groups needed to achieve 80% power for various SRM designs. The table shows that more groups are needed to achieve 80% power for the block design than for the round-robin design. For example, for partner variance, 33 groups of four people are needed for the symmetric-block design, compared to just 17 groups for the round-robin design. It is clear that the round-robin design's statistical advantages over the symmetric block are substantial.

Not surprisingly, power is largely a function of the number of data points present in the design. The half-block design has the fewest data per research group, the symmetric-block design has more data than the half-block design, and the round robin has more data than any block design. However, not all of the differences can be attributable to differences in the number of data points. Consider the symmetric-block design and the round-robin design. When $n = 4$, there are 33% fewer observations per group in the symmetric-block design than in a round-robin design, yet as shown in Table 8.8, approximately twice as many groups are needed in the block design than in the round-robin design. When $n = 12$, there are 45%

TABLE 8.8. Estimated Number of Groups Required for .80 Statistical Power for SRM Parameter Estimates by Research Design Type

	SRM parameter							
	Variance				Covariance			
	Actor[a]		Partner[b]		Actor–Partner[c]		Dyadic[d]	
	Group size							
Design	4	12	4	12	4	12	4	12
Symmetric block	158	7	33	4	686	30	293	14
Half block	311	12	64	6	—	—	—	—
Round robin	69	5	17	3	324	20	136	8

[a]Actor variance set to 0.1.
[b]Partner variance set to 0.3.
[c]Actor–partner covariance set to 0.05.
[d]Dyadic covariance set to 0.1.

fewer observations in the block design, yet the relative power advantage of the round-robin design drops dramatically.

Which is more advantageous in terms of power, a large number of small groups or a few large groups? For all the SRM designs, a few large groups are preferable to many small groups (logistical and substantive matters aside). The larger the research group, the more data there are per group. The more data per group, the more stable the SRM parameter estimates become. Thus the distribution of those parameter estimates has smaller variance, resulting in greater power for significance tests. To determine the statistical power, a computer program, AID-SRM, has been written. It can be downloaded off the web at *http://davidakenny.net/srm/srmp.htm*.

MODEL ASSUMPTIONS

The SRM has built into it a series of assumptions about the nature of two-person relationships. Following Kenny and La Voie (1984), the major assumptions are:

- Social interactions are exclusively dyadic.
- Persons are randomly sampled from some population.
- There are no order effects.
- The effects combine additively and relationships are linear.

We now consider these assumptions in greater detail.

The interaction between persons is presumed to be solely a function of the two persons in the interaction, and therefore there are no extra-dyadic effects. Persons are presumed not to influence the interactions of dyads to which they do not belong. When persons are members of long-standing groups, this assumption would not be true. We would expect persons to communicate with each other and influence each other's perceptions of third parties. For example, A and B may discuss person C. In terms of the model, A and B's relationship effects with C would be correlated. If this correlation is strong enough, estimates of the partner effect will be biased. For instance, if people in a group communicate about person A and come to a consensus about A's standing on a trait, then A will have a spurious partner effect. These extradyadic effects may also bias the actor effects. Their presence can distort the estimates of variance components.

There is no foolproof way to control for extradyadic effects. (Holland and Leinhardt, 1981, have argued that triadic and higher level effects are weak for sociometric data.) If one can specify the type of extradyadic effects, they can be measured and controlled. Consider the Curry and Emerson study (1970) in which eight persons represent four sets of roommates. There might be extradyadic effects between roommates. That is, the two roommates communicate with each other about the other six persons. It turns out that the relationship effects of pairs of roommates are correlated. After 1 week of being roommates, the correlation is .21, and it increases to .27 after 8 weeks. Similar correlations are found in Kenny and Kashy (1994). Although not very large, these correlations do provide evidence of extradyadic effects. As is said all too often, more research on this topic is needed, and we encourage it. Although extradyadic effects are a serious problem, the problem can be solved within the SRM if we allow for extradyadic effects but limit them to a few dyads (e.g., roommates). Also Hoff (2005) and Bond, Horn, and Kenny (1997) have developed methods that allow for triadic effects.

Another assumption of the SRM is that persons are randomly sampled from some population. Normally, most social scientists, with the exception of survey researchers, are rather cavalier about random sampling. We rarely even attempt to sample randomly. However, the SRM focuses on estimating variance, and if persons are nonrandomly sampled, the variance component estimates could be seriously distorted. For instance, if persons in the group were pairs of married couples, then the actor and partner variance would likely be underestimated because couples should have similar effects. Thus the use of intact groups violates the assumption of random sampling. This problem was particularly apparent in the analysis of data gathered by Kenny and Lowe (1979). The participants in each group were two pairs of roommates. When analyzed as a round robin, very anomalous results occurred. The similarity of the roommates and their high level of attraction distorted the results.

The SRM represents an essentially static view of interpersonal behavior. However, it requires multiple interactions with different partners that are necessarily sequentially ordered. Yet the model as stated ignores any order effects caused by repeated interactions. Normally, order effects are conceived of as constant effects added to scores. (A discussion of more complex order effects follows.) For instance, with repeated interactions people may increase their rate of self-disclosure. We know of no general strategy for controlling for these types of order effects in the round-robin design. It would seem that some type of modified Latin-square approach could solve the problem, but this solution has yet to be developed.

More problematic than the simple order of interaction effects are the subtle order effects, such as contrast and context effects. In a *contrast effect*, one's response reverses across repeated interactions. For instance, in Kenny and Bernstein's (1982) research, persons interacted with two opposite-sex partners. There was some evidence that participants compared the two persons with whom they interacted. They rated one high and the other low. This contrasting of the two partners artificially depresses actor effects. A *context effect* is a subtle, distorting effect that can occur when the order of partners is counterbalanced. It presumes that persons rate their first partner near the midpoint of the scale. Then all subsequent interactions are rated in that context. For instance, for peer ratings, if the first partner is high on the scale, he or she is rated near the midpoint, and the remaining partners tend to be rated below the midpoint. The first partner, then, anchors the rating scale. A context effect can produce spurious actor effects.

The model as stated presumes that the actor, partner, and relationship effects are additive. It may be the case, however, that the effects combine in a multiplicative manner, as was discussed in Jackson's (1972) model of inferential accuracy. An empirically based method for determining nonadditivity (Tukey, 1949) has been adapted by Hoff (2005). Researchers need to consider whether an additive formulation is reasonable.

Finally, dyadic reciprocity is assumed to be linear. However, there is good reason to believe that reciprocity might be nonlinear. Cappella (1981) discussed the two sides of reciprocity. If A likes B, does B like A? (This can be called *positive reciprocity*.) Also, if A dislikes B, does B dislike

A? (This can be called *negative reciprocity.*) It would seem likely that positive reciprocity would be stronger than negative reciprocity. This would result in a nonlinearity that cannot as yet be measured.

SOCIAL RELATIONS ANALYSES: AN EXAMPLE

In this section we discuss the results from a simple fictitious example involving a single group of six individuals who interact in a round-robin fashion. The example study examines the correspondence between ratings of liking, the degree to which individuals smile when interacting, and age. Six individuals (A, B, C, D, E, and F) are recruited to serve as participants. The six individuals are broken into dyads (A with B, C with D, and E with F). The three dyads are videotaped while interacting for a period of 5 minutes, after which each person rates how much he or she likes his or her partner. Then dyad composition rotates, and interactions and ratings are again obtained. This procedure is followed until each individual has interacted with every other individual in the group, and thus each person participates in five interactions. The videotapes of the interactions are then coded by independent coders on a 9-point scale for the amount each dyad member smiles. The fictitious data set generated by this example study is given in Table 8.9. Note that because individuals did not provide data about how much they liked (or smiled at) themselves, the diagonal in Table 8.9 is empty, and correlations between the individual-level effects

TABLE 8.9. Fictitious Round-Robin Data Set of Participant Ratings of Liking and Coded Ratings of Smiling during Dyadic Interactions

| Actor | Age | Partner | | | | | |
		A	B	C	D	E	F
A	26	—	$6,^a 7^b$	6,6	4,7	8,6	6,5
B	22	8,5	—	7,4	7,6	6,5	8,4
C	17	5,3	7,5	—	3,4	5,3	4,5
D	19	5,4	9,5	6,4	—	9,4	7,3
E	25	6,5	7,4	6,5	8,6	—	5,4
F	22	4,2	6,5	5,4	6,4	8,3	—

[a]Ratings of the degree to which the actor liked the partner on 9-point scales.
[b]Independent observer's codings of the degree to which the actor smiled at the partner on 9-point scales.

and self-data cannot be estimated. The age of the participants was also measured and is included in the table.

The group mean for liking was $M = 6.23$, and the mean for smiling was $M = 4.57$. The SRM variances and correlations are presented in Table 8.10. Examination of the variance partitioning for liking indicates that, in this fictitious data set, such judgments largely depend on actor and relationship effects. About one-quarter of the variation in ratings of liking is accounted for by who the rater or actor was. Only about 11% of the variation is dependent on the partner, indicating that there was a rather weak tendency for some group members to be liked by everyone, whereas others were liked by no one. Clearly, however, the majority of liking variance is at the level of the dyad or relationship (plus error).

The variance partitioning for smiling indicates that 47% of the total variation for this variable was accounted for by actor. Some individuals were "smilers" (they smiled at all of their partners), and others were "nonsmilers." The 14% partner variance shows a tendency for some individuals to elicit smiling from all of their partners. The remaining 39% of the variation in smiling was accounted for by the relationship plus error.

The generalized reciprocity correlation for liking is quite large and positive. This result indicates that individuals who liked all of their partners tended to be liked by their partners. The generalized reciprocity correlation for smiling is relatively small and negative, implying that individuals who smiled at all of their partners were not generally smiled at by all of

TABLE 8.10. Social Relations Model Estimates for the Round-Robin Data Set in Table 8.9

Variance partitioning: Absolute (percentages)		
	Actor	Partner	Relationship/error
Liking	.644 (25.0)	.278 (10.8)	1.656 (64.2)
Smiling	.717 (46.8)	.217 (14.1)	.600 (39.1)

Reciprocity correlations		
	Generalized	Dyadic
Liking	.775	.255
Smiling	−.190	.194

Correlations with age		
	Age–actor	Age–partner
Liking	.342	.484
Smiling	.746	−.585

their partners. In contrast, the positive dyadic reciprocity correlation for smiling indicates that individuals reciprocated relational smiling. That is, if a person smiled a great deal at a particular partner, the partners reciprocated by smiling back a great deal. Liking was also positively reciprocated at the dyad level such that, if one person indicated an unusually high level of liking, his or her partner also indicated an unusually high level of liking. The divergence of the smiling findings for generalized and dyadic reciprocity in the fictitious data set demonstrates how SRM analyses can simultaneously model different processes that occur at the individual and dyad levels.

The final set of correlations in Table 8.10 assesses the degree to which age relates to the two individual-level effects, actor and partner. The positive correlation between age and actor effects in liking implies that older persons tended to rate all of their partners as more likable than did younger persons. Similarly, the positive correlation between age and actor effects in smiling indicates that older persons tended to smile at all of their partners more than did younger persons. Age was positively related to partner effects for liking and negatively related to partner effects for smiling. These correlations indicate that older persons were generally liked more but were smiled at less by all of their partners.

The multivariate correlations for this fictitious data set are presented in Table 8.11. The individual-level correlations, those correlations involving actor and partner effects, are in the top portion of the table. The largest correlation is between the actor effect in liking and the partner effect in smiling: People who like others tend to receive more smiles. The weakest correlation is between the partner effect in liking and the actor effect in smiling: People who are liked by others tend to smile less. Recall that ordi-

TABLE 8.11. Multivariate Correlations

Individual			Smiling	
			Actor	Partner
Liking	Actor		.257	.937
	Partner		.056	.374
Relationship				
		Intrapersonal	.084	
		Interpersonal	.175	

narily these correlations should be computed only if the SRM component explains at least 10% of the variance.

There are two multivariate relationship correlations in Table 8.11, an intrapersonal correlation and an interpersonal correlation. They are both weak, but we interpret them nonetheless. The intrapersonal correlation indicates that if A especially likes B, then A especially smiles at B. The interpersonal correlation indicates that if A especially likes B, then B especially smiles at A.

SUMMARY AND CONCLUSIONS

In this chapter we have introduced the Social Relations Model (SRM), which is a model of dyadic behavior that allows researchers to partition dyadic data into individual- and dyad-level effects. An important requirement of the SRM is that each person participates in more than one dyad, and in this chapter we describe five data structures that are commonly used with the SRM: round robin, half block, symmetric block, asymmetric block, and block–round robin. We then introduced the components of the SRM, including the group mean, actor and partner effects, and the relationship effect. We noted that, whereas actor and partner effects are individual-level effects that describe a person's general tendencies, the relationship effect refers to the unique combination of two individuals, and so it is inherently dyadic.

Our discussion of how the SRM is estimated used the simplest SRM design, the half block, to introduce computation of actor, partner, and relationship effects. The SRM can be treated as a two-factor random-effects ANOVA, with actor as one factor, partner as the other, and relationship as the interaction between actor and partner. We then generalized this approach to the more complex case of round-robin data structures. After presenting the actor, partner, and relationship effect estimates, we described the SRM variances. An important part of this discussion included descriptions of typical variance partitioning results for perception data, metaperception data, and behavioral data. We also detailed how the SRM models reciprocity at both the individual and dyadic levels. Dyadic reciprocity is particularly important because it represents the unique adjustments that two people make to each other.

We then turned to a series of statistical issues, including software. We also described a general approach to significance testing in which group is the unit of analysis. Power considerations were also addressed, and we came to the perhaps surprising conclusion that having fewer, larger groups may result in higher power than having many small groups. Finally, before presenting a detailed example, we discussed the assumptions inherent in the SRM.

The SRM provides the most complete and most complicated analysis of nonindependence of dyadic data. Nonindependence due to reciprocity, actor, and partner can be studied. Given all of these exciting possibilities, there are a multitude of formulas and terms in this chapter. We must admit that the SRM can be confusing and at times difficult to understand. Sometimes we have difficulties understanding some subtle feature of the model. However, the model offers so much that the complications are well worth the effort of mastering it. Often the model forces researchers to think of new and interesting facets of dyadic processes.

In the next chapter, we continue our consideration of the SRM. There, we consider the case in which members are distinguishable. As will be seen, such a design is particularly important for the analysis of family members' perceptions of each other.

NOTE

1. In fact, we believe that the variance and covariance components of the asymmetric block design can be estimated by using SPSS or SAS. Additionally, all the components for the round-robin design except actor–partner covariance can be estimated. The reader should consult the website at *http://davidakenny.net/ kkc.htm* for details.

9

Social Relations Designs with Roles

The preceding chapter presented the original version of the Social Relations Model (SRM), a model that is used with a group of individuals who are indistinguishable from one another. However, the SRM can also be applied to groups whose members are distinguishable by their roles within the group. Roles can be extremely important determinants of behavior, as illustrated by Zimbardo's (Zimbardo, Banks, Haney, & Jaffe, 1973) classic study in which volunteers were randomly assigned to the roles of either prisoner or guard. In some groups, such as families, individuals within the group are naturally distinguishable by their roles (e.g., mother, father, older child, younger child). Another example of naturally existing role variation within groups is supplied by Bagozzi, Ascione, and Mannebach (2005). These researchers studied medical committees that were composed of a physician/chairperson, a physician/nonchairperson, a pharmacist, a nurse, and an administrator. The SRM with roles can also be used to study groups in which individuals within each group are assigned specific roles for purposes of the study (e.g., task leader, socioemotional leader, worker). SRM analysis of such data can address important questions about the special features of role relations; for example, how a person's behavior changes when interacting with a spouse or with a stranger (Fitzpatrick & Dindia, 1990).

Although the basic aspects of the SRM remain the same, application of the model to individuals who hold particular roles requires several modifications. For example: (1) variation in average responses from group to group may be of greater interest and importance; (2) the actors and partners represent particular roles within the group;

223

and (3) the data-analytic approach differs from that described in Chapter 8. Although our examples in this chapter focus primarily on the family group and familial roles, the application of the SRM to other types of groups with roles is a straightforward translation of the family model.

We begin with a brief review of several studies in which the SRM has been applied to family relationships and discuss the types of questions the analysis can address. The more formal aspects of the model are then presented, followed by an illustration using data on family members' security of attachment to each other. We first consider four-person families and then three-person families. Finally, we discuss how effect estimates can be computed and interpreted. This chapter is largely an update and elaboration of a previous article (Kashy & Kenny, 1990a).

SRM STUDIES OF FAMILY RELATIONSHIPS

From the advent of the family systems perspective (e.g., Bowlby, 1949) through the high point of behaviorism (e.g., Patterson, 1976), families have been understood as complex organizations in which socially and biologically prescribed role requirements and processes of positive and negative feedback have dramatic effects on family members' behavior. The hallmark of the family systems perspective is that the behavior of an individual cannot be understood apart from the interpersonal behavioral systems in which he or she is embedded. Because the SRM allows for the evaluation of behavioral stability across time and relationships and at multiple levels of analysis (group, individual, and relationship), and because it allows for the measurement of dynamic feedback processes (e.g., reciprocity), utilizing it to test the systemic nature of family relationships represents a major advance in family science.

Applications of the SRM to family relationships have yielded a number of insights into the complex nature of the family system. For instance, reciprocity of negativity has been found for fathers and for adolescents at the individual level of analysis. This indicates that fathers and adolescents who are negative toward other family members in general tend to elicit negativity from them. On the other hand, reciprocity of negativity occurs at the dyadic level for husband–wife relationships, indicating that husbands who are especially negative toward their wives (more negative than the husband is to other family members and more negative than other family members are to the wife) have wives who are especially negative toward them (Cook, Kenny, & Goldstein, 1991). For other measures of relationship quality, dyadic reciprocity has been found in dyads from the same generation (e.g., the mother–father dyad and the sibling dyad), but not across generations (Ross, Stein, Trabasso, Woody, & Ross, 2005). SRM analysis of perceived coerciveness in family relationships (Cook, 1994) suggests that reciprocal processes govern adolescent behavior at the individual level of analysis such that adolescents who think that all of their family members are coercive tend to be seen as coercive by members of their families. In addition, adolescent–father dyads show reciprocity of coerciveness at the dyadic level of analysis: In families in which the adolescent thinks the father is especially coercive, the father thinks the adolescent is especially coercive.

SRM-based studies of perceived control and attachment security have demonstrated the important role of partners in eliciting interpersonal perspectives (Cook, 1993, 2000). For example, regardless of whether the perceiver is the mother, father, older sibling, or younger sibling, the sense of control is determined by characteristics of the partner and is often due to relationship-specific effects (Cook, 1993). That is, family members' sense of control in a relationship very much depends on who the other person in the relationship is. Partner effects have also been shown to partially explain family members' attachment security in relationship to each other, raising questions about how "internal" internal working models of attachment really are (Buist, Dekovic, Meeus, & van Aken, 2004; Cook, 2000). In contrast to the view that perceptions of others are entirely subjective, the proportion of variance in perceptions of conscientiousness explained by partner characteristics is larger in absolute size than the amount explained by perceiver characteristics (Branje, van Aken, van Lieshout, & Mathijssen, 2003). Thus research using the SRM with families has shown that these constructs vary in important ways beyond individual differences in the perceivers. Finally, research using the SRM with roles has also demonstrated that outcomes for children may be affected more by the characteristics of the family as a group than by the characteristics of the child or parents as individuals or by their relationships to each other (Delsing, Oud, De Bruyn, & van Aken, 2003).

DESIGN AND ANALYSIS OF STUDIES

The most common design for SRM analysis of group data in which each individual has a specific role is the round-robin design. As noted in Chapter 8, in a round-robin design data are collected on each individual's behavior in relation to each of the other group members. In family studies, round-robin designs typically involve three or four family members, but they may include more. When there are three roles involved, the round-robin data include six directed relationship measures (e.g., mother's security of attachment to father, mother's security of attachment to the child, father's security of attachment to mother, father's security of attachment to the child, child's security of attachment to mother, and child's security of attachment to father). In four-person family groups, a round-robin data structure involves 12 such relationship measures.

Block and half-block designs can also be used to study groups with roles, in some cases increasing efficiency of data collection. For example, an asymmetric block design might be used if one were interested only in parent–child relationships. In this case, one would collect data on the father's relationships with each child, the mother's relationships with each child, the older child's relationship with each parent, and the younger child's relationship with each parent. Data on the marital or sibling relationships would not be collected (Cook & Douglas, 1998). This design reduces the number of directed relationships measured per family from 12 to 8 (see also Stevenson, Leavitt, Thompson, & Roach, 1988).

Limitless possibilities could be attempted. For instance, Sabatelli, Buck, and Kenny (1986) were interested in the ability of married couples to read each other's nonverbal behavior. They gathered dyadic judgments from the married couples (as senders and receivers of behavior), as well as judgments by and of strangers, and analyzed those judgments using confirmatory factor analysis (CFA). They were able to examine dyadic and individual differences in nonverbal sensitivity (see also Thomas & Fletcher, 2003).

THE MODEL

As originally presented by Kenny and La Voie (1984), and as discussed in the previous chapter, in the SRM every dyadic score is composed of four different effects: an actor effect, a partner effect, a relationship effect, and a group-mean effect. As an example, consider the variable of "mother's attachment security to father." There should be considerable variability across families in how secure the mothers are in their marital relationships. One major purpose of the SRM is to identify the sources of this variability. In groups with distinguishable roles, however, each of the SRM components is estimated for each role or combination of roles.

The Components

The *actor effect* describes a person's general level of response across partners. Thus one element that may contribute to mother's security with father could reflect her general level of security independent of whether the partner is her husband, her son, or her daughter—a kind of cross-situational (viz. cross-relationship) consistency. In the SRM model with roles, actor effects are computed for each role, and so within a family there is an actor effect for mother, an actor effect for father, and so on.

The *partner effect* describes the way people generally behave (think or feel) toward a particular partner. In other words, it reflects the partner's tendency to elicit similar responses from all other members of the group. Thus another component that may contribute to the mother's attachment security to the father might reflect the father's general tendency to make all other family members feel secure. As with actor effects, partner effects are computed for each role, and so the model posits a partner effect for mother, a partner effect for father, and so on.

The *relationship effect* describes the unique relationship of an actor to a partner after both actor and partner effects have been removed. Thus the relationship effect for mother's attachment security to father assesses her unique level of security in this particular relationship, controlling for her general tendencies to be securely attached to everyone (her actor effect) and his general tendency to support a secure attachment (his partner effect). It would be her unique adjustment to him. Note that the relationship effect is directional. Her attachment security in relationship to him is not identical to his attachment security in relationship to her; because it is specific to a particular relationship, the level of analysis is the dyad. The actor and partner effects, however, reflect individual differences and are therefore analyzed at the individual level. The SRM with roles contains a relationship effect for each combination of roles. Thus, in the family design, there are relationship effects for mother with father, father with mother, older child with mother, mother with older child, and so on.

The final component is called the *group mean* and reflects the average level of the outcome score for the group, averaging across all relationships in the group. For the security of attachment example, the group mean measures the average level of security in the family. To a certain extent, groups such as families can be small cultures or societies. They can have their own norms, shared goals, and values. For example, some families may create a culture of responsiveness through their attempts to support each other. In these families everyone would be highly secure in each of their family relationships. Other families may create a culture of resistance or control. In these families attachment security would be low in all relationships. Assuming that some families are somewhere between these two extremes, we would expect there to be group-level differences in attachment security. In the SRM with roles the group or family-level effect can be an important variable, and so, unlike the original SRM, in the model with roles, the group or family mean is computed, and variance across groups or families can be estimated.

Generalized and Dyadic Reciprocity

As in the traditional SRM, the SRM with distinguishable group members permits estimation of both generalized and dyadic reciprocity. *Generalized reciprocity*, sometimes called individual reciprocity, is measured by the correlation between a person's actor effect and that person's partner effect. For example, generalized reciprocity measures whether a mother who is secure in her attachment to all other family members supports a sense of security in all family members' relationships with her. There are separate generalized reciprocity correlations for each role.

Dyadic reciprocity is measured by the correlation between the two relationship effects that represent the two sides of a given relationship. For example, dyadic reciprocity in the marriage is measured by the correlation of the mother–father relationship effect with the father–mother relationship effect. It therefore examines whether women who are securely attached to their husbands have husbands who are securely attached to them, independent of the more general characteristics of mothers or fathers as individual actors and partners. In the four-person family, there are six estimates of dyadic reciprocity: mother–father with father–mother, mother–older child with older child–mother, and so on.

Estimation of Variance in the SRM with Roles

The SRM was originally designed to evaluate dyadic data derived from groups of people in which the group members were not distinguished by roles. Because group members are interchangeable in the traditional SRM, estimates of the variance in the SRM components (i.e., actor, partner, and relationship variance) are pooled across individuals within each group, as well as between groups. For example, estimates of actor effects from members within the same group and across the groups are pooled into a single measure of actor variance.

The key way in which the SRM with roles differs from the standard model is that individuals are not interchangeable within each group. Because individuals are distinguishable, pooling of estimates of the various SRM effects across roles within groups may be inappropriate. Instead, estimates of variance in the SRM effects are computed across groups for each role. In the family context, this means that the actor variance for mothers is computed by estimating the variance in the actor effects for mothers across families. Using the example of attachment security, having little actor variance for mothers would mean that, across families, mothers are relatively similar in the amount of security they generally feel. Finding substantial partner variance for fathers would mean that the fathers in some families are a greater source of security for all family members than the fathers in other families are; fathers are not similar across families.

In addition to actor and partner variance for each role, we can estimate relationship variance for each dyadic combination of roles (e.g., mother–father, mother–older child, father–mother, and so on). For example, variance in the mother–father relationship effect for attachment security means that some mothers feel more security that is specific to their relationship with their husbands than do other mothers. This variance in attachment security cannot be attributed to characteristics of mothers as individual actors or fathers as individual partners or to the families as groups. Rather, it reflects differences at only the relationship level of analysis, and to generalize beyond this relationship would be incorrect. Note that the absence of variance in an SRM component (i.e., an actor, partner, or relationship effect) essentially identifies the effect as a constant across groups, rather than a variable.

Family Subsystems

One factor that may distinguish family groups from other types of groups (either with or without roles) is the presence of a generational boundary. This generational boundary between the parent and child can be defined in terms of age, life experiences, control of resources (i.e., power), and numerous other variables. The existence of such differences between the generations suggests a certain level of similarity within generations. For example, parents tend to be of similar age, and so do siblings. On the other hand, members of the same generation may also be systematically different from each other (Kashy & Kenny, 1990a). For example, if one parent is highly persuadable (i.e., everyone is able to influence this person), the other parent might compensate by being more rigid or strict (Cook, 2001). This would be reflected in a negative correlation between the mother's and father's partner effects. Siblings may also be systematically similar to or different from each other, as when a rebellious child rejects normative behavior in an attempt to be different from an overly conformist sibling. The implication is that the analysis of these subsystems may reveal important aspects of family process. Thus a comprehensive model of the family system should take into account not only group, individual, and dyadic level effects but also the effects of subsystem dynamics.

Additional questions may develop that require modifications to the model. For example, differences in the amount of actor (and partner) variance for different roles can be examined. Differences in actor variance between mothers and fathers might indicate that, across families, mothers tend to be consistent in the behavior they initiate, whereas fathers are much more variable. Similarly, differences in the degree of relationship variance between two dyads within the family—mothers with daughters compared with fathers with daughters, for example—might indicate that the mother–daughter relationship is fairly similar across families, whereas the father–daughter relationship varies from family to family.

The researcher may also have reasons to test various correlations not specified in the standard SRM family model. These can generally be classified as individual-level second-order factors and dyadic-level second-order factors. Individual-level second-order interdependence is represented by correlations between actor effects or between partner effects. The intragenerational subsystem correlations discussed earlier (i.e., the negatively correlated partner effects for mothers and fathers) represent individual-level second-order interdependencies. However, an alternative model can test individual-level second-order correlations that cross the generations. For example, mothers and daughters may be similar in their ability to support attachment security in others, in which case they would have correlated partner effects. Second-order dyadic-level factors involve correlating relationship effects across dyads (i.e., other than the dyadic reciprocity correlations). For example, if mother's unique relationship with father is secure, does father have a more secure unique relationship with his son or daughter (Kenny, 1990b)?

Other possibilities that have received even less consideration include correlations of effects at different levels of analysis. For example, a study of interpersonal influence in families (Cook, 2001) reported a significant correlation between the partner effect for the older sibling (i.e., older sibling influenceability) and the father's unique relationship to the older sibling (i.e., father–older sibling influence). Without theoretical guidance, such correlations are difficult to interpret and should be viewed cautiously. Moreover, the ability to test these correlations depends on the design and, in particular, the number of roles in each group. In general, four-person groups (or larger) are required to test these alternative effects.

APPLICATION OF THE SRM WITH ROLES USING CONFIRMATORY FACTOR ANALYSIS

As the preceding discussion indicates, the analysis used in standard round-robin designs is inappropriate for designs in which group members have roles. Instead, a confirmatory factor analysis (CFA) is needed (see Chapter 5). In CFA, the researcher specifies exactly which observed variables load on which factor in the model. Consider, for example, the measure of mother's security in relationship to father. This variable is composed of information concerning the family mean (i.e., perhaps this is a family of very secure individuals), the mother's actor effect (i.e., the mother is secure with the father in part because she is secure with everyone), the father's partner effect (i.e., the mother is secure with the father because he elicits such behavior, and so everyone in the family is securely attached to the father), and the mother–father relationship effect (i.e., the mother is uniquely secure with the father).

In a CFA, the mother–father measure is allowed to load on the family factor, the mother-actor factor, and the father-partner factor. The mother–father relationship variance is then the unique variance in the mother–father measure that is not explained by the family mean, the mother-actor factor, and the father-partner factor. Likewise, the father's security of attachment to the mother is specified to load on the family factor, the father-actor factor, and the mother-partner factor. Again the father–mother relationship variance is the unique variance in the father–mother measure. Thus, four-person family data consists of 12 observed relationship measures, each of which loads on three factors: the family factor and the respective actor and partner factors. The variance in the errors or unique effects of the 12 measures estimates the 12 relationship variances.

Importantly, each factor included in the CFA must have at least two observed scores as indicators to be identified. For example, the measures for the mother–father relationship, the mother–older child relationship, and the mother–younger child relationship all load on the mother-actor factor. Thus, the mother-actor factor represents the common variance found in measurements for which mother is the actor. Similarly, the mother–father, older child–father, and younger child–father measures load on the father-partner factor, and thus the father-partner factor represents the common variance in measurements for which father is the partner. The details for creating separate relationship factors are presented later in the chapter.

In an SRM analysis, the sizes of the factor variances are of vital interest. For example, the variance in the mother-actor factor estimates the variance in the corresponding SRM component (the mother-actor effects) and can address questions such as, Do mothers vary across families in their general degree of attachment security? The ratio of the variance estimate for a factor over the standard error of this estimate, or Z-test, provides a preliminary test of whether the factor variance is reliable. Structural equation modeling (SEM) programs (e.g., Amos, EQS, or LISREL) generally provide the Z-test for this ratio. If the Z-test is greater than 1.645 (because variances are in principle non-negative, the test is one-tailed), the factor variance can be tentatively viewed as reliable (i.e., that there is reliable variation across families for the factor). A stronger conclusion about the reliability of a factor can be obtained by the model comparison procedures discussed later.

Several important issues arise in CFA of the SRM. The first concerns whether the model is identified. As mentioned, for a factor to be identified, it must have a minimum of two indicators (or observed measures) that load on it. It is for this reason that a three-person group with roles is the smallest group for which this model can be estimated. For example, in a three-person family design in which each family includes a mother, a father, and a child, only two measures load on the mother-actor factor: the mother–father measure and the mother–child measure. Similarly, two measures identify the father-partner factor: the mother–father measure and the child–father measure. However, these factors are identified only if the factor loadings are fixed to 1. In the three-person SRM with roles, all the loadings must be fixed. In a four-person SRM with roles design, there are three indicators for each factor because each actor has three partners and each partner is experienced by three actors. The consequence of having more actors and more partners is that two of the three loadings can be freed (i.e., estimated rather than fixed to 1), although this is not usually done for reasons of parsimony and simplicity.

The size of the group also determines the number of factors that can be included in the model. In a three-person group, each measure can load on only two factors. This has typically meant that the family factor is dropped from the model and only actor, partner, and relationship variances are computed. However, as discussed later in this chapter, other solutions are possible. When there are four family members in the group, there are sufficient degrees of freedom for a family factor and all the other components (i.e., actor and partner factors and relationship variances) to be estimated. Model identification is a complex topic, and the reader may wish to consult texts on SEM (Bollen, 1989; Kenny, 1979; Kline, 2005). Throughout the remainder of this chapter, we discuss the identification status of the models that we propose.

Significance testing is another important issue in CFA. First, the over-all fit of the SRM should be evaluated by a chi-square goodness-of-fit test. This test assesses the ability of the model to reproduce the observed correlations or covariances between the measured variables. A statistically significant chi-square test indicates that there are significant discrepancies between the covariances among the measured variables and covariances as predicted by the model; the model has not adequately explained the correlational structure of the data. This is often the case with family data because so little is known about family systems. In this case, post hoc specifications may need to be made (i.e., specifying a correlation that is not specified in the standard SRM model). There are other measures of model fit besides the chi-square test. In a large enough sample ($N > 200$), even accurate models may be unlikely to fit. Thus alternative indicators of the adequacy of the model have been proposed. One of these is the comparative fit index (CFI; Hu & Bentler, 1998), which is analogous to an R^2 measure of explained variance (and covariance). In general, the CFI should be .95 or larger.

The goodness-of-fit chi-square test can be used to compare two alternative models, one model being a simpler version of the other. For example, the SRM without a mother-actor factor is a simpler model (a submodel) than the full model. Two models must be estimated, one in which the variance of the mother-actor factor is included (i.e., the full model) and one in which this parameter is set to zero (the submodel), thus obtaining two chi-square values. The difference between these two chi-squares is itself a chi-square, and the degrees of freedom for this test equal the degrees of freedom for the simpler model minus the degrees of freedom for the full or larger model. If this differenced chi-square is statistically significant, the parameter that has been set to zero (e.g., the mother-actor factor) is concluded to be significant in that removing it significantly worsens the fit of the model. This procedure can be performed for all of the key components of the model (i.e., each factor and each correlation between factors). In this way, an initial model can be modified, and the changes can be evaluated.

The computer program LISREL (Jöreskog & Sörbom, 1984) is used in our discussion of the estimation of the SRM parameters, model fit, and model comparisons specified in the following. Other computer programs, such as EQS (Bentler, 2004), Amos (Arbuckle & Wothke, 2003), Mplus (Muthén & Muthén, 2001), Mx (Neale, 1991), and CALIS (Hatcher, 1994) can also be used. In a chapter such as this, it is impossible to present a thorough discussion of CFA or its implementation in a computer program. Readers who are unfamiliar with these topics should consult the statistical program manuals and other appropriate references.

In the remaining sections of this chapter, we elaborate on the proposed analytical techniques, illustrate the method using an example data set, discuss the various questions that can be examined, and review the constraints and limitations of this method. Group or family size is an important constraint on the types of models that can be specified. Consequently, we first discuss the analysis of data from four-person families from which all the key parameters can be estimated. We then discuss data from three-person groups (e.g., mother, father, and child) and how the smaller group size affects the modeling procedure.

THE FOUR-PERSON DESIGN

As we have described, for a given variable, a four-person round-robin design with roles produces 12 directed relationship measures; there are four persons, and each has three partners. Using the abbreviations of "M" for mother, "F" for father, "O" for older sibling, and "Y" for younger sibling and allowing the abbreviation for the actor to always come first and the abbreviation for partner second (e.g., for MF mother is actor and father is partner), the 12 relationships in a four-person family are MF, MO, MY, FM, FO, FY, OM, OF, OY, YM, YF, and YO. To illustrate, Table 9.1 presents a correlation matrix of the 12 relationships. The measured variable is a relationship-specific measure of attachment security (RS-Anxiety; Cook, 2000) derived from the Anxiety dimension of the Collins and Read (1989) Adult Attachment Scale.

TABLE 9.1. Correlations among Measures of Relationship-Specific Anxiety for Members of 208 Four-Person Families

	1	2	3	4	5	6	7	8	9	10	11	12
1. MF	1.00											
2. MO	.36	1.00										
3. MY	.31	.34	1.00									
4. FM	.32	.08	.08	1.00								
5. FO	.08	.24	.07	.32	1.00							
6. FY	.05	.04	.25	.28	.50	1.00						
7. OM	.26	.38	.08	.14	.18	.03	1.00					
8. OF	.30	.25	.11	.08	.27	.09	.56	1.00				
9. OY	.19	.24	.14	.05	.15	.20	.54	.55	1.00			
10. YM	.20	.14	.24	.10	.00	.15	.16	.06	.22	1.00		
11. YF	.14	.08	.20	.05	.02	.26	.10	.16	.28	.53	1.00	
12. YO	.05	.16	.07	.04	.01	.06	.14	.15	.29	.40	.35	1.00
Mean	1.83	1.75	1.85	1.89	1.90	2.00	1.48	1.74	1.88	1.73	1.96	2.07
SD	0.88	0.71	0.78	0.91	0.70	0.74	0.62	0.74	0.75	0.73	0.83	0.77

Note. M, mother; F, father; O, older child; Y, younger child.

The Base Model

The SRM with roles attempts to account for the correlational structure in Table 9.1. Tables 9.2, 9.3, and 9.4 present the specifications for the CFA that accomplishes this task (Kashy & Kenny, 1990a). Table 9.2 presents the loading matrix that indicates which measured variables load on which factors. Along the far left side of the table are the rows for the measured variables, and across the top row of the table are column labels for the factors in the SRM. A variable is specified to load on a factor if there is a "1" in the cell in which the respective row and column cross.[1] Looking across the rows, one can see that each of the measured variables loads on three factors: a family factor, an actor factor, and a partner factor. For instance, in the row for the mother–father (MF) variable, there are 1's in the columns for the family factor, the mother-actor factor, and the father–partner factor. All the other cells in this row contain 0's. Note that every measured variable is hypothesized to load on the family factor, as indicated by 1's in every cell of the first column. This factor would have a large variance if there were some degree of similarity among all family members and if there were large differences in level across families.

A close examination of the correlations in Table 9.1 confirms the underlying factor structure in the data. For instance, select any three RS-

TABLE 9.2. Parameter Specifications for Four-Person Family: Loading Matrix

	Family	Actor				Partner			
		M	F	O	Y	M	F	O	Y
MF	1	1	0	0	0	0	1	0	0
MO	1	1	0	0	0	0	0	1	0
MY	1	1	0	0	0	0	0	0	1
FM	1	0	1	0	0	1	0	0	0
FO	1	0	1	0	0	0	0	1	0
FY	1	0	1	0	0	0	0	0	1
OM	1	0	0	1	0	1	0	0	0
OF	1	0	0	1	0	0	1	0	0
OY	1	0	0	1	0	0	0	0	1
YM	1	0	0	0	1	1	0	0	0
YF	1	0	0	0	1	0	1	0	0
YO	1	0	0	0	1	0	0	1	0

Note. A "1" indicates that the variable loads on the respective factor, and a "0" indicates that it does not load on the factor.

TABLE 9.3. Parameter Specifications for Four-Person Family: Factor-by-Factor Covariance Matrix

	Family	Actor				Partner			
		M	F	O	Y	M	F	O	Y
Family	f								
Actor									
M	0	a							
F	0	0	a						
O	0	0	0	a					
Y	0	0	0	0	a				
Partner									
M	0	g	0	0	0	p			
F	0	0	g	0	0	0	p		
O	0	0	0	g	0	0	0	p	
Y	0	0	0	0	g	0	0	0	p

Note. The term f indicates the estimate of family-group variance; a indicates estimate of actor variance for roles; p indicates estimate of partner variance for roles; g indicates estimate of actor–partner covariance (generalized reciprocity).

TABLE 9.4. Parameter Specifications for Four-Person Family: Measure-by-Measure Covariance Matrix

	MF	MO	MY	FM	FO	FY	OM	OF	OY	YM	YF	YO
MF	r											
MO	0	r										
MY	0	0	r									
FM	d	0	0	r								
FO	0	0	0	0	r							
FY	0	0	0	0	0	r						
OM	0	d	0	0	0	0	r					
OF	0	0	0	0	d	0	0	r				
OY	0	0	0	0	0	0	0	0	r			
YM	0	0	d	0	0	0	0	0	0	r		
YF	0	0	0	0	0	d	0	0	0	0	r	
YO	0	0	0	0	0	0	0	0	d	0	0	r

Note. The term *r* indicates estimate of relationship variance for 12 dyads, and *d* indicates estimate of relationship–relationship covariance (dyadic reciprocity).

Anxiety variables that have the same person as the actor (e.g., MF, MO, and MY), and the correlations between these variables are positive and relatively large. The reason is that they all, to some extent, measure characteristics of the mother as an actor. This is specified in Table 9.2 by the 1's in the column for the mother-actor factor. If the correlations were small or negative, it would suggest that there would be little or no variance in the actor effects for mothers. Similarly, any three variables that have the same person as the partner (e.g., MF, OF, and YF) would tend to correlate positively if there were variance in the partner effects. Note that the rows for the three relationships in which father is the partner (MF, OF, YF) all have 1's in the column for the father-partner factor in Table 9.2. It should be kept in mind that each factor is estimated while controlling for the other factors that account for the particular dyadic relationship. Consequently, whether or not the correlations in Table 9.1 are significant does not by itself provide an adequate picture of the underlying factor.

Estimates of family variance, as well as actor and partner variances for each role, are found on the diagonal of the factor-by-factor covariance matrix (see Table 9.3). This matrix is analogous to the factor correlation matrix in traditional factor analysis, but because the factors are not standardized, the matrix is a covariance matrix. The family-factor variance (denoted by *f* in Table 9.3) measures between-family differences that are a function of the family as a group. Family members as a group may tend to be more secure in some families than in other families. The actor variance for any given role (denoted by *a*) measures the degree of variation in actor effects for that role. Some mothers may be highly secure in their attachment to all other family members, whereas other mothers are not secure in any relationship. Similarly, the partner variance (denoted by *p*) measures the variability in partner effects for each role.

Estimates of generalized reciprocity for each role (the covariance between actor and partner effects) can be found in the off-diagonal values of this matrix and are denoted by *g*. Positive generalized reciprocity for mothers, for example, would indicate that mothers who are secure in their attachments elicit a sense of security from others.

Relationship variances consist of the variance in a variable that is unexplained by the individual-level and family-level factors. The relationship variance for mother–father attachment security, for example, is the variation in the observed measure that is not explained either by the family factor, the mother-actor factor, or the father-partner factor. The relationship variance is therefore a measure of the unique dyadic adjustment of one family member to another. Estimates of relationship variance are found on the diagonal of the measure-by-measure covariance matrix (see Table 9.4) and denoted by *r*. Relationship effects are directional, so mother's unique adjustment to father is not the same as father's unique adjustment to mother. The four-person family design contains 12 relationship variances, one for each directed relationship. The six dyadic reciprocity correlations, MF–FM, MO–OM, MY–YM, FO–OF, FY–YF, and OY–YO, are based on correlations among these 12 variances, one for each side of the six dyads involved. They can be found in the off-diagonal elements of Table 9.4 denoted by *d*. Dyadic reciprocity measures the degree of similarity in two individuals' relationship components and thus measures, for example, the degree to which mothers and fathers are mutually secure in the marriage, independent of their family or individual characteristics.

The relationship component has been operationalized as that part of the score that is not accounted for by the family, actor, and partner factors. However, some of this residual variance is error variance. To separate the true relationship variance from error variance, a separate factor must be created for each directed relationship. As discussed in Chapter 8, this requires having a minimum of two measures of each relationship. In other words, mother's security in relation to father must be assessed with two different measures. Two strategies can be used to obtain the replication measures needed to measure relationship effects. One option is to measure each variable at two or more points in time. In this case, the relationship factor would be based on temporal stability in the relationship. A second option is to obtain two or more indicators of the same construct at the same point in time. This can be achieved by splitting multi-item scales into two half scales (Cook, 1993) or by using measures of two different but overlapping constructs, such as criticism of performance and criticism of personality. Either way, there must be replications, either over time or across measures, for each relationship variable in order to separate true relationship effects from error.

Thus, to separate relationship variance from error variance, each of the 12 directed relationships would need to be measured twice, resulting in a set of 24 variables. Twelve relationship factors would then be added to the factor-loading matrix in Table 9.2, and each relationship factor would have two indicators. Note, too, that the loadings for the family mean, actor factors, and partner factors also change, such that the family mean factor will have 24 indicators and each actor and partner factor will have 6 indicators. The factor-by-factor covariance matrix would then have an additional 12 rows and columns, and the values on the diagonal for the relationship factors provide estimates of relationship variance. The dyadic reciprocity covariances would be found as six off-diagonal elements. Finally, the diagonal values of the measure-by-measure covariance matrix would simply be error variances for the 24 measured variables. We return to estimation of relationship variance when we discuss three-person family models.

ILLUSTRATION OF THE FOUR-PERSON FAMILY DESIGN

This illustration uses previously published data on the security of attachment in family relationships (Cook, 2000). The mother, father, older child, and younger child from 208 families from the United States reported on their security of attachment to each other. The data are analyzed as a round-robin family design. The mean age of the parents was 45.4 years for mothers and 49.5 years for fathers. The sample of older children consisted of 81 young men and 127 young women (mean age 19.1). There were 102 boys and 106 girls in the sample of younger children (mean age 16.0). The families were predominantly middle-class and Caucasian, with an average income of between $50,000 and $60,000 in 1995. The adults were almost always the biological parents of the adolescent and college-age "children," although stepparents and adopted parents were not excluded from the study. SRM analysis was performed on the 12 measures of relationship-specific fear of rejection (RS-Anxiety; Cook, 2000). Derived from items on the Adult Attachment Scale (Collins & Read, 1990), the RS-Anxiety scale consists of items such as "I feel that (insert name of family member) is reluctant to get as close as I would like." Table 9.1 presents the correlation matrix, means, and standard deviations for these data. Note that relationship effects cannot be partitioned from error in this illustration because each directed relationship is measured only one time.

Model Evaluation

CFA is typically conducted using maximum likelihood estimation, which involves an iterative search for parameter estimates that result in the best-fitting model (i.e., a model that can reproduce a version of the variance–covariance matrix that is similar to the actual observed variance–covariance matrix of the measures). Thus testing the fit of the SRM involves finding values for the SRM parameters (i.e., the family variance, the actor variances, the partner variances, and so on) that are maximally consistent with the correlations and variances in Table 9.1. There are 31 unknown parameters in the four-person univariate SRM: 1 family variance, 4 actor variances, 4 partner variances, 12 relationship/error variances, 4 generalized reciprocity covariances (actor–partner), and 6 dyadic reciprocity covariances. There are 78 known variances and covariances, (12)(13)/2. The model is overidentified, with 47 degrees of freedom (78 − 31).

The model was estimated using the 12×12 variance–covariance matrix of family members' attachment security (RS-Anxiety) using the EQS (Bentler, 2004) software. The χ^2 test was well within the acceptable range: $\chi^2(47) = 45.10$, $p = .55$, with a CFI of 1.00. The fit of this model is excellent.

Parameter Estimates

The parameter estimates of the variances for the family, actor, partner, and relationship-residual effects are reported in Table 9.5. These estimates are measures of between-family variance in the SRM factors. Because variance is, in principle, non-negative, a one-tailed Z-test is used to determine whether the effects differ from zero. Alternatively, a chi-square difference can be used. We can also run a combined test of effects (e.g., all the actor variances are zero).

As can be seen in the table, all the factor variances are statistically significant, indicating that there are between-family differences for each of

TABLE 9.5. Social Relations Analysis
of Relationship-Specific Anxiety

SRM component	Variance[a]
Family	0.039
Actor	
Mother	0.163
Father	0.217
Older child	0.215
Younger child	0.232
Partner	
Mother	0.044
Father	0.056
Older child	0.064
Younger child	0.079
Relationship	
Mother–father	0.491
Mother–older child	0.223
Mother–younger child	0.338
Father–mother	0.616
Father–older child	0.170
Father–younger child	0.205
Older child–mother	0.107
Older child–father	0.204
Older child–younger child	0.205
Younger child–mother	0.204
Younger child–father	0.336
Younger child–older child	0.356

[a]All variances statistically significant ($p < .05$).

the SRM effects. Consequently, when trying to explain attachment relationships among family members, one should take into consideration explanations appropriate to each of the factors (family, actor, partner, and relationship). Thus some mothers are more secure in relationship to their husbands (the father) than are other mothers, in part because of family traits (e.g., SES), mother's actor characteristics (i.e., her general level of attachment security), father's partner characteristics (i.e., the amount of security he affords others in general), and the mother–father relationship (i.e., the unique characteristics of the mother's relationship to the father). Similarly, some husbands are more secure in relationship to their wives than other husbands because of family traits, the husband's general level of attachment, the wife's characteristics as a partner, and the unique characteristics of the husband–wife relationship.

Knowing that the factor variance is statistically significant does not reveal much about the relative importance of the effect. A better understanding of the size of a factor can be obtained by calculating the percentage of the variance in the observed measure accounted for by each of the four SRM factors. The calculation of the percentage of variance explained by each component is very simple. First, one sums the variances for the components specified to account for a particular measured variable. For example, variance in mother–father anxiety is a function of variance in the family factor (.039), the mother-actor factor (.163), the father-partner factor (.056), and the mother–father relationship residual (.491). The sum of these variances equals .749, and the ratio of each of the individual variances to this sum is the percent of variance accounted for by the component. Thus the family factor accounts for .039/.749, or 5.2%, of the variance; the mother-actor factor accounts for .163/.749, or 22.8%; the father-partner variance accounts for .056/.749, or 8.0%; and the relationship-residual term accounts for .491/.749, or 66.0%. The percentage of variance explained by each of the components for each of the relationships is presented in Table 9.6. Alternatively, the variances can be presented in a figure (e.g., Branje, van Aken, & van Lieshout, 2002). Note that, in general, the relationship-residual variances are very large and the family variance is relatively small.

TABLE 9.6. Percentage of Variance in Relationship-Specific Anxiety That Is Explained by the Components of the Social Relations Model

| Relationship | SRM components | | | |
	Family	Actor	Partner	Relationship
Mother–father	5	22	8	66
Mother–older child	8	33	13	46
Mother–younger child	6	26	13	55
Father–mother	4	24	5	67
Father–older child	8	44	13	35
Father–younger child	7	40	15	38
Older child–mother	10	53	11	26
Older child–father	8	42	11	40
Older child–younger child	7	40	15	38
Younger child–mother	8	45	8	39
Younger child–father	6	35	8	51
Younger child–older child	6	34	9	52

Note. Because entries are percentages, the rows sum to 100.

TABLE 9.7. Generalized and Dyadic Reciprocity
Correlations for Relationship-Specific Anxiety

Reciprocity	Reciprocity correlation	Z
Generalized		
Mother	.40	1.96*
Father	.03	0.16
Older child	.51	3.14*
Younger child	.54	3.52*
Dyadic		
Mother–father	.35	3.86*
Mother–older child	.16	1.12
Mother–younger child	−.00	−0.04
Father–older child	.22	1.71†
Father–younger child	.19	1.70†
Older child–younger child	.05	0.49

Note. The Z tests whether the covariance on which the correlation
is based differs significantly from zero.
†p < .10; *p < .05.

The actor–partner correlations, which represent reciprocity at the
individual level of analysis, are presented at the top of Table 9.7. The statistical significance of these correlations is tested by a Z-test, which evaluates whether the covariance is significantly different from zero. An alternative test would be to estimate the model with a particular covariance set to
zero to determine whether the fit significantly worsens compared with the
full model (i.e., a chi-square difference test). Reciprocity correlations for
the mother, older sibling, and younger sibling are statistically significant.
The reciprocity correlations at the relationship level of analysis are also
presented in Table 9.7. Reciprocity of attachment security is statistically
significant only in the husband–wife relationship, although two of the
other correlations (father–older child and father–younger child) approach
statistical significance.

Respecifications of the Base Model

Once the base model has been estimated, alternative versions of the model
can be tested. The first series of tests are equality-of-parameter tests. In
these tests, one takes a given set of parameters (e.g., actor variances, partner variances, and so on) and forces them to equal the same value. By comparing the fit of this restricted version of the base model with the base

model itself, one can evaluate whether or not these parameters differ significantly by role. As an example, this type of test is used to determine whether there is more actor variance for mothers than for fathers. In this test, one would compare the chi-square value for the unrestricted model (the model in which the actor variances for mother and father are free to differ) with the model that forces these two variances to be equal. If the chi-square difference test is significant, the restriction on the model significantly worsens the fit, and one would then conclude that there are differences in actor variance for mothers and fathers. Even if one can conclude that they are not significantly different, theoretical considerations would generally argue against treating mothers and fathers as "the same." Note that restricting their variances to be equal is not the same as restricting the correlation between their actor effects to 1.0.

For the example, the chi-square difference test of four equal actor variances is $\chi^2(3) = 2.34$, $p = .50$; the test of four equal partner variances is $\chi^2(3) = 1.79$, $p = .62$; the tests of equal relationship/residual variances is $\chi^2(11) = 112.42$, $p < .001$; the tests of equal actor–partner correlations is $\chi^2(3) = 6.89$, $p = .07$; and the test of equal dyadic reciprocity correlations is $\chi^2(5) = 9.75$, $p = .08$. Therefore, we conclude that, except for the relationship-residual variances, the variances and covariances do not differ much by family role.

A second way in which the model can be respecified is to allow some of the factor loadings to vary. In such models, for each factor, one loading is set to 1 (i.e., a marker variable), and the other loadings on that factor are free to vary. Consider the case of father's security of attachment in relationship to mother, older sibling, and younger sibling (FM, FO, and FY, respectively). These three variables load on the father-actor factor. Permitting the loadings to vary in this case might involve setting the loading of FM on the father-actor factor to 1 and allowing the loadings of FO and FY on the father-actor factor to be free. If the loading for FO is found to be smaller than the loading for FM (which is fixed to 1), then the father's actor effect is more apparent when he is interacting with the mother than when he is interacting with his child. That is, men who are secure in their attachments are even more secure in relationship to their wives. When we estimate a model that allows the loadings to vary, we find $\chi^2(20) = 10.71$, $p = .95$. Using the chi-square difference test, we obtain $\chi^2(27) = 34.38$, $p = .16$, and we conclude that allowing the loadings to vary does not significantly improve the fit of the model. There are 27 degrees of freedom in this test, because 8 loadings are set equal for actor (2 for each role), 8 for partner (2 for each role), and 11 for the mean factor.

We also have found it useful to test for intragenerational similarity. This is accomplished by specifying correlations between the mother and father actor effects, the older child and the younger child actor effects, the mother and father partner effects, and the older child and younger child partner effects. The chi-square difference between the model with the intragenerational correlations and the model without them was not significant, $\chi^2(4) = 2.12$, $p = .71$. Thus there is no evidence for intragenerational similarity. Despite our failure to find intragenerational similarity in this data set, we often do find it (e.g., Cook, 2001). We urge family researchers to always examine these effects in their data.

THE THREE-PERSON DESIGN

Not all the components of the SRM with roles can be simultaneously estimated when there are just three people in the group. Moreover, certain theoretical questions might drive the decision to select a particular configuration of roles. For instance, a family study of intergenerational transmission of attachment security might best be approached using a design involving mothers, grandmothers, and daughters. A study of single-parenting mothers might involve the mother, a child, and the child's best friend, or a mother, her sister, and the child. All of the SRM variances and covariances, except the family variance, can still be estimated as long as data are obtained on each relationship in the group. Our example has families that include a mother, a father, and a child.

In the three-person family, there are six possible relationships: mother–father (MF), mother–child (MC), father–mother (FM), father–child (FC), child–mother (CM), and child–father (CF). Note that, as before, the first letter in these abbreviations corresponds to the actor (the person initiating the behavior) and the second letter corresponds to the partner (the person eliciting the behavior).

Base Model

In the base model we assume that there is no family factor, so each variable (e.g., MF) loads on two general factors, an actor factor and a partner factor. Thus mother's attachment security in relationship to father would load on both the mother-actor factor and the father-partner factor. Recall that the actor effect measures the average level of attachment security for a particular individual (e.g., mother) based on that person's relationships with all of his or her partners. The partner effect measures a person's (e.g., father's) tendency to elicit that behavior (or feeling) from all the persons with whom he or she interacts. We add to this model the specifications for relationship factors. We could have had relationship factors for a four-person model, but we have deferred that discussion until now.

As noted earlier, for the relationship factors to be identified, there must be at least two measures of each relationship. In this example we accomplished this by using the average of the first three items of the relationship-specific attachment scale as one measure and the average of the second three items as the second measure. This was done for each of the six family relationships. Table 9.8 presents the loading matrix for the three-person family design with the relationship factors included. Note that there are now two measures of mother's attachment security to father (MF1 and MF2) and that they both load on the mother-actor factor, the father-partner factor, and the mother–father relationship factor. Similarly, the two measures of father's attachment security to mother (FM1 and FM2) load on the father-actor factor, the mother-partner factor, and the father–mother relationship factor. We could have created two actor factors for each family role, one for each measure and two partner factors. We did not do so, and thereby are implicitly assuming that the correlation between the two factors is one.

TABLE 9.8. Parameter Specifications for a Three-Person Family Design with Replications: Loading Matrix

	Actor			Partner			Relationship					
	Mother	Father	Child	Mother	Father	Child	MF	MC	FM	FC	CM	CF
MF1	1	0	0	0	1	0	1	0	0	0	0	0
MF2	1	0	0	0	1	0	1	0	0	0	0	0
MC1	1	0	0	0	0	1	0	1	0	0	0	0
MC2	1	0	0	0	0	1	0	1	0	0	0	0
FM1	0	1	0	1	0	0	0	0	1	0	0	0
FM2	0	1	0	1	0	0	0	0	1	0	0	0
FC1	0	1	0	0	0	1	0	0	0	1	0	0
FC2	0	1	0	0	0	1	0	0	0	1	0	0
CM1	0	0	1	1	0	0	0	0	0	0	1	0
CM2	0	0	1	1	0	0	0	0	0	0	1	0
CF1	0	0	1	0	1	0	0	0	0	0	0	1
CF2	0	0	1	0	1	0	0	0	0	0	0	1

Note. A "1" indicates that the variable loads on the respective factor, and a "0" indicates that it does not load on the factor.

In the base model, there are three factors for actor (M, F, and C actor) and three factors for partner (M, F, and C partner). As with the four-person family model, all the factor loadings are set to 1. Estimates of the actor and partner variance for each role, as well as the relationship factor for each relationship, are found on the diagonal of the factor-by-factor covariance matrix. As in the four-person model, the generalized (actor–partner) reciprocity covariances are found in the off-diagonal cells of this matrix, labeled g in Table 9.9. Relationship reciprocity covariances are also specified in the off-diagonal cells of this matrix (labeled d). The diagonal of the measure-by-measure matrix in Table 9.10 specifies error variances (labeled e). Correlations among these error variances are indicated in the off-diagonals (labeled c). These correlations measure method variance due to the use of the same items. For example, MF1, MC1, FM1, FC1, CM1, and CF1 all use the first three items in the RS-Anxiety scale. No family factor and no intragenerational similarity covariances have been specified in this model due to limitations imposed by the smaller group size. Modifications

TABLE 9.9. Parameter Specifications for a Three-Person Family Design with Replications: Factor-by-Factor Covariance Matrix

	Actor			Partner			Relationship					
	M	F	C	M	F	C	MF	MC	FM	FC	CM	CF
Actor												
M	a											
F	0	a										
C	0	0	a									
Partner												
M	g	0	0	p								
F	0	g	0	0	p							
C	0	0	g	0	0	p						
Dyad												
MF	0	0	0	0	0	0	r					
MC	0	0	0	0	0	0	0	r				
FM	0	0	0	0	0	0	d	0	r			
FC	0	0	0	0	0	0	0	0	0	r		
CM	0	0	0	0	0	0	0	d	0	0	r	
CF	0	0	0	0	0	0	0	0	0	d	0	r

Note. The term a indicates estimate of actor variance for roles; p indicates estimate of partner variance for roles; g indicates estimate of actor–partner covariance (generalized reciprocity); r indicates estimate of relationship variance for 6 dyads; and d indicates estimate of relationship–relationship covariance (dyadic reciprocity). The family factor cannot be estimated in this model.

TABLE 9.10. Parameter Specifications for a Three-Person Family Design with Replications: Measure-by-Measure Covariance Matrix

	MF1	MF2	MC1	MC2	FM1	FM2	FC1	FC2	CM1	CM2	CF1	CF2
MF1	e											
MF2	0	e										
MC1	c	0	e									
MC2	0	c	0	e								
FM1	c	0	c	0	e							
FM2	0	c	0	c	0	e						
FC1	c	0	c	0	c	0	e					
FC2	0	c	0	c	0	c	0	e				
CM1	c	0	c	0	c	0	c	0	e			
CM2	0	c	0	c	0	c	0	c	0	e		
CF1	c	0	c	0	c	0	c	0	c	0	e	
CF2	0	c	0	c	0	c	0	c	0	c	0	e

Note. The term e indicates the estimate of error variance in the observed measures, and c indicates correlations among these error terms.

in the model that allow for the estimation of some of these effects are discussed later in this chapter.

Illustration

The same family data on relationship-specific attachment security were used to illustrate the three-person model with the exceptions that relationships involving the older siblings were dropped and two measures of each relationship (i.e., replications) were included. The fit of the model was in the acceptable range, $\chi^2(18) = 17.55$, $p = .49$, and the CFI was at its maximum of 1.00. The variance estimates for the SRM factors are presented in Table 9.11.

The results of an SRM analysis of a three-person group are generally different from those for four-person groups. Because the components of the three-person group model do not control for a family factor, the actor and partner variances may be larger. Also, the more partners a person has, and the more actors whose relationships with a partner are measured, the more stable the estimates of the actor and partner variances are. As can be seen in Table 9.11, the actor variances for the three-person model are all reliable, but in contrast to the four-person model, the father-partner variance is now only marginally reliable. Although the absolute value of the father-partner variance is larger than in the four-person model (0.071 vs.

TABLE 9.11. Social Relations Analysis:
Three-Person Families

SRM component	Variance
Actor	
Mother	0.208*
Father	0.193*
Child	0.300*
Partner	
Mother	0.073*
Father	0.071†
Child	0.146*
Relationship	
Mother–father	0.399*
Mother–child	0.178*
Father–mother	0.515*
Father–child	0.136*
Child–mother	0.055
Child–father	0.214*

Note. Error variances not shown.
†$p < .10$; *$p < .05$.

0.056), so is its standard error (0.046 vs. 0.021). Consequently, the reliability of the smaller partner variance (the variance estimate divided by its standard error) is greater (0.056/0.021 = 2.634) than that of the larger partner variance (0.071/0.046 = 1.528).

In contrast to the prior analysis of the four-person model, the relationship variances and variances due to errors of measurement have been separated in the three-person model. Thus this analysis gives a more complete view of the importance of unique relationships in determining attachment security. The results show that all the relationship variances are reliable sources of attachment security, with the exception of the child's security in relationship to mother. Because the variance in the child–mother relationship factor is unreliable, the relationship-reciprocity covariance in the mother–child dyad cannot be computed. This is indicated in Table 9.12 as "NA." When one of the components is unreliable, the estimate of the reciprocity correlation is often out of range (e.g., the absolute value of a correlation greater than 1.0). Statistically significant or at least marginally significant variance in both components has generally been sufficient to produce valid covariances. The other reciprocity correlations in Table 9.12 are valid. The generalized reciprocity correlations (i.e., actor–partner cor-

TABLE 9.12. Reciprocity Correlations
for the Three-Person Model

Reciprocity	Reciprocity correlation	Z
Generalized		
Mother	.75	2.654**
Father	.27	0.859
Child	.44	2.993**
Dyadic		
Mother–father	.34	2.440**
Mother–child	NA	NA
Father–child	.16	0.558

Note. The Z tests whether the covariance on which the correlation is based differs significantly from zero. The mother–child relationship reciprocity correlation is undefined or "not available" due to insufficient variance in the child–mother relationship factor. **$p < .01$.

relations) for the mother and the child were reliable, as was the mother–father dyadic reciprocity correlation.

Alternative Three-Person Models

In most of the studies published so far, the variance due to family factors has tended to be small, whereas the actor, partner, and relationship variances have tended to be larger. Thus the assumption of no family variance for the three-person family model may be reasonable. However, for some variables, the family effect may be very important. For example, suppose the variable was "going to church." Family members might rate how often they go to church with each of the other family members. Going to church might be something that families do as a group more than in pairs. In this case, the variance would be more at the family level than at the individual or dyadic levels. It might, therefore, be important to include a family-level factor. However, with three-person family data, it is not possible to estimate a family factor in addition to all the other components and correlations.

There are three ways that we know of to estimate a family factor with three-person family data. In the first model, the individual level (actor–partner) covariances are dropped from the model, and the family, actor, partner, and relationship variances are estimated (Delsing, Oud, De Bruyn,

& van Aken, 2003). This approach would be viable only if there were a considerable degree of positive reciprocity. Variables involving affectivity (e.g., positivity and negativity) are good candidates for this approach. If the reciprocity of affect tended to engulf the family as a whole, a family-level factor would result. Variables related to interpersonal influence or control, because they tend to elicit compensatory processes, are not good candidates for this approach. Family members are unlikely to be similar to each other when measured on constructs on which one person's high score tends to imply a low score for the partner.

In the second model, the actor factors are dropped from the model, and the family, partner, and relationship factors are estimated. If there are no actor variances, the actor–partner covariances are undefined, and so they too must be dropped. For example, church attendance may depend on a family member who organizes the activity. Whenever anyone goes to church, they are likely to go with this person, so there will be partner variance. Consequently, the partner factors should not be dropped. But if the actor factors can be dropped, the family factor can be estimated, thus capturing the tendency of families to go to church as a group. We would judge this as the least plausible way to add a family factor.

In the third model, the partner factors are dropped, and the family, actor, and relationship factors are estimated. Without partner variances, the actor–partner covariances are again undefined, and so they too must be dropped. Variables based on skills or competencies do not tend to be affected by partner traits, thus allowing one to drop the partner factor. For example, assertiveness tends to be expressed similarly across a person's family relationships but also tends to be unaffected by general characteristics of the partner (Cook & Douglas, 1998). Accordingly, it might be justifiable to drop the partner factor and estimate the family, actor, and relationship variances. All three alternative approaches allow for the estimation of relationship reciprocity correlations.

How does the researcher know whether dropping a set of variances (e.g., actor or partner factors) or covariances has produced an invalid model? Suppose that the actor variances have been dropped from the model and that the family, partner, and relationship factors have been estimated. If the actor variances were sufficiently large, the model would not fit the data, and the chi-square test would be significant. The covariance matrix of the residuals (standard in the output of SEM programs) is one place to look for clues about such misspecifications. Most CFA software also includes modification indexes (called Lagrangian multipliers in EQS) that aid in the identification of misspecifications. However, because a complete model cannot be identified with three-person groups, it is fundamentally impossible to know whether the correct model has been specified.

MULTIPLE PERSPECTIVES ON FAMILY RELATIONSHIPS

In the typical SRM study of family relationships, the respondents report either on their own thoughts, feelings, or behavior toward the other family members or they report on or observe themselves as the target of the thoughts, feelings, or behavior of other family members. In either case, the data are dyadic. In some cases, however, a third person might report on the relationship between two other family members, in addition to how they and their partners respond to each other. When three or more raters provide information on a given relationship, it is possible to determine the shared perspective on the relationship, a perspective that might be more "objective" than the individual perspective of any particular family member. Studies using such data have typically used CFA to test latent variable models of the multitrait-multimethod matrix (e.g., Cole & Jordan, 1989; Cook & Goldstein, 1993).

Data involving multiple perspectives on family relationships have also been used in SRM analyses. For example, mother reports and father reports have been used to provide the replications needed to partition relationship factors from variance due to errors of measurement (Cook et al., 1991). Alternatively, separate SRM analyses of each perspective can also be used to assess the factors associated with agreement in the perspectives of family members. In this case, the perspectives of the respondents are not assumed to be equivalent (which is assumed when two family members provide replications of each other's perspective). Rather, the goal is to assess the equivalence of perspectives and sources of similarity of these perspectives within the SRM framework. To accomplish this, each person must provide reports on all the relationships in the group. For example, the adolescent, mother, and father might each report on how negative mother is toward father and toward the child, how negative father is toward mother and toward the child, and how negative the child is toward mother and toward father. These kinds of reports have been termed *triadic data* (Bartle-Haring, Kenny, & Gavazzi, 1999).

In the triadic SRM for family data (Bartle-Haring et al., 1999), an SRM is fitted separately to each person's ratings. Thus there are separate mother, father, and child actor factors for each rater (nine actor factors altogether); there are separate mother, father, and child partner factors for each rater (nine partner factors altogether); and there are six relationship factors (mother–father, mother–child, father–mother, father–child, child–mother, and child–father) for each rater (18 altogether). There are also three rater factors, which assess each family member's tendency to view all relationships similarly. Correlations among the three actor factors for a particular role (e.g., the three actor effects for father) provide information on how similar the three perspectives of the actor are. Correlations among the three partner factors for a given role indicate similarity of perspectives on the degree to which the partner elicits or affords certain behaviors. And correlations among the three relationship factors for each dyad (e.g., mother-to-child negativity from mother's, father's, and child's perspectives) provide information on agreement about the unique adjustment the actor makes to the particular partner, controlling for actor and partner effects. Bartle-Haring and colleagues (1999) found an average correlation of .44 for actor factors, suggesting that agreement among family members in how they viewed a person's relationships was largely due to agreement in their view of the actor's characteristics.

MEANS AND FACTOR SCORE ESTIMATION

So far, the SRM has been discussed in terms of the variances and covariances of the components. That is, we have focused on whether there are differences between families in the group effect and in the actor, partner, and relationship effects for the various family members. However, each of these variances measures deviations around a mean effect—an effect that describes the "average" family. There is an average family effect, an average actor effect for mothers, an average partner effect for fathers, and so on. This section presents the method for calculating this factor score for each of the SRM components across all families and for each individual family. These techniques allow researchers to address additional important questions about family relationships. For example, by comparing the means for the mother and father partner effects, one can evaluate whether mothers, on average, differ from fathers in the average amount of anxiety (or security) that they elicit from other family members. Also, by converting the SRM factor scores to Z scores for a particular family, one can evaluate whether the family differs from the norm in some respect. Thus the factor scores can be used for the purpose of identifying exceptional family relationships. We present a brief overview of this topic, and the interested reader should consult Cook and Kenny (2004) for more details.

Imagine the raw scores for each of the relationship-specific measures of attachment security from a particular family organized in a two-way table in which the rows are the actors and the columns are the partners, as in Table 9.13. There are four actors or perceivers (mother, father, older sibling, and younger sibling) and four partners (the same as the actors). For each family member, a row mean is calculated, representing the average of that person's scores across their three partners. Similarly, for each family member a column mean is calculated that represents the average score of that person as a partner in relationships with the other family members. Finally, the grand mean represents the average relationship in the family.

We can view the entries in Table 9.13 as a two-way ANOVA design. Given a sufficient number of families, one most basic analysis would determine whether there is a main effect for actor, a main effect for partner, and an interaction effect. We are specifically interested in whether particular rows (e.g., mothers as actors) differ from the grand mean, whether particular columns (e.g., fathers as partners) differ from the grand mean, and whether specific cells of the table (e.g., the mother × father interaction) differ from row and column means.

TABLE 9.13. Round-Robin ANOVA Table for a Single Family's Attachment Security Scores

Actor	Partner				
	Mother	Father	Older Child	Younger Child	
Mother		1.00	1.00	2.00	Row Mean Mother
Father	1.17		1.50	3.83	Row Mean Father
Older Child	1.09	1.33		2.83	Row Mean Older Child
Younger Child	1.17	4.83	3.33		Row Mean Younger Child
	Column Mean Mother	Column Mean Father	Column Mean Older Child	Column Mean Younger Child	Grand Mean for Family

An important feature of this table is that empty cells are located where an individual's row and column intersect (i.e., along the main diagonal). The cells remain empty because a person never has him- or herself as a partner. This produces a "missing partner" bias (Warner et al., 1979). If it were not for the missing score, the row mean could be interpreted as an actor effect (the family member's average behavior or perceptions across all partners), and the column mean could be interpreted as that family member's partner effect (how the person is perceived or acted on, averaged across all other actors). The effect of the missing partner has been compared to the effect on a baseball team's batting average that results from having the best pitcher in the league (Kenny & La Voie, 1984). Because they do not have to bat against the best pitcher in the league (i.e., their own pitcher), members of this team tend to have higher batting averages. Similarly, the person who is perceived as most anxious by other family members would tend to have a relatively small row mean because he or she does not rate the most anxious family member.

The next step in the process is to apply the formulas for the group mean (i.e., family mean) and actor, partner, and relationship effects to the appropriate relationship measures from the round-robin family design. These formulas were originally presented by Warner and colleagues (1979) for use in social psychology studies and were subsequently applied to family relationship data (Cook & Dreyer, 1984). As in Chapter 8, the estimate for actor effect for actor i is

$$
\begin{aligned}
\text{Actor effect}_i = \ & (n-1)^2/[n(n-2)]\,\text{row mean}_i \\
& + (n-1)/[n(n-2)]\,\text{column mean}_i \\
& - (n-1)/(n-2)\,\text{grand mean}, \qquad (9.1)
\end{aligned}
$$

where n is the number of group or family members. There are three steps in computing an estimated actor effect, each step corresponding to a row in Equation 9.1. For any given family member i, the actor effect is a function of the average of the person's score with each of the $n-1$ other family members, that is, the row mean. The actor effect is the row mean adjusted by the column mean for that person, to remove the bias due to the missing partner score. It is then differenced from the mean for the family, the grand mean. A particular actor effect can be either positive or negative. If the person were generally the source of scores that are greater than the average family score, the actor effect would be positive. If the actor has scores that are less than the family mean, the actor effect would be negative. In other words, actor effects are relative to the average score for all relationships within the family.

The formula for the partner effect is based on the column mean for each person in the same way the actor effect is based on the row mean:

$$\text{Partner effect}_i = (n-1)^2/[n(n-2)]\text{column mean}_i$$
$$+ (n-1)/[n(n-2)]\text{row mean}_i$$
$$- (n-1)/(n-2)\text{grand mean}, \qquad (9.2)$$

where n is the number of the group or family members. Because the column mean does not include scores reflecting the person as an actor or rater, it is adjusted by the row mean. The grand mean is then subtracted, in Equation 9.2, from the adjusted column mean. If the person receives scores from other family members that exceed (or are less than) the family mean, the partner effect would be positive (or negative). Thus, like the actor effects, partner effects are relative to the average family relationship.

If a person has a low score in one relationship (e.g., mother–father negativity), a relatively high score in another relationship (e.g., mother–older child negativity), and an average score in a third relationship (e.g., mother–younger child negativity), the row mean can be the same size as that for an actor who has moderate scores in all three relationships. The same logic applies to column means and partner effects. If one family member has a high score with a particular partner, one family member has an average score with that partner, and another family member has a relatively low score with that partner, the column mean for that partner would be the same as for a partner with whom everyone has moderate scores. It is therefore important to know how particular relationships affect actor and partner effects. The estimates for relationship effects provide this information:

$$\text{Relationship effect}_{ij} = X_{ij} - \text{actor effect}_i - \text{partner effect}_j - \text{grand mean.} \qquad (9.3)$$

In Equation 9.3, the actor effect for person i, the partner effect for person j, and the grand mean are differenced from the raw score for a particular actor with a particular partner (X_{ij}). In other words, the effects of the family mean, the actor, and the partner are removed from the relationship score. What remains is the effect for that particular relationship. Consequently, if an actor effect or partner effect has been affected by a particular relationship, the relationship effect would be large. Like actor and partner effects, relationship effects can be positive or negative. Thus the person whose actor effect is of average size because he or she has one relationship high in negativity and one relationship low in negativity can be distinguished from the person who has moderately negative scores in all his or her relationships.

Constraints on the SRM Effects

In the SRM with roles analysis, an actor effect is computed for each member of the family, a partner effect is computed for each member, and a relationship effect is computed for each directed dyadic relationship. A two-parent, two-child family will include 1 family effect, 4 actor effects, 4 partner effects, and 12 relationship effects. There are 21 effects and only 12 data points! Because we have 12 pieces of information, we must place constraints on the 21 effect estimates. Referring to Table 9.13, it should be apparent that the average of the row means would equal the grand mean for the family, as would the average of the column means. As a consequence, if we know three of the row means, the fourth can be calculated as the difference of the first three from the grand mean. In other words, for an independent variable with four levels, there are three degrees of freedom. These constraints are the same as in the standard ANOVA model, on which the SRM is based. In a round-robin family design, the degrees of freedom for actor and partner effects are each $n - 1$, where n equals the number of family members providing data. Accordingly, for a family of 4, there are $4 - 1$, or 3, degrees of freedom. Thus there can be three independent row means or column means, but the fourth mean has to be that number which, when averaged with the other 3, results in the grand mean. This constraint shows up in the actor effects such that the sum of the actor effects equals zero. It shows up in the partner effects in the same way; that is, the sum of the partner effects also equals zero. Consequently, a large and positive actor effect for father must be compensated for by the other actor effects. For example, the mother's actor effect might be equal in size but negative. There is no particular pattern to how the actor effects sum to zero, so it can be accomplished by various combinations.

There are also constraints on the relationship effects. If we add all of the relationship effects for a given actor, the result equals zero. For example, the father–mother, father–older child, and father–younger child relationship effects sum to zero. Similarly, if we add the relationship effects in which a particular person, such as the father, is the partner, this sum also equals zero. Thus the relationship effects of the other family members' unique adjustments to father sum to zero.

Estimation of SRM Effects for a Particular Family

Not only can we estimate the actor, partner, and relationship effects for a particular family but we can also apply the very same formulas to the sample means and assess the average actor effect for adolescents in general, the average partner effect for fathers in general, the average family effect for families in general, and so on. By using the norms generated by estimating these effects in a representative sample, we can determine, for a given family, which of the SRM effects are unusual. This is useful for purposes of assessment (Cook & Kenny, 2004).

Consider the responses for family 382 from our example data set, whose raw scores were presented in Table 9.13. The first column of numbers in Table 9.14 presents the family-specific SRM effects for this family. We see that the younger child, a daughter, has the largest absolute actor effect of 1.448: She reports more relationship anxiety than the other family members. The second column of numbers presents the SRM effects for the average family in the sample, which serve as norms. These mean SRM effects can be computed by applying the SRM formulas to the means presented at the bottom of Table 9.1. We see that the average actor effect for younger siblings, 0.117, is smaller than the one for the younger child in our example family. As shown in the next column to the right (SRM′), there is a difference of 1.331 points. The younger child's actor effect for relationship anxiety is 1.331 scale points greater than the average for younger children. The last column provides the Z-score for this effect (see Cook & Kenny, 2004). It is statistically significant, $Z = 2.578$. Thus this result demonstrates that this family is extreme in the degree of relationship anxiety experienced by the younger child. With respect to the effect of partners on attachment security, mother has the lowest partner effect, −1.355, which is statistically lower than the partner effect for the average mother, −0.169, $Z = -3.390$. She elicits less anxiety than the average mother, SRM′ = −1.187. Other statistically notable effects include the mother-actor effect, the younger child–partner effect, the older child–mother relationship effect, the younger child–mother relationship effect, and the younger child–father relationship effect.

In summary, the formulas presented here provide the SRM effects for a family. They could, therefore, be used to identify families with extreme group means (family effects); extreme actor and partner effects for mothers, fathers, and children; and extreme relationship effects for all relationships measured. Families may differ from each other on any of these effects; hence, for purposes of family assessments, any of these effects may identify the source of family dysfunction.

TABLE 9.14. Social Relations Analysis of Relationship-Specific Anxiety: Family 382

SRM effect	Family-specific effects	All families	SRM′	z
Family	2.090	1.838	0.252	0.646
Actor				
Mother	−1.208	−0.087	−1.122	−2.441
Father	0.198	0.103	0.096	0.195
Older child	−0.438	−0.134	−0.305	−0.643
Younger child	1.448	0.117	1.331	2.578
Partner				
Mother	−1.355	−0.169	−1.187	−3.390
Father	0.365	0.038	0.327	0.962
Older child	−0.292	0.022	−0.313	−0.829
Younger child	1.282	0.109	1.177	3.131
Relationship				
Mother–father	−0.247	0.040	−0.286	−0.763
Mother–older child	0.410	−0.028	0.437	1.366
Mother–younger child	−0.163	−0.012	−0.151	−0.438
Father–mother	0.233	0.116	0.118	0.298
Father–older child	0.497	−0.066	−0.430	−1.334
Father–younger child	0.263	−0.050	0.313	1.027
Older child–mother	0.783	−0.059	0.842	2.843
Older child–father	−0.683	−0.003	−0.680	−2.210
Older child–younger child	−0.100	0.062	−0.162	−0.466
Younger child–mother	−1.017	−0.057	−0.960	−2.884
Younger child–father	0.930	−0.037	0.966	2.727
Younger child–older child	0.087	0.094	−0.007	−0.018

Note. The SRM′ difference scores were obtained by subtracting the mean of each of the 12 relationship scores before applying the SRM formulas. A Z score of plus or minus 2.0 indicates that the effect is 2 standard deviations above or below the sample mean for the effect.

POWER AND SAMPLE SIZE

Because the round-robin SRM with roles design requires data from multiple group members in relation to each of their partners, the design is difficult to implement. The unit of analysis is the family or group, so to obtain a sample size of 60, a study of 4-person families would require the participation of 240 persons. On the other hand, the SRM components are estimated using SEM, a method that generally requires sample sizes of 200 or more (e.g., Bollen, 1989). A sample of 200 three-person families would require the participation of 600 people, and a sample of 200 four-person families would require 800 participants. Clearly, obtaining such large samples of families would be burdensome. It is therefore important to know precisely how many families are necessary to provide sufficient power for an SRM analysis. We should note that larger sample sizes are needed for CFA models in which factor loadings are free to vary. Because the base family SRM model fixes all the loadings to the same value, sample sizes smaller than 200 have acceptable levels of power.

In determining power, the size of the variances of the SRM components (e.g., family, actor, and partner) is the effect size. Following Cohen (1988), relative variances of .1 are small effects, relative variances of .3 are medium effects, and relative variances of .5 or more are large effects. Using the Satorra and Saris (1985) method of computing power in covariance structure models, an 80% chance of detecting a small effect would require 619 families. However, detection of a medium-size effect requires only 66 families and of a large effect, only 22 families. We would conclude that a small sample size of families is 40, a medium sample size is 80, and a large sample size is 200.

SUMMARY AND CONCLUSIONS

In this chapter we have discussed the use of the SRM with groups in which there are clearly delineated roles (i.e., the group members are distinguishable). Although the SRM procedures for indistinguishable (see Chapter 8) and distinguishable group members are very similar, there are some striking differences. First, because there are model effects for each role, the model with distinguishable members has many more parameters. In families, for example, separate actor and partner effects are estimated for mothers, fathers, and the children. Second, the group-level effect may be more meaningful because families (and perhaps other groups as well) may create microcultures that affect the behavior of all group members in the same way. Third, data analysis is performed using CFA, not ANOVA-like methods. As noted in Chapter 8, however, it is possible to estimate the parameters of the SRM using multilevel modeling techniques. In the future we expect that the multilevel modeling approach will be used more often in groups with distinguishable roles.

In addition to its ability to assess differences in the "cultures" of small groups (i.e., group-level variances), we have described how the SRM can be used to identify and assess subsystems within groups. When defined in terms of group processes (rather than group roles), subsystems include the components of positive and negative feedback loops. It is by virtue of processes of feedback that we can say that a group has a self-organizing capacity, which is one way of defining something as "systemic." Most important in this regard are the SRM estimates of reciprocity. For example, when adolescents reciprocate coerciveness (Cook, 1994), they perpetuate the presence of coerciveness in the family system. Other second-order SRM factor correlations may also identify subsystems within the family. For example, a process in which parents compensate for each other's controllability, perhaps reflecting a struggle over strictness and leniency in parenting, was identified by the correlation of mothers' and fathers' partner effects (Cook, 2001). As we have shown, the SRM can provide estimates of reciprocity and other second-order factors at both the individual and dyadic levels of analysis.

Certainly, the SRM provides a very detailed examination of family members' behavior with or perceptions of one another. In particular, we can examine whether actor, partner, and relationship variances differ by role. We have also presented a way to analyze the means for the SRM components within families and other groups. We have shown two ways to do this. Using the methods of CFA, it is possible to obtain estimates for the average of the group, actor, partner, and relationship effects within a sample of groups. This method allows one to determine, for example, whether adolescents generally perceive their families more negatively (an actor or perceiver effect) than does the average family member (the family group effect). The other way is to use the formulas for the SRM to obtain estimates of the group, actor, partner, and relationship effects for the members of a particular group. This latter approach can provide information on the dynamics of individuals and relationships within a particular family, thus facilitating clinical applications (Cook, 2005; Cook & Kenny, 2004).

The SRM is currently the most comprehensive method of investigating patterns and dynamics of family systems. Other approaches (e.g., sequential analysis) are generally limited to the assessment of the single dyad. In fact, if sequential analysis (see Chapters 13 and 14) were performed on all dyads in a family in a round-robin design, the SRM could be applied to the data to assess the individual and dyadic factors affecting processes of reciprocity and interpersonal influence (Cook, 2001). From this example it can be seen that the SRM and sequential analysis are complementary approaches to data analysis that can be integrated in ways that address issues more complex than either method alone can address. The SRM is also complementary to behavior-genetic analysis because it provides the means to address substantially more sophisticated questions (Manke & Plomin, 1997). Specifically, the assessment of the genetic basis for sibling similarity in what is elicited from the family environment (i.e., correlated partner effects) can be analyzed independently from the genetic basis for similarity in what siblings bring to the family environment (i.e., correlated actor effects). We hope that these examples of the analysis of family groups will inspire the application of the SRM to other types of groups in which the group members are distinguishable by their roles. Clearly, there is a place for this method in studies of business relationships, military units, medical treatment teams, and other organizations.

NOTE

1. Unlike traditional factor analysis, all of the nonzero loadings are fixed to one. This is permissible because the factors are not standardized. As a consequence, however, the factor loadings are not correlations. In effect, the unit of measurement of the factor corresponds to the scale of the measured variables. All the measured variables should be measured using the same scale (e.g., a 5-point Likert scale). If one of the measured variables has a different scale of measurement, some accommodation must be made in terms of its loading. For example, if the design allows, the loadings may be freed (all but one loading per factor being free to vary).

10

One-with-Many Designs

In the one-with-many design, a person is in multiple dyadic relationships, but each of the person's partners is in a relationship with only that one person. In our survey of 75 studies (see Chapter 1), we found that 16% of studies used the one-with-many design. We refer to the person who has multiple partners, the "one," as the *focal person* and to the multiple others, the "many," as the *partners*. As explained in Chapter 1, the one-with-many design is a blend of the standard dyadic and Social Relations Model designs; it is similar to the standard design in that each partner is paired with only one person, and it is like an SRM design in that the focal person is paired with many partners.

Examples of the one-with-many design are:

An individual reports how jealous he or she felt in each of his or her past relationships (Hindy & Schwarz, 1994).

A person's personality is evaluated by several of his or her friends (Vazire & Gosling, 2004).

Patients of an obstetrician are asked how satisfied they are (Roter, Geller, Bernhardt, Larson, & Doksum, 1999).

A person describes the drinking behavior of his or her friends (Mohr, Averna, Kenny, & Del Boca, 2001).

A person reports on the truthfulness of his or her everyday interactions with different partners (DePaulo & Kashy, 1998).

A mother is asked how secure her attachment is to three different family members (Cook, 2000).

263

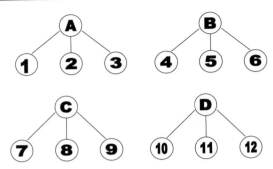

FIGURE 10.1. Illustration of the one-with-many design in which persons A through D are the focal persons and 1 through 12 are the partners.

In each case, data are gathered about one person, the focal person, who is linked to at least two partners but whose partners are linked only to the focal person. The basic structure of the design is illustrated in Figure 10.1. Focal persons A, B, C, and D are each linked to three different partners.

The reader needs to be forewarned that much of the material in this chapter is dense. Additionally, because the one-with-many design is a "new" design, it has its own vocabulary, which might seem foreign to most readers. Much of the material needs to be studied quite carefully.

DESIGN ISSUES

There are three basic variants of the one-with-many design. In the first, all of the measurements are taken from the focal person. That is, the focal person provides data about each of his or her partners. This is the most common variant of the one-with-many design. One good example of this variant is egocentric network research in which the focal person (the ego) lists members of his or her social network and then judges how much social support each member provides. Kenny and Winquist (2001) refer to this design as a 1PMT, or one-perceiver, many-targets, design.

A second variant is one in which the source of the data is the partners and the focal person does not provide data. For example, data might be gathered from the patients of a doctor. Kenny and Winquist (2001) refer to this design as an MP1T design, or a many-perceivers, one-target design. Sometimes *hidden nesting* (Rosenthal & Rosnow, 1991) occurs in the MP1T design. For example, patients from the same physician are measured but the link due to the physician is ignored, and the data are analyzed treating patient as the unit of analysis. In this case, the hidden-nesting variable would be physician.

In the third variant of the one-with-many design, data are gathered from both the focal person and his or her partners, and, therefore, the data structure is reciprocal. An example of such a design is a study of adolescents' family relationships in which the child reports on the quality of his or her relationships with three family members and each of the three family members also report on the quality of their relationships with the child. Kenny and Winquist (2001) refer to this design as a 1PMT–MP1T design, or a reciprocal design. This design is not used very frequently. For instance, in the 12 one-with-many design studies that we found in our survey (see Chapter 1), only one used a reciprocal design (Golombok, MacCallum, & Goodman, 2001). In that study, children were the focal persons, and their partners were the children's fathers and mothers. Both children and their parents were asked about the quality of the parent–child relationship.

As another example of the variants of the one-with-many design, if 20 teachers in 20 classrooms rated the students in their classrooms, the design would be a 1PMT design. If the students rated their teachers, the design would be an MP1T design. Finally, if the student and teacher made judgments on the same variables, the design would be reciprocal.

There are several other design considerations in the one-with-many design. One key question is whether the number of partners per focal person is constant or variable. Sometimes the number of partners is fixed to be the same, as would be the case in a study in which each focal person is asked to recall his or her last four romantic relationships. Even when the number of partners is experimentally set to be the same, missing data can create differences in the number of partners per focal person. For instance, although people are asked to recall their previous four relationships, some may give data for only two or three.

Another design issue is whether the partners[1] are distinguishable or indistinguishable. If the partners were distinguishable, we would say that they take on *roles* (see Chapter 9). For instance, a researcher might ask a college student to state his or her emotional closeness to his or her lover, father, best friend, and roommate. In cases in which partners are distinguishable, the number of partners per person, k, is the same for all focal persons, unless there are missing data. An example of indistinguishable partners would be patients of a doctor. When partners are indistinguishable, they all have the same role relationship with the focal person.

In this chapter, we denote the total number of focal persons as n and the number of partners for focal person j as k_j, or just k when the number of partners per focal person does not vary by focal person. We use N to denote the total number of partners in the study. Thus N equals Σk_j when the number of partners varies by focal person, and N equals nk when the number of partners does not vary by focal person. Note that in several chapters n refers to the number of dyads, but in this chapter n refers to the number of focal persons.[2]

The data can be organized in one of two ways. Each data record may refer to a different focal person with separate variables for each partner. In this case, focal person is the unit of analysis. Alternatively, there might be a separate record for each partner. There would need to be a variable on each record that denotes which focal person is linked to the partner. In this case, partner is the unit of analysis.

As an example, we use part of Cook's (2000) relationship-specific anxiety data, discussed in Chapter 9. We consider only the relationship-specific anxiety that the mother experiences in her relationships with the father, the older child, and the younger child. Thus we have a 1P3T, or one perceiver (the mother) and three targets (the father and the two children) design. There are a total of 208 focal persons and 624 partners. In our analysis, gender and age of the targets, as well as age of the perceiver, serve as predictor variables.[3] At times in this chapter, we denote predictor variables that refer to the partners (e.g., age and gender of the partner) as X variables and predictor variables that refer to the focal person (e.g., age of mother) as Z variables. (We do not consider gender of the perceivers because all mothers are obviously female.) The partners are distinguishable, but for illustration purposes, we sometimes ignore that fact. Also, when we consider the analysis of the reciprocal one-with-many design, we use the relationship-specific anxiety ratings made by each of the three family members about the mother: the father's anxiety with the mother, the older child's anxiety with the mother, and the younger child's anxiety with the mother.

We begin our discussion with a description of ways to measure nonindependence of the partner observations. These methods are the same regardless of whether only the focal person generated all of the data or whether the partners generated all of the data. We then describe the analysis of a single variable for the typical one-with-many designs (i.e., when only the focal person supplies data or when only the partners supply data). We first consider the case in which partners are indistinguishable and then the case in which they are distinguishable. Finally, we consider the analysis of the reciprocal one-with-many design and also the analysis of multivariate designs.

MEASURING NONINDEPENDENCE

In Chapter 2, we discussed measuring nonindependence for the reciprocal standard design. Here we consider measuring nonindependence for the nonreciprocal one-with-many design. In this design, the nonindependence at issue is the nonindependence that occurs among the scores of the partners who are all linked to the same focal person. In this context, we consider the issue for indistinguishable and distinguishable partners. In the final part of this section, we discuss the conceptual meaning of nonindependence for the one-with-many design.

Indistinguishable Partners

As we did in Chapter 2, we use the intraclass correlation as a measure of nonindependence, although its measurement and interpretation are quite different. Readers might wish to review the discussion of the intraclass correlation in Chapter 2.

There are three methods for estimating the intraclass correlation. The first approach uses ANOVA, and the intraclass that is estimated using this approach is symbolized by r_I. We start with a partner data set in which each record refers to a different partner. To estimate the intraclass correlation using ANOVA, focal person is treated as the independent variable in a one-way, between-subjects ANOVA in which each score refers to the response of a different partner. Thus the independent variable would have n levels. The partners, who are nested within focal person, provide the "outcome scores" for the ANOVA. From this analysis we obtain a mean square between groups, or MS_B, and a mean square within groups, or MS_W. In terms of formulas, with these two mean squares, we estimate the intraclass correlation, or r_I:

$$r_I = \frac{MS_B - MS_W}{MS_B + (k-1)MS_w},$$

where k is the number of partners per focal person, which is assumed not to vary across focal persons. If number of partners varies by focal person, k' is substituted for k in the preceding formula, where the value of k' is defined as $M_k - s_k^2/(NM_k)$, and where M_k and s_k^2 are the mean and variance, respectively, of the number of partners per focal persons (Kenny & La Voie, 1985; Snijders & Bosker, 1999).

The formula for the intraclass correlation presented in this chapter is slightly different from the one presented in Chapter 2. Note that when k is equal to 2, the two formulas are identical,[4] and so the formula in this chapter can be viewed as the more general formula. Chapter 2 also presents the formulas for the confidence interval.

The limits of the intraclass correlation are 1 and $-1/(k-1)$. Notice that if the number of partners per focal person is two, then the intraclass correlation varies from 1 to -1. However, if k were greater than two, then the lower limit would be less than -1. For three partners, the lower limit of the intraclass correlation is $-.5$: If partner A is very different from both partners B and C, then B and C cannot also be very different from each other. The intraclass correlation equals 1 when all the partners' scores for a focal person equal the same value and the averages of the partners' scores differ across focal persons ($MS_{BG} > 0$ and $MS_{WG} = 0$; e.g., all patients like their doctor to the same degree, but some doctors are liked more than others); the intraclass correlation is at its minimum when the averages of the partner scores for each focal person all equal the same value but the partner scores vary ($MS_{WG} > 0$ and $MS_{BG} = 0$; e.g., all doctors are equally liked on average, but not all patients like their doctor to the same extent).

Testing the intraclass correlation for statistical significance also uses the mean squares from the ANOVA that treats focal person as the independent variable. The test is an F-test, computed as MS_B/MS_W with $n-1$ degrees of freedom in the numerator and $N-n$ degrees of freedom in the denominator, where n is the number of focal persons. However, if the intraclass correlation were negative, then this F-test would be less than 1. Thus, if the intraclass correlation were negative, the F-test would be computed as MS_W/MS_B, with a corresponding flip in the degrees of freedom. Therefore, unlike the usual F-test in ANOVA, the test should be two-tailed, and the usual p value should be doubled. However, as we discuss later, negative nonindependence is relatively rare for the one-with-many design. The researcher may want to consider a one-sided test in which r_i is only positive. Also, as we discussed in Chapter 2, one might wish to adopt a more liberal value of alpha because of the costs of falsely concluding that the data are independent. In fact, as shown in Kenny and colleagues (1998), the bias increases as the number of partners increases.

To illustrate the computation of the intraclass correlation, we use data on mother's relationship-specific anxiety in relation to three specific family members: father, older child, and younger child. Note that we are ignoring the fact that the partners are actually distinguishable for this example. As mentioned, in this example, n equals 208 mothers and k equals 3 partners. To compute the intraclass correlation, a one-way ANOVA is run with focal person (mother) as the independent variable. From that analysis, the MS_B = 1.048, and MS_W = 0.423, making r_I equal to .330. The test of statistical significance is $F(207, 416) = 2.48$, $p < .001$. Thus the correlation is statistically significant, and we conclude that there is a moderate amount of consistency in the anxiety that mothers feel across their family relationships.

The second method of computing the intraclass correlation involves using the pairwise method. The pairwise intraclass correlation, symbolized as r_P, is computed using an ordinary Pearson product–moment correlation, but the data are duplicated and reordered. For the one-with-many design, as k increases, this method becomes increasingly cumbersome. We need to artificially create $k(k - 1)/2$ dyads among the partners for each focal person (note that these paired partners are not actually partners with one another in the data set); then, for each artificial dyad, the data need to be double-entered from each dyad. We do not detail the computation and testing of this measure here, but instead we refer the reader to Griffin and Gonzalez (1995).

We computed the pairwise correlation for the relational anxiety data set (again, for the purposes of this example, we are ignoring the fact that partners are actually distinguishable). To do so, we had to create three different sets of dyads (partner 1 with partner 2, partner 1 with partner 3, and partner 2 with partner 3) and double their data. Thus, if partner 1's (e.g., father's) anxiety with mother is a 3, and partner 2's anxiety score with mother is a 5, then (3,5) and (5,3) represent two of the pairs of scores used in the analysis. The pairwise correlation equals .328, a value only slightly different and predictably smaller than the ANOVA value of .330.

Later in this chapter, we also discuss how the intraclass correlation can be computed within multilevel modeling (MLM). We shall see that the MLM intraclass correlation is a variant of both the ANOVA intraclass and pairwise correlations. The one major advantage of the MLM approach is that it allows for missing data.

Distinguishable Partners

When partners are distinguishable (as they are in the example: father, older child, and younger child), we treat each partner as a separate variable. We can measure nonindependence by computing the bivariate correlations among the k different partners, and thus nonindependence is assessed by testing whether each of $k(k - 1)/2$ correlations differ significantly from zero. For Type I error protection, we can perform a Bonferroni adjustment by dividing alpha, usually .05, by the number of tests.

For the relational anxiety data, we have three partners (father, older child, younger child) and three correlations (mother–father with mother–older child, mother–father with mother–younger child, and mother–older child with mother–younger child). We divide alpha by 3 to obtain a Bonferroni adjusted alpha of .0167. The three correlations are .357 between mother–father and mother–older child, .306 between mother–father and mother–younger child, and .345 between mother–younger and mother–older child. All these correlations are statistically significant, $p < .001$.

Structural equation modeling (SEM; see Chapter 5) can be used to conduct a single test of nonindependence when partners are distinguishable. The variance–covariance matrix is read into an SEM program (e.g., AMOS, EQS, or LISREL) or is computed by that program. A model that includes no latent variables is estimated. All the covariances between the variables are fixed to be zero, and all variances are set to be free. Note that if a covariance between variables were zero, then the correlation between those variables would also be zero. Some programs refer to this model as the *independence* or *null model*, because if all the correlations were zero, the variables would be independent. The number of degrees of freedom for such a test is $k(k-1)/2$. If the chi-square test were statistically significant, then we would conclude that one or more of the correlations is nonzero.

For some analysis strategies that are discussed in this chapter (e.g., repeated-measures ANOVA), we assume that the correlational structure takes on the form of *compound symmetry*. This assumption is that the k variances are all equal and that the $k(k-1)/2$ covariances (correlations times the product of the two variables' standard deviations) also have the same value. A consequence of this assumption is that all the correlations are equal to each other. Again, a convenient way to test this hypothesis is to use an SEM program (e.g., AMOS, EQS, or LISREL). One sets the variances equal to each other and then sets the covariances equal to each other. The chi-square test of compound symmetry has $k(k+1)/2 - 2$ degrees of freedom. If the chi-square test were statistically significant, then we would conclude that the assumption of compound symmetry is not met.

Returning to the Cook (2000) study of mothers' anxious attachment, using SEM to test whether the set of three correlations are all zero, we find a $\chi^2(3) = 63.64$, which is statistically significant, $p < .001$. Thus there is strong evidence of a correlation among the three scores. As mentioned, we can also test compound symmetry using SEM. For this model, the variances are all equal, as are the correlations. Using SEM, we find $\chi^2(4) =$

11.94, which is statistically significant, $p < .001$. Thus compound symmetry cannot be assumed for this data set. However, when we test that the variances are unequal but the covariances equal, we obtain a good-fitting model, $\chi^2(2) = 0.48$, $p = .788$.

We can extend the compound-symmetry assumption to a statistical determination of whether the partners are distinguishable or indistinguishable. We add to the test of compound symmetry a test of equality of the means of the k measures. Again using SEM with the Cook (2000) data, we find $\chi^2(6) = 14.86$, which is statistically significant, $p = .021$. Thus the dyad members cannot be treated as if they were indistinguishable.

THE MEANING OF NONINDEPENDENCE IN THE ONE-WITH-MANY DESIGN

To understand nonindependence in the one-with-many design, it is helpful to review the sources of nonindependence in the standard reciprocal dyadic design. In the standard design, there are only two persons, and both are sources of data. For example, we might measure marital satisfaction of both the husband and the wife in a sample of couples. These two measures are likely to be correlated (i.e., nonindependent), because the two persons are directly linked to each other. For the one-with-many design, the linkage is indirect. Because the two individuals are not partners to one another but rather to a third party (the focal person), they do not influence each other. Instead, the two partners share an indirect linkage. Thus the nonindependence is mediated by the common fate (see Chapter 1) of a linkage to the focal person.

The meaning of this common-fate effect changes depending on the type of design. In the 1PMT design, the focal person is the source of the data on his or her relationship to each of the three partners. Because the focal person is a common source for all three measures, we would expect there to be shared variance across the measures. Thus the interdependence among the three measures is due to consistency in the way the focal person feels about or perceives others. The nonindependence in this design can be viewed as similar to the actor effect in the SRM (see Chapter 8). The actor effect reflects the tendency for a person to see or treat all others in the same way.

In the MP1T design, the sources of the data are the partners. Each partner rates or interacts with the focal person. What the measures have in common is the focal person as the target. Consequently, the correlation between the ratings is assumed to be due to characteristics of the focal person that affect all the partners. The source of nonindependence in this design can be viewed as a partner effect in the SRM (see Chapter 8). The partner effect reflects the tendency for a person to be viewed or treated the same way by others.

If the design is reciprocal, there then are three different types of nonindependence. First, there are actor effects, because the focal person provides data for each partner. Second, there are partner effects, because each of the partners provides data for the focal person. Third, there is the usual nonindependence, because two people, the focal person and the partner, each provide data about the relationship. As seen later in this chapter, these three types of nonindependence can be examined by an analysis that is similar to the SRM (see Chapters 8 and 9).

In Chapter 1, we suggested that one source of nonindependence, commonly called *assortative mating* in the marriage literature, is due to nonrandom assignment of persons to dyads. Nonrandom assignment is also relevant in the one-with-many design in that it refers to how partners are assigned to focal persons. Consider a study of patients' ratings of their doctor. If patients were not randomly assigned to physicians, one reason why some doctors would be seen negatively and others would be seen positively might be this nonrandom assignment.

UNIVARIATE ANALYSIS
WITH INDISTINGUISHABLE PARTNERS

We now turn our attention to estimating the effects of predictor variables within the one-with-many design. For instance, we might be interested in whether male or female patients are more or less satisfied in their interactions with male or female doctors, or we might be interested in whether salespersons devote more time to clients who are demographically similar to them.

We discuss three different ways to approach a univariate analysis of the nonreciprocal one-with-many design with indistinguishable partners: naive analysis, between–within analysis, and multilevel analysis. As is discussed later in the chapter, we think the naive method is deficient and should almost never be used. The between–within method of analysis is statistically acceptable, but it has interpretative difficulties. Because MLM provides statistically correct and interpretable estimates, we recommend this method for the analysis of the one-with-many design with indistinguishable partners.

We focus in this section on the analysis of a single outcome or dependent measure from a one-with-many design in which the partners are indistinguishable. In later sections, we consider the multivariate analysis of the one-with-many design and the analysis when partners are distinguishable. We denote the outcome variable as Y and the causal variables as X (partner variables) or Z (focal-person variables). For the relationship anxiety data, Y is relationship-specific anxiety, the two X variables are age and gender of the partner, and the Z variable is age of the mother.

Naive Analysis

One approach to the analysis of the one-with-many design is to do separate analyses for partners and focal persons. In the partner-as-unit analysis, each partner's Y is regressed on X and Z. In the satisfaction-with-physician example, this would involve computing a regression based on N observations in which each patient's satisfaction is predicted as a function of his or her gender and the physician's gender. In the focal-person-as-unit analysis, the means of X and Y are computed, and M_Y is regressed on M_X and Z. For our example, this would involve computing a regression based on n observations in which the physician's average satisfaction rating is predicted to be a function of that physician's gender and the mean of the gender of his or her patients.

The partner-as-unit analysis is a very common approach to analyzing data from the one-with-many design, whereas it is much less common for researchers to conduct an analysis using the means of the focal person. Researchers often assert that "Because I am only interested in individuals (i.e., partners), I did an analysis with individual as the unit." However, such an approach is indefensible because of the violation of the independence assumption. Even if the substantive interest is the behavior of individuals, the violation of the independence assumption invalidates significance-testing results (see Chapter 2). In fact, if there are many partners per focal person, the bias in the p values can be considerable (see Kenny et al., 1998, Table 4). For instance, if 40 focal persons have 5 partners each and the intraclass correlation is .45, then the effective alpha is .25, rather than the nominal alpha of .05. Clearly, there would be a serious inflation of Type I errors if this strategy were employed.

Moreover, the two analyses are at least partially redundant. Because focal-person effects are contained in the partner scores, the partner level is confounded with the focal-person level (Glick & Roberts, 1984). To understand this, consider the extreme situation in which each of the partners of a given focal person has exactly the same score on the independent and the dependent variables. In such a case, the regression coefficients (or mean differences if the independent variable were categorical) would be the same in the partner as unit of analysis as in the focal person as unit of analysis.

An analysis with partner as the unit of analysis would be justifiable if observations were independent. Some (Anderson & Ager, 1978; Myers, 1979) have recommended a two-step approach to the analysis of this type of design. First, test for nonindependence by the methods that we have described in the previous section. Myers (1979) recommends that this test be done using a liberal alpha of .20. If the data are independent, then the partner-as-unit analysis is not problematic, and it can proceed as described earlier with partner as the unit of analysis. If there were evidence of nonindependence, then focal person would need to be the unit of analysis. This would be accomplished by conducting an analysis on the means for each focal person, aggregating across the focal person's partners.

There are two major drawbacks with this approach. First, let us presume that we find that the partners' scores are nonindependent and that we must use means of the partners' predictor variables as predictors and means of the partners' outcome scores as the outcomes. If there were a purely "within focal person" causal variable (i.e., a variable that does not vary between focal persons, only within) and we computed means for each focal person, we would be unable to test the effect of this variable because it has no between-focal-person variance.

The second problem with this approach is that it presumes that there is sufficient power to test for nonindependence. Kenny and colleagues (1998) have shown that, particularly when many partners are involved, power is typically insufficient to test for consequential nonindependence (see Chapter 2). Thus we think that the two-step approach is flawed and should be avoided.

Despite its serious deficiencies, we performed a naive analysis for illustrative purposes. We computed the partner-as-unit analysis by regressing the partner's age and gender (both X variables) and the focal person's age (a Z variable) on the relationship-specific anxiety score. This analysis has 624 cases. As seen in the first column of Table 10.1, we found no statistically significant effects in the partner-as-unit analysis. We then computed means for partner age and gender for the 208 focal persons, as well

TABLE 10.1. Effects of Age of Mother and Partner and Gender of Partner on Relationship-Specific Anxiety Using Different Methods of Analysis

| | Analysis | | | | | | | |
| | Partner | | Focal person[a] | | Within | | Multilevel | |
Effect	b	t	b	t	b	t	b	t
Age of mother[b]	0.089	1.22	0.287	2.22*	—	—	0.088	0.94
Age of partner[b]	−0.007	−0.29	−0.485	−2.16*	−0.010	−0.48	−0.008	−0.39
Gender of partner[c]	−0.051	−1.33	0.072	0.77	−0.081	−2.21*	−0.067	−1.95†

†$p < .10$; * $p < .05$.
[a]Between-focal-person analysis.
[b]Age measured in 10-year intervals.
[c]Gender coded as −1 for males and 1 for females.

as means for the mothers' anxiety. We used these means, as well as focal-person age, to conduct the focal-person-as-unit analysis. Here we find statistically significant effects for age of focal person and age of partner. The age-of-mother (Z) effect indicates that older mothers reported higher levels of anxiety across all three partners than did younger mothers, and the age-of-partner effect (M_X) suggests that anxiety was lower across partners when the partners, on average, were older.

Between–Within Analysis

The prior method has statistical problems due to violations of the independence assumption. A second approach, known as a *between–within analysis*, is not subject to this statistical problem and is a better approach.

If we examine the formula for the ANOVA intraclass correlation, we see that it partitions the variance in the outcome variable into two sources: between and within groups, where focal person takes on the role of group. We have also noted that the variation of a mixed independent variable is composed of both between- and within-focal-persons variation (see the pooled regression approach, Chapter 7). In essence, a between–within analysis uses the between-focal-person variation in the independent variable to predict the between-focal-person variation in the outcome measure; it also uses the within-focal-person variation in the independent variable to predict the within-focal-person variation in the outcome measure.

As we have just implied, in a between–within analysis, two analyses are done. In the between analysis, the focal-person means are analyzed. Thus we compute the X and Y means for each focal person, and then the X

mean (M_X) is used to predict the Y mean (M_Y). (In principle, we should weight these means by the number of partners.) There would be $n - p - 1$ degrees of freedom in the between analysis, where n is the number of focal persons and p represents the number of X variables that have variation at the level of the focal person.

For the within analysis, the focal-person mean is subtracted from each score. Thus $X - M_X$ is computed for each partner, as is $Y - M_Y$. Then the deviation score for the independent variable is used to predict the deviation score on the outcome measure. The degrees of freedom for the within analysis are $N - n - p - 1$, where p represents the number of predictors that have variation across partners within focal persons.

Once we have computed the within and between scores for both the independent and dependent variables, we run two regression analyses, one between and one within. There is a statistical complication for the within analysis. A total of $n - 1$ dummy codes indicating focal person should be included in the within analysis to make sure that the degrees of freedom are correct, even though these variables would not explain any of the variance. They are included to create the proper degrees of freedom for the within analysis.

Even though this analysis method represents a statistically adequate solution to nonindependence, the approach has drawbacks. The two analyses examining the effect of X on Y may lead to different results. However, there is no direct statistical test of differences between the effects of the two analyses. Even if we knew there was a difference, it would be difficult to understand the meaning of such a difference. Additionally, it can be cumbersome to keep the degrees of freedom correct and to weight the between analysis properly. Likely because of these difficulties, this method is used very infrequently.

For the relationship-specific anxiety example, we performed a between–within analysis. We have already reported the between analysis (it is the same as the focal-person-as-unit analysis discussed previously; see the second column of results in Table 10.1). The within analysis is presented in the third column of Table 10.1. We first note that there is no effect of age of the focal person, because that variable does not vary across partner within focal person. We do see that there is an effect due to gender of partner: Mothers experience less relationship anxiety with female than with male family members. However, because the members are actually distinguishable, it would probably be more accurate to say that mothers experience less relationship anxiety with their children than with their husbands.

Multilevel Analysis

Chapter 4 provides an overview of MLM for the standard design. In Chapter 7, we present a fairly detailed discussion of the method, and in this chapter we extend that discussion to the one-with-many design. MLM is a relatively new data-analytic approach that can be used when data have a hierarchically nested structure. Data from the one-with-many design are hierarchically structured because partners are tied to a focal person. There are two levels in the one-with-many design: the focal person and the partners. In this section, we describe the MLM approach for one-with-many data (Raudenbush & Bryk, 2002; Snijders & Bosker, 1999).

The Model

The one-with-many design has two levels. Level 1, sometimes called the *lower level*, is partner. Level 2, sometimes called the *upper level*, is focal person. In MLM, the analysis has two stages, the first at level 1 and the second at level 2. As an example, we denote age of partner as X, relationship-specific anxiety as Y, and age of the mother as Z.

The first stage of the estimation, called a *level-1 analysis*, involves computing a separate regression equation for each focal person. Thus, in the first stage, for each focal person, partner's age is used to predict the mother's relationship anxiety with that partner. The variable X (i.e., partner age) is called a *level-1 variable* because it is assumed to vary across partners within focal person. The equation for partner i with focal person j is

$$Y_{ij} = b_{0j} + b_{1j}X_{ij} + e_{ij}.$$

Each of these first-stage analyses results in an intercept, b_{0j}, and a slope, b_{1j}, for each focal person j. So b_{1j} refers to effect of partner age on anxiety for mother j. The term b_{0j} refers to expected level of relationship-specific anxiety of mother j for partners whose age is zero. To make this intercept more interpretable, it is generally advised to center the X variables by subtracting the overall partner mean. If partner age were centered, then b_{0j} refers to expected level of relationship-specific anxiety of mother j when partner's age is average (27.95 years old). The term e_{ij} represents the error or residual for partner i with focal person j.

The second stage of estimation involves analyzing the first-stage results across focal persons. The most basic second-stage analysis simply involves averaging the first-stage coefficients (the intercept and the slope for X) and testing whether the average of either differs from zero. More commonly, the intercept and slope for X are each treated as outcome variables, and any variable that varies only at the focal-person level is used to predict those coefficients. In this second stage, the "observations" are the first-stage intercepts and regression coefficients, and the unit is focal person. The predictors in these second-stage equations are called Z variables.

The second-stage equations, one for intercepts and one for slopes from stage 1, are

$$b_{0j} = a_0 + a_1 Z_j + d_j,$$
$$b_{1j} = c_0 + c_1 Z_j + f_j.$$

For the relationship-specific anxiety example, the Z variable is mother's age, which has been centered (i.e., the mean across all mothers in the sample is subtracted). The coefficient a_0 is akin to the grand mean; it is the intercept of the intercepts and is the predicted maternal relationship anxiety that mothers of average age experience with family members of average age. The coefficient a_1 measures the effect of mother's age on her level of relationship-specific anxiety. The coefficient c_0 measures the average effect of partner's age on the mother's level of anxiety. Finally, the coefficient c_1 measures the degree to which the relationship between partner age and anxiety varies as a function of mother's age. Thus this coefficient represents the interaction of a level-2 variable (mother's age) with a level-1 variable (partner age) on anxiety.

A key distinction in multilevel models is between fixed and random effects. The fixed effects in the model are the overall intercept, or a_0; the overall slope for the predictor variable X, or c_0; the effect of Z on the intercept, or a_1; and its effect on the slope, or c_1. The residuals from the level-1 equation (e_{ij}) and from the level-2 equations (d_j and f_j) are random effects. For fixed variables, the key parameter is the regression coefficient, whereas for random variables the key parameter is the variance of that variable.

The presence of variance in the first-step intercepts, or variance in d_i, indicates variability in average relationship-specific anxiety scores from focal person to focal person after controlling for the focal person's score on Z (i.e., the mother's age). The presence of variance of the first-step slopes, or variance in f_i, indicates that the relationship between partner age and anxiety varies across focal persons. That is, some mothers may feel more anxious with older partners, whereas other mothers may feel less anxious with older partners. If there are relatively few partners per focal person, allowing such a variance may not be possible. Recall that k refers to the number of partners per focal person. To treat *all* the slopes as random for p predictor variables, k must be at least $p + 2$. (See Chapter 13, in which we discuss potential estimation difficulties with many random variables.) We do not have to assume that slopes vary by focal person, and if we decide not to make that assumption, we can have many level-1 predictors, many more than the number of partners per focal person. In general, we recommend no more than $k - 2$ level-1 random predictor variables.

As discussed in Chapter 4, although the slopes can be constrained to be equal for each focal person, it is almost always advisable to presume that the intercepts vary across focal persons. Though it is not obvious, the variation of the intercepts models the nonindependence in the data. Consider the simplest multilevel model, one with no X or Z variables. Such a model is called the *unconditional model* (Raudenbush & Bryk, 2002) or the *empty model* (Snijders & Bosker, 1999). From such a model we can compute the variance of the intercepts, or s_d^2, and the error variance, or s_e^2. If we compute the ratio of variance due to the intercept to the total variance, or $s_d^2/(s_d^2 + s_e^2)$, that quantity provides an estimate of the intraclass correlation, the measure of nonindependence. If there are any predictor variables at either the upper or lower levels (i.e., Xs or Zs), in order to increase comparability to the unconditional model, these predictor variables should be centered about their grand means before computing the ratio of the variance of the intercepts to the sum of variance of the intercepts and the error variance. The intraclass correlation then becomes a partial intraclass (see Chapters 2 and 3). This ratio represents the proportion of variance due to the focal persons after controlling for the effects of the independent variables.

It is important to note that, by definition, a ratio of the variance of the intercepts to the total variance must be non-negative, and this method presumes that the intraclass correlation cannot be negative. Normally, we would not expect the intraclass correlations to be negative for the one-with-many design. However, treating nonindependence as a variance precludes the possibility of any negative nonindependence. Later we suggest a strategy to circumvent this limitation.

It is possible to treat the mean of the X variable for each focal person, or M_X, as a predictor in the second stage of the multilevel analysis (Raudenbush & Bryk, 2002). For the example, we might include the mean age of the partners as a level-2, or Z, predictor variable. Consider the effects of partner age and mean partner age. The effect of partner age examines the effect of the particular partner's age on anxiety. The effect of mean partner age examines the effect of age of the other family members. As we discussed in an earlier section on between–within analysis, there are two different types of effects for an X variable. There is the within effect, or the effect of partner's age on relationship anxiety estimated across relationships within each mother, and a between effect, or the effect averaged across the mother's relationships. By examining the effect of the mean we see whether the between and within effects are equivalent. For gender we find that the two effects are equal, whereas for age they are not.

Estimation

Estimation of the multilevel parameters a_0, c_0, a_1, c_1, σ_d^2, σ_f^2, σ_{df}, and σ_e^2 is typically accomplished using the method of maximum likelihood. Although we have presented MLM as a two-step procedure, in most estimation methods a single multilevel equation that includes parameters from both "steps" is estimated (see Chapter 4). MLM programs generally use either maximum likelihood or restricted maximum likelihood (REML) estimation. Both use an iterative solution to derive estimates of random effects (e.g., variances and covariances). REML is the default estimation technique in most multilevel programs and is generally preferred over maximum likelihood because estimates of fixed effects using maximum likelihood tend to be biased, particularly with small data sets.

As explained in Chapter 4, one advantage of this estimation approach is that the degree to which the model does not totally explain the data, called the model's *deviance* (which equals −2 times the log likelihood of the model), can be computed for each model. The deviance provides a badness-of-fit index. That is, the larger the deviance, the worse the model is. The deviances of alternative models can be compared to examine the relative fit. In fact, if two models are nested in the sense that one is a simpler version of the other, the difference between the deviances of the two models has, under the null hypothesis, a chi-square distribution that evaluates whether the additional parameters in the more complex model, relative to the simpler model, are statistically unnecessary. The degrees of freedom of the chi-square equal the number of additional constraints made in the simpler model.

However, as explained in Chapter 4, this differencing of deviances can be used only to compare models that involve differences in parameters estimated using maximum likelihood (or GLS for MLwiN). Thus, if one wishes to compare two models that differ in their fixed effects, maximum likelihood would have to be specified as the estimation approach. Note that both maximum likelihood and REML (or RGLS for MLwiN) approaches provide *t*-tests of individual fixed effects.

We next consider estimating two types of multilevel models using SAS and SPSS. In the first we allow for positive nonindependence (i.e., the intraclass correlation is positive). In the second, we allow for either negative or positive nonindependence. Although we provide syntax for only these two data-analysis programs, the one-with-many design can be estimated with virtually any MLM program (e.g., HLM6 or MLwiN).

For our example data, we create a variable called FP that identifies the focal persons (i.e., it ranges in values from 1 to 208). Mother's age is FPAGE, partner's age is PARTAGE, partner's gender is PARTGEN, and relationship-specific anxiety is ANX. If we want to allow for only positive nonindependence, we would use the following PROC MIXED statements for SAS:

```
PROC MIXED COVTEST;
    CLASS FP;
    MODEL ANX = FPAGE PARTAGE PARTGEN
        / SOLUTION DDFM = SATTERTH;
    RANDOM INTERCEPT / SUBJECT=FP;
```

The COVTEST option requests that SAS present Z-tests evaluating the statistical significance of the variance components. The CLASS FP statement makes focal person a categorical variable. The MODEL statement specifies the causal equation. In this model, relationship anxiety is determined by age of the focal person (FPAGE), age of the partner (PARTAGE), and partner gender (PARTGEN). Note that SAS (or SPSS) makes no distinction between level-1 and level-2 predictors. The SOLUTION option in the MODEL statement requests that the estimates for the fixed-effects parameters be printed, and the DDFM = SATTERTH option requests the Satterthwaite approximation (1946) to determine the degrees of freedom for the fixed effects (Kashy & Kenny, 2000; see also Chapter 7).[5] The RANDOM statement allows for the fact that the intercept may vary by focal person. Notice that in this specification, we have not allowed for random slopes. To do so, the partner variables for which random slopes are desired are added to the random statement. For example, the statement

```
RANDOM INTERCEPT PARTGEN / SUBJECT = FP;
```

allows for the effect of partner gender on relationship-specific anxiety to vary across focal persons. This specification also allows the slope and intercept to be correlated.

The parallel syntax in SPSS 12.0 for the model in which the intercept is a random variable (but not partner's gender) is

```
MIXED
    ANX WITH FPAGE PARTAGE PARTGEN
    /FIXED = FPAGE PARTAGE PARTGEN
    /PRINT = SOLUTION TESTCOV
    /RANDOM INTERCEPT | SUBJECT(FP) COVTYPE(VC).
```

As we stated in Chapters 4 and 7, SPSS treats tests of variance as one-tailed, and so p values should be doubled.

One strategy that accommodates negative nonindependence is to use the REPEATED statement for PROC MIXED within SAS, rather than the RANDOM statement. That is, the syntax for SAS is identical except that the last statement is removed and replaced by

```
REPEATED / TYPE = CS SUBJECT = FP;
```

The REPEATED statement treats the partner scores as a repeated measure within focal person, and CS implies what is called compound symmetry (discussed earlier), which means that all partners' scores are equally correlated. By using this option, nonindependence is modeled as a correlation between partners' scores and not as a variance of intercepts. For SPSS 12.0, the last line of the syntax would be dropped, and the following line would be substituted:

```
/REPEATED = PARTID | SUBJECT(FP) COVTYPE(CS).
```

where PARTID is a variable that identifies the partners within focal persons. Thus, for the Cook (2000) data, the PARTID variable might be 1 for fathers, 2 for older children, and 3 for younger children.

Example

The last column of Table 10.1 presents the MLM results in which focal person's age, partner's age, and partner's gender are used to predict the mother's relationship anxiety. We used SAS's PROC MIXED program, but we would have obtained essentially the same results if we had used some other MLM program.

We find that partner gender has a marginally significant effect such that mothers experience less relationship-specific anxiety with female partners. The model's deviance is 1416.60. We test the hypothesis that the three fixed-effects coefficients are all zero by estimating two models, one with the three predictors and one without. We estimated each of these models using maximum likelihood, and the difference in deviances yielded a $\chi^2(3) = 5.29$, $p = .152$. Because we are comparing a model with no predictors with a model with all three predictors, this test is analogous to the test of the multiple correlation for the three predictors with relationship-specific anxiety. Notably, the test is not statistically significant, indicating that these three predictors together do not explain a significant proportion of the variation in mothers' anxiety with their family members. This fact is bolstered by the fact that the pseudo R^2 for the model (see Chapter 4 for formula) is only .001.

In terms of the random effects, we estimate the variance of the intercepts, or s_d^2, as 0.2090 and the error variance, or s_e^2, as 0.4175. The resulting intraclass correlation is .337. The test that σ_d^2 is zero is $\chi^2(1) = 62.30$, $p < .001$. The value of the intraclass correlation for the unconditional, or empty, model is .328, which differs from the ANOVA value only due to rounding error. Recall that the ANOVA estimate of the intraclass correlation is a REML estimate and that the pairwise intraclass is a maximum likelihood estimate.

We did separately examine whether the effects of partner age and gender were random. That is, we examined whether their effects were different for different mothers. Although we found no evidence that the partner gender effect was random, $p = .36$, we did find evidence that the age of partner effect is significant, $p = .003$. Likely the source of the effect is that some mothers are more anxious with their husbands than with their children, whereas for other mothers the pattern reverses.

Finally, we fitted a model that included the means of the two partner variables, age of partner and gender of partner, as level-2 predictors. Thus this model has three focal-person variables (mother's age, average age of the partners, and average gender of the partners) and two partner-level variables (partner's age and partner's gender). The results of this multilevel analysis are presented in Table 10.2. We see that there are some major changes, although, like the focal-person analysis in Table 10.1, the age of the mother effect is still significant such that older mothers experience greater anxiety. The partner age effect now emerges as an effect of average partner age rather than particular partner age. Finally, mothers report more anxiety with male partners.

TABLE 10.2. Multilevel Analysis Including Means of Partner-Level Variables as Predictors

	b	t
Age of mother[a]	0.287	2.22*
Age of partner[a]	−0.010	−0.48
Gender of partner[b]	−0.081	−2.21*
Mean age of partner[a]	−0.474	−2.11*
Mean gender of partner[b]	0.153	1.53

* $p < .05$.
[a]Age measured in 10-year intervals.
[b]Gender coded as −1 for males and 1 for females.

UNIVARIATE ESTIMATION WITH DISTINGUISHABLE PARTNERS

The previous section presumes that the partners are indistinguishable. However, in dyadic research, partners are often distinguishable. In the example, each mother is asked to state her relationship-specific anxiety with her husband and with her older and younger children. Therefore, partners are distinguished by their role relationship to the mother. In this section, we discuss the statistical analysis of one-with-many designs with distinguishable partners. We note that because the previous analyses reported in Tables 10.1 and 10.2 ignored role, they are likely quite misleading.

Repeated-Measures Analysis of Variance and MANOVA

Perhaps the simplest analysis when partners are distinguishable is a repeated-measures ANOVA. We treat the distinguishable partners as the repeated measure, and focal person is the "subject" or the unit of analysis. For the example, the repeated measure would be the family role—father, older child, and younger child—and the "subject" would be the mother. When there are more than the two partners, such an analysis presumes equal correlation across roles and equal variance for each role, previously described as the compound-symmetry assumption.[6] Generally, the compound-symmetry assumption is not true, and repeated-measures analysis yields results that have too liberal (i.e., too small) p values (Maxwell & Delaney, 2004; Myers, 1979).

Because the compound-symmetry assumption so rarely holds when there are more than two partners, it is generally advised to conduct a multivariate analysis of variance (MANOVA). We treat each of the different partners as separate outcome variables. If we seek to test the effect of the distinguishing variables, we need to do the following: We compute difference scores between pairs of the repeated measure. If we have k repeated measures, we compute $k - 1$ difference scores. For the example, we might compute the older child minus younger child and the father minus the average of the two children. The multivariate test that the mean of the $k - 1$ difference scores equals zero evaluates the main effect of the repeated measure. (Most repeated-measures programs routinely provide the multivariate test of the repeated measure.)

Let us consider the example without any covariates. When we test the effect of role using repeated-measures ANOVA in our example, we find that there is no effect due to role, $F(2, 414) = 1.474$, $p = .230$. Using MANOVA results in the same conclusion, $F(2, 206) = 1.743$, $p = .178$. Thus there are no statistically meaningful differences in mother's relationship anxiety between roles.

There are potentially two types of covariates in the analysis. One type, denoted as Z, is not repeated and refers to the focal person, and the other type, denoted as X, is repeated and refers to the partner. Usually when running a MANOVA, covariates are generally all treated as Z covariates. It can then be difficult to interpret effects from a MANOVA with covariates.

We reran the MANOVA with four covariates: mother's age and the ages of the three partners. Again we found no effect due to role, $F(2, 202) = 0.209$, $p = .81$. The only covariate that was statistically significant was mother's age, $F(1, 203) = 4.665$, $p = .032$.

Multilevel Analysis

An alternative strategy is to perform a multilevel analysis, as was described in the previous section when we discussed the analysis of indistinguishable partners. The analysis is quite similar to the indistinguishable case, except that we now include $k - 1$ additional dummy variables to code for role effects, one less dummy variable than the number of roles. This analysis presumes equal correlation across roles and equal variance, the compound-symmetry assumption. Some multilevel programs do allow for the testing and relaxation of that assumption. For instance, within SAS, we can allow the covariance structure to take on any form. Thus, for instance, the following SAS code allows for a general covariance structure:

```
PROC MIXED COVTEST;
    CLASS FP;
MODEL ANX = FPAGE PARTAGE PARTGEN FATHER OLDERC
    / SOLUTION DDFM = SATTERTH;
REPEATED / TYPE = UN SUBJECT = FP;
```

To estimate the effects of the distinguishing variable, two coded variables are included. The variable FATHER contrasts the father role with the two child roles. The variable OLDERC contrasts the older child with the younger child. The part of the last statement that says TYPE = UN allows for a relaxing of the compound-symmetry assumption (TYPE = CS) by specifying any pattern of correlations among family members, as well as different variances.

For SPSS, the parallel syntax commands are as follows:

```
MIXED
    ANX WITH FPAGE PARTAGE PARTGEN FATHER OLDERC
    /FIXED = FPAGE PARTAGE PARTGEN FATHER OLDERC
    /PRINT = SOLUTION TESTCOV
    /REPEATED = ROLE | SUBJECT(FP) COVTYPE(UN).
```

Returning to the relationship-anxiety data, when we test for compound symmetry by using a difference between deviances, using either SAS or SPSS, we find $\chi^2(4) = 11.71$, $p = .020$. Thus the assumption of compound symmetry cannot be made. Table 10.3 presents the estimates of

TABLE 10.3. Effects of Age of Mother and Partner, Gender of Partner, and Role on Relationship Anxiety Using Multilevel Modeling

	b	t
Age of mother[a]	0.006	0.06
Age of partner[a]	0.186	2.01*
Gender of partner[b]	−0.070	−2.12*
Father[c]	−0.404	−2.09*
Older child[d]	−0.078	−2.29*

* $p < .05$.
[a]Age measured in 10-year intervals.
[b]Gender coded as −1 for males and 1 for females.
[c]Father coded as 1 and children as −0.5.
[d]Older child coded as 1, younger child as −1, and father as 0.

fixed effects when we allow for a more complex error structure. We see that the father and the older child create lower relationship anxiety for the mother than does the younger child. Controlling for role, we also see that mothers in general experience more relationship anxiety with older partners and with male partners. Note that the partner effect for age is positive. Mothers feel more anxiety with older partners.

Structural Equation Modeling

Usually, the most straightforward method for analyzing the data when partners are distinguishable[7] is SEM (see Chapter 5). In this case, each distinguishable partner becomes a variable. Again referring to the example data set, there would be three variables, one for the father, one for the older child, and one for the younger child.

The basic model is as follows: There is a latent variable that causes the score for each partner. The variance due to the focal person is contained in this latent variable. If the design were 1PMT, the factor would be interpreted as "actor" (see Chapter 8), and if it were MP1T, the factor would be interpreted as "partner." We suggest, in the base model, assuming equal loadings by fixing all of the loadings to 1 and allowing the error variances to be unequal. However, if there are three or more partners, the equal-loading assumption can be relaxed. With four or more partners, a test of whether a single latent variable factor explains the covariation between partners can be conducted.

When we estimate the single-factor model with equal loadings and unequal error variances for the Cook (2000) attachment data, we find $\chi^2(2) = 0.48$, $p = .788$; CFI = 1.00; RMSEA = 0.0. The good fit of the model implies that the equal-loading assumption is consistent with the data. The common factor explains approximately 27% of the variance of the father measure, 40% for the older child, and 33% for the younger child.

The inclusion of covariates greatly complicates the SEM analysis. If covariates are to be considered, the means should be included in the model, because the covariates can potentially explain the differences between the roles.

For Z covariates (i.e., covariates that refer to the focal person), we have two different models in Figure 10.2. In the first model, shown in Figure 10.2A, Z affects the latent variable and so indirectly affects the measures. In the second model, shown in Figure 10.2B, Z affects the different measures and not the latent variable. In this second model, Z is un-

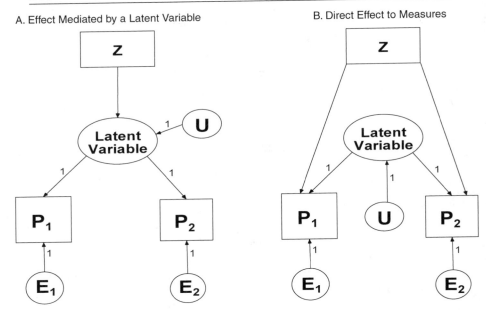

FIGURE 10.2. Two structural equation models for the focal person covariate (Z).

correlated with the latent variable. We can view this second model as one in which Z interacts with partner role, whereas the first model evaluates whether Z has the same effect on each role. The relative fit of the two models evaluates whether the effect of Z varies by partner role.

Sometimes there are X covariates, or covariates that are measured for each partner. There are many different models for X covariates, and we warn the reader that the remainder of this section is quite technical.

Figure 10.3 contains three different models for an X variable. In the model in Figure 10.3A, each X variable causes its own Y variable. This is the simplest model, and we refer to it as the *pair model* because each Y measure is paired with an X measure. For the example, a partner's age affects how much relationship anxiety the mother experiences with that partner. The k different X variables are correlated with each other and with the Z variables but uncorrelated with the general factor. Additionally, we can test a model in which the k paths are equal and compare the fit of the models, one in which the paths are equal and one in which the paths are unequal. The degrees of freedom for such a test are k − 1.

A. Pair Model

B. Saturated

C. Mediated

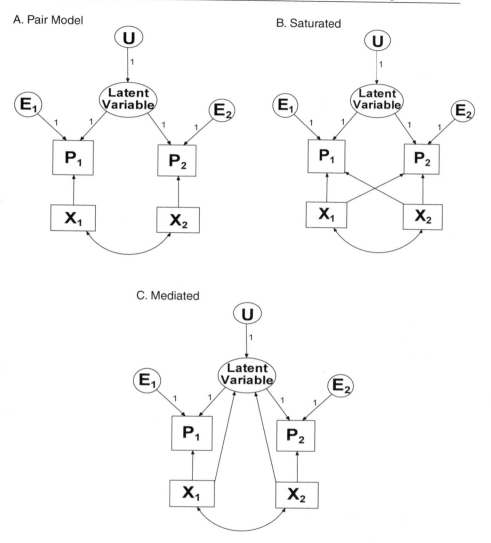

FIGURE 10.3. Three structural equation models for the partner covariates (X).

The second model, Figure 10.3B, shows paths from the X variable of one partner to the responses of the other partners. We call this the *saturated model* because all possible paths are estimated. In our example, the age of one partner is specified to predict the anxiety experienced by the mother with another partner. The third model, Figure 10.3C, contains paths from each X to the general factor, but the "partner" paths in Figure 10.3B are no longer present. We call this model the *mediated-effects model*, because the effect of X on the Y's is mediated by the general factor. Note that models in Figures 10.3B and 10.3C are identical in terms of model fit when paths are set equal.

THE RECIPROCAL ONE-WITH-MANY DESIGN

The one-with-many design has three major variants. The focal person can serve as the source of the data, as the target of the data, or as both the source and the target—the reciprocal design. In this section, we discuss the analysis of the reciprocal design.

The strategy for the analysis of the reciprocal design is to consider it as a nonreciprocal one-with-many design that contains two variables. One variable would be the measures in which the focal person is a source, and the other variable would be the measures in which the focal person is the target. For instance, for the relationship-anxiety data set, one variable would be the ratings by the mother of the other three family members, and the other variable would be the ratings by the three family members of the mother. We now consider the bivariate analysis of the one-with-many design—first with indistinguishable partners and second with distinguishable partners.

Indistinguishable Partners

Generally, multilevel models are the most appropriate to use with indistinguishable partners.[8] Some MLM programs provide the option of analyzing multiple variables simultaneously. Alternatively, sometimes the analyst has to "trick" the computer program into thinking that there is only a single variable. The approach is an extension of the two-intercept approach discussed in Chapters 4 and 6.

The method to be described is complicated and not very obvious. First, $2k$ dummy variables are created for each focal person. The first k

dummy variables refer to the k partners and variable 1 (e.g., mother's relationship anxiety with her partners), and the second k dummy variables refer to the k partners and variable 2 (partner's relationship anxiety with mother). We refer to the $2k$ dummy variables as X_1 through X_{2k}. (Note that this X has a very different meaning from X covariates that were discussed earlier in this chapter.) The variable X_1 would equal 1 if the score were for variable 1 and partner 1, and it would be 0 otherwise. The variable X_2 would equal 1 if the score were for variable 1 and partner 2, and it would be 0 otherwise. The variable X_k would equal 1 if the score were for variable 1 and partner k and would be 0 otherwise. The variable X_{k+1} would equal 1 if the score were for variable 2 and partner 1 and would be 0 otherwise. Finally, the variable X_{2k} would equal 1 if the score were for variable 2 and partner k and would be 0 otherwise. The variables X_1 through X_{2k} would be predictors in the equation, they would be treated as random variables, and there would be no intercept (at least in the usual sense) or error term.

Second, we would make several constraints on the $2k$-by-$2k$ covariance matrix of the X variables. They are as follows:

> The variances of X_i ($i = 1$ through k) are equal.
> The variances of X_i ($i = k + 1$ through $2k$) are equal.
> The covariances of X_i with X_j ($i = 1$ through k; $j = 1$ through k; $i \neq j$) are equal.
> The covariances of X_i with X_j ($i = k + 1$ through $2k$; $j = k + 1$ through $2k$; $i \neq j$) are equal.
> The covariances of X_i with X_j ($i = 1$ through k; $j = k + 1$ through $2k$; $i + k \neq j$) are equal.
> The covariances of X_i with X_j ($i = 1$ through k; $j = i + k$) are equal.

In effect, a single actor variance and a single partner variance are created, and they are allowed to correlate with each other. The constraints serve to eliminate any partner-specific effects. These equality constraints can be made within SAS's PROC MIXED, but not simply. To the best of our knowledge, the constraints cannot be made within SPSS or HLM6. However, it is a relatively simple matter to do so with the computer program MLwiN.

We used MLwiN for the relationship anxiety example with the reciprocal design. We now have a data set with 1,296 cases, because we have 208 families, 3 partners, and 2 variables. Table 10.4 presents the 6 × 6 covariance matrix with the appropriate constraints.

TABLE 10.4. Variance–Covariance Matrix for the Reciprocal One-with-Many Design and Indistinguishable Partners Estimated by MLwiN

	X_1	X_2	X_3	X_4	X_5	X_6
X_1	0.630					
X_2	0.207	0.630				
X_3	0.207	0.207	0.630			
X_4	0.193	0.078	0.078	0.609		
X_5	0.078	0.193	0.078	0.060	0.609	
X_6	0.078	0.078	0.193	0.060	0.060	0.609

Note. Measures 1 through 3 refer to mother's rating of relationship anxiety, and measures 4 through 6 refer to ratings of family members of the mother. Note that measures 1 and 4, as well as 2 and 5 and 3 and 6, refer to the same dyad.

We find that mothers report more anxiety with family members, 1.808, than other family members report with the mother, 1.698. The covariances in Table 10.4 have an SRM interpretation (see Chapters 8 and 9).

> Covariances of X_1, X_2, and X_3: mother-actor variance, or how much relationship anxiety a mother experiences.
> Covariances of X_4, X_5, and X_6: mother-partner variance, or how much relationship anxiety family members experience with the mother.
> Covariance of X_1 with X_4, X_2 with X_5, and X_3 with X_6: dyadic reciprocity; or whether, if the mother experiences anxiety with the family member, that family member also experiences anxiety with the mother.
> Other covariances: generalized reciprocity, or whether, if the mother generally experiences anxiety with all other family members, the other family members generally experience anxiety with the mother.

The estimate of the actor variance is 0.207, $p < .001$, which compares quite favorably with the estimate obtained in the previous chapter of 0.178. The estimate of the partner variance is 0.060, $p = .027$, which also compares quite favorably with the estimate obtained in the previous chapter of 0.059. The actor–partner covariance is 0.078, $p = .001$, which results in an actor–partner correlation of .700, a value quite different from the correlation obtained in the complete SRM model ($r = .28$). Because the one-with-many design does not permit estimation of the family variance, estimates of actor and partner variances are inflated somewhat, and estimates of the actor–partner correlation are inflated to a much greater extent.

Distinguishable Partners

One can also use SEM to analyze the data when partners are distinguishable. As will be seen, the model is very similar to the SRM model of roles that was discussed in the previous chapter. The model contains two latent variables that correspond to the "actor" and "partner" factors of the SRM. A measure loads on the actor factor if the measure comes from the focal person, or the measure loads on the partner factor if the measure is about the focal person. Initially, we fix all loadings to 1, although that assumption can be tested. We correlate the two factors to obtain an actor–partner covariance. We also correlate the "errors" of the two measurements from the same partner (e.g., the mother's anxiety with the father and the father's anxiety with the mother). The correlation between these errors represents dyadic reciprocity. With the reciprocal one-with-many design, we can estimate most of the SRM variances and covariances for the model with roles (see Chapter 9). However, we have to assume that there is no variance due to "group," and we estimate variances and covariances for a single role (e.g., the mother for the example data set).

The model, without X and Z variables, is shown graphically for the example data in Figure 10.4. We first fitted a model that allowed the loadings to vary, but forcing the loadings to be equal to 1.0 results in no loss of fit, $\chi^2(4) = 1.96$, $p = .74$. The model with equal loadings fits quite well for the Cook (2000) data, $\chi^2(9) = 8.18$, $p = .516$; CFI = 1.00; RMSEA = 0.0. The estimate of the actor variance is 0.206, $Z = 5.96$, $p < .001$, which is comparable to the estimate obtained in the previous chapter of 0.178. The estimate of the partner variance is 0.073, $Z = 2.98$, $p = .001$, which is similar to the estimate obtained in the previous chapter of 0.059. The actor–partner correlation is .636, $Z = 3.56$, $p < .001$, which is quite different from the correlation obtained in the model estimated in Chapter 9, $r = .28$. It is interesting to note that the estimates for the variances and covariances using SEM are very similar to those obtained by MLM that were presented in Table 10.4.

The "error variances" in this model contain relationship plus either actor (for MP1T studies) or partner (for 1PMT studies) variance. Also, the error covariances measure not only dyadic reciprocity but also the actor–partner correlation for that family role. Those correlations are .271, $Z =$

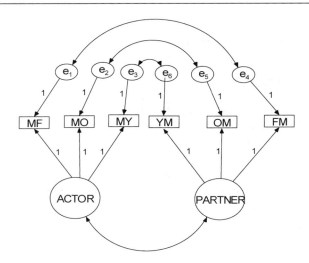

FIGURE 10.4. Structural equation model for the reciprocal one-with-many design.

3.34, $p < .001$, for the father; .296, $Z = 3.08$, $p = .002$, for the older child; and .142, $Z = 1.67$, $p = .095$, for the younger child.

SUMMARY AND CONCLUSIONS

The one-with-many design is a commonly used design in dyadic analysis (about 16% of the studies in our survey), but discussions of its statistical analysis are very rare. It is the "forgotten" dyadic design. As far as we know, this is the first extended treatment of this design explicitly written for researchers interested in dyadic data. Most treatments of dyadic analysis presume that the data are either the standard or the SRM design (see Chapter 1). The one-with-many design allows for a much more detailed analysis of dyadic processes than the standard design, but it is not nearly as complex to analyze as SRM designs. Still, we have seen that the analysis of data from the one-with-many design can be rather complicated; our discussion has included estimation methods involving ANOVA, multilevel models, and SEM. Much of the choice in methods is based on whether partners are distinguishable from one another or whether they are indistinguishable. Typically, with indistinguishable members, the data can be most easily analyzed by MLM, and with distinguishable members, by SEM. We hope that this chapter can aid in the analysis of this very useful design.

Because the example data set contained only three partners, we did not emphasize the possibility of testing for random effects. Characteristics of partners—what have been designated as X variables—can be allowed to vary across focal persons. For instance, we could test whether the gender differences in satisfaction vary by physician; that is, whether some physicians have satisfied male patients and others have satisfied female patients.

In the next chapter on the analysis of social network data, we return to the round-robin design in which everyone is paired with everyone else in the group. Unlike Chapters 8 and 9, in Chapter 11 we consider categorical variables such as "like" versus "do not like."

NOTES

1. A separate issue is whether the focal person and his or her partner are distinguishable. This issue is relevant only when the design is reciprocal, and we discuss it in that section.

2. We can view the structure of one-with-many data as similar to group data. The partners of each focal person can be viewed as members of a group, even if the partners have never interacted or even met each other. Because of this similarity, we adapt in this chapter some of Kenny, Mannetti, and colleagues' (2002) analysis of the group design to the one-with-many design.

3. There were some missing data in the predictor variables, but to make the analyses easier, we inserted the mean in the analysis.

4. However, as discussed in Chapter 15, their interpretations are quite different.

5. We should note that, for complicated large sample studies, the Satterthwaite approximation can be computationally intensive and very time-consuming and so is impractical.

6. Actually, the assumption is called *homogeneity of treatment-difference variances* (Maxwell & Delaney, 2004, p. 539) and is more general than compound symmetry.

7. We could also use SEM when partners are indistinguishable through the Olsen and Kenny (2006) approach described in Chapter 5.

8. One could also adapt the Olsen and Kenny (2006) method (see Chapters 5 and 7) to this case.

Social Network Analysis

Relationship research and theory typically ignores the fact that relationships are embedded within a social network. To study a relationship in isolation is to miss something essential: the social context of interpersonal behavior. The prototypical variable in social network research is "liking": Each member of a social group is asked whom in the group he or she likes. Social network analysis provides methods of summarizing these relationships and quantifying aspects of the social context. Kilduff and Tsai (2003), Scott (1991), and Wasserman and Faust (1994) have written entire books on this topic, and one single chapter cannot begin to summarize the vast amount of existing knowledge concerning the analysis of network data. In this chapter, we introduce the central concepts of network analysis; we do not provide all of the technical details, but we do provide the relevant references to more advanced treatments of this topic.

DEFINITIONS

A specialized terminology is associated with social network analysis, and understanding these terms is critical. We begin with the definition of a social network: A social network is a set of ties, connections, or links between persons in a group. Note that although social networks can be networks of countries, corporations, or businesses, most social networks refer to persons, and we limit our discussion to networks of people. Three general types of networks or groups have been studied: open networks, closed networks, and ego-centered networks. An open network does not restrict people from naming those to whom they have ties. If, for example, the researcher asks with whom a person drinks alcohol and then seeks out those people and asks them the same question, the network would be open. In a closed network, the members of the networks are fixed. For example, if a classroom is studied, and children are asked whom they like, the network would be considered open if children could nominate anyone they like. However, if children were restricted to choosing from only those in their class, then the network would be closed. In the study of an ego-centric network, the researcher elicits from each respondent the persons to whom that respondent has ties. Egocentric networks are commonly utilized for research on social support. In this chapter we consider closed networks, because most network methods were developed for the analysis of this type of network. As we explained in Chapter 10, methods for the analysis of the one-with-many designs can be used to analyze data from egocentric networks. As far as we know, there is relatively little work on the statistical analysis of open networks.

The ties between persons can be thought of as "verbs" linking together a "subject" and an "object" (i.e., another person). Therefore, if John likes Jim, the tie would be "liking." We should note that the absence of a tie does not imply disliking. To measure dislike would necessitate the researcher asking persons whom they dislike. Besides liking and disliking, many other ties are possible. We could determine whether John asks for help from, respects, shoots heroin with, or kisses Jim. Some ties are directional. Liking is usually directional, in that John might like Jim but Jim might not like John. "Sits next to" is a nondirectional tie, because if John sits next to Jim, then Jim must also sit next to John. Typically in network analysis, the ties are discrete. Either there is a tie or there is not (i.e., one is present or absent), and the strength of a tie is usually not measured.

The objects that are linked in a social network are called *nodes*. In fact, the nodes in a network need not even be persons but might be countries or corporations. As mentioned, in this chapter we consider only networks in which persons are nodes. If the tie is directional, it is helpful to distinguish the two persons. We refer to the actor as the *sender* and the other person as the *receiver*. So if John likes Jim, John would be called the *sender*, and Jim would be called the *receiver*.

One might wonder how network data are collected. A fairly common way is to obtain data from senders. Each person might be asked whom in the group he or she likes. It is also possible that receivers might be asked, "Who in the group likes you?" Sometimes restrictions are placed on informants, for example, telling a sender to state the three persons in the group whom the sender likes. Alternatively, someone outside the network might serve as an informant who provides the information about the network ties.

At times, the informants can provide information about the entire network. For instance, Bernard, Killworth, and Sailer (1980) asked 58 members of fraternities how much time each member spent with each other member. One key question addressed in this research was how much the informants agreed with each other. Although some have argued that there is little or no agreement in these networks (Bernard & Killworth, 1977), others (Kashy & Kenny, 1990b) have argued that there is substantial agreement. Regardless, the degree of agreement and disagreement can itself be an interesting question (Krackhardt, 1987).

THE REPRESENTATION OF A NETWORK

There are two fundamental ways to summarize the ties of a closed network. First, we can represent the set of ties in a sociomatrix. As the name suggests, a sociomatrix is a person-by-person matrix in which "1" signifies a tie and "0," the absence of a tie. A row of the sociomatrix represents the sender, or the subject of the sentence, and a column represents the receiver, or the object. Thus, if John likes Jim, there would be a 1 placed in the John row, Jim column.

Alternatively, we can represent the network by a picture called a *sociogram*. In a sociogram, a connecting line represents a tie between persons. If the tie were directional, the line would be an arrow going from the sender to the receiver. If the tie were nondirectional or reciprocal, the arrow would be double headed. Self- or reflexive ties are rather uncommon, but in some applications (particularly those in which the nodes are organizations and not persons), such reflexive ties can be informative, and they would be represented by a circular arrow.

As an example, in this chapter we use a social network that has received considerable attention. Samuel Sampson (1968) conducted his study of a Roman Catholic monastery[1] in the late 1960s. Eighteen monks participated in the study, and they are denoted here as A through R. Each monk nominated three other monks that he liked. Two of the monks, denoted as C and J, chose four monks. Even monks do not follow the rules! The ties were directional in that if monk B chose monk D, monk D did not necessarily choose monk B.

During Sampson's stay at the monastery, considerable dissension resulted in the expulsion of four monks (monks B, C, Q, and R) and the voluntary departure of several others (monks A, G, N, O, and P). In the end, only four monks (E, F, J, and L) remained. We return to these events later in this chapter.

The sociomatrix for the 18 monks is presented in Table 11.1 and the sociogram in Figure 11.1. The sociogram was drawn by the computer program PAJEK (Slovenian for "spider"), which is available on the World Wide Web[2] at no cost for noncommercial use. Quite clearly, the most prominent feature of the data is subgrouping. When the data were gathered, the monastery was undergoing widespread controversy, and the monks divided into two factions—the "Old Guard," those on the right of Figure 11.1, and the "Young Turks," those on the left of the figure. We repeatedly use this data set throughout this chapter.

In the first section of this chapter, we consider measures that can be obtained from a network. We organize this section by level of analysis: the individual, the dyad, the triad, the subgroup, and the entire network. In the second section, we consider one relatively complicated but very useful

TABLE 11.1. Sociomatrix for the Sampson (1968) Monastery Data: Does Monk A (Row) Like Monk B (Column)?

	A	B	C	D	E	F	G	H	I	J	K	L	M	N	O	P	Q	R
A	0	0	1	0	0	0	0	0	0	0	0	1	0	1	0	0	0	0
B	1	0	0	0	0	0	1	0	0	0	0	1	0	0	0	0	0	0
C	1	0	0	0	0	0	0	0	0	0	0	0	1	0	0	0	1	1
D	0	0	0	0	1	1	0	0	0	0	1	0	0	0	0	0	0	0
E	0	0	0	1	0	0	0	0	1	0	1	0	0	0	0	0	0	0
F	0	0	0	1	1	0	0	0	1	0	0	0	0	0	0	0	0	0
G	0	1	0	0	0	0	0	0	0	0	0	1	0	0	0	1	0	0
H	0	0	0	1	0	1	0	0	1	0	0	0	0	0	0	0	0	0
I	0	0	0	0	1	0	0	1	0	0	0	1	0	0	0	0	0	0
J	0	0	0	1	1	0	0	0	1	0	0	0	1	0	0	0	0	0
K	0	0	0	0	1	0	0	1	0	0	0	0	0	1	0	0	0	0
L	1	1	0	0	0	0	1	0	0	0	0	0	0	0	0	0	0	0
M	0	0	0	0	1	0	1	0	0	0	0	0	0	0	0	0	0	1
N	1	0	0	0	0	0	0	0	0	0	0	1	0	0	1	0	0	0
O	0	1	0	0	0	0	1	0	0	0	0	1	0	0	0	0	0	0
P	0	1	0	0	0	0	1	0	0	0	0	0	0	0	1	0	0	0
Q	0	1	1	0	0	0	0	0	0	0	0	0	0	0	0	0	0	1
R	0	1	1	0	0	0	0	0	0	0	0	0	0	0	0	0	1	0

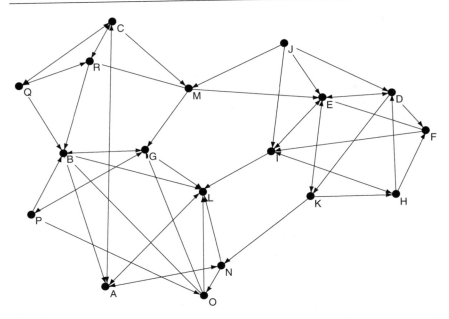

FIGURE 11.1. Sociogram for directional liking ties between 18 monks (A through R) in the Sampson study (drawn by PAJEK).

model of a network, the p_1 model. We shall see that this model can be viewed as a dichotomous version of the Social Relations Model (SRM) that we extensively discussed in Chapters 8 and 9.

We denote the number of persons or nodes in the network as k and the number of potential ties as n, which equals $k(k-1)$ when ties are directional and $k(k-1)/2$ when ties are nondirectional. We denote the total number of actual ties as t. Accordingly, for the Sampson (1968) data, k is 18, n is 306, and t is 56. Note that the number of potential ties, n, assumes that there are no limits on the number of receivers (within the closed network) that each sender can nominate. Recall that in the example, however, each sender was supposed to limit himself to three nominations, and, therefore, the value of t is $18 \times 3 = 54$ plus the two extra nominations, which makes $t = 56$. At times, we transform the sociomatrix by making it symmetric. One way of doing so would be to assume that there is a nondirectional tie between A and B if either A is tied to B or B is tied to A. Turning the directional ties into nondirectional ties results in t, the number of ties, becoming 82 and n, the total number of possible ties, becoming 153.

NETWORK MEASURES

A wide variety of measures can be created from a social network. We consider some of the most important ones in this section. However, we consider only a very small subset of such measures. One way of conceptualizing the differences between network measures is the level of analysis. Some of the measures focus on the individual (e.g., centrality), others on the dyad (e.g., reciprocity), others on triads (e.g., transitivity), still others on subgroups, and, finally, some treat the entire network (e.g., density) as the unit of analysis. Ultimately, there are methods of looking at networks that consider multiple levels of analysis simultaneously (e.g., the p_1 model and the analysis of roles). We discuss all of these levels in the next section. Most of the computations in this chapter were performed using the computer program UCINET VI (Borgatti, Everett, & Freeman, 2002), which can be purchased[3] for less than $200.

Centrality

One question in network analysis is how important or key each person is in the network: The degree of importance is called *centrality*. Although centrality is a measure of the individual, it represents the individual embedded within the group.

The simplest measure of centrality is the number of ties to a person. If ties are directional, we want to differentiate the ties that lead in from those that lead out. The number of ties that a receiver has is called *indegree*, and the number of ties that a sender has is called *outdegree*. To control for the size of the network, we might wish to divide the indegree or outdegree by the number of persons in the group minus one. Alternatively, the measure can be standardized, or Z-scored, within each network.

We computed the outdegree measure for the Sampson (1968) data. The outdegree score is 3 for all monks except monks C and J, who have 4 each. More interesting in terms of centrality is the indegree measure. In Table 11.2, we present the indegree measure for each monk. The larger the score, the more often the monk is chosen, and the more central he is. We see that monks B, E, and L have the highest score, a 6. They are the most central monks, at least according to this measure. We also see that monk J has an indegree of zero, and he is called an *isolate*. Note that there is not much variance in the indegree scores. For 13 of the monks, the scores range only from 2 to 5.

TABLE 11.2. Centrality Measures for the Sampson (1968) Data Set

Monk	Indegree	Closeness	Betweenness
A	4	36	97.167
B	6	35	34.167
C	3	45	97.167
D	4	58	19.167
E	6	46	63.750
F	2	71	1.917
G	5	35	22.000
H	2	71	3.500
I	4	58	37.333
J	0	306	0.000
K	2	60	27.833
L	6	29	52.500
M	2	57	68.000
N	2	42	29.000
O	2	50	4.083
P	1	51	4.333
Q	2	58	0.500
R	3	56	5.833

However, not all ties are the same. That is, a tie to someone who has more ties is a more valuable tie than a tie to someone who has few ties. It is not so much how many people you know, but rather whom you know. If a person has ties to people who have many ties, that person is relatively central. However, if a person has ties to persons who have very few ties, then the person is not very central. One way to capture this is to determine the geodesic: The geodesic between two persons is the smallest number of paths connecting them. The geodesic is identical to the lay concept of "degrees of separation," which has gained a fairly wide degree of publicity from the movie *Six Degrees of Separation* and the "Kevin Bacon game" (i.e., picking a movie star and seeing how many links there are between him or her and actor Kevin Bacon). A geodesic is sometimes colloquially referred to as the "Kevin Bacon number."

How is the geodesic determined? If ties are symmetric, one simply determines the minimum number of links, just as in the Kevin Bacon game. To determine the geodesic from A to B, one first looks for an arrow from A to B. If there is not a direct tie from A to B, then one looks for an arrow to some other person, X, and then an arrow from person X to B. This is continued until a link is obtained.

Consider the sociogram in Figure 11.1 and the sociomatrix in Table 11.1. We see that the geodesic from A to C is 1 and is also 1 from C to A. What is the geodesic between monks A and E? We go from A to C, from C to M, and from M to E, producing a score of 3. The largest value that the geodesic can take is the number of persons in the network less one, and, consequently, for the Sampson data that value would be 17. Note that sometimes there is no way to connect one person to another. In this case, the convention is to set the geodesic to the largest possible value plus 1.

One measure of centrality, called *closeness*, is the sum of the geodesics for each person with every possible partner in the network. The greater the value of closeness, the less central the person is. Table 11.2 presents the closeness measure of centrality for the 18 monks in the Sampson data. We see that there are some similarities between the geodesic measure and the indegree measure, but the two are different. The correlation between indegree and closeness is −.542, a strong, but hardly perfect, correlation.

Another way to determine the importance of someone (i.e., centrality) is to determine how often the person appears in other persons' geodesics. To do this, we first determine all the geodesics, and then we count the number of times that a person appears in other persons' geodesics. Sometimes there is more than one geodesic; for instance, in Figure 11.1, the geodesic between D and M is 2, because D and M are both linked to E and J and because there is no direct link between D and M. For this example, E and J are in .5 of the geodesics between D and M. The total number of times that a person appears in the geodesics for pairs of others is called *betweenness*. Table 11.2 presents the betweenness scores for the 18 monks. Although there is some similarity among the three measures of centrality in Table 11.2, there are indeed differences. The correlation between indegree and betweenness is .456, and that between closeness and betweenness is −.336. Note that, for indegree, monks B, E, and L have the three highest scores; for closeness, B, G, and L have the three lowest scores; and for betweenness, A, C, and M have the three highest scores. The different measures of centrality result in different answers. However, all three measures agree that monk J is the least central, a fact not surprising, given that no monks chose him.

Each of these centrality measures could be correlated with other measures. For instance, personality measures or social status measures could be correlated with centrality measures. Centrality scores can have a practical use. For example, if the behavior or attitude of the most central member of the network could be changed, the entire network might follow along. Centrality then can be used to predict the likelihood of the diffusion of innovation.

Reciprocity

A key concept in dyadic research is *reciprocity*, defined as the exchange of similar behavior. Given that ties are directional, we can ask: If A has a tie to B, is B more likely to have a tie to A? Examples of reciprocity are: If A likes B, does B like A? If A helps B, does B help A? And if A smiles at B, does B smile at A? Some types of ties are very unlikely to be reciprocated, and, instead, they may reflect *compensation* or *complementarity*. For example, if A asks B for advice in the workplace, B may be less likely to ask A for advice. Also, for the tie of "gives orders to," there may be compensation in that people may not take orders from those to whom they give orders.

There are two ways to test whether reciprocity occurs in the social network. We first describe the simpler way. There are a total of $n/2$ pairs of scores or dyads, where, again, n equals $k(k-1)$, k being the number of persons or nodes and n being the potential number of ties. There are three possibilities for each of the $n/2$ dyads:

- Reciprocity (e.g., A likes B and B likes A); the number of pairs for which there is reciprocity is n_r.
- A lack of reciprocity (e.g., A likes B, but B does not report liking A); the number of pairs for which there is no reciprocity is n_n.
- No tie (e.g., A does not report liking B and B does not report liking A); the number of pairs for which there are no ties is n_0.

Note that $n_r + n_n + n_0 = n/2$. We again denote the number of actual ties as t. If ties were totally random, then n_r would be expected to equal

$$\frac{t(t-1)}{2(n-1)}.$$

If n_r is appreciably larger than its expected value, we conclude that there is reciprocity in the network. If n_r is appreciably smaller than its expected value, then there is evidence of compensation or complementarity. Scott (1991) details more formal tests of statistical significance.

For the Sampson (1968) data, n_r is 30, n_n is 26, and n_0 is 97. The chance value of n_r is equal to (56*55)/(2*305), or 5.049. Because n_r is more than five times greater than its chance value, we conclude that there are more reciprocal ties than would be expected by chance.

The preceding method assumes a null model in which ties are random. However, ties are not typically random, because some people have more ties than others (i.e., are more central than others). This is, in fact, the case that we saw earlier when we discussed the indegree measure of centrality. So the assumption of random ties is likely false, not necessarily because there are reciprocal ties but because of popularity and other factors. To remedy this problem, the p_1 model, described later in this chapter, can be used. Alternatively, Wasserman and Faust (1994) discuss alternative ways to test reciprocity.

Triads

For reciprocity, we look at dyads, but for transitivity, we look at triads. Transitivity embodies the notion that if A and B are friends and B and C are friends, then A and C are likely to be friends. Transitivity requires an examination of triads. Recall that for dyads there are only three possibilities: reciprocal ties, nonreciprocated ties (or one tie), and no ties. For triads with directional ties, there are 16 different possibilities. We need to perform what is called a *triad census*. Let us adopt the following notation: For each triad and its three dyads, we count the number of reciprocal ties, nonreciprocated ties, and no ties. Accordingly, the designation 300 means that the three dyads of a given triad all have reciprocal ties; the designation 021 means that two pairs have a single tie, and one pair has no ties.

We discuss here the simpler case in which ties are nondirectional and only four possibilities exist for a given triad. Using the preceding notation, the possible triad types are 003, 102, 201, and 300. Note that because the ties are nondirectional, there can be no nonreciprocated ties. If there were perfect transitivity in relationships, there should be no triads of the "201" type. A 201 triad would mean that A and B like each other, as do B and C, but A and C do not like each other.

Table 11.3 depicts the number of different types of triads for the Sampson (1968) data if we designate the ties to be nondirectional. Using UCINET VI (Borgatti et al., 2002), we have also computed the chance values for each of the four types. We see that, although there are many triads that are intransitive—the 201 type—there are many fewer than would be expected by chance. So although there is not perfect transitivity, most of the triads are transitive.

If all the ties were transitive, there would be cohesive subgroups. That is, there would be subgroups of persons all of whom had ties to each other but no ties to members of other subgroups. In the next section we consider the topic of subgroups and of cohesive subgroups in particular.

TABLE 11.3. Triad Census of the Symmeticized
Sampson (1968) Data

	Observed	Expected
Transitive		
102[a]	412	355.32
300[b]	22	14.86
003[c]	293	317.77
Intransitive		
201[d]	89	128.04

[a]One pair likes each other, and the other two do not.
[b]All three people like each other.
[c]None of the three like each other.
[d]Two pairs like each other, and the other does not.

Subgroups

As can be seen in Figure 11.1, the monks form two distinct subgroups. In all probability, this subgroup formation is the dominant feature of the network and is the feature that was most predictive of what eventually happened in the network. One strategy in network analysis is to determine the extent to which subgroups exist. We need to distinguish the different ways to define subgroups. There may be overlapping subgroups, nonoverlapping subgroups, cohesive subgroups, or nonoverlapping, noncohesive subgroups. We explain each in turn.

Overlapping subgroups are usually called *cliques*. Cliques can be operationally defined in several ways. We can require that all members of a clique have ties to all other members of the clique. We can relax the criterion and require that each person have direct ties to all but q members of the clique. The value of q is usually a small number, such as 1. An individual can be a member of one or more cliques or not a member of any clique. In contrast, for *nonoverlapping* subgroups, each individual is a member of one and only one subgroup.

Cohesive subgroups require that persons within the subgroup have ties to each other and that members of different subgroups do not have ties to one another. Such a pattern best describes the Sampson (1968) data that have been reordered in Table 11.4, with the rows and columns now sorted into the two subgroups. The members of the first subgroup are the monks J, K, E, D, I, F, and H, who were called the "Old Guard," and the monks of the other subgroup are C, G, A, B, L, M, N, O, P, Q, and R, who were called the "Young Turks." Only 4 of the 56 ties are outside the subgroups. Note that all of the monks who were later expelled and most of those who left shortly after that were members of the Young Turks.

Networks can sometimes be partitioned into subgroups with the constraint that, both within and across subgroups, the relationships are homogeneous. For cohesive groups, persons have ties to members of their group but not to members of other groups. However, other patterns are possible. If, for instance, the ties consisted of dislike, then people would not have ties to members of their own group but would have ties to members of other groups.

Table 11.5 presents different examples of subgroup formation for four subgroups within the network. Elements of the 4-by-4 matrix tell us whether ties exist between members of the subgroups. The diagonal represents ingroup ties, and the off-diagonal represents outgroup ties. A zero for row 2 and column 3 implies that there are no ties from members of subgroup 2 to the members of subgroup 3. The table presents idealized patterns, as real data do not exactly conform to such patterns.

As illustrated in Table 11.5, there are several distinct possibilities. The first is the pattern of cohesive subgroups. For such a pattern, the members

TABLE 11.4. Sociomatrix of the Sampson (1968) Data Rearranged to Show Subgrouping

	J	K	E	D	I	F	H	C	G	A	B	L	M	N	O	P	Q	R
J	0	0	1	1	1	0	0	0	0	0	0	0	1	0	0	0	0	0
K	0	0	1	0	0	0	1	0	0	0	0	0	0	1	0	0	0	0
E	0	1	0	1	1	0	0	0	0	0	0	0	0	0	0	0	0	0
D	0	1	1	0	0	1	0	0	0	0	0	0	0	0	0	0	0	0
I	0	0	1	0	0	0	1	0	0	0	0	1	0	0	0	0	0	0
F	0	0	1	1	1	0	0	0	0	0	0	0	0	0	0	0	0	0
H	0	0	0	1	1	1	0	0	0	0	0	0	0	0	0	0	0	0
C	0	0	0	0	0	0	0	0	0	1	0	0	1	0	0	0	1	1
G	0	0	0	0	0	0	0	0	0	0	1	1	0	0	0	1	0	0
A	0	0	0	0	0	0	0	1	0	0	0	1	0	1	0	0	0	0
B	0	0	0	0	0	0	0	0	1	1	0	1	0	0	0	0	0	0
L	0	0	0	0	0	0	0	0	1	1	1	0	0	0	0	0	0	0
M	0	0	1	0	0	0	0	0	1	0	0	0	0	0	0	0	0	1
N	0	0	0	0	0	0	0	0	0	1	0	1	0	0	1	0	0	0
O	0	0	0	0	0	0	0	0	1	0	1	1	0	0	0	0	0	0
P	0	0	0	0	0	0	0	0	1	0	1	0	0	0	1	0	0	0
Q	0	0	0	0	0	0	0	1	0	0	1	0	0	0	0	0	0	1
R	0	0	0	0	0	0	0	1	0	0	1	0	0	0	0	0	1	0

TABLE 11.5. Different Patterns of Subgroup Formation
with Four Subgroups

Cohesive subgroups

1	0	0	0
0	1	0	0
0	0	1	0
0	0	0	1

Hierarchy

1	0	0	0		0	0	0	0
1	1	0	0		1	0	0	0
1	1	1	0		1	1	0	0
1	1	1	1		1	1	1	0

Neighborhood subgroups

1	1	0	0
1	1	1	0
0	1	1	1
0	0	1	1

Mixed cohesive and hierarchical subgroups

1	0	0	0
1	1	1	0
0	0	1	0
0	0	1	1

Note. Rows represent subgroups of senders, and columns represent subgroups of receivers.

have ingroup ties, the diagonal values are all 1, but there are no outgroup ties, as all the off-diagonal ties are 0.

The table also presents two examples of hierarchy. In the one on the left, the measure might be "likes." People like everyone in their subgroup, and they like people who are in higher status groups. For the one on the right, the measure might be "takes orders from." A person may only take orders from their superiors. For instance, the subgroups might be the different ranks of military officers.

The next example is one of neighbors. The subgroups are arrayed on a line, and individuals engage in the behavior with members of their own subgroup, as well as with their neighbors who are members of an adjacent subgroup.

The final example in Table 11.5 contains a mixture of two types of subgroups. There are two cohesive subgroups. However, the two subgroups have, within each of them, a hierarchy. Subgroup 1 is superior to subgroup 2, and subgroup 3 is superior to subgroup 4.

Density

This is a very simple measure, but one that is key to many network computations. Density simply equals the total number of ties divided by the total number of possible ties, or t/n. For the monastery data, there are 56 ties and 18 times 17, or 306, possible ties. Therefore, the density of this social network is .183. The measure of density for the Sampson liking matrix is not very informative, because the researcher determined the total number of ties by limiting the monks to three ties each. However, in other applications it can be important. For instance, one might want to investigate whether fewer friendships are formed in larger organizations than in smaller organizations.

THE p_1 MODEL

It might have occurred to the reader that the structure of a sociomatrix is quite similar to the round-robin design that was extensively discussed in Chapters 8 and 9. The major difference between the two is that in a sociomatrix the measurements are categorical (e.g., dichotomous for the example data set), whereas the analysis methods discussed in Chapters 8 and 9 presume an interval level of measurement. There is a network model that is very similar to the SRM but that allows for the fact that the measures are dichotomous. We warn the reader that this section is much more difficult than the material in the previous sections. Again, we do not provide the complete details, and the interested reader should consult Scott (1991) for a more detailed introduction to the topic and Wasserman and Faust (1994) for a more advanced presentation.

The Model

The model we consider is called the p_1 model, developed originally by Holland and Leinhardt (1981). The p_1 model is quite similar to the SRM and can be viewed as an extension of that model, where the variable is a dichotomy. The extent to which there are many ties in the network is denoted as *theta*, or θ, in the p_1 model. The extent to which a sender has more ties is referred to as *expansiveness*, and the extent to which a receiver receives more ties is referred to as *popularity*. These terms make more intuitive sense when the measure is liking; nonetheless, the terms are also used for measures other than liking. Expansiveness is referred to as *alpha*, or α, and popularity as *beta*, or β. Finally, the reciprocity of ties is measured and is called *rho*, or ρ (not to be confused with the intraclass correlation; see Chapter 2). Expansiveness is similar to the actor effect in the SRM, popularity is similar to the partner effect, θ is similar to the grand mean, and ρ is similar to dyadic reciprocity. The p_1 model has no parameter similar to the actor–partner correlation.

To estimate the p_1 model, we need to create a somewhat strange four-way table of frequencies, denoted as f_{ijkm}. For each pair of persons, i and j, we define the following frequency values:

- $f_{ij11} = 1$ if i has a tie to j and j has a tie to i; otherwise, $f_{ij11} = 0$.
- $f_{ij10} = 1$ if i has a tie to j and j does not have a tie to i; otherwise, $f_{ij10} = 0$.
- $f_{ij01} = 1$ if i does not have a tie to j and j has a tie to i; otherwise, $f_{ij01} = 0$.
- $f_{ij00} = 1$ if i does not have a tie to j and j does not have a tie to i; otherwise, $f_{ij00} = 0$.

Thus, i and j refer to persons, and k and m refer to the presence or absence of a tie. The entries in the table are dyadic in the sense that they measure the correspondence between the ties between two people. Upon reflection, the reader should realize that the sum of the values of the preceding four frequencies is 1; that is, $f_{ij11} + f_{ij10} + f_{ij01} + f_{ij00} = 1$. Also observe that $f_{ij10} = f_{ji01}$. We have, then, a four-way table of senders (subscript i), receivers (subscript j), ties from sender to receiver (subscript k), and ties from receiver to sender (subscript m). We denote this table as ABCD, where A is sender, B is receiver, C is whether the sender has a tie to the receiver, and D is whether the receiver has a tie to the sender. If the number of senders is denoted as n, the dimensions of the table are n by n by 2 by 2.

We can also form subtables. Consider the subtable of CD. The entry f_{++11} refers to the number of pairs of nodes who both have ties to one another. Actually, because each person is both a sender and a receiver, the term equals twice the number of reciprocated ties. Thus the CD table refers to reciprocity. Other subtables are not as interesting. Consider the AB subtable, all of whose entries equal 1.

The p_1 model uses log-linear modeling to estimate the parameters of the model. We described log-linear models briefly in Chapter 6 (see also Chapter 14). Here we briefly describe how log-linear models can be used to estimate and test the p_1 model. We begin with a table of counts. For network data, we have a four-way table of ABCD, where there are four variables, A, B, C, and D. In a log-linear model, we try to develop a model that fits the subtables of the larger table. For instance, one might fit a model that contains all the two-way tables: AB, AC, AD, BC, BD, and CD. The adequacy of such models is assessed by a goodness-of-fit test that compares the similarity of the observed frequencies in the ABCD table to the expected frequencies in the predicted ABCD table derived on basis of the model containing all two-way tables. To determine fit we use the likelihood ratio test, or G^2 (see Chapter 6 for the formula), which is analogous to but different from the more conventional chi-square goodness-of-fit test. The fit of nested models can be compared.

The standard p_1 model requires the estimation of the log-linear model that fits all of the two-way tables: AB, AC, AD, BC, BD, and CD. The likelihood ratio chi-square, or G^2, for such a model must be divided by 2 because each data point is entered into the ABCD table twice due to the earlier mentioned constraint that $f_{ij10} = f_{ji01}$. The degrees of freedom for this model are $(3k^2 - 7k)/2$, where again k is the number of persons. Because of the small size of the cells (recall that typically the tests of goodness of fit require an expected value of at least 5 per cell, and for p_1 the largest cell size is only 1), one does not interpret the G^2 but rather compares alternative models. In particular, we can test for reciprocity by not fitting the CD table. This model has its own G^2 value and degrees of freedom of $(3k - 1)(k - 2)/2$. Its degrees of freedom are 1 more than that of the model that fitted the CD table. We can subtract the G^2 from the two models and use the G^2 difference to evaluate the null hypothesis of no reciprocity. The difference is treated as a χ^2 with 1 degree of freedom. If the fit of the model significantly worsens by not including that table, then we conclude that there is reciprocity of choices in the network. We can also test whether people differ in their popularity by not fitting the AD and BD tables and whether people differ in their expansiveness by not fitting the AC and BD tables.

We applied the p_1 model to the Sampson (1968) data set and used the computer program UCINET VI (Borgatti et al., 2002). We found a G^2 of 236.93 with 390 degrees of freedom. This indicates a good-fitting model. When we estimate the model without fitting the CD table, we find a G^2 of 267.34 with 391 degrees of freedom. When we compute the chi-square difference test, we obtain a value of 30.41 with 1 degree of freedom. Thus we conclude that liking is reciprocated.

In Table 11.6, we have the expansiveness and popularity effects that are analogous to indegree and outdegree measures. The expansiveness effects do not vary a great deal, except for the fact that monk J has a large one. Remember that monk J chose four other monks, not three. The popularity effects vary to a much larger extent, and they parallel the indegree and the closeness measures. In fact, the correlation of the popularity effects with the indegree measure is .987, and it is −.606 for the closeness measure. Thus the popularity effect is virtually identical to the indegree measure of centrality.

There is one complication in the computation of popularity effects for the Sampson example. Recall that monk J is an isolate in the sense that no one chose him. Technically, his popularity effect is minus infinity. For this reason, we have left his popularity effect blank. The analysis was done throwing out person J as receiver. Consequently, there is one less receiver, and that is why the degrees of freedom do not equal 423 but only 390.

TABLE 11.6. p_1 Expansiveness and Popularity Parameters for the Sampson (1968) Data

Monk	Expansiveness	Popularity
A	−0.302	0.489
B	−0.742	1.252
C	0.480	−0.253
D	−0.302	0.489
E	−0.742	1.252
F	0.225	−0.619
G	−0.535	0.897
H	0.225	−0.619
I	−0.302	0.489
J	1.157	—[a]
K	0.225	−0.619
L	−0.742	1.252
M	0.225	−0.619
N	0.225	−0.619
O	0.225	−0.619
P	0.496	−1.535
Q	0.225	−0.619
R	−0.045	0.001

The value of theta is large and negative, equaling –2.504. When theta is less than 1, the density is less than .5, which is the case for this data set. We can estimate the density as

$$\frac{e^{\theta/2}}{1+e^{\theta/2}},$$

where e approximately equals the number 2.718. For the example in which $\theta = -2.504$, the estimated density equals .222, which is close to the simple density estimate of .183 reported previously.

The value of ρ, or reciprocity, is 3.153, and it is a logit difference. It represents the logarithm of the odds of a reciprocated relationship. If we compute $e^{\rho/2}$ we can determine the estimated odds that a relationship would be reciprocated, assuming that the density is .50. The value is 2.20, indicating very strong reciprocity. The probability that a relationship is reciprocated is 2.20/(1 + 2.20), or .68.

The p_1 model incorporates many of the parameters of network models. It includes density in the θ parameter, centrality in the popularity and expansiveness parameters, and reciprocity in the ρ parameter. It can even incorporate subgrouping and triadic features (see Holland & Leinhardt, 1981). It is a very general model for the analysis of sociometric data.

Relation to the SRM

The reader might wonder what would happen if we performed an SRM analysis on the Sampson (1968) data. As we said earlier, such an analysis is not entirely appropriate, because the SRM presumes that the data are at the interval level of measurement, whereas in social network research the data are typically at the nominal level.

There are some interesting relationships between actor and partner effects and measures from a sociomatrix. We find that

Actor = indegree + outdegree/(k – 1) – density (k – 1)/(k – 2),
Partner = outdegree + indegree/(k – 1) – density (k – 1)/(k – 2).

Note that these are applications of the formulas for the estimation of actor and partner effects from Chapters 8 and 9.

When we apply an SRM analysis to the Sampson (1968) data, we find that there is no actor variance. This is not surprising because of the constraint of each sender nominating the same number of persons. There is partner variance, but it represents only 1% of the total variance. We correlated the SRM estimated partner effects with the p_1 popularity effects, and that correlation is .98. Thus little or no difference exists between the p_1 estimate of popularity and the SRM estimate for this data set. As in the p_1 model, considerable dyadic reciprocity exists, $r = .472$. We can treat the dyadic reciprocity correlation as an intraclass correlation (see Chapter 8), and the value is statistically significant, $F(135, 136) = 2.79$, $p < .001$.

There is one technical difference between the SRM and p_1 models. The SRM model is a random-effects model, and, accordingly, it presumes that the results generalize beyond the specific actor and partners who are studied. However, the p_1 model is a fixed-effects model, and its results refer to the specific senders and receivers studied. That is, the SRM estimates actor and partner variances, whereas p_1 estimates expansiveness and popularity effects for the particular members of the network. Be aware that the standard SRM estimates presume that the level of the measurement is the interval level, something not true for the Sampson (1968) data. In this chapter we do not discuss the p_2 model (van Duijn, Snijders, & Zijkstra, 2004) and p^* (Snijders, 2002), which are both random-effects models that can be viewed as logistic versions of the SRM.

Another Look at the Sampson Data

Finally, we can view the Sampson (1968) data as two different networks, the Old Guard and the Young Turks. When we run the p_1 model separately on each of the two groups, we find that θ, or density, is -0.258 for the Old Guard and -2.185 for the Young Turks. Note that θ is more positive (i.e., less negative) because of more in-group (members of the same subgroup) than out-group (members of the other subgroup) choices. The value of ρ, or reciprocity, is 0.921 for the Old Guard and 3.009 for the Young Turks. These levels of reciprocity of choice are less than that found for the overall model, because the reciprocity is enhanced by excluding members of the out-group. We do note that the Young Turks show more reciprocal choices than the Old Guard. The G^2 is 41.39 with 38 degrees of freedom for the Old Guard and 104.33 with 143 degrees of freedom for the Young Turks.

SUMMARY AND CONCLUSIONS

Social behavior is embedded within a social context, and in this chapter we have discussed social network analysis as a method for quantifying that context. The basic data from a social network are the links between network members, and these links can be represented in a sociomatrix or sociogram. In this chapter we defined many of the basic terms in network analysis. We discussed several types of networks, including open, closed, and ego-centered networks. We have also provided various network measures for individuals, dyads, triads, subgroups, and the entire network.

At the individual level, we discussed several measures of centrality, which is the degree to which an individual is important in the network. *Indegree* and *outdegree* were defined as the number of links to an individual and the number of links from an individual, respectively. Other measures of centrality, such as closeness and betweenness, use the concept of geodesics to quantify an individual's importance. Dyadic reciprocity in a social network (if person A is linked to B, is B linked to A) was also presented. At the level of the triad, we introduced the idea of transitivity. We also discussed measures that can be used to identify subgroups or cliques. Finally, we described the log-linear p_1 model and its measures of expansiveness (akin to the actor effect in the SRM) and popularity (akin to the partner effect in the SRM).

We have outlined many different network measures in this chapter. Each of these measures can be estimated for a single network. Perhaps more interestingly, these measures can be computed for each network, and then properties of the network, such as size and type, can be used to explain variation across networks.

This chapter, although it provides a good deal of information, has only begun to scratch the surface of network analysis. The reader is referred to the introductory texts by Scott (1991) and Kilduff and Tsai (2003), as well as to the much more advanced text by Wasserman and Faust (1994). These texts provide the details of the analyses that we have presented, and they also describe other analyses that we do not discuss.

Outside of a small network of researchers, primarily sociologists and anthropologists, little utilization of social network analysis takes place. Sadly, and ironically, only a small clique of researchers performs network analysis. This is quite unfortunate, as much can be learned by using network models. A little-known fact is that the identification of AIDS as a sexually transmitted disease was facilitated by the sociologist William W. Darrow at the U.S. Centers for Disease Control using methods of network analysis (Shilits, 1987). Additionally, several researchers (e.g., Barabasi, 2002; Watts, 2003) have recently suggested that network analyses can be used to understand a wide range of topics, from the spread of viruses on the World Wide Web to the effect of a stroke on the brain. Hopefully, this chapter may play a small role in stimulating interest in this topic. Previous attempts to stimulate interest (e.g., Kanfer & Tanaka, 1993) appear to have not been particularly successful, although we still remain optimistic.

In the next three chapters, we consider idiographic analyses, in which effects are measured for each dyad. Chapter 12 considers the measurement of similarity in dyadic relationships.

NOTES

1. The data set we used from UCINET VI is "Sampson Data Set" and SAMPLK1.

2. The website to download the computer program PAJEK is *http://vlado. fmf.uni-lj.si/pub/networks/pajek/default.htm.*

3. The website for UCINET VI is *http://www.analytictech.com/downloaduc6. htm.* Purchasers of the program can also obtain the Sampson data set.

Dyadic Indexes

Questions concerning correspondence or similarity between dyad members are common in dyadic research. In studies investigating such questions, two sets of scores are often obtained, one set from each member of the dyad,[1] and a measure of correspondence between these two sets is determined. We refer to such a measure as a *dyadic index*. Many of the important concepts in relationship research, such as reciprocity, mutuality, accuracy, understanding, agreement, synchrony, similarity, perceived similarity, sensitivity, empathy, and assumed reciprocity, are measured by some type of dyadic index. It should then come as no surprise that many of the most important studies of couples (e.g., Levinger & Breedlove, 1966; Murstein & Beck, 1972) use dyadic indexes.

Consider various examples of dyadic indexes in the recent literature:

- Accuracy: Husbands and wives attempt to predict their partners' responses to a marital values questionnaire (Acitelli, Kenny, & Weiner, 2001).
- Similarity: Two friends answer a behavioral inventory, and the degree to which they respond the same way is determined (Wakimoto & Fujihara, 2004).
- Agreement: Parents of children with attention-deficit/hyperactivity disorder complete a discipline survey, and agreement[2] on that survey is correlated with marital satisfaction (Harvey, 2000).
- Sensitivity: A person attempts to guess how happy his or her partner is during a 15-minute interaction (Levenson & Ruef, 1992).

317

- Synchrony: The correspondence in the movements of dancers is measured by a correlation coefficient (Boker & Rotondo, 2003).
- Perceived similarity: The degree to which a supervisor believes he or she is similar in personality to a subordinate is related to more positive performance ratings (Strauss, Barrick, & Connerley, 2001).

The key feature of a dyadic index is that it provides an assessment of the correspondence between two sets of measures. Although dyadic indexes tap a multitude of theoretical constructs, in this chapter we refer to the index as *similarity* or *dissimilarity*, even though in many applications the index may refer to a different concept.

Computing a dyadic index implies an idiographic analysis in that the index is computed for each couple separately. In this chapter we describe several dyadic indexes, including correlational measures and discrepancy or distance measures, to name two. In each case, the dyadic index (e.g., correlation, discrepancy) is computed for each dyad. For example, if the measure assesses husbands' and wives' preferences for a series of foods, the idiographic approach might measure the degree of similarity for each couple across foods. This stands in contrast to the *nomothetic* approach, which would assess the degree to which, across couples, husbands and wives agree in their ratings of a single food item. A nomothetic analysis precludes comparing dyads on the dyadic index. Thus, if the research focus is on whether there are differences between dyads on the dyadic index (e.g., are some couples more compatible in their food preferences than others?), then the nomothetic approach should not be used.

One key question that needs to be answered before computing any dyadic index is whether an index should even be computed. Often, an alternate form of analysis can avoid the many complications discussed in this chapter. One alternative is a nomothetic analysis in which a measure of correspondence is computed across dyads. This can be done one item at a time, or it can be done on a combination of the items (e.g., a summary score, such as an average, could be computed for each individual), and then the index of correspondence could be computed across dyads. For such an approach, dyad is the unit of analysis, and correspondence can be computed using an ordinary correlation coefficient when dyad members are distinguishable or an intraclass (see Chapter 2) or bivariate intraclass (see Chapter 6) correlation when dyad members are indistinguishable. Note that an average would be preferred if all the items measured the same construct (e.g., how much they like their partners), but an item-by-item analysis might be required if the items measured different constructs (e.g., how much they like different foods). One good way to determine whether the items measure the same construct is to factor analyze them and determine whether there is one strong factor; if there is, then all the items tap the same construct.

Dyadic indexes are particularly useful when assessing similarity (or dissimilarity) across a set of items for each dyad. This context arises when researchers are interested in treating the dyadic index as a variable in and of itself. For example, one might examine whether couples who are more similar stay together longer (a correlation between relationship length and the dyadic index measuring similarity of the partners). Another question might involve examining mean differences in a dyadic index across some relevant variable, such as marital therapy condition.

This chapter considers a series of issues in the use of dyadic indexes. First, we examine measurement considerations for the items used to create the index. Second, guidelines for selecting the particular type of dyadic index are considered. Third, stereotype accuracy and its effect on dyadic indexes are discussed. Fourth, pseudo-couple analysis, an alternative approach to the estimation of dyadic effects, is described. Finally, we return to the issue of idiographic versus nomothetic analysis.

Throughout the chapter, we refer to the items on which each member is measured. The dyadic index is the gauge of how similarly the dyad members respond to those items. We let k be the number of items that are used to form the dyadic index and n be the number of dyads.

ITEM MEASUREMENT ISSUES

In computing the dyadic index, we have two sets of items, and the items within each set must be measured in the same units. For example, if all the items were on 9-point scales, then the units would be the same. However, if the units were different, the methods described in this chapter would likely be misleading. A study of the similarity of married couples with the measures of each member's age, weight, IQ, and height would present serious problems of comparability of measurement. The mean differences between the items would not have a meaningful interpretation, and variation around this mean would be determined more by differences in metrics than by substantive factors. Consequently, the covariation across sets used to measure similarity would not be meaningful.

If the units of measurement are different but it still makes sense to compute similarity, transformations might be employed to make the units comparable. One brute-force strategy for creating metric equivalence is standardization. Each item is standardized by subtracting that item's mean based on the entire sample of individuals and dividing by the item's standard deviation (again based on the entire sample). Alternatively, the measures could be made comparable by a rational strategy. Imagine 10 items, 5 measured on a 7-point scale (1 to 7) and the other 5 on a 10-point scale (1 to 10). We could convert the 10-point scale to a 7-point scale by using the transformation $(6/9)(X - 1) + 1$, where the 6/9 is the range of the new scale divided by the range of the old scale. In this way, the ranges of different scales can be made equivalent. Another alternative would be to equate the actual ranges of scales instead of the theoretical ranges.

One further possibility is that the weights for transformation could be estimated using the data. For each score, a transformation of item X_i into item Y_i would be conducted. The formula would be $Y_i = a_i + b_i X_i$, where the coefficients of a_i and b_i would be chosen empirically. Perhaps the criterion for choosing the coefficients would be to maximize the size of the average dyadic index (e.g., the correlation coefficient).[3] Although we know of no empirical use of the method of an empirically derived transformation before computing a dyadic index, we believe that the strategy deserves investigation.

In this chapter we assume that all the items are measured at the interval level of measurement. If the items were measured at the nominal level (e.g., religion), then the methods described in this chapter would be inappropriate. However, very often the items used to form a dyadic index are dichotomous (e.g., agree/disagree or yes/no), and the methods described in this chapter have been used. Because most of the methods in this chapter require interval measurement, it is uncertain what the effect of violating this assumption would be.[4]

Scale reversal of the items may be necessary. Items generally vary on a positive–negative or good–bad dimension, and if higher scores on some items indicate a positive outcome but higher scores on other items indicate a negative outcome, then reorientation of some items is necessary so that high scores consistently indicate the same type of outcome (e.g., all items might be scaled so that higher numbers indicate more positive outcomes). Scale reversal can be easily accomplished by subtracting each score from the sum of the upper limit (the largest possible score) and the lower limit (the smallest possible score) for the item.

Sometimes, items do not clearly vary on a positive–negative dimension, and it is not immediately evident which items require reversal. In this case, another criterion for assessing the orientation of the items is necessary. One possibility is to examine the correlations among the items to determine which items relate positively to one another and which relate negatively. Negatively related items are candidates for reversal. Another option is to use factor analysis. The researcher computes the first principal factor (not component!) and reverses those items that have a negative loading on that first factor. If, for some reason, the researcher decides not to use scale reversal prior to computing the dyadic index (something we do not advise), the researcher should recompute the dyadic index with reversal to determine whether results are affected.

Redundancy of items is also an issue. Sometimes essentially the same question is asked more than once, and that one item has more weight than it likely deserves. We suggest examining the correlation matrix between items with person as the unit of analysis. If some pairs of items correlate too highly (Kenny & Acitelli, 1994, suggest .70 as a cutoff) and those pairs of items have very similar content, then one of the items should be deleted or the two combined.

MEASURES OF PROFILE SIMILARITY

In this section we consider the many different types of dyadic indexes, or, as they are sometimes called, measures of *profile similarity*. We describe them and discuss how to determine which one to use.

Types

There are a number of different dyadic indexes, which can be divided into two types. We call the first type *dissimilarity* measures:

- Discrepancy[5]: the sum of absolute differences divided by the number of measures.
- d^2: the sum of squared differences between measures.
- Distance: the square root of the sum of the squared differences.

As the name suggests, the defining feature of dissimilarity measures is that smaller values imply greater similarity. The second type of dyadic index we call *similarity* measures:

- Correlation: the Pearson product–moment correlation between two sets of scores.
- Covariance: the sum of the product of mean-deviated scores, divided by sample size less one.
- Intraclass correlation: $(MS_B - MS_W)/(MS_B + MS_W)$ (see Chapter 2 for a description of these terms).

As the name suggests, the defining feature of similarity measures is that larger values imply greater similarity. The final similarity measure presumes that there is a causal direction between the measures:

- Regression coefficient: one measure is used to predict the other.

For this type of dyadic index, one measure must cause or be antecedent to the other. For instance, in accuracy research, the criterion may be used to predict the judgment. Although this list contains most of the possible measures found in the literature, it is not at all exhaustive. Virtually any measure of association can be, and probably has been, used to compute a dyadic index.

There is a fundamental difference between similarity and dissimilarity indices. A dissimilarity index starts by assuming perfect similarity and then measures how dissimilar the two sets of items are. A similarity index starts with assuming that there is no similarity (although the different types of indexes define "no similarity" differently) and then measures how similar the two sets of items are. Some of the similarity measures are standardized in that they are divided by the maximum possible similarity between the measures. The correlation and intraclass correlation are standardized measures, whereas the covariance is not.

How many items are needed to compute the dyadic index? It depends on what measure is used. One advantage of the dissimilarity dyadic indexes is that only one item is needed. For the other measures, more are needed, but it is difficult to give a specific number. One thing to realize is that the usual rules of thumb for computing correlations and regression coefficients do not apply to a dyadic index. Much smaller sample sizes can be used. We would suggest that four items is the absolute minimum and that at least eight items is a practical minimum. However, this is just a rough guide, and a simulation study would be informative in helping to determine the minimum number of items.

Some of the similarity measures are undefined when there is no variability across a set of items for an individual. The correlation coefficient is undefined when either person in the dyad has no variability across the items. The regression coefficient is undefined when the predictor items do not vary. The usual convention is to set the dyadic index to zero in these cases. It is better, however, to treat the dyadic index as a missing value, because it cannot be computed.

Measurement error can cause problems with indexes of similarity and dissimilarity. Consider, for example, a correlational dyadic index. Measurement error attenuates correlational measures of association. One might want to consider a correction for attenuation (Nunnally & Bernstein, 1994). For the correlation coefficient, the correction is to divide the correlation by the product of the square root of the reliabilities. For the regression coefficient, the correction for attenuation is to divide by the reliability of the predictor variable. However, there might not be reliability measures, particularly for each dyad.

Table 12.1 presents data for five dyads, I through V, on a measure that has six items, A through F. To help in the comparison of the dyadic index measures, the data for the first member of the dyad (person 1) are always the same across the five dyads. We have also graphed the data for dyads II through V in Figures 12.1 to 12.4. In each of the four figures, the solid line always represents person 1's data. Table 12.2 presents the values of the different types of dyadic indexes for the five dyads presented. Quite clearly, the particular measure affects the conclusions drawn about the rank ordering of dyads in terms of similarity. For example, ignoring dyad I (which is a special case because person 1's scores exactly equal those of person 2), the discrepancy measure indicates that dyad III is the most similar, whereas the correlation measure indicates that all four dyads are equally

TABLE 12.1. Hypothetical Data to Illustrate the Different Dyadic Indexes

	Dyad								
	I		II		III		IV		V	
Item	P1	P2	P1	P2	P1	P2	P1	P2	P1	P2
A	6	6	6	8	6	8	6	2	6	11
B	8	8	8	10	8	9	8	6	8	12
C	10	10	10	12	10	10	10	10	10	13
D	14	14	14	16	14	12	14	18	14	15
E	12	12	12	14	12	11	12	14	12	14
F	10	10	10	12	10	10	10	10	10	13

Note. P1, Person 1; P2, Person 2. The data for Person 1 are the same across the five dyads.

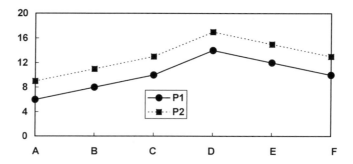

FIGURE 12.1. Data from dyad II (see Table 12.1) with the same shape but different levels.

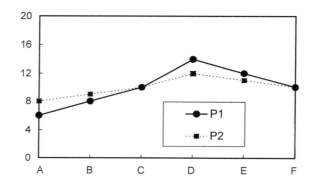

FIGURE 12.2. Data from dyad III (see Table 12.1) with the same shape but different spreads.

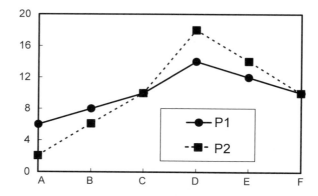

FIGURE 12.3. Data from dyad IV (see Table 12.1) with the same shape but very different spreads.

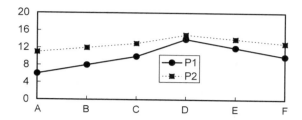

FIGURE 12.4. Data from dyad V (see Table 12.1) with the same shape but different levels and spreads.

similar. We do note that if the set of scores are identical, as in the case for dyad I, all measures indicate perfect similarity.

Which Measure to Use?

Why do the measures differ, and how is a researcher to decide which measure to use? Following Cronbach and Gleser (1953), three crucial factors influence the size of the measure: level, spread, and shape. *Level* refers to the mean, or average value, of the scores across items. *Spread* refers to the variability of the scores across the items. *Shape* refers to the pattern of differences, the ups and downs, between the scores across the items. Generally, correspondence in shape is thought to be the most important component of the dyadic index: The more similar the shape, the greater the similarity. The critical issue in dyadic indexes is how differences in level and spread are handled.

To see how level matters in determining similarity, consider the data in Figure 12.1, from dyad II in Table 12.1. Note that the two shapes are the

TABLE 12.2. Different Dyadic Indexes Computed for the Dyads in Table 12.1

Measure	Dyad				
	I	II	III	IV	V
Discrepancy	0.00	2.00	1.00	2.00	3.00
Distance	0.00	4.90	3.16	6.32	8.00
d^2	0.00	24.00	10.00	40.00	64.00
Correlation	1.00	1.00	1.00	1.00	1.00
Covariance	8.00	8.00	4.00	16.00	4.00
Intraclass correlation	1.00	0.77	0.83	0.83	0.26
Regression coefficient	1.00	1.00	0.50	2.00	0.50

same. They both peak for item D and are lowest for item A. However, the levels differ: The mean level for person 2 is greater than for person 1, differing by two units. We see that the dissimilarity measures are nonzero, indicating some dissimilarity, whereas the correlation measure is a perfect 1, indicating complete similarity. Note also that the intraclass correlation is less than perfect. Like the discrepancy measure, the intraclass correlation is lowered by a difference in levels.

Figures 12.2 and 12.3 contain the data from dyads III and IV in Table 12.1 and illustrate the effect of spread on measures of similarity. The shapes are all the same: They all peak for item D and are lowest for item A. Additionally, the levels are the same for all four persons, their means all being 12.0. However, the spreads differ. Person 2 from dyad III has less spread than person 1 does, and person 2 from dyad IV has more spread than person 1. Because the shapes are the same, the correlation measure is a perfect 1.0 for dyads III and IV. However, the dissimilarity measures do not equal zero because the spreads differ. Note that the intraclass correlation is less than perfect because of the differences in spread. The covariance measure is also affected by spread: Assuming some similarity of shape, the greater the spread, the greater the covariance. Thus the covariance for dyad IV is greater than the covariance for dyad III because the data for person 2 in dyad IV is more spread out than that for person 2 in dyad III.

Finally, Figure 12.4 presents the data from dyad V in Table 12.1. The two shapes are the same, but both the levels and spreads differ. The level for person 1 is lower than the level for person 2; the spread for person 1 is greater than the spread for person 2. Note that differences between spread and level obscure the correspondence of shapes. Also, notice that, whereas the correlation is 1 because the shapes are identical, the dissimilarity measures are greater than 0, and the intraclass correlation is very small, despite identical shapes.

In summary, if the researcher's interest is in the similarity of the shapes of the two sets of items, then the correlation coefficient is the best dyadic index. If the level is the most relevant, then the correlation, regression, and covariance are inappropriate measures because the means are subtracted before computing the index. Instead, an intraclass correlation or some type of dissimilarity measure, a distance, discrepancy, or d^2, should be used. If only differences in level are of concern, then the researcher should simply average scores across the items for each individual and compute a discrepancy measure. If the two sets of items differ due to spread and the researcher believes that the difference is meaningful, then a dissimilarity or intraclass correlation index should be used. If shape is important and level is not, and if it is believed that shape should be weighted by greater spread, then a covariance measure is more appropriate (Chaplin & Panter, 1993).

When should we use a dissimilarity measure? These measures should be preferred whenever similarity in all three of the factors that influence the size of the dyadic index (i.e., shape, level, and spread) is required. The distance measure would generally be preferred over the discrepancy and d^2 because distance has a spatial interpretation. The discrepancy measure can be used when the response items are dichotomous because it can be interpreted as a measure of the number of disagreements. Finally, d^2 can be used if the researcher desires to interpret the dissimilarity measure in terms of variance unexplained.

The intraclass correlation is very much like a dissimilarity measure in that it should be used when shape, spread, and level are all relevant (Robinson, 1957). Unlike the dissimilarity measures, this dyadic index is normalized by the spread such that 1.0 indicates exact similarity, −1.0 indicates maximal dissimilarity, and 0 indicates chance similarity.

If there is a causal direction between the two sets of items, then the regression coefficient is to be preferred. Although a regression coefficient of zero means no association, there is no upper or lower limit. Sometimes choice of the most appropriate dyadic index is unclear. Empirical analysis can sometimes be useful in determining the best measure. That is, several dyadic indexes can be estimated, and the index that yields the most plausible correlates and pattern of results can be selected. If this strategy is used, the researchers should discuss how it is they picked an index. Ideally, results would be cross-validated.

MEAN AND VARIANCE OF THE DYADIC INDEX

Two summary statistics are of particular interest when working with a dyadic index: the mean and the variance. The mean tells us the average of couples on the dyadic index, and the variance tells us how much couples differ, that is, how heterogeneous they are.

Average Measure

Usually the focus of research that utilizes a dyadic index is on understanding the factors that produce greater similarity or the effects of similarity on other dyadic outcomes. For example, we might want to know if more similar couples are more satisfied. Thus the focus is on moderators of the dyadic index. However, the following question can be interesting: What is the average level of similarity across all dyads, and is it above chance? This question is particularly important in studies of accuracy, synchrony, and reciprocity. For instance, the research topic under investigation might be whether persons are accurate overall in perceiving their partners.

Some measures (e.g., correlation and regression coefficients) have a natural chance score of zero. Thus one can conduct an analysis to determine whether the mean of the dyadic index is different from zero. For the correlation, r, the sampling distribution is known, and the scores have a normal distribution. Therefore, one can adopt the following strategy when the dyadic index is a correlation. The correlation for each dyad is converted to a Fisher's z value. As discussed in Chapter 2, that transformation is $\ln[(1 + r)/(1 - r)]/2$, where ln is the natural logarithm and r is the Pearson product–moment correlation. The mean z is computed across the sample, and one then tests that the mean z is different from zero by multiplying it by $n/(k - 3)$, where n is the number of dyads and k the number of items that are used to compute the correlation coefficient. The resulting value has a standard normal, or Z, distribution under the null hypothesis that the average correlation is zero.

Generally, when researchers wish to test the null hypothesis that the mean of the dyadic index equals some a priori value (usually zero), a one-sample t-test can be computed. The formula for this t-test is

$$t(n-1) = \frac{M-\mu}{s/\sqrt{n}}.$$

In this t-test, n is the number dyads, M is the mean of the dyadic index across the sample, s is the standard deviation of the index across the sample, and μ is the theoretical value against which the test is being conducted (e.g., often $\mu = 0$).

For some measures (e.g., distance and discrepancy), no baseline or theoretical value (such as $\mu = 0$) exists. It is therefore difficult with these measures to know whether, on average, members are similar. To form a baseline measure of such indexes, one may have to create pseudo-couples, a method discussed later in this chapter.

Tests of Heterogeneity

The spirit of a dyadic index is that the size of the index differs from dyad to dyad (i.e., it is idiographic). In studies of similarity, such variation might reflect the fact that some couples have more interests in common or have more similar tastes in food. One of the primary goals of research using dyadic indexes is to understand factors that produce variation in the index. That is, the major hypothesis is one of moderation: The association found in the dyadic index is explained by some other factor. Common moderator variables might be relational closeness or length of the relationship; for example, one might find that similarity in food preferences is stronger for couples who have been married longer. However, before moderation is tested, we recommend that a test of homogeneity be conducted. This test determines whether or not there is any variation in the dyadic index to be explained by moderators. The test of heterogeneity assesses the degree to which the dyadic index varies more than would be expected by chance.

The most general way to determine heterogeneity is to show that the dyadic index is reliable. This is not done by showing that the set of items themselves are reliable (i.e., via Cronbach's alpha) but rather by assessing whether the dyadic index itself is reliable. For instance, we can use split-half procedures to compute the index twice. Thus we could use half of the items to form one estimate of the index, and we could use the other half to form the second estimate of the index. We would then compute a split-half correlation coefficient, r^*, between the two estimates. Using the Spearman–Brown prophecy formula, the reliability of the overall dyadic index would be $2r^*/(1 + r^*)$. Of course, for this procedure to be reasonable, there need to be enough items. Assuming that there are enough, the Spearman–Brown reliability estimate establishes whether there is sufficient variability in the dyadic index.

The distributions for some dyadic indexes are known, so we can actually compute what the variation in the index would be even if there were no real differences (i.e., if the only differences were due to sampling error). For the correlation coefficient, we transform each dyad's correlation using a Fisher's z. As noted earlier, that transformation is $\ln[(1 + r)/(1 - r)]/2$, where ln is the natural logarithm. We then compute $(k - 3)\Sigma(z - M_z)^2$, where k is the number of items, M_z is the mean of the Fisher's z values across the dyads, and the summation is across dyads. Under the null hypothesis that there are no differences between couples in the correlation, this quantity is distributed as χ^2 with $n - 1$ degrees of freedom (n being the number of dyads). Notably, a very small amount of variance can yield a statistically significant chi-square value. An alternative measure is the proportion of variance in the z's that is meaningful. Such a measure can be interpreted as a reliability. That measure of reliability is

$$\frac{s_z^2 - (k-3)}{s_z^2},$$

where s_z^2 is the variance in the Fisher's z's and $k - 3$ is the theoretical variance of z. Larger values of this statistic indicate increased meaningful variation in the correlations. We do not recommend using the correlational dyadic index in a moderation analysis unless its reliability is at least .50.

For regression coefficients, we do something akin to a test of homogeneity of slopes in analysis of covariance. Essentially, this would involve estimating the regression with an interaction in the model. A slope is computed for each dyad by regressing the set of Y measures on the set of X measures. The null hypothesis would be that these slopes do vary by dyad. Thus we test whether X interacts with the $n - 1$ dummy variables coding for dyad membership. A statistically significant interaction between the dyad membership variables and X implies that the regression slope between X and Y differs across dyads. A similar analysis could be accomplished via multilevel modeling. Within a multilevel model, we estimate the effect of X on Y for each dyad. We can then estimate the variance in the resulting slopes. We can also test whether the variance in the slopes is statistically significant. We discuss this strategy extensively in the next chapter, in which we consider cross-lagged over-time analyses and growth-curve analyses.

As we noted earlier, we strongly suggest that an analysis of homogeneity–heterogeneity of the dyadic index be conducted prior to any analysis of moderator variables. Once such an analysis has established that the dyads do vary in their levels of similarity (or dissimilarity), analyses in which explanatory variables are used to model the differences can be illuminating. For instance, do spouses in satisfied couples understand their partners better than dissatisfied spouses? Such an analysis can be viewed as a moderator analysis in that marital satisfaction moderates the amount of accuracy. However, if the dyadic index does not vary (i.e., is homogeneous), then a moderator analysis should not be conducted.

STEREOTYPE ACCURACY

As Cronbach (1955) noted, one key but often neglected factor that can affect a dyadic index is stereotype accuracy: Members of a dyad might appear to be similar not because they are really similar but because they respond in a stereotypical fashion. In this context, *stereotype* means the typical or normative responses persons tend to give for a set of variables (rather than the more common definition of an oversimplified shared view of a group).

The problem of stereotype accuracy is most evident with correlational dyad indexes. Consider as an example the correspondence between husbands' and wives' food preferences. Finding that husbands and wives on average have similar food preferences may not be as interesting as it might appear, because such a finding can result simply because most people generally like ice cream and do not like liver. Ordinarily, we do not merely want to know whether dyad members are similar to one another; rather, we want to know whether they are more similar to one another than are members of a randomly paired dyad.

Consider the data in Table 12.3. We have five male–female dyads, and each person completes a five-item questionnaire. If we compute the mean score for men and the mean score for women for each item and then correlate these means, we find that the correlation between the mean responses is .916. The correlation between mean judgments is the standard measure of stereotype accuracy. Because the correlation is strongly positive, we judge that stereotype accuracy exists, indicating that the men's typical or average responses were very similar to the women's typical or average responses. The presence of stereotype accuracy can seriously inflate correlational measures of dyadic indexes. Moreover, the failure to adjust for stereotype accuracy can lead to biased correlations of the dyadic index with other measures.

TABLE 12.3. Hypothetical Data to Illustrate Stereotype Accuracy

	Dyad											
	I		II		III		IV		V		Average	
Item	M	F	M	F	M	F	M	F	M	F	M	F
A	4	3	3	5	2	4	2	3	4	5	3.0	4.0
B	5	5	7	6	4	3	6	7	4	3	5.2	4.8
C	7	8	6	7	6	5	7	6	5	6	6.2	6.4
D	6	5	4	3	5	6	5	4	4	3	4.8	4.2
E	3	3	3	4	2	3	3	4	5	4	3.2	3.6
F	4	4	2	5	1	2	2	3	3	2	2.4	3.2
r	.924		.583		.783		.883		.752		.916[a]	
r'	.371		.447		.627		.604		.690		—	

Note. r is the correlation between scores, and r' is the correlation adjusted for stereotype accuracy by subtraction of item means.
[a]Measure of stereotype accuracy.

We should note that if level differences are considered meaningful, then adjustments for stereotype accuracy are problematic because the adjustments (described later) essentially remove the average effect from the person's score. Thus when level differences are meaningful but stereotype accuracy may distort the estimates of similarity, correlational indexes are undesirable. Instead, discrepancy, distance, d^2, intraclass correlation, or the intraclass covariance should be considered as options for the dyadic index.

The standard way to control for stereotype accuracy is a pseudo-couple analysis, which we discuss later in this chapter. Another, and we think better, way is to simply subtract the sample means of the items before computing the dyad index.

Questions arise concerning which means should be subtracted. Consider the questions of whether roommates have the same personalities and the question of whether a parent and child have the same personalities. For a given personality measure (e.g., extroversion), we would compute the mean for all roommates, so there would be just one mean. However, for parent–child dyads, there may be a difference between the means, and, for the measure, there would one mean for parents and another for children. In general, if dyad members are indistinguishable (e.g., best friends) and the dyadic index relates the same two items to one another (e.g., it is a similarity or agreement index rather than an accuracy index in which one item is an "X" score and the other is a "Y" score), then the means of the two sets of items should be treated as the same. However, if either the members are distinguishable (e.g., husbands and wives) or the index is the association between two different items, as in accuracy or assumed similarity, the means may be different. Of course, in this case it is an empirical question whether the means are in fact different. A multivariate analysis of variance can be conducted on the difference scores (e.g., husband's score minus wife's score) to determine whether statistical differences exist between the two types of dyad members on the two sets of items. If the members of the dyad were parent and child, the child's score would be subtracted from the parent's score for each dyad on each item. Then we would have k scores for each dyad, and we conduct a multivariate analysis of variance that all the means of these difference scores equal zero.

To be clear, one way to adjust for stereotype accuracy is to compute the mean for each item (e.g., for distinguishable dyads a separate mean for each item is computed for men and women); then the appropriate mean is subtracted from the individual's score before we compute the dyadic index. In Table 12.3 we present the correlations for the five dyads, with and without adjusting for stereotype accuracy. The average correlation declines from .785 to .548. It is rather typical for correlations unadjusted for stereotype accuracy to be .70 or .80 and then, following adjustment, to be only .20 or .30.

Controlling for stereotype accuracy can substantially reduce the level of similarity. Consider, for example, the study by Deal, Halverson, and Wampler (1999) on child-rearing practices. They asked mothers and fathers to report on the behaviors that they employed while raising their children. These authors used the correlation coefficient as their dyadic index. Parents appeared to agree substantially in their preferences for child-rearing strategies, the average correlation being .61. However, when stereotype accuracy was removed, the agreement declined to .13, an 80% reduction of the correlation! Clearly, making adjustments for stereotype accuracy can dramatically change the conclusions that are drawn from the research.

Corrections for stereotype accuracy seem to have some benefits that are not immediately obvious. One advantage of the mean subtraction is that it tends to solve the reversal problem. If one fails to reverse items, the overall similarity score is affected very little when a correction for stereotype accuracy has been made. So, if the adjustment for stereotype accuracy is completed, the value of the dyadic index is very much the same whether items are reversed or not. However, if there is no such adjustment or variable reversal, the size of the dyadic indexes are often inflated.

A second "advantage" of adjusting for stereotype accuracy is that correlations of a dyadic index with other measures are much lower than without the adjustment. The reason for this is quite complex (see Acitelli et al., 2001, for a discussion), but it appears that the correction removes artifacts that lead to spurious correlation. As an example of this effect, in the Deal and colleagues (1999) study, many of the statistically significant correlations with the agreement measures disappeared after adjustment.

Stereotype accuracy affects the different types of dyadic indexes differently. Note that the dissimilarity measures are not affected at all if the same means for the two sets of items are subtracted. However, if different means were subtracted, then dissimilarity measures would be smaller after adjustment. The mean subtraction affects the similarity measures even more. As was true for the correlation, the average value of other similarity measures often becomes much smaller after adjustment. Moreover, adjustment may render many of the statistically significant correlations of other variables with the similarity measures nonsignificant. Thus the adjustment appears to be removing more than the bias due to stereotype accuracy.

It is possible, but unlikely, that controlling for stereotype accuracy might increase the level of agreement. Heterosexual couples may disagree substantially in their preference for leisure activities because of gender differences. On average, men may prefer to watch sports more than they like to shop, and women may like to shop more than they like to watch sports. Thus the stereotype correlation may be negative. However, once the gender stereotype is removed, similarity might increase. We know of no case in which removing stereotype accuracy increases similarity, but it is theoretically possible. If corrections for stereotype accuracy are increasingly used, we should see examples of increasing correlations after stereotype accuracy is controlled.

Funder (2001) has argued that corrections for stereotype accuracy may do more harm than good and thus should sometimes be avoided. He gives an example in which a woman exactly predicts her partner's responses. Using the correlation coefficient as the measure of accuracy, the person's accuracy is 1.00. However, after making adjustments for stereotype accuracy, the person's accuracy would likely decline. We do not accept this argument. Any type of adjustment raises some scores and lowers others. The procedure is not invalidated simply because it lowers one hypothetical score. Moreover, because stereotypes are usually shared, the correlation for this hypothetically accurate judge would probably be lowered only trivially.

Funder (2001) makes a second argument that stereotype accuracy is real accuracy in that it represents knowledge of what people are like in general, and so it should not necessarily be adjusted away. We agree that stereotype accuracy can be viewed as real accuracy, but we nevertheless think a separation in the accuracy score is valuable. We need to know how it is that people know their partners: Is it that they know people in general, or that they have unique insight into their particular partners?

DIFFERENTIAL ENDORSEMENT OF THE STEREOTYPE

Kenny and Acitelli (1994) have suggested that the effect of stereotype accuracy may vary by person. In essence, the stereotype can be viewed as reflecting a very general cultural belief that members share. However, members may vary in their endorsement of that stereotype such that some individuals endorse the stereotype more than others do. Kenny and Acitelli describe a fairly complicated method that allows for such a differential endorsement. The general stereotype is estimated by the mean response, which is then used to predict each person's response. So, if the coefficient for a person is less than 1, then the person endorses the stereotype less than others in the sample do. If the coefficient is 0, then the person does not endorse the stereotype at all.

The Kenny and Acitelli (1994) method is equivalent to the following analysis: We take the correlation between husband and wife and partial out the mean response. Thus the dyadic index correlation is a partial correlation. For an example study using this strategy, the reader might consult Krueger (1996).

We refer the interested reader to Kenny and Acitelli (1994) for a detailed description of this method. However, we have found that a simple subtraction of the means is typically just as effective as their more complicated method. Thus the more complex Kenny and Acitelli analysis appears to be unnecessary. For instance, when we performed the Kenny and Acitelli analysis for the data in Table 12.3, the average similarity was not very different using the two methods.

There is one final point to make in the case that adjustments are made for stereotype accuracy. Ordinarily, the variance of a Fisher's transformed correlation is $k - 3$ (recall that k is the number of items). If we make adjustments for stereotype accuracy (i.e., by computing partial correlations), we recommend replacing the $k - 3$ with $k - 4$. In a sense, one item or degree of freedom is lost by such an adjustment.

PSEUDO-COUPLE ANALYSIS

A simple yet very insightful idea is the pseudo-couple analysis. Corsini (1956) is usually credited with developing this analysis, in which each person is randomly paired with a person who is not his or her actual partner. If the original dyads were distinguishable, then the pseudo-couples would also distinguishable (i.e., if the original couples were marital dyads, each pseudo-couple would be a woman paired with another person's husband). The advantage of this analysis is that it can be used to determine the potential bias in a measure that is due to stereotype accuracy. For example, Corsini was interested in the similarity in couples, and he found that the average similarity correlation between real couples was .36. Notably, he also found that the correlation between pseudo-couples was .30, and he concluded that much of the similarity observed in real couples was artifactual.

One difficulty that arises with the dissimilarity indices—discrepancy, d^2, and distance—is that they have no natural chance values. Thus there is no obvious way to test whether couples are less (or more) dissimilar than would be expected by chance. However, the pseudo-couple analysis provides a way of generating the necessary chance values to conduct such a test. First, the researcher computes the dyadic index (e.g., discrepancy) for each dyad. Then the researcher randomly pairs each dyad member with another partner (i.e., creates a pseudo-couple for each individual) and computes the same measure. In this way, each real dyad has three scores: their actual discrepancy, the man's pseudo-couple discrepancy, and the woman's pseudo-couple discrepancy. The two pseudo-couple discrepancy scores are averaged together to form a dyad-level measure of pseudo-couple dissimilarity, resulting in each couple having an actual score and a pseudo-couple score. A paired t-test can be conducted to test whether the average of the actual dyadic index is different from the average index derived from the pseudo-couples. Note that if there are sufficient resources, the researcher might benefit from creating multiple pseudo-couples and averaging their scores.

There are some difficulties in pseudo-couple analysis. Perhaps the most obvious difficulty is that such analysis is computationally tedious and cumbersome. Another disadvantage of the pseudo-couple analysis is that the results depend on the pairing of persons. The results from two different pseudo-couple analyses of the same data are slightly different. The careful researcher repeats the analysis and determines whether the results change with a different random pairing. Of course, researchers should never repeat the analysis until the results look "good." The analysis chosen should be a representative analysis.

One approach might be to adapt Little and Rubin's (1987) missing-data strategy to the analysis with pseudo-couples. That is, we compute a pseudo-couple analysis five times, five being the number recommended by Little and Rubin. For each analysis, we save the dyadic index estimate, as well as the standard error of the estimate. The standard error is a combination of the standard errors from the five analyses plus the degree to which the estimates differ across the five pseudo-couple analyses. The reader should consult Little and Rubin for details.

A pseudo-couple analysis often points to potential biases in the analysis. If one finds a bias based on a pseudo-couple analysis, the careful researcher should attempt to understand what that bias is and then find some way of correcting it. For instance, frequently a pseudo-couple analysis is performed to control for stereotype accuracy. Very often, a pseudo-couple analysis is not a complete solution to a problem; rather, it is a procedure that points to how a real solution to the problem can be obtained. Of course, it may not be obvious how to correct for the bias, and so only a pseudo-couple analysis can be used.

Pseudo-couple analysis can be used as a validation tool for a methodological correction procedure (e.g., subtracting the means). That is, we attempt the analysis using both a pseudo-couple analysis and the methodological correction. If they yield the same result, then we become more confident in the methodological correction procedure.

IDIOGRAPHIC VERSUS NOMOTHETIC ANALYSIS

The major impetus for computing a dyadic index is the wish to study how that index varies from couple to couple. For instance, we may want to show that couples who understand each other are more satisfied. The focus is said to be *idiographic* in that we measure a process for each couple and see how it varies. More traditionally in research, the approach is nomothetic. With a nomothetic analysis, we assume that the process is the same for all couples.

Let us be clear what we mean practically by the difference between these two types of analyses. Imagine that we have k items for both husbands and wives and that we are interested in similarity. In an idiographic analysis, we would compute similarity for each couple by using a correlation coefficient. We could average the correlations and also could correlate them with couple characteristics (e.g., relationship satisfaction).

In a nomothetic analysis, for each of the k items, we compute the similarity between the husband and wife for each item. In this way, we get one estimate of similarity across couples for a given item. We might then examine how similarity differs across the k items.

Kenny and Winquist (2001) have extensively analyzed the differences between nomothetic and idiographic analyses. Space precludes us from giving a detailed description here of those analyses, but we can restate two of their important conclusions. First, researchers should prefer an idiographic analysis if the expectation is that the index differs by couple, and researchers should prefer a nomothetic analysis if the expectation is that the process differs by item. What if both are expected to differ? Then we have a problem, because an idiographic analysis presumes no difference by item, and a nomothetic analysis presumes no difference by couple.

Second, after suitable corrections are made (something that we explain next), an idiographic and a nomothetic analysis both yield essentially the same overall effect. That is, if we compute the average similarity of couples from an idiographic analysis and the average similarity across items in a nomothetic analysis, the two values are very close. Thus the analyses are not nearly as different as it might seem. Now what do we mean by "suitable corrections"? For the idiographic analysis, we must control for stereotype accuracy, a topic discussed earlier in the chapter. For the nomothetic analysis, we must control for differential elevation, a person's average response across the k items. This can be done simply by computing for each person a mean across the k items but subtracting the mean before computing the relationships across dyads. The details are spelled out in Kenny and Winquist (2001).

ILLUSTRATION

In this section, we illustrate an analysis using a dyadic index with a data set gathered by Acitelli and colleagues (2001).[6] These researchers gathered 14 items assessing marital values for 238 married and dating heterosexual couples. Among the values studied were "having enough money," "being sexually satisfied," "talking about things that are important," and "raising children." The value-endorsement measurements were performed by a mixture of rating and rank ordering (see Acitelli et al., 2001). The resulting scores ranged from 1 to 7 for each item.

We begin by examining the redundancy in the items. We performed this portion of the analysis separately for men and women. Three of the goals were highly correlated ("making each other feel good," "caring about each other," and "getting along"), and we averaged them to create a single goal item. We next considered item reversal. Because all the items were measured on a scale of endorsement of values, we did not think any reversal was necessary.

We computed the mean endorsement across men and women for the 11 values and found a strong correlation of .973 between the two means. This result demonstrated a cultural stereotype that some values were generally more important than others in marriage. We tested whether gender differences existed in the means. The multivariate test that there were no gender differences in all values was statistically significant, $F(10, 2370) = 3.65$, $p < .001$. To explore the gender differences, we followed up the multivariate test with a series of univariate t-tests but set alpha at .05/11, or .0045, a Bonferroni correction. Using this stringent criterion, there was only one value difference that was statistically significant: Women valued "talking about things that are important" more than men did.

In our analyses that controlled for stereotype accuracy, we subtracted the male mean from the men's value ratings and the female mean from the women's ratings. We used the correlation coefficient as the dyadic index. Using the correlation as our index implies that we do not think that level or spread differences are meaningful. Level differences are not really meaningful as, in this instance, they likely merely reflect scale usage. Spread differences might be meaningful, but we do not think it likely.

The average correlation without adjusting for stereotype accuracy is .453. We transformed the correlations to Fisher's z's and tested whether this average correlation is significantly greater than zero, and it was, $p < .001$. Thus couples are fairly similar in their values. However, when we adjust for stereotype accuracy by subtracting the mean scores, the average correlation is reduced to .210, but it is still statistically significant, $p < .001$. Thus there is evidence that men and women in heterosexual couples share similar values, but the association is rather weak—over half of the similarity is due to shared stereotypes.

Next we tested whether the similarity varied significantly across couples. The test that the unadjusted correlations only vary due to chance is $\chi^2(237) = 280.057$, which is statistically significant, $p = .029$. The test that the adjusted correlations only vary due to chance is $\chi^2(236) = 318.294$, which is also statistically significant, $p < .001$. However, the reliability of the unadjusted correlation is only .154, and the reliability of stereotype-adjusted correlation is .255. As indicated by these low reliabilities, the evidence that similarity is greater in some couples than in others is weak, and it is likely unprofitable to search for variables that correlate with similarity. Thus a moderation analysis is not warranted in this case. However, for illustration purposes, we correlated the unadjusted similarity dyadic indexes with relationship satisfaction, and that correlation is .197 for women and .203 for men, both statistically significant, $p < .002$. Adjusting for stereotype accuracy made a difference, as the correlations became much smaller, .084 for women and .102 for men, both $p > .10$. As we stated earlier, adjusting for stereotype accuracy typically reduces correlations with dyadic indexes, something that we find in these analyses.

SUMMARY AND CONCLUSIONS

In this chapter we discussed many issues involved in measuring the correspondence between sets of scores from dyad members. We described this analysis as an idiographic one, because each dyad's data are analyzed separately and a dyadic index is computed for each dyad. Before discussing specific dyadic indexes, we first overviewed a number of measurement issues that need to be considered, including equality of measurement units across items, item reversal, and redundancy of items.

Our discussion of specific dyadic indexes argued that such measures can be conceptualized as measures of similarity or dissimilarity. Correlations, covariances, intraclass correlations, and regression coefficients were described as measures of similarity, whereas discrepancy, d^2, and distance were called measures of dissimilarity. An important section of this chapter was our discussion of the three factors that influence each of these measures: level, shape, and spread. We argued that similarity in shape is typically the type of similarity that researchers want to assess, but differences in level and spread also affect estimates of the various dyadic indexes. We then discussed ways of testing means and variances of the dyadic indexes across dyads.

One major issue in the assessment of dyadic indexes is stereotype accuracy, which occurs when dyad members are similar only because both members respond in a stereotypical fashion. We discussed two approaches that can reduce the impact of stereotype accuracy. The first option was simply to subtract the sample means on the items before computing the index. The second, more complicated method was a pseudo-couple analysis. The chapter concluded with a detailed illustration.

Despite its simple naive appeal, the interpretation of a dyadic index is very complex. We are faced with a myriad of choices about what dyadic index we should compute. We also need to figure out how best to test whether the index is greater than chance, whether the variance in the index varies more than expected by chance, and how to handle stereotype accuracy. Many researchers have been misled by naively thinking that using a dyadic index is easy and straightforward. This chapter has illustrated several errors that must be avoided.

The chapter clearly illustrates that caution should be taken about the whole enterprise of computing a dyadic index. Because of the methodological traps that are detailed in this chapter, the approach is looked upon with suspicion by some (e.g., Cronbach, 1955). Very often, the methodological shortcomings of these measures can be controlled. However, once these controls are undertaken, the conclusions drawn from the research are often not nearly as interesting as they would be without these controls. We believe that with proper analyses much more may be learned through the study of dyadic indexes.

In this chapter we considered how relationships between sets of variables varied by couple. In the next two chapters, we consider over-time analyses of dyadic data. Much of the focus is on idiographic analysis; in the following two chapters we consider the analysis of within-dyad change over time, how processes of change vary across couples, and how the measure of change (i.e., a regression coefficient) can be estimated by multilevel analyses.

NOTES

1. Sometimes in dyadic research the two sets of scores come from the same person, as in the case of assumed similarity and assumed reciprocity. The methods described in this chapter can also be applied to these measures.

2. Following Kenny and Acitelli (1994), *agreement* refers to correspondence when two judges are evaluating the same object, whereas *similarity* refers to correspondence when two judges are evaluating a different object that has the same relationship to each of them. So, if parents were evaluating their child's personality, the measure would be agreement, but if they were evaluating their own personalities, it would be similarity.

3. Later in this chapter, we discuss strategies for removing stereotype accuracy, which is accomplished by having the mean of each item equal zero. Thus, if there is a desire to eliminate stereotype accuracy, a_i and b_i should be chosen so that the mean of Y is zero.

4. Later we consider the discrepancy measure that, with dichotomous measures, can be viewed as an index of disagreement.

5. In the multidimensional scaling literature, this measure is sometimes called the *city-block* measure.

6. The results from the analyses presented here differ slightly from those presented in Acitelli and colleagues (2001) because we do not consider the data that came from a person guessing the partner's values.

Over-Time Analyses
Interval Outcomes

Like our discussion of dyadic indexes in Chapter 12, the methods presented in this chapter are idiographic in nature. However, whereas the dyadic indexes were computed across items or variables for each dyad, in this chapter and the next we consider the analysis of over-time dyadic data. That is, this chapter describes analyses that are appropriate for observations that are gathered across multiple time points from both members of the dyad.

We presume in this chapter that the outcome variable is measured on an interval or ratio scale, such as marital satisfaction. In the next chapter we consider outcome variables that are dichotomous (e.g., positive vs. negative speech acts). For each of the methods described in these two chapters, the behaviors of both members of the dyad are observed repeatedly over time such that for each member there is literally a stream of recorded behavior, commonly called a *time series*. Some examples are:

- The members' responses to their partners' criticism during a conversation (Gottman, Swanson, & Swanson, 2002).
- One person's competitiveness as a response to his or her partner's competitiveness in a game situation (Cook, 1988).
- Level of aggressiveness of one person in response to the partner's level of aggressiveness (Leonard, 1984).

- Cycles in the intensity of mother–infant interactions (Lester, Hoffman, & Brazelton, 1985).
- Changes in marital satisfaction over years of marriage (Kurdek, 1998).

The analysis of over-time data from individuals is very complex, and entire books have been written on this topic. Adding the complications of dyadic data analysis makes a difficult topic even more challenging. Moreover, methodologists have not yet come to a complete consensus on which data-analytic techniques are most appropriate. Devoting only two chapters to covering this topic necessarily means that the discussion is brief and preliminary.

We adopt the following notation. For dyad i, members 1 and 2 are each measured up to T times. It need not be the case that all persons are measured at each of T time points. Generally, we assume that dyad members are distinguishable, but we occasionally consider the case of indistinguishable dyad members.

A fundamental idea in working with over-time data is the concept of *lagging*. If we have a measure of Y_{1ti} that is a measure of Y for person 1 of dyad i at time t, its lagged value would be $Y_{1,t-1,i}$ (the previous observation). Note that there is no lagged value for the first observation, Y_{11i}. If we have T observations, we have $T - 1$ observations with complete data if we lag back one time point.

There are many different types of nonindependence in over-time dyadic data. The first is the usual type of nonindependence: dyadic nonindependence. Scores from the two members of the dyad are likely nonindependent, and so the two scores, Y_{1ti} and Y_{2ti}, might well be correlated. Moreover, any parameter that is estimated for each person, for example, a slope or an intercept, might be correlated across the two members. That correlation is *usually* a positive correlation, but it might be negative.

There is a second type of nonindependence called *autocorrelation*. There is probably no more reliable finding in the social and behavioral sciences than the fact that the best predictor of future behavior is past behavior. Statistically, autocorrelation is the association between a measure taken at one point in time and the same measure taken at another point in time. As with other forms of nonindependence of observations, it can be a problem for statistical analysis. The correlation between these observations must be controlled. However, as with other analyses, nonindependence in a time-series analysis may be interesting in its own right (Warner,

1998). In this chapter and the next, we discuss many different ways to model autocorrelation.

As is true of the majority of research in which the effects of time are considered, we adopt what are called *first-order* models. For these models, any nonindependence between observations separated by two or more time points is assumed to be explained by the intermediate time point. For example, the correlation between $Y_{1,t-2,i}$ and $Y_{1,t,i}$ is explained by $Y_{1,t-1,i}$. Because the data are dyadic, it is also assumed that the correlation between $Y_{1,t-2,i}$ and $Y_{2,t,i}$ is explained by $Y_{1,t-1,i}$ and $Y_{2,t-1,i}$.

The combined presence of dyadic dependence and autocorrelation makes the analysis of over-time dyadic data especially difficult. In this chapter, we consider five types of analyses: cross-lagged regressions, the standard Actor–Partner Independence Model (APIM) growth-curve modeling, cross-spectral analyses, and nonlinear dynamic modeling. However, only the first three topics are covered extensively. We introduce each of the remaining two topics, but the reader is advised to consult other sources for details before attempting such analyses. Three of the models, cross-lagged regressions, standard APIM, and nonlinear dynamic modeling, can be considered to be longitudinal variants of the APIM. Growth-curve modeling emphasizes trends in time series, whereas cross-spectral analysis emphasizes cycles.

We again advise the reader that the models discussed in this chapter are complicated, perhaps the most intricate models discussed in this book. Moreover, our use of multilevel modeling (MLM) in this chapter is much more complicated than it was in Chapters 4 and 7. We also suggest that interested readers consult Laurenceau and Bolger (2005) for an introduction to this topic.

CROSS-LAGGED REGRESSIONS[1]

The cross-lagged regression model for distinguishable dyad members is contained in Figure 13.1. In this model, we have a person's behavior, Y, at times t and $t - 1$, for members 1 and 2. For example, the time points may be days, and Y might be the level of stress experienced by each member of the dyad. The APIM serves as the conceptual model for the cross-lagged regression analysis. The actor effects are the effects from $Y_{1,t-1}$ to $Y_{1,t}$ and from $Y_{2,t-1}$ to $Y_{2,t}$ and the partner effects are from $Y_{1,t-1}$ to $Y_{2,t}$ and from $Y_{2,t-1}$ to $Y_{1,t}$. The two equations for dyad i are

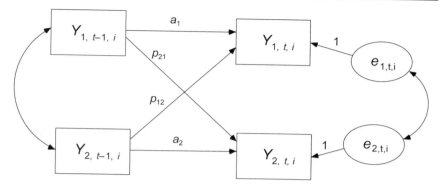

FIGURE 13.1. APIM for over-time data.

$$Y_{1ti} = c_{1i} + a_{1i}Y_{1,t-1,i} + p_{12i}Y_{2,t-1,i} + e_{1ti},$$
$$Y_{2ti} = c_{2i} + a_{2i}Y_{2,t-1,i} + p_{21i}Y_{1,t-1,i} + e_{2ti},$$

where a_{1i} and a_{2i} represent actor effects and p_{21i} and p_{12i} represent partner effects. Actor effects are interpreted as stability effects, and partner effects represent cross-partner influence, or reciprocity (Cook & Kenny, 2005). Because the data are measured over time, the model can be estimated for each dyad, which is the reason the paths in the model are subscripted with an i. We adopt the convention that a_{1i} refers to the stability for member 1 in dyad i and that a_1 refers to the average value of the actor effects for member 1 (e.g., for husbands) across dyads. There are six parameters for each dyad i:

- Actor effect for person 1, or a_{1i}.
- Actor effect for person 2, or a_{2i}.
- Partner effect from person 1 to person 2, or p_{12i}.
- Partner effect from person 2 to person 1, or p_{21i}.
- Intercept for person 1, or c_{1i}.
- Intercept for person 2, or c_{2i}.

Each of these terms may vary across dyads. Accordingly, if a_1 varies, then that implies that for some 1's (e.g., some husbands), there is more stability than there is for other 1's. Similarly, there might be variance in the partner effects such that individuals in some dyads may be more responsive or reactive to their partners than are individuals in other dyads. Finally, the intercepts may also vary.

It is very important in an over-time model to make certain that we have centered or subtracted off the mean of $Y_{1,t-1}$ and $Y_{2,t-1}$, making sure we use a common value (i.e., the same value is subtracted from person 1's data and person 2's data). Thus we compute a mean for both Y_1 and Y_2 and average them. With centered values for the lagged values of Y, the intercepts estimate the average or typical value. Centering is also important to make the variance of the six effects interpretable.

These six terms (two actor, two partner, and two intercepts) may also covary with each other. For instance, the intercepts of member 1 and member 2 might be correlated. In principle, there is a six-by-six variance–covariance matrix of terms. Later we discuss different patterns of covariation among these effects.

The two APIM equations for each dyad also include two error terms, one for person 1 and one for person 2, and these two errors might be correlated. This correlation between the errors, or r_{ee}, tests a key question because it measures the extent to which the two dyad members are especially similar to one another at a particular time point. It is important to distinguish the correlation of the intercepts, or r_{cc}, from the correlation of the errors. For example, suppose that stress is measured each day for husbands and wives. Then r_{cc} would measure the extent to which husbands who experience more stress *overall* have wives who also experience more stress *overall*. In contrast, r_{ee} would measure the extent to which, if the husband experiences more stress *on a particular day* than one would expect given his prior value and his wife's prior value, then his wife would also experience more stress *on that same day* than one would expect given her prior value and her husband's prior value. Thus the unit for r_{cc} is the person, and the unit for r_{ee} is time within person. Note that either correlation can be negative, and, ideally, the statistical analysis procedure should allow for that possibility.

The saturated cross-lagged regression model is quite complex, having a total of 8 (the 6 effects and 2 errors) variances and 16 covariances (15 for the effects and 1 for the errors). There are also 6 fixed effects: the 2 average actor effects, the 2 average partner effects, and the 2 average intercepts. Thus the total number of potential parameters is 30. However, simpler versions of the model can be estimated. First, it may be the case that the actor, partner, and intercepts do not vary by dyad. For instance, the partner effects may be the same for all persons, and their partner variances would be set to zero. Alternatively, we can set pairs of variances, pairs of covariances, or pairs of fixed effects equal. For example, wife-to-husband partner variances might be set equal if wives do not differ in the degree to which they influence their husbands. If variances are set equal, it may make sense to force certain covariances to be equal. As discussed in Chapter 4, we can test whether setting a pair of variances or covariances equal is empirically supported by comparing the change in the deviances for the models with and without the equality constraint. In the extreme case, in which we want to treat dyad members as indistinguishable, we would have just 3 fixed parameters (intercept, actor, and partner effects), 4 variances (intercept, actor, partner, and error), and 10 covariances. Thus the complete model with 30 parameters would be reduced to a model with only 17 parameters.

Analysis Model

In over-time data from dyads, we have three factors: time, person, and dyad. Researchers often make the mistake of considering these data to be a three-level nested model in which time points are nested within persons and persons are nested within dyads. The problem is that time and person are usually crossed, not nested. That is, for a given dyad, the level of time is the same for the two persons at each time point. If the three-level nested model is mistakenly assumed, then the correlation between the two partner's intercepts, r_{cc}, is constrained to be positive (because it is estimated as a variance), and the correlation between the two members' errors at each time, r_{ee}, is assumed to be zero.

An alternative approach that does not force these constraints is an extension of the two-intercept model described in Chapters 4 and 7. To apply the two-intercept model in this context, two dummy variables are created. One dummy, what we call M1 (member 1), is set to 1 when the score is obtained from member 1 and set to 0 otherwise. The other, what we call M2 (member 2), is set to 1 when the data are obtained from member 2 and to 0 otherwise. These two terms are then multiplied by the predictor variables (i.e., the actor's and partner's scores for the prior trial). Consequently, for every point in time at which member 1's outcome is the dependent variable (Y_{1t}), member 1's prior score ($Y_{1,t-1}$) is one of the independent variables (representing the actor variable), and member 2's prior score ($Y_{2,t-1}$) is the other independent variable (representing the partner variable). Correspondingly, for every point in time at which member 2's outcome is the dependent variable (Y_{2t}), member 2's prior score ($Y_{2,t-1}$) and member 1's prior score ($Y_{1,t-1}$) are, respectively, the actor and partner variables. In this way, actor and partner effects can be estimated for the two members.

To allow for correlated errors, we create a variable that takes on the values 1 and −1 to contrast the two dyad members. We call this variable MM. Recall that in Chapter 7, when our distinguishing variable was gender, we created a variable MALE, which was 1 for male partners and 0 for female partners. We also created a similar variable, FEMALE. We then noted that a simpler analysis could be done using the variable GENDER, coded −1 for men and 1 for women. In the current discussion, M1 is analogous to MALE, M2 is analogous to FEMALE, and MM is analogous to GENDER.

Computer Programs

In this section, we discuss the use of MLM programs to estimate the cross-lagged regression model. We first note that we are creating a data file in which each unit refers to a "person time point." If we have 50 couples measured at 10 time points, we would begin with 1,000 units.

The first step involves creating a variable that we call OBS_ID, which creates a unique code for each pair of observations obtained from each dyad at each time point. This code is the same for the two dyad members at a particular point in time, but it varies across dyads so that it ranges from 1 (the observation identification number for dyad 1 at time 1) to the number of time points times the number of dyads (i.e., the observation identification number of the last dyad at their last time point). The observation identification code for each pair of observations can be computed using the formula OBS_ID = TIME_ID + NT(DYAD_ID − 1), where NT is the number of time points, TIME_ID is a variable that codes for the time point of the observation (which varies from 1 to T), and DYAD_ID is the dyad number. Therefore, if 50 couples are measured at 10 times, there would be a total of 1,000 observations, and OBS_ID would then vary from 1 to 500. However, because one time point for each dyad is lost due to lagging, only 900 observations are actually used in the analysis.

Each data record would contain Y_t, $Y_{a,t-1}$, $Y_{p,t-1}$, M1, M2, MM, DYAD_ID, TIME_ID, and OBS_ID, where Y_t is the score at time t, $Y_{a,t-1}$ is the prior score for the person, and $Y_{p,t-1}$ is the prior score of the person's partner. Thus the data set is structured in a time-as-unit format, sometimes called a *person–period data set*, with one record for each time point for each dyad member. As we stated earlier, the lagged values of Y should be centered, that is, have the grand mean subtracted from them.

There are six variances in the model, and it may be that some of them are very small. Small variances create estimation difficulties for MLM programs. For instance, if there were little or no variance in the partner effects (i.e., the partner effect is essentially the same for all dyads), the computer program may not run. Sometimes the program runs for a very long time but does not converge (i.e., it fails to yield a solution). This is what typically happens with SAS, MLwiN, and HLM. At other times, the program converges, but there are warnings in the solution. This is typically what happens with SPSS. To obtain a meaningful solution, we need to trim the terms that have very small variances out of the model. Typically, problems in estimation are due to the presence of too many terms in the model (Singer & Willett, 2003).

We are faced with a "catch 22." For the program to run, we need to eliminate terms that have zero variance. However, to find those terms, we need to run the program. We suggest the following approach to get around this difficulty: First, the researcher runs a saturated model, a model with all of the terms. If it runs, then there is no problem. However, if there are estimation difficulties, we need to consider running a simpler model. A model with just a few random terms or a model in which the covariances are set to zero (although that option is not currently available with HLM6) can be run.

SPSS

In Chapters 4 and 7 we discussed the estimation of multilevel models for dyadic data with SPSS. When time is added to the model, the SPSS syntax becomes more complex:

```
MIXED
    Y BY MM WITH TIME_ID YA YP
    /FIXED = MM TIME_ID MM*YA MM*YP | NOINT
    /PRINT = SOLUTION TESTCOV
    /RANDOM MM MM*YA MM*YP | SUBJECT(DYAD_ID)
        COVTYPE(UN)
    /REPEATED = MM | SUBJECT(DYAD_ID*OBS_ID)
        COVTYPE(CSH) .
```

where the variables are as follows: Y is the outcome variable, YA is the lagged value of Y for the actor, and YP is the lagged value of Y for the partner. Note that this SPSS code uses MM and is analogous to the syntax for the two-intercept model in Chapter 7 that uses GENDER rather than

MALE and FEMALE. In the fixed section, the MM*YA term enables estimation of separate actor effects for the two members, and the MM*YP enables estimation of separate partner effects for the two members. Note also that TIME_ID is in the model. It represents a linear trend in the data, and it should be centered.

In the RANDOM statement, the corresponding terms (MM*YA and MM*YP) enable estimation of variance in the actor and partner effects. The COVTYPE(UN) allows for the six random effects to be correlated. Notice that the time effect is not random. When we discuss growth-curve models later in the chapter, the time effect is random. The final statement is the most complicated statement. It states that for each dyad at each time, the two observations might well be correlated. Using CS allows for that correlation to be negative, and the H of the CSH allows for heterogeneous variances. Instead of the CSH option, we could have also used the unrestricted, or UN, option.

SAS

Not surprisingly, the code for SAS is similar to that for SPSS. Again, we create an observation identification variable, or OBS_ID = TIME_ID + NT(DYAD_ID − 1), where NT is the number of time points. The SAS code is:

```
PROC MIXED COVTEST;
CLASS DYAD_ID OBS_ID MM;
MODEL Y = MM TIME_ID YA*MM YP*MM / NOINT S
   DDFM = SATTERTH ;
RANDOM MM YA*MM YP*MM / SUB=DYAD_ID;
REPEATED MM / TYPE=CSH SUBJECT=OBS_ID R;
```

Because there is no intercept in the model (NOINT), the program estimates separate intercepts for the distinguishing variable (MM), as well as separate actor and partner effects.

HLM

For the computer program HLM, two data sets must be created. First, there must be an observation or a time data set similar to the one created for SPSS and SAS. In addition, there must be a dyad data set that includes two dummy variables for the two dyad members, what we have called M1 and M2. Member would be treated as a repeated measure within this formulation. We can run the two-intercept model that we described in Chapter 4 with HLM. We advise centering the lagged Y variables and time before reading them into HLM and not to allow the program to center the variables.

MLwiN

One of the main advantages of the computer program MLwiN is that we can place constraints on the covariance matrix. It is easy to set values to zero and to set values equal to each other. The equality constraints are particularly useful in testing differences between distinguishable members. Currently, we see this program as the most flexible program for the analysis of dyadic over-time data. However, as we discussed in Chapter 4, it is not an easy program to use.

Structural Equation Modeling

Although we have emphasized the use of MLM, SEM can also be used to estimate dyadic over-time models. This estimation technique is particularly useful when the number of time points is relatively small, and it can be used for as few as two (Cook & Kenny, 2005). With this technique, we do not allow for actor and partner effects to vary by person or dyad. However, we can allow for actor and partner effects to vary between different pairs of waves; for example, the actor effect from wave 1 to wave 2 may be greater than that from wave 2 to wave 3. Cook and Kenny (2005) illustrate the possibility that actor effects (i.e., stabilities) increase over time; that is, persons change less as they age.

Example

We analyze a data set, gathered by Leonard (1984), of dyads that were randomly paired. In the subset of the data considered here, one member of 10 male dyads was given 1.5 ounces of vodka for every 40 pounds of body weight, enough to become legally intoxicated. The other member was not given any alcohol, and thus the dyad members can be distinguished by their alcohol levels. They were then put in a situation in which they chose the level of electric shock to administer to each other, the shock intensity being rated from 1 to 10. There were a total of 25 trials. The data set is rather small, only 10 dyads, and its size creates estimation problems.

First, we create a data set in which the observations are gathered for each person in a dyad at each time; thus, for a data set with 10 dyads, each giving 25 trials, the number of records in the data set would be $2 \times 10 \times 25 = 500$. The observed variable is SHOCK level. Next, we create two new variables using the lag transform function. One of these variables is the person's prior behavior at time $t - 1$, ASHOCK, and the other variable is the person's partner's prior behavior at time $t - 1$, PSHOCK. We then delete from the data set all time-1 observations, because at time 1 there is no prior behavior.

For this analysis we create three dummy variables: INTOX, which is 1 for the intoxicated dyad member and 0 for the sober member; SOBER, which is 1 for the sober person and 0 for the intoxicated person; and INTOXSOB, which is 1 for the intoxicated person and −1 for the sober person. We compute an observation identification number as described earlier (OBS_ID), and we also have a TRIAL_ID variable that varies from 1 to 25. The variable DYAD_ID varies from 1 to 10. As mentioned, the observed variable is shock level, or SHOCK. We computed the mean SHOCK level across all the dyads and all the times ($M = 5.34$) and subtracted that value from the lagged values (i.e., we mean-centered ASHOCK and PSHOCK). Note that we subtracted the same value from both the intoxicated and the sober members. Even though dyad members are distinguishable, we still want the units of measurement of the shock variables to be the same. We centered the TRIAL_ID variable (i.e., subtracted 13 from each TRIAL_ID score). Centering the predictor variables is crucial, as we have random intercepts and we want to interpret those intercepts as if they reflect the average response (i.e., the mean) of each person.

We have the traditional APIM framework (see Figure 13.1, as well as Figure 7.1), in which the horizontal paths are actor effects (a_S and a_I) and the crossing paths are partner effects, with p_{SI} being the path from the intoxicated to the sober member and p_{IS} being the path from the sober member to the intoxicated member. For the Leonard (1984) data, we can view the partner effect as a measure of retaliation: If the intoxicated member gave the sober member a strong shock, does the sober member respond with a strong shock at the next trial? Because the members are distinguishable, we can test whether the stability effects, a_S and a_I, are the same and whether the partner effects, or retaliation effects, are the same, $p_{SI} = p_{IS}$. Moreover, we can test whether the intercepts for the sober and intoxicated individuals are equal, a test that evaluates whether the sober or intoxicated member administered more severe shocks. All of these effects are fixed effects.

We are estimating a plethora of random effects for the model. They include:

- Variance of the actor effect of the sober member, or the variance of a_S.
- Variance of the actor effect of the intoxicated member, or the variance of a_I.
- Variance of the partner effect of the sober member, or the variance of p_{SI}.
- Variance of the partner effect of the intoxicated member, or the variance of p_{IS}.
- Variance of the intercept for the sober member.
- Variance of the intercept for the intoxicated member.

Moreover, the preceding six terms can be correlated, resulting in 15 different covariances. Additionally, there are two error variances:

- Error variance for the sober member.
- Error variance for the intoxicated member.

Finally, these two error variances can be correlated. Accordingly, the complete model contains 8 variances and 16 covariances. The reader should be happy that we did not treat trial as random (but we do so later when we consider growth-curve models).

We first estimated the full model with the 8 variances and 16 covariances. However, we had considerable difficulty fitting such a model. When we ran the model with SAS and HLM6, it never converged, and within SPSS standard errors for some parameters could not be estimated. We also had estimation difficulties with MLwiN and could not get the program to converge. When we estimated a model in which the six effects were uncorrelated, we noted that the variances of the partner effects were smaller than the other effects. Thus it appears that the two partner effects do not vary by dyad. We then estimated a model in which actor effects and intercepts were random (i.e., had a variance) but partner effects were not. When we ran this model we noted that the actor effects were essentially uncorrelated with intercept effects. So in our final model the partner effect was not random, and there were no correlations between intercepts and actor effects. The results of this model, as estimated by SPSS and SAS, are presented in the first column of Table 13.1. The results using MLwiN were very similar, but not exactly identical, to those from SPSS and SAS. The SAS code for the run is:

TABLE 13.1. Fixed Effects from the Cross-Lagged Regression Analysis of the Leonard (1984) Study

	Estimate	
Fixed effects	Distinguishable	Indistinguishable
Effect of trial	−0.032*	−0.028*
Intercept		5.395*
Sober	5.520*	
Intoxicated	5.484*	
Actor effect		0.216*
Sober to sober	0.252*	
Intoxicated to intoxicated	0.188†	
Partner effect		0.271*
Sober to intoxicated	0.234*	
Intoxicated to sober	0.316*	

†$p < .10$; *$p < .05$.

```
PROC MIXED COVTEST;
CLASS DYAD_ID OBS_ID INTOXSOB;
MODEL SHOCK = TRIAL_ID INTOXSOB INTOXSOB*ASHOCK
    INTOXSOB*PSHOCK / NOINT S DDFM=SATTERTH;
RANDOM INTOXSOB / SUB=DYAD_ID TYPE=UN GCORR;
RANDOM INTOXSOB*ASHOCK / SUB=DYAD_ID TYPE=UN GCORR;
REPEATED INTOXSOB / TYPE=CSH SUBJECT=OBS_ID R;
```

Note that we include two RANDOM statements, one for the intercepts and one for the actor effects, each with a TYPE=UN, or unstructured covariance matrix. This allows the intercepts to be correlated and the actor effects to be correlated while constraining the intercepts to be uncorrelated with the actor effects. We also add in the RANDOM statements the option GCORR, which gives the correlation of the effects.

To test whether there were differences between the intoxicated and the sober member, we reparameterized the model by creating interaction terms. This required the following SAS syntax:

```
PROC MIXED COVTEST;
CLASS DYAD_ID OBS_ID INTOXSOB;
MODEL SHOCK = TRIAL_ID INTOXSOB ASHOCK INTOXSOB*ASHOCK
    PSHOCK INTOXSOB*PSHOCK / SDDFM=SATTERTH;
RANDOM INT INTOXSOB / SUB=DYAD_ID TYPE=UN GCORR;
RANDOM ASHOCK INTOXSOB*ASHOCK / SUB=DYAD_ID TYPE=UN
    GCORR;
REPEATED INTOXSOB /TYPE=CSH SUBJECT=OBS_ID R;
```

In this formulation, we do not estimate two intercepts (note that we no longer include the NOINT option), but rather we have all effects interact with the INTOXSOB variable. We note that the two models are the same in that the parameters from one solution can be derived from the other. We also note that the deviances (see Chapter 4) of the two models are identical. We use the first model to obtain estimates for the sober and the intoxicated members, and we use the second model to determine whether there are statistically significant differences for the two types of members.

In all the analyses, we controlled for the linear effect of trial (i.e., the effect of TRIAL_ID, which was centered and which assesses the tendency to administer more or less severe shocks over time). The shock level declined by about 0.76 units across the 25 trials.

In Table 13.1 we see from the intercepts that the sober and intoxicated members shocked each other at about the same level. There is no statistically significant difference between these two average shock levels, $p = .90$. As indicated by the actor effects, there was some degree of stability in both members' behavior: If a member shocked his partner at a high level in the previous trial, then he persisted on the next trial. Again, there is no statistically significant difference in the stability of the intoxicated and the sober persons, $p = .58$. The partner effects indicate that both members retaliated against their partners. It appears that the sober members retaliated more, but the difference between the two partner effects is not statistically significant, $p = .25$. Note also there is some indication of a couple-oriented model in that actor and partner effects have nearly the same value. Aggression begets aggression, whether the aggression comes from oneself or the other.

In terms of the random components, we see in Table 13.2 that considerable variability exists in the intercepts for both the sober and the intoxicated members. Some people tend to shock their partners more than others. Interestingly, there is a very strong correlation of .975 in these "individual" differences across trials. Thus we conclude that the differences are due to dyad much more than they are due to the person. Having seen these results, we could assume that the two intercepts are equal and then estimate the model with a dyadic intercept and single dyadic variance rather than two individual intercepts and their covariance. To accomplish this in SAS or SPSS, we would not estimate an MM (INTOXSOB) main effect, we would drop the NOINT option, and we would allow the intercept to be a random variable across dyads.

There is some correlation between actor effects: If the sober member is stable, the intoxicated member is also stable. However, the correlation is not statistically significant. Note also that there is little or no correlation

TABLE 13.2. Random Effects from the Cross-Lagged Regression Analysis of the Leonard (1984) Study

	Estimate	
Random effect	Distinguishable	Indistinguishable
Variance		
Intercept		2.359*
Sober	1.519†	
Intoxicated	3.035*	
Actor effect		0.058*
Sober to sober	0.082†	
Intoxicated to intoxicated	0.048†	
Error		1.856*
Sober	1.883*	
Intoxicated	1.813*	
Correlations		
Intercepts	.975†	.951*
Actor effects	.433	.603
Errors	−.019	−.036

†$p < .10$; *$p < .05$.

between the errors. Thus, once the intercepts are controlled, there is no correlation in shock levels for any given trial.

We also present in Tables 13.1 and 13.2 the estimates of the effects of treating the dyad members as if they were indistinguishable, using the program MLwiN to estimate these models. We placed equality constraints where appropriate. When we estimated a model in which there was variance due to the partner effects, that variance was only 0.001; we again set the partner variance to zero. In Table 13.2, we see the estimates of the random effects for the two members. The pattern is similar to that for distinguishable members. The largest systematic variance is in the intercepts: Some persons are more aggressive than others. However, given the strong correlation between dyad members, it is more accurate to say that some dyads are more aggressive than others.

OVER-TIME STANDARD APIM

In the previous section, we have a version of the APIM in which the prior Y's cause the current Y's. In the standard APIM only the X's, either current or prior, cause the current Y's. Consider the following examples:

- Married couples guess each other's emotions at various times (Neyer, Banse, & Asendorpf, 1999; Wilhelm & Perrez, 2004).
- The stress that couples experience during the day determines their moods at night (Thompson & Bolger, 1999).

This model contains actor effects (e.g., Does my stressful day lower my mood?) and partner effects (e.g., Does my stressful day lower my partner's mood?). Such models are very common in diary studies.

There are several issues in analysis of the over-time standard APIM. They include the specification of error structure and measurement of the causal variable. We discuss each in some detail.

Specification of Error Structure

In some ways, the analysis of the standard APIM is no different from the cross-lagged regression model. We have six random effects of two actors, two partners, and two intercepts. We need to center the Xs (i.e., subtract off the average of two means across couples and time). We could combine the cross-lagged regression model with the standard APIM, but such a model may be too complex to run. It would have 10 random variables and 45 covariances. There is, however, one key difference between the standard APIM and the cross-lagged model, and that is the problem of autocorrelation in the errors.

In the cross-lagged regression model, prior Y causes current Y. The actor effect models the autocorrelation in the data. In the cross-lagged model, the pattern of autocorrelation is called a first-order *autoregressive model*. In the standard APIM design, the value of Y at time $t - 1$ is not a predictor of Y at time t. Consequently, the standard APIM needs some way to model the correlation between the current Y and the Y that immediately preceded it, and one way of doing that is to allow the errors to be autocorrelated.

One way of modeling the correlations of the error is the model initially suggested by Bolger and Shrout (in press). In this model, the error structure is defined as a lag 1 autoregressive structure, and in SAS this is accomplished by the TYPE = UN@AR(1) option in the repeated statement. The SAS code for a generic APIM follows. In this code, MM is the variable that codes for the distinguishing factor (e.g., 1, −1 for husbands and wives), XA is the actor's predictor score at a particular time point, XP is the partner's predictor score at that time point, TIME_ID is the variable that specifies the particular time point, and Y is the outcome for the actor at that same time point.

```
PROC MIXED COVTEST;
CLASS DYAD_ID MM TIME_ID;
MODEL Y = MM MM*XA MM*XP TRIAL_ID / S DDFM=SATTERTH;
RANDOM MM MM*XA MM*XP / TYPE = UN G GCORR SUB =DYAD_ID;
REPEATED MM TIME_ID / SUB = DYAD_ID TYPE = UN@AR(1);
```

Note that TRIAL_ID equals TIME_ID. So far as we know, this model cannot be estimated using any other MLM program.

Measurement of the Causal Variable

Consider a study that examines the effect of work stress on mood, both participant mood and partner mood. We might measure the work stress each day and see whether it affects the person's mood that night. However, it is possible, and even likely, that stress from the prior day can carry over to the next day. That is, it might be the accumulated stress that causes mood. Therefore, instead of using today's stress as the predictor, we should use the stress of the previous 3 days, or perhaps a weighted average of 4 days (e.g., .5 times the current day plus .33 times the previous day plus .08 times each of the 2 days preceding). Thus a key concern is how to measure the X variable. The investigator needs to carefully consider how to compute the X variable and not just routinely use current or prior X.

If X were a lagged composite, we would be lagging back over time. Whenever we lag, we lose observations. Thus, if we have T observations for a dyad and we lag back 3 days, we would have $T - 3$ observations for analysis.

Example

We use the Leonard (1984) data as an example, even though they are not entirely appropriate (because the data really only contain the observations for Y and there is no X variable), but it can illustrate the SAS syntax. We estimate the partner effects, the effect of partner's shock level on the previous trial, but not the actor effect. The nonindependence of observations is handled by the autoregressive structure. The SAS code is:

```
PROC MIXED COVTEST ;
CLASS DYAD_ID INTOXSOB TIME_ID;
MODEL SHOCK = TRIAL_ID INTOXSOB INTOXSOB*PSHOCK /
    NOINT S DDFM=SATTERTH;
RANDOM INTOXSOB / SUB=DYAD_ID TYPE=UN GCORR;
REPEATED INTOXSOB TIME_ID / TYPE=UN@AR(1)
    SUBJECT=DYAD_ID R;
```

The partner effect for the sober member is .269 and for the intoxicated member is .352, and both are statistically significant. The autoregressive coefficient is .088 and is marginally significant. This marginally significant coefficient indicates that the residual for the amount of shock administered at a particular time, controlling for how much the partner shocked the person at the previous time point, is correlated with the residual from the previous time point. The correlation between the intercepts is .920, $p = $ .053, and between the errors is $-.045$, $p = .49$.

GROWTH-CURVE ANALYSIS

In the prior two sections we examined predictive over-time effects. In this and the next section, we do not consider causal effects, but rather we assume that change occurs in a regular, deterministic fashion. Consider the variable of marital satisfaction, measured on heterosexual couples every 6 months over a period of 2 years, resulting in five measurements. We could fit a straight line to each husband's satisfaction scores. Like any regression line, there are two parameters, a slope and an intercept. The slope represents the rate of change per unit; for example, how much more or less satisfied the husband becomes for each year of marriage. Some husbands may have a negative slope, indicating that they are becoming less satisfied. Others are becoming more satisfied and have a positive slope. Still others may have a zero slope because they showed no change over the course of the study.

The central idea of growth-curve analysis is that we fit a function to a set of observations. The simplest function is a linear, or straight-line, function. With that function, each person has a slope and an intercept parameter. With dyadic data, we can examine the correlation of these parameters. For instance, in couples in which the husband's marital satisfaction is declining, we can determine whether the wife's satisfaction is also declining.

There are two alternative methods of estimating growth-curve models: SEM and MLM. SEM is easiest when dyad members are distinguishable (though see Olsen & Kenny, 2006, for an example of SEM growth-curve model with indistinguishable dyad members), when the temporal spacing is the same for each member, and when there are not too many time points. Before we describe each method, we first discuss two central issues in growth-curve analysis: definition of time zero and functional form.

Definition of Time Zero

The intercept represents the level of response predicted for "time zero." The researcher must decide how to define the zero point in the time variable. Very often it is set at the time of the first measurement. However, there are alternatives that should be considered. One possibility is to define time zero as the middle of the study; another is to define time zero as the end of the study. Time zero can also be extrapolated to some idealized point before or after measurements were made; for example, the time at which the couple was married. In this case, time zero would be a different point in real time for each couple. Sometimes in developmental research, time zero is defined as the time of birth, or, in other cases, the time of starting school. The researcher has considerable flexibility in determining time zero. The important point to remember is that the first time point need not automatically be time zero.

The choice of time zero affects not only the average intercept but also the variance in the intercepts and the covariance of the slope and intercept. It does not, however, affect the mean of the slopes or the variance of the slopes. Because the choice of time zero affects both the variance of intercepts and the covariance of slope and intercept, it is inadvisable to set either the variance of the intercept or the covariance of slope and intercept to zero. These parameters should be kept in the model even if tests of statistical significance for these two components are nonsignificant. However, if there is evidence that the slopes have zero variance and, accordingly, the slope variance is set to zero, it would be permissible to test the intercept variance and trim it out of the model if is not statistically significant.

We could choose time zero as the point that minimizes the variance in the intercepts (see Singer & Willett, 2003, pp. 186–187). Note that if there is a time point at which the intercepts have zero variance, we can interpret that point as a point of *common origin*. The time point in which the variance of the intercepts is at a minimum is the time of $C(a,b)/V(b)$, where $C(a,b)$ is the covariance of intercept and slope and $V(b)$ is the variance of the slope. We take the time measure and subtract $C(a,b)/V(b)$ from it, and zero becomes the time point at which the intercept variance is at a minimum.

Functional Form

Typically, growth-curve models are assumed to be linear. That is, the relationship between time and the outcome is a straight line. However, linearity is only an assumption, and the researcher needs to examine this assumption very critically. The researcher should consider alternative functional forms and should statistically evaluate whether there are detectable deviations from linearity. Later in the chapter we discuss how to test statistically for nonlinearity. In this section, we consider alternative functional forms.

There are three ways in which to allow for nonlinearity in the growth curve: (1) to transform the outcome variable, (2) to transform the time variable, and (3) to include nonlinear terms through the use of polynomials. We discuss each in turn.

Transformation of the Outcome

If the relationship between T, time, and Y, the outcome, is not a straight line, one possibility is to turn it into a straight line through the transformation of the outcome variable. Let us consider three examples. First, if the outcome measure is a count (e.g., number of health service visits), one might compute the square root of Y or take the logarithm of $Y + 0.5$ to create a functional relationship between T and transformed Y that is relatively linear. Second, if the outcome is a proportion (e.g., the number of pills taken divided by the number of pills prescribed), one might want to consider a logit or log odds transform. In this case, we compute $\ln[p/(1 - p)]$, where "ln" is the natural logarithm and p is the proportion. A logit removes the floor of 0 and the ceiling of 1 in a proportion. Third, if the outcome is a rate, for example, the number of physician visits during a 1-year period, we might want to consider the reciprocal of the rate measure, or $1/Y$. Such a transformation would measure the time interval between visits. Singer and Willett (2003) provide an extensive discussion of possible transformations of the outcome variable.

Transformation of Time

To straighten a nonlinear relationship, we can transform the predictor variable instead of the outcome variable. For instance, instead of computing the square root of the Y, we could instead compute the square of T. Basically, if the function is accelerating (i.e., more change at later time points), T would need to be raised to a power larger than 1 (i.e., squared), but if the function is decelerating (i.e., more change at earlier time points), T would need to be raised to a power less than 1 (e.g., square rooted or reciprocal). The potential advantage of transforming T instead of Y is that the results may well be more interpretable because the outcome variable is left in its more "natural metric."

Consider the functional form of a negative exponential[2] in which the outcome variables decelerate toward an asymptote. To model this non-linearity, we can create exponential time (Kenny et al., 2004). We transform T by the function $-p^T$, where p is a specific value between 0 and 1. One way of approximating p would be to take the ratio of the amount of change from time 1 to time 2 to the amount of change from time 0 to time 1. Thus p measures the rate of deceleration. Greater values of p correspond to weaker deceleration. The researcher can experiment with different values and determine what value best describes the pattern of change. Note that with exponential time, time 0 becomes the asymptote. Consequently, for this growth model, the intercept refers to the theoretical limit that each person or dyad would eventually reach if they lived forever. The slope would represent the total amount of change from the beginning of the study to the asymptote.

A situation for which we might expect exponential change occurs when regression toward the mean (see Campbell & Kenny, 1999, especially Chapter 8) is plausible. Because scores in many dyadic studies are selected to be extreme, regression toward the mean is all but inevitable. Consider the example of marital satisfaction measured over time. For instance, it is known that for the typical couple, satisfaction declines after marriage (e.g., Kurdek, 1998). Because satisfaction is relatively high at the point of marriage, much of this decline can be attributed to regression toward the mean. As another example, marital satisfaction is also often tracked in marital therapy. Because marital satisfaction is relatively low at the point at which couples enter therapy, much of the improvement of couples in therapy is also due to regression toward the mean and not due to the effects of therapy. In both of these cases, we would expect regression toward the mean—in the first example, downward (the loss of newlywed bliss), and in the latter case, upward (hitting bottom and going to therapy). If regression toward the mean is at all plausible, the researcher should consider exponential growth or decay. Note that regression to the mean over time implies nonlinear growth because there is more change earlier than later.

Polynomial Regression

The standard approach to nonlinearity (e.g., Francis, Fletcher, Stuebing, Davidson, & Thompson, 1991) is to add polynomials to the model, for example, the square of time and the cube of time. Thus, if we denote time as T, we enter T, T^2, and T^3 in the model. Such an approach is costly in terms of parameters because we would have to estimate the means of each component, as well as their variances and all of their covariances. For instance, if we allow a squared term, we add three parameters; and we if we allow for a squared and a cubed term, we add seven parameters.

The difficulty with fitting polynomials, in addition to the large number of parameters, is that it is an empirically based method of estimating a growth curve and not a theoretical one. Because the approach capitalizes on chance, the probability that replication would fail is increased. Given a new sample, the findings may change dramatically when polynomials are used to model nonlinearity.

Structural Equation Modeling

Both SEM and MLM have been proposed for the analysis of growth-curve data. The major advantage of MLM is that the number of time points and the spacing between time points can be different for each dyad, whereas SEM performs best when the spacing is the same for each dyad. In this section we introduce growth-curve models within SEM.

Figure 13.2 presents a path diagram for a model of growth in husbands' and wives' marital satisfaction scores measured at three points in time. The essential features of this model are the four latent variables, represented by large circles; the six observed variables, represented by squares; and the six residual factors, represented by the small circles. The model specifies that each of the observed variables is caused by three factors: (1) an intercept, or constant; (2) a rate of change, or a slope; and (3) unknown residual causes. There are several correlations in the model. As is typical in growth-curve models, the intercept and slope are correlated. Also, slope and intercept factors are correlated across members. Finally, with dyadic data, it makes sense to correlate the errors of the same measure at the same time from two different persons. All nine correlations are represented in Figure 13.2 by curved lines.

As is typical of SEM for dyadic data, we analyze a dyadic data set with all six measures in each record (H1, H2, H3, W1, W2, and W3). For growth-curve models, we analyze the variance–covariance matrix and the means. Notice that each of the loadings for the latent variable intercepts are all fixed at 1.0. To interpret this intercept value, we need to know what time zero is. Time zero is determined by the time point that has a zero loading on the slope factor. We see in Figure 13.2 that there are zero load-

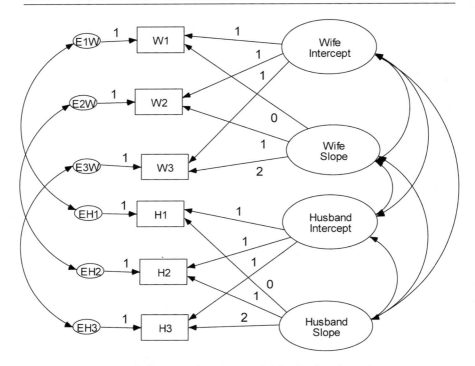

FIGURE 13.2. Growth-curve model for husbands and wives.

ings on the slope factors at time 1. Under this specification, the mean of the intercept factor refers to the predicted marital satisfaction at the first time point. If we were to change the slope loadings to -1, 0, and $+1$, the mean of the intercept factor would refer to the expected value of the middle wave. Finally, if we were to change the slope loadings to -2, -1, and 0, the mean of the intercept factor would refer to the expected value for the last wave. Recall that there is a variance associated with the intercept factor that represents the degree to which, for example, husbands (or wives) differ from dyad to dyad in the average value of their satisfaction at time zero. By making changes in the designation of time zero, the variance of the intercept changes, as does the covariance of slope and intercept. In fact, by changing time zero, it is easy to change the sign of the covariance between slope and intercept (see Singer & Willett, 2003).

To interpret the latent variable for slope, it is necessary to examine the factor loadings of that factor. What is not explained by the constant factor (i.e., the intercept) is the degree to which the three observed variables differ from each other, or, in other words, whether husbands' marital satisfaction changes over time. This information is captured by the slope factor. Observe that the loadings for the slope factor go from 0 to 1 to 2, a simple linear pattern. These loadings imply that the level of husbands' marital satisfaction at time 2 is greater (or smaller) than it was at time 1, and husband's marital satisfaction at time 3 is greater (or smaller) than it was at time 2. If most husbands' satisfaction scores decrease, the mean of the slope factor would be negative. The factor mean for the slope is interpreted as the average level of change in marital satisfaction for one unit in time for the average husband and is comparable to an unstandardized regression coefficient and interpreted accordingly. For example, if the average slope for husbands is 1.288, then for each 6 months (the time between measurements), husbands' marital satisfaction increases 1.288 units on average. The variance associated with the slope factor measures the extent to which the slope is the same for all husbands. If the slopes were the same for all husbands, the variance would be zero. If the marital satisfaction of some husbands has grown (or declined) at rates different from that of others, the variance would be nonzero. In fact, growth-curve analysis of marital satisfaction indicates that for both husbands and wives, marital satisfaction declines over the first few years of marriage (Karney & Bradbury, 1997; Kurdek, 1998).

A comprehensive growth-curve analysis should include a test of nonlinearity, which implies either acceleration or deceleration of change. It addresses questions such as: Does the rate of decline in wives' and husbands' marital satisfaction increase or decrease over time? As shown in Figure 13.2, the slope factor was estimated by measures loading 0, 1, and 2 on a latent growth variable. We can test for nonlinearity by freeing one of the loadings—for example, the loading of 2—for both members and observing what happens to the fit of the model. If the fit improves by freeing up the loading, one can interpret the effect as nonlinearity or as a transformation of the time variable. Therefore, if the linear loading that was forced to be 2 before were now estimated as 1.5, then we would conclude that time "slowed down" between the second and third wave of the study. If, however, it were 3.0, change would be accelerating.

Alternatively, a second growth-factor slope could be estimated for each dyad member. This slope factor would measure the quadratic growth function. With four time points, the loadings could be chosen from a table of orthogonal polynomials (e.g., 1, −1, −1, 1) by squaring the linear loadings (e.g., 0, 1, 4, 9) or by centering and then squaring (e.g., −2.25, −0.25, 0.25, 2.25). Note that although these loading options are different, they are fundamentally the same. More complex curves corresponding to more complex growth processes (e.g., cubic functions) may also be modeled. The quadratic factor may have a variance, and it can be correlated with the intercepts and linear slope factors. To be able to estimate a simple linear growth curve minimally requires three waves of data. The estimation of curvilinear growth patterns requires four or more waves of data.

With dyadic data, there are two growth curves, one for each dyad member. An interesting empirical question is the degree to which the members of the couples have the same or different growth curves: For example, do husbands and their wives have the same slopes or intercepts? We might ask, for instance, the following questions about marital satisfaction: Is the decline in marital satisfaction, as measured by the slope, greater for husbands or for wives? Additionally, is the level or average of marital satisfaction, as measured by the intercept, greater for husbands or for wives? One should not assume a priori that the growth curves are identical. Rather, this is an assumption that should be tested by determining whether the correlation between the factors is 1. We ordinarily estimate two models, one that constrains the correlation to 1 and another that leaves it free. If the correlation is less than 1, the latter model should fit better than the former.

The slope and intercept factors can be treated as outcome variables. For example, we can examine whether age of the spouses predicts either their slopes or intercepts. As is generally advisable in prediction, the predictors should be centered variables, or, at the very least, zero should be a meaningful value.

We can also use the slopes and intercepts from one variable to predict the slopes and intercepts of another variable. For example, in Raudenbush and colleagues (1995), the growth in husbands' and wives' job-role quality was used to predict growth in husbands' and wives' marital satisfaction. Specifically, it was hypothesized that growth in a husband's marital satisfaction might be caused by either growth in his own job-role quality or growth in his wife's job-role quality. Similarly, it was hypothesized that growth in a wife's marital satisfaction is caused by either growth in her job-role quality or growth in her husband's job-role quality.

The reader may recognize the essential ingredients of the APIM in the Raudenbush and colleagues (1995) study. The extent to which growth in husband's marital satisfaction is predicted by growth in his job-role quality is an actor effect, and the extent to which growth in his marital satisfaction is predicted by growth in his wife's job-role quality is a partner effect. Raudenbush and colleagues found significant actor effects (i.e., growth in job-role quality predicts growth in own marital satisfaction) but no partner effects. Kurdek (1998) has also combined the APIM and growth-curve analysis to test whether growth in husbands' and wives' depressive symptoms predicts change in their marital satisfaction. He also found significant actor effects for both husbands and wives (i.e., growth in one's own depression predicts decline in one's marital satisfaction) but no reliable partner effects. These studies demonstrate that the APIM and growth-curve modeling are not competing methods of conceptualizing and analyzing interpersonal relationship data but, rather, address different, complementary questions and, as in the preceding cases, can be profitably combined.

Multilevel Modeling

Due to its multilevel nature, growth-curve analysis is often performed using MLM software such as MLwiN (Rasbash, Steele, Browne, & Prosser, 2004), HLM6 (Raudenbush et al., 2004), SAS, or SPSS. In the context of growth curves, level 1 refers to time, and level 2 refers to dyad. The level-1 models for the two dyad members' scores for dyad i at time t would be

$$Y_{1ti} = c_{1i} + b_{1i}T_{ti} + e_{1ti},$$
$$Y_{2ti} = c_{2i} + b_{2i}T_{ti} + e_{2ti},$$

where T is a time variable, c is the intercept, and b is the slope. Note that both slopes and intercepts may be random variables and may have variances and covariances. We use a person–period data set; that is, each observation refers to one time point of one person.

Earlier we introduced a dummy variable M1 that is 1 for person 1 and 0 for person 2. We had a similar variable, M2. The variable MM was 1 for person 1 and −1 for person 2. Using these variables, the SPSS code for a model that allows for different slope and intercepts for the two members is

```
MIXED
Y BY MM WITH TIME_ID M1 M2
/FIXED = M1 M2 M1*TIME_ID M2*TIME_ID | NOINT
/PRINT = SOLUTION TESTCOV
/RANDOM M1 M2 M1*TIME_ID M2*TIME_ID | SUBJECT(DYAD_ID)
     COVTYPE(UN)
/REPEATED = MM | SUBJECT(DYAD_ID*TIME_ID) COVTYPE(CSH).
```

Note that this is the saturated model that treats the slope and intercepts for the two members as random variables that may be correlated. The last line allows for correlated errors across dyad members, what we called r_{ee} earlier in the chapter.

The comparable SAS code is

```
PROC MIXED COVTEST;
CLASS DYAD_ID OBS_ID MM M1 M2;
MODEL Y = M1 M2 M1*TIME_ID M2*TIME_ID
    /S DDFM=SATTERTH NOINT;
RANDOM M1 M2 M1*TIME_ID M2*TIME_ID
    / SUB=DYAD_ID TYPE=UN;
REPEATED MM / SUB=OBS_ID TYPE=CSH R;
```

General Error Models

With over-time data, responses are nonindependent because the data come from the very same person (i.e., autocorrelation). This nonindependence implies that the elements of the variance–covariance matrix of errors are nonzero. The cross-lagged and growth-curve models have specialized models of the variance–covariance matrix of errors. However, these are only two of many possible models than can be specified. In terms of the extremes, there could be models in which no correlation in errors occurs or models in which the variances of the errors are different at each time and all the pairs of covariances are different.

Singer and Willett (2003) present an extended discussion about the choice of error model. For instance, one classic model, the one assumed by repeated-measures ANOVA, is that of compound symmetry (see Chapters 6 and 10): The variances are equal to the same value, and the covariances are equal to the same value. The most general model of errors is the model that is unstructured (i.e., covariances of different pairs of errors are allowed to be different), the model assumed by MANOVA. For this structure, if there were 10 time points, there would be 10 variances and 45 covariances, and all of them would be free parameters. For a model that places no constraints on the covariance of errors, we cannot estimate any random over-time effects. Consequently, we could not allow for individual differences in growth-curve parameters nor allow for actor effects in the cross-lagged regression model. It is only by placing constraints on the structure of errors that we can estimate these parameters.

Singer and Willett (2003) have claimed that the choice of error structure does not greatly affect the estimation of the fixed effects. We agree that it does not usually have much of an impact on the estimates of the fixed effects, but it can have a dramatic impact on the standard errors. For instance, it is well known that if the assumption of compound symmetry is violated, standard errors can be grossly inflated (Maxwell & Delaney, 2004).

Example

We reanalyzed the Leonard (1984) data using MLM of growth curves. As before, we centered the time variable, and thus time zero is defined as the midpoint of the study, or the 13th trial. Note that if we had left time as originally coded (from 1 to 25), the intercept would refer to a point before the study began. The SAS code (variables defined earlier in the chapter) is as follows:

```
PROC MIXED COVTEST;
CLASS DYAD_ID OBS_ID INTOXSOB;
MODEL SHOCK = TRIAL_ID INTOXSOB TRIAL_ID*INTOXSOB /
    NOINT S DDFM=SATTERTH;
RANDOM INTOXSOB TRIAL_ID*INTOXSOB / TYPE = UN
    SUB = DYAD_ID GCORR;
REPEATED INTOXSOB / SUB=OBS_ID TYPE=CSH R;
```

Using MLM, we first estimated separate curves, both slope and intercept, for both the intoxicated and sober partners in the 10 dyads. However, we had difficulty getting the model to run with multilevel programs (e.g., SAS and SPSS). Moreover, when the program did run, we found evidence for variation across dyads in the slope and intercept parameters for both members, and we found a virtually perfect correlation between the two intercept parameters ($r = .978$) and between the two slope parameters ($r = 1.000$). Thus it seemed sensible to treat the data as if there were a common slope and intercept parameter for each dyad.

The code for the analysis in which both partners have the same slope and intercept but in which these common slopes and intercepts are allowed to vary across dyads, using SAS's PROC MIXED, is

```
PROC MIXED COVTEST ;
CLASS DYAD_ID OBS_ID INTOXSOB;
MODEL SHOCK = TRIAL_ID / S DDFM = SATTERTH;
RANDOM INTERCEPT TRIAL_ID / TYPE = UN SUB = DYAD_ID
    GCORR;
REPEATED INTOXSOB / SUB=OBS_ID TYPE=CSH R;
```

We also estimated the same model using SPSS and MLwiN.

The results of the model with a common growth curve for the sober and intoxicated members are as follows: The overall intercept is 5.316. Recall that the range of possible responses is from 1 to 10, which puts the intercept near the scale midpoint of 5.5. The intercept refers to the predicted level of shock given on at the 13th trial. The average effect of time is −0.041. This implies a decline across the 25 trials of 0.98 points on the shock scale. Although the correlation between the slopes for the sober and intoxicated members was perfect, the mean of the slopes was different for sober and intoxicated members. The decline for intoxicated members' shock level was 1.70, whereas the sober members declined only 0.27 points. It is confusing that the two slopes differ yet their correlation is perfect. Note that a perfect correlation implies relative and not absolute equality.

Both the intercept and slope varied from dyad to dyad, and their variances were statistically significant. Thus some dyads tended to increase shock levels and others tended to decrease them. The correlation between slope and intercept is .572, indicating that those who lowered their shock levels more over time tended to have lower shock scores at trial 13 and those who increased shock levels had higher shock levels at trial 13. This correlation, however, is not statistically significant, $p = .155$. The correlation between errors in the shock levels was −.054, and this small correlation is marginally significant, $p = .061$.

The estimate of the variance of the intercepts at trial 13 is 8.50. Note that there is about four times as much intercept variance as error variance, and, accordingly, dyad explains about 80% of the variance in shock level. If we were to change time zero to the first trial, the intercept variance would be 6.26; if we were to change time zero to the last trial, the variance becomes 12.46. These results suggest that the dyad differences in aggression are widening over time. This is what some have called *fan spread* in that dyads differ more later on than they differ initially.

Finally, we also tested for nonlinearity by including a square term for trial (i.e., time). Although there was evidence of a small amount of curvilinearity, such that the shock level went up and then down, for ease of presentation we presented only the simpler linear model.

CROSS-SPECTRAL ANALYSIS[3]

In cross-lagged regression analysis, the role of time is primarily to establish which behavior came first and which followed; thus temporal precedence in the causal or influence process is the focus of the analysis. Time plays a much more important role in some processes, however. For instance, an infant may enjoy the playful attention of a caregiver—up to a point—but may eventually become overstimulated and withdraw from interaction. Thus, over time, the caregiver's attention is transformed from something positive to something aversive to the infant (Brazelton, Koslowski, & Main, 1974). If only the infant's behavior were observed, one might find that there is a pattern in the data such that for some period of time the infant is engaged with the caregiver, followed by a period of disengagement, followed by a period of engagement, and so on. In other words, the behavior ebbs and flows, or cycles. Figure 13.3 illustrates such a cyclical pattern in mother–infant interactions. The Y-axis is affective tone of expressive behavior, ranging from negative engagement (e.g., averting gaze) to neutral to positive engagement (direct gaze), and the X-axis is time, measured in seconds. Notice that the Y variable must be measured on an interval scale for the gradual rise and fall (or wave) to be observable.

If we tried to fit a linear regression line to this plot with time as the independent variable, the slope of linear time would be near zero. Every rise (i.e., more positive involvement) is counterbalanced by a fall (i.e., more negative involvement, or disengagement). Thus there is no consistent linear trend in the data because the data are nonlinear. Although it is not obvious, the data are so nonlinear that they cannot be modeled by the squared and cubed (i.e., polynomial) functions. Waves or cycles in over-time data are typically modeled by the sinusoid functions (i.e., the sine and the cosine).

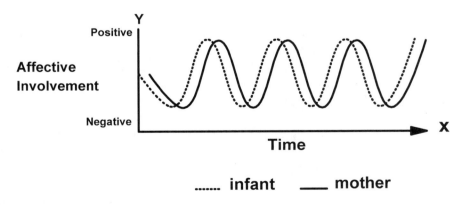

FIGURE 13.3. Cycles in mother and infant behavior.

The presence of cycles in the data implies a very particular correlational structure. Imagine blood pressure data measured every hour, and assume that these data have a strong daily cycle. More temporally adjacent observations—for example, an hour apart—would be very highly correlated. However, as the time lag increases, the correlation weakens and becomes strongly negative, becoming most negative with a lag of 12 hours. Then, for longer lags, the correlation strengthens, and for a lag of 24 hours the correlation would be very strong. Cycles are seen in the correlations, as well as in the raw data.

In dyadic analysis we are not so much interested in the cycles in one person's behavior as in the degree to which the behavior of two persons cycle together. A strong association between the cycles for two people is called *synchrony*. Lester and colleagues (1985) studied synchrony of affective involvement in 40 mother–infant dyads when the infants were 3 and 5 months old. The scale measuring affective involvement ranged from 1 (avoidant behavior) to 13 (positively engaged). In 20 dyads, the infant had been born prematurely, and in the other 20 dyads, the infant was full term. The researchers hypothesized that there would be greater synchrony in the mother–infant dyads with full-term infants than in those with premature infants because of the full-term infants' greater neurological development and information-processing capacity. Cross-spectral analysis is the method used to test their hypothesis. However, before one can investigate the association of two persons' cycles using cross-spectral analysis, one must first have adequate descriptors of each individual's cycling. We therefore discuss the analysis of individual cycles using harmonic analysis and spectral analysis.

Three parameters are involved in the description of a sinusoid. The horizontal distance from the top of one wave (i.e., the peak) to the top of the next is called the *period*. It is the length of the cycle measured either in number of observations or in units of time, and it is symbolized by τ. For example, Lester and colleagues (1985) identified a period for infant affective involvement that was approximately 10 seconds long; 10 seconds elapsed from peak of positivity to peak of positivity. The *frequency* is measured by the inverse of the period, or $1/\tau$, and is symbolized as ω. So if the period for the infant's affective involvement were 10 seconds, the frequency would be (1/10), or .10 cycles per second. One cycle per second is called a hertz and is abbreviated as *Hz*. (The reader probably is familiar with the term megahertz, from audio equipment.) The *phase* of the sinusoid locates the peak relative to the zero point on the time scale. Finally, the amplitude is the height of the peak. It is the distance from the mean of the waveform (halfway between the peak and trough) to the peak, measured in the unit or scale of the outcome variable. Amplitude is analogous to the slope in regression analysis. It measures the ability of the sinusoid to explain variance in the response. If the frequency, phase, and amplitude are known, then the sinusoidal cycle can be computed.

Suppose that on the basis of the Lester and colleagues (1985) findings, we hypothesize that there is a 10-second period in infant affective involvement. We can test this hypothesis by fitting a sinusoid function to the infant's behavior observed over time, a procedure called *harmonic analysis*. Harmonic analysis is accomplished by creating predictor variables that represent the sine and cosine of time for a given frequency, denoted as ω. The equation (adapted from Warner, 1998) is as follows:

$$Y_t = a + b[\sin(\omega t)] + c[\cos(\omega t)] + e_t.$$

The equation is not nearly as complicated as it looks, and we have graphed it in Figure 13.4. In this equation, Y_t is the value of the infant's affective involvement at different times ($t = 1, 2 \ldots T$, or 1 to 60 in Figure 13.4) in the series. It is an ordinary multiple regression equation with an intercept (the typical value of Y), a (see Figure 13.4), and two predictors, the sine and cosine functions. There are two regression coefficients, b and c. What is complicated are the two predictor variables, one involving a sine function and one involving a cosine function. They convert the time variable (t) into a sine wave and a cosine wave using the frequency, denoted as ω (or $1/\tau$), transforming the frequency into an angle (Warner, 1998). The combination of these two waves creates a single wave that accounts for variance in Y.

By fitting both the sine and cosine waves to the data, one obtains two coefficients, b and c. These coefficients are used to compute the amplitude and phase of the cycle. The amplitude of the cycle, R (see Figure 13.4), is equal to $b^2 + c^2$. The phase denoted as ϕ is equal to arctan($-c, b$). The phase is important to the analysis of interpersonal influence and is to be discussed later. A large amplitude means that the sinusoid for the period (in this case, 10) explains much of the variability in the person's scores. If the hypothesized period were incorrect (i.e., the behavior cycles at a different frequency or does not cycle at all), the amplitude would be small. Including the sine and cosine wave functions in the equation removes from the outcome variable any variance due to a cycle of the specified length in the

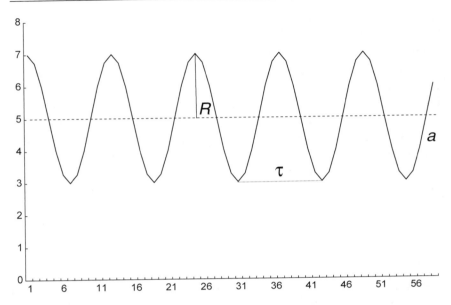

FIGURE 13.4. Graph of a sinusoid function with a period (τ) of 12, intercept (*a*) of 5, and amplitude (*R*) of 3.

data (in this case, every 10 seconds), thus correcting for nonindependence of observations due to that cycle. Warner (1998) provides a more detailed explication of a harmonic analysis.

With most time-series data, the length of the cycle is not known. Part of what spectral analysis does, as opposed to harmonic analysis, is to determine empirically what periods (there may be more than one) explain the most variance in the data (i.e., have the largest amplitudes). For a given series with T time points, $T/2$ cycles can be estimated. Each of these cycles is tested for statistical reliability, thus identifying potentially important cycles. For example, Lester and colleagues (1985) found reliable cycles in infant affective involvement at three different frequency ranges. We already mentioned one cycle that was approximately 10 seconds long. This is a relatively fast cycle. They also found cycles of approximately 0.05 Hz (midrange cycles with periods of roughly 20 seconds) and cycles of approximately 0.025 Hz (slow cycles with periods of roughly 45 seconds).

As mentioned earlier, the larger goal is understanding the dynamics of dyadic behavior—in this case, associations between partners' cycles. Lester and colleagues (1985), for example, hypothesized about the synchrony of affective involvement in mother–infant dyads and how it might differ for preterm and full-term infants. If one is interested in whether the behavior of two people is coordinated or coupled, it is necessary to measure the degree to which the two sets of waves rise and fall together, like the waves in Figure 13.3. The estimation of the coupling in the waves is done using cross-spectral analysis. Cross-spectral analysis involves taking the cross-product of the mother's and infant's amplitudes for selected frequencies (viz., those identified as reliable). These cross-products are used in the calculation of covariances, from which we can determine the amount of variance in one person's cycle that overlaps with the other person's cycle. This measure of correspondence between two sets of waves is called *coherence*. If there were high coherence, then the two waves would move together and have the same cycles.

When there is high coherence between the two sets of data (i.e., they are *in phase* with each other), we say their behavior exhibits *synchrony* (Bakeman & Gottman, 1997). For example, we have already determined that the infant has a 10-second period. If mother and infant behaviors were coupled, the mother would also have a 10-second period. If this were so, then the measure of coherence for the 0.10 Hz frequency would be high. Note, however, that this coherence is specific to the 10-second period. In cross-spectral analysis, coherence is measured for each of the $T/2$ frequency bands in an exploratory fashion. Thus the investigator must choose which of these frequency bands should be interpreted. As mentioned earlier, interpretation is usually limited to only those frequencies that are relatively powerful predictors (or descriptors) of individual behavior (i.e., that have a high amplitude).

It is also possible to estimate the extent to which one person's waves systematically lead or lag behind those of the partner, suggesting a process of interpersonal influence. If the amount of time the mother makes eye contact with her infant begins to decrease after she notices that the infant has begun to avoid eye contact with her, the cycles describing her behavior would lag slightly behind those of her infant. The formula for phase (earlier called ϕ) is central to the determination of lag and lead. Lag (or lead) refers to the difference in phase at which the two individual cycles have the greatest coherence. In other words, coherence is estimated while controlling for the difference in the phase of the two cycles. As can be seen in Figure 13.3, the infant's behavior changes first, followed shortly by a change in the mother's behavior. Lag–lead relationships between sets of cyclical data are also analyzed using cross-spectral analysis. Warner (1998) provides a clear and comprehensive introduction to these methods.

We need to be clear about causation in lead–lag relationships. It is not at all clear who is influencing whom. Suppose the mother and child both show a cycle length of 10 seconds, and the peaks in the infant's cycles lead the peaks in the mother's cycles by 3 seconds. Under certain circumstances you might view the infant's behavior as pulling the mother's behavior along, and under other circumstances, you might view the mother's behavior as pushing the infant's behavior along. In the absence of strong theoretical guidance, it is best to say that the two are entrained in a shared cycle. Nonetheless, theory and common sense may dictate that one person be viewed as influencing the other.

A fundamental assumption of cross-spectral analysis is that both time series are stationary. That is, the mean, variance, and covariances do not change over time. Boker, Xu, Rotondo, and King (2002) discuss the relaxation of this assumption.

NONLINEAR DYNAMIC MODELING

There has been increasing interest in nonlinear dynamic models of dyadic data (Felmlee & Sprecher, 2000). Here we discuss the approach that Gottman, Swanson, and Swanson (2002) have developed, because it has been featured most prominently. As described by Gottman and colleagues, nonlinear dynamic modeling is a qualitative method that uses differential equations to plot the influence two partners have on each other. It is idiographic in that the influence of one person on another is measured for each person. We present a brief description of the technique, and we refer interested readers to Gottman and colleagues for more details. We assume that Y_{1t} for person 1 and Y_{2t} for person 2 are measures of positivity–negativity. (We omit here the subscript for dyad.) Lower scores would indicate negative behavior, and higher scores would indicate positive behavior.

There are two equations, one for each partner's outcomes. The outcome variable in each equation (e.g., person A's behavior at time t or Y_{1t}) is a function of the intercept of the regression equation, which is denoted as a, and is referred to as the person's *uninfluenced steady state* or *emotional inertia*. Additionally, a person is influenced by his or her past behavior, $Y_{1,t-1}$. In equation form we have

$$Y_{1t} = a + rY_{1,t-1} + e_t.$$

The intercept and the autoregressive coefficient, r, are estimated using ordinary regression analysis. Note that the partner's behavior is not entered into the equation.

In the next step, the partner's influence is calculated separately at each point in time over the course of the interaction. This involves subtracting the uninfluenced steady-state component, a, and the effect of the person's own past behavior, $rY_{1,t-1}$, for each of the time-specific observations of person 1. This leaves, for each point in time, a residual effect, or e_t; that is, the component of the dependent variable (person 1's score) that is not accounted for by either the uninfluenced steady state (what person 1 brings to the interaction) or person 1's emotional inertia. The dynamic-systems model specifies that this residual effect e_t is due to the prior behavior of the partner, or $Y_{2,t-1}$. However, we take $Y_{2,t-1}$ and break it up into categories, create dummy variables, and estimate the effects of "discretized" Y on e_t. We denote these effects as I_{12}, or the influence of person 2 on person 1.

For instance, if the scale for the partner's behavior, Y_2, ranges from 0 to 4, the I_{12} coefficient can be estimated for every level of Y_2, producing four different values. We can then graph these effects where the X-axis is the level of Y_2 and the Y-axis is the mean value of the residual. Each of these means is an influence effect, I_{12}. In this manner, one can qualitatively evaluate whether the degree of influence changes for different levels of the partner's prior behavior. If interpersonal influence is nonlinear, the function on the graph is not a straight line. For example, the effect of the partner may be greater when his or her prior behavior is at higher values (i.e., more negative) than at lower values. It may also be that the partner has no influence at all until he or she manifests a certain level of negativity, which would be indicated by the point at which the line begins to slope upward. This point is called a *negativity threshold*. A second component reflecting sensitivity to positive behavior (called a *positivity threshold*) can also be determined. A parallel analysis can be conducted using person 1 to predict person 2.

In several papers, Gottman and colleagues (2002, 2003) have suggested a simpler version of their model. They propose what is called a *bilinear model*, in which partner's lagged effect is linear but the effect is different when lagged Y is positive than when it is negative. We discuss the estimation of the bilinear model using an APIM framework.

First, two different predictor variables are created. The variable Y_p equals Y when Y is positive and elsewhere is zero; the variable Y_n equals Y

when Y is negative, or else it is zero. To test whether the slopes of Y_p and Y_n are different—bilinearity—we estimate a model with lagged Y and Y_p (or Y_n) as predictors, and we test to see whether lagged Y_p has an effect. If Y_p has an effect, bilinearity is indicated.

To measure bilinearity, we create two dummy variables, $P_{2,t-1,i}$ and $N_{2,t-1,i}$ where P equals 1 if the partner's behavior was positive and 0 otherwise, and N equals 1 if the partner's prior behavior was negative. The dummy variable Q is 1 if the behavior is positive and -1 if negative. The equations that we gave earlier for the cross-lagged regression model would be modified as follows:

$$Y_{1ti} = c_{1i} + a_{1i}Y_{1,t-1,i} + p_{P21i}Y_{2,t-1,i}P_{2,t-1,i} + p_{N21i}Y_{2,t-1,i}N_{2,t-1,i} + b_{1i}Q_{2,t-1,i} + e_{1ti},$$
$$Y_{2ti} = c_{2i} + a_{2i}Y_{2,t-1,i} + p_{P12i}Y_{1,t-1,i}P_{1,t-1,i} + p_{N12i}Y_{1,t-1,i}N_{1,t-1,i} + b_{2i}Q_{1,t-1,i} + e_{2ti}.$$

The null hypothesis is for the bilinear hypothesis that $p_{P21} = p_{N21}$ and $b_1 = 0$. In other words, the null model states that the effect of the partner's positive behavior is the same (has the same slope) as the effect of the partner's negative behavior.

Although this dynamic-systems model appears to be very different from the cross-lagged regression model, we can view the approach within the APIM. Basically, the dynamic-systems approach postulates that the partner effect is nonlinear and that it varies by dyad. We believe that the dynamic-systems model might be better estimated by MLM. Moreover, we think it problematic that effects are not centered and that the residuals are analyzed, as opposed to simultaneously estimating actor and partner effects.

Again we reiterate that our discussion of dynamic modeling is very brief. To apply this technique, the reader needs to consult the sources that we cited or attempt our APIM adaptation.

SUMMARY AND CONCLUSIONS

We have discussed five different models for the over-time analysis of dyadic relationships with interval variables: cross-lagged regressions, standard APIM, growth-curve analysis, cross-spectral analysis, and dynamic-systems analysis. Many of the models extend the APIM to over-time data. The cross-lagged regression examines the effect that the person's past behavior and the partner's past behavior have on the person's current behavior. The model of nonlinear dynamic systems presumes that partner effects are nonlinear. Both cross-lagged regressions and dynamic growth models are stochastic in the sense that a person adjusts to the random changes of the partner.

The growth-curve model and the cross-spectral analysis model make different assumptions about the functional relationship between the dyad members' behavior and time. In growth-curve modeling, the functional form is usually assumed to be linear or exponential. In cross-spectral analysis, the assumption is that the functional form is cyclical (i.e., sinusoidal). Both growth-curve modeling and spectral analysis presume a deterministic growth pattern. Individuals are on track and continue along that track over time. A central question in all analyses is whether both members of the dyad have the same functional relationship; for example, the same rate of growth or the same cycle in their behaviors. If dyad members vary in their functional relationship, then we want to know whether there is any covariation in those functions.

We have seen that both MLM and SEM are used to estimate these models. There are analysis complications of centering, negative variances, and covariation between terms. However, resolving these difficulties is well worth the effort, as we learn a great deal about the structure of change in dyadic processes.

The methods that we have discussed in this chapter are complex, perhaps the most complicated in the book. However, even more complicated methods exist that we have not discussed. For instance, it is possible to combine the cross-lagged regression and growth-curve models (Curran & Bollen, 2001). Additionally, Boker and Laurenceau (2006) present an elaborate approach that blends nonlinear dynamical systems and MLM, and Ferrer and Nesselroade (2003) discuss dynamic factor analysis.

Additionally, one point that we discussed in Chapter 7 is that the standard APIM does not allow for measurement error in the predictors. We do note that the Ferrer and Nesselroade (2003) approach can be viewed as a latent variable, over-time APIM, thus controlling for measurement errors in the predictors.

In the next chapter, we consider over-time data with categorical outcomes: for example, studies of competition versus cooperation. We discuss a method of estimating the cross-lagged regression model with dichotomous outcomes, a procedure more generally known as sequential analysis. We consider estimating the model by both log-linear analysis and MLM. We also consider event-history analysis that treats time as a continuous variable.

NOTES

1. We wish to acknowledge the extensive feedback and advice that we received from Niall Bolger on this and the next section of the chapter.

2. The standard functional form for negative exponential is ae^{-bt}, where e is the transcendental number that approximately equals 2.718. The specification that we have introduced based on regression toward the mean is that cd^t. The negative exponential formulation is identical to the regression toward the mean formulation given that $c = a$ and $d = -\ln(b)$.

3. The material in this section was adapted from Cook (2003).

Over-Time Analyses
Dichotomous Outcomes

In the previous chapter, we described analytic techniques that are appropriate for data from two-person interactions that are measured over time on an interval-level variable. In this chapter, we consider the analysis of categorical outcomes, focusing much of our discussion on outcomes that are dichotomies. Most of this chapter is devoted to sequential analysis, or the study of behavior measured at multiple points in time. Our discussion highlights two different statistical estimation techniques: log-linear analysis and multilevel modeling (MLM).

As discussed in Cook (2003), two different approaches for sampling observations from the stream of behavior produced by dyadic interaction have been widely applied. In one approach, the behavior of both persons is coded or rated at specific intervals of time, such as every 15 seconds. In the other approach, the observations are coded at the onset of each new behavior or event. These two approaches are referred to as *interval sampling* and *event sampling*, respectively (Bakeman & Gottman, 1997). Interval sampling requires cutting the stream of behavior into units of equal duration, called *epochs*. An observer codes the behavior of interest for each epoch. Interval sampling of two-person interactions produces two parallel streams of behavior, as illustrated in Figure 14.1.

Rather than defining an observation unit as a specific time interval, event sampling defines an observation unit as a specific event. Conversational data are a good example, because in most cases only one person

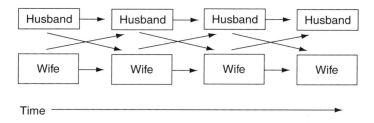

FIGURE 14.1. Interval sampling over time.

speaks at a time, resulting in a series of turn taking. For example, a boy might speak for 20 seconds, followed by his mother speaking for 15 seconds, followed by the boy speaking again for 5 seconds, followed by his mother speaking for 45 seconds, and so on. The pattern of exchange in the dialogue is often a central issue of the research. Thus, irrespective of its duration, the nature of each person's speech act (e.g., warm vs. cold) can be coded, and the boundary of each speech act (the unit of coding) is defined by the onset of the next speech act. This use of the onset of a new event to determine the unit of coding is the defining feature of event sampling. Thus coding each person's speech acts over the course of the conversation represents one type of event sampling. In conversations, the overall pattern is one of alternation between partners, and the stream of behavior resembles the pattern shown in Figure 14.2.[1]

There is one other type of strategy for coding events as they occur over time. Instead of thinking about whether the event does or does not occur at a given time, we can think in terms of how long it takes for the event to happen. Thus we measure how long it takes for an event, such as a couple breaking up, a woman having a baby, or a person dying, to occur. We discuss event-history analysis for the analysis of this type of data in the last section of the chapter.

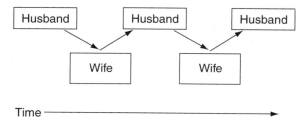

FIGURE 14.2. Event sampling over time.

The primary data-analytic approach taken in this chapter is cross-lagged regression (see Chapter 13) with dichotomous outcomes for both members. Such analyses are commonly called *sequential analyses*, and we consider applications of log-linear and MLM strategies. As we discussed in the previous chapter, over-time analysis is a very complex topic. Combining the complications of dyads with those of dichotomous outcomes makes the topic even more difficult. The reader should realize that one chapter cannot comprehensively discuss all of the issues involved in such analyses, and this chapter should be viewed as only an introduction.

Before we begin, we mention briefly what has been called *lag sequential analysis* (Sackett, 1979). This method is used to study interpersonal behavior by measuring the number of times certain behaviors precede or follow a selected behavior. A key measure in lag sequential analysis is the conditional probability of an event. As an example, a researcher might code parent–child interactions for such behaviors as smiles, gazes, and touches. In a lag sequential analysis, the following sequence might occur relatively frequently: child gazes, the mother smiles, and the child touches the mother. A more contemporary version of lag sequential analysis is *t*-system analysis (Anolli, Duncan, Magnusson, & Riva, 2005). This approach uses a sophisticated computer program called *Theme* that searches for recurring sequences in dyad behavior.

SEQUENTIAL ANALYSIS

In the social sciences, the most common form of dyadic time-series analysis is sequential analysis. Although many scholars have contributed to the development and refinement of sequential analysis, its popularity can be largely credited to John Gottman (1979; Bakeman & Gottman, 1997; Gottman & Roy, 1990). Sequential analysis provides estimates of one person's influence on another based on categorically coded observations of their interaction. By far the most difficult task involved in sequential analysis is obtaining reliable and valid observations over time. The reader should consult the book by Bakeman and Gottman (1997) called *Observing Interaction: An Introduction to Sequential Analysis* for an excellent introduction to the concerns of systematic observation and the development of coding schemes for observing dyads. The current chapter provides an introduction to the statistical analysis of these types of data.

The data that are used in sequential analysis are categorical and, most often, dichotomous codes. These codes may identify a person's affective, cognitive, or behavioral state at a particular point in time. For example, if a person says something unkind to a partner, that person might be coded as being "cold" at that moment. Of course, when a dyad is being observed, both persons' states are coded over time.

The Model

Figures 14.1 and 14.2 are illustrations of common forms of the data collected within interval-sampling and event-sampling designs, but they are not the analytic model that is estimated and tested. Analytically, both types of data can be treated as versions of the Actor–Partner Interdependence Model (APIM). However, when event sampling is conducted on data from a dialogue, a particular type of event never follows itself in the stream of behavior. Rather, each observation is terminated by the onset of a new event, and the data are usually coded and organized such that with each new event the identity of the person observed switches (e.g., husband, wife, husband, wife, husband, wife, and so on). Thus, in contrast to the standard version of the APIM (see Figure 13.1), the path diagram resembles Figure 14.3. That is, there are three time points included in the model. First is the husband's (or wife's) behavior at time t, then the wife's (or husband's) behavior at time $t - 1$, then the husband's (or wife's) behavior at time $t - 2$.

Figure 14.3 illustrates the case in which the husband's behavior at time t is being predicted from his wife's behavior at time $t - 1$ and his own behavior at time $t - 2$. The path from husband's behavior at time $t - 2$ to husband's behavior at t corresponds to the actor effect in the APIM, and its path measures and controls for serial dependency in the data. Conceptually, the path reflects stability in the husband's behavior independent of the wife's behavior. The path from the wife's behavior at time $t - 1$ to the

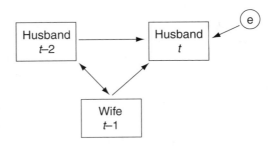

FIGURE 14.3. Model of over-time effects.

husband's behavior at time t corresponds to the partner effect in the APIM and measures interdependence in the data. However, unlike the standard APIM, in sequential analysis this path is not usually interpreted as the partner's influence on the person. Rather, the path is interpreted as the person's reciprocity of his or her partner's prior behavior.

One might be tempted to interpret the correlation between husband's time $t - 2$ behavior and the wife's time $t - 1$ behavior as measuring the wife's reciprocity of her husband's prior behavior. Note, however, that we have not controlled for the serial dependence (i.e., the actor effect) in the wife's data. Consequently, it is not a valid estimate of the wife's reciprocity (Allison & Liker, 1982). For this reason a double-headed arrow connects these variables, indicating a correlation rather than a causal effect.

Some might think that autocontingency (i.e., an actor effect) does not have to be controlled when estimating cross-lagged dependency (i.e., a partner effect) in the analysis of event-sampled time-series data. This argument is based on the observation that the codes for the actor's behavior never follow each other contiguously. In other words, the linkage between the actor's state at one point in time and his or her next state is always mediated by the intervening state of the partner. However, this position confuses two meanings of the term *mediation*. In terms of observational coding, an observation of the partner always separates observations of the actor. However, in the causal sense of mediation, whether the partner's state at one point in time "mediates" the stability or consistency in the state of the actor must be determined statistically. For example, the husband may remain in a bad mood over the course of a conversation despite the wife's attempts to cheer him up.

The stability of one person's mood is modeled by the path from the actor's state at time $t - 2$ to his or her state at time t. The effect of the partner's mood is modeled by the path from the partner at time $t - 1$ to the actor at time t. It should not be assumed that, just because the coded observations imply a mediational model, the variable in the role of mediator has a significant effect. In interpersonal behavior, autocontingency (or consistency) is probably the rule rather than the exception. Evidence of the statistical significance of autocontingency in event-based sequence analysis was found for both mothers and adolescents in a sample of high-risk treatment-seeking families (Cook, Strachan, Goldstein, & Miklowitz, 1989). Consistent with the views of Warner (1998), these autocontingency effects also had important clinical and theoretical implications.

To say that a particular pattern of interaction exists between two people, one must demonstrate that there is a statistically reliable pattern in the codes for their behavior. Although we may be somewhat interested in patterns of the partners' concurrent behaviors, we are usually more concerned with patterns that exist over time (e.g., addressing the question, Does the wife's behavior at one point in time predict the husband's behavior at the next point in time?). Sequence analysis requires observations of transitions; that is, changes in the state of the wife's behavior at one point in time to the subsequent behavior of her husband. A single observation that a negative statement by the wife is followed by a negative speech act by the husband is not sufficient to establish the reliability of a pattern. Instead, the goal is to make a generalization about the husband–wife dyad that is predictive of their future interactions. To do so requires a sample of the transitions in their behavior sufficient for statistical analysis.

A *transition* is an observation of two temporally separated observations in a system over time. In time-sampling designs, a transition is usually the observation from one epoch to the next, and in event-sampling designs it is usually the observation of one event to the next. In some cases, the transition may not be between temporally contiguous observations but rather between two observations that have a longer period of separation. For example, in the event-sampling procedure, the path for temporal stability (or the actor effect) is based on transitions from the actor's behavior at time $t - 2$ to his or her behavior at time t, skipping the partner's behavior at time $t - 1$.

Illustration

To illustrate the extraction of sequences from two-person time-series data, we use data from a study of spouse interactions involving the prisoner's dilemma game (Cook, 1988). On each of 32 trials of this game, the husband and wife had to choose to either cooperate (a C choice) or compete (i.e., defect; a D choice). The choices were made simultaneously. If both spouses chose C, they both received 3 points. If one spouse chose C and the other chose D, the first spouse would receive −3 points, and other spouse would receive 5 points. Thus choosing D is a competitive option insofar as it provides an opportunity to gain more points than the partner gains. However, the dilemma in the prisoner's dilemma game is that if both partners choose D, they both lose 3 points. Consequently, if you know your partner is going to be cooperative, you could gain more by being competitive; but if both are competitive, both have worse outcomes. The choices made by one of the couples, whom we call "Mike" and "Sarah," are presented in Table 14.1. Mike and Sarah's choices were recorded for each of 32 trials of the prisoner's dilemma game. Because their choices were

TABLE 14.1. Choices of Mike and Sarah over 32 Trials
of the Prisoner's Dilemma Game

Trial	Choices		Prior choices	
	Mike t	Sarah t	Mike $t-1$	Sarah $t-1$
1	C	C		
2	C	D	C	C
3	D	C	C	D
4	D	D	D	C
5	C	C	D	D
6	C	D	C	C
7	C	D	C	D
8	D	C	C	D
9	D	D	D	C
10	D	D	D	D
11	C	C	D	D
12	D	C	C	C
13	D	D	D	C
14	D	D	D	D
15	C	C	D	D
16	C	C	C	C
17	C	C	C	C
18	C	D	C	C
19	D	C	C	D
20	C	D	D	C
21	D	C	C	D
22	D	D	D	C
23	C	D	D	D
24	C	C	C	D
25	C	C	C	C
26	C	C	C	C
27	C	D	C	C
28	D	C	C	D
29	D	D	D	C
30	D	C	D	D
31	D	C	D	C
32	D	C	D	C

Note. C, cooperate; D, compete.

made simultaneously, their time series are parallel. On trial 1 Mike chose C, and Sarah also chose C. The table also includes what each person chose on the prior trial; Mike and Sarah's $t - 1$ choices are listed under the heading "Prior Choices." Thus Sarah's time $t - 1$ entry for trial 3, a D, is the same as her time t entry for trial 2. Obviously, there are no prior choices for trial 1.

We first discuss the analysis using log-linear analysis because, historically, it has been the dominant approach. In the second section, we discuss the use of MLM of dichotomous outcomes. Even if the reader is primarily interested in MLM, we still recommend reading the log-linear section, as it discusses the model, its parameters, and their interpretation.

STATISTICAL ANALYSIS OF SEQUENTIAL DATA: LOG-LINEAR ANALYSIS

Ever since the seminal critique of lag sequential analysis by Allison and Liker (1982), log-linear analysis has been the preferred method for analyzing sequential dyadic time-series data. As we discussed in Chapters 6 and 11, log-linear analysis is a data-analytic method for analyzing the effects of multiple independent variables on nominal- and ordinal-level data. In a sense, log-linear analysis is to an ordinary chi-square analysis of a 2×2 table what multiple regression analysis is to a Pearson correlation. Like an ordinary chi-square analysis, log-linear analysis estimates the association between cells in tabled data. Like regression analysis, logit analysis within log-linear analysis permits estimation of the effects of multiple independent variables, each controlled for the other. These are exactly the statistical features needed to test the APIM on Mike and Sarah's choices. Specifically, we want to simultaneously estimate the effects of Mike and Sarah's trial $t - 1$ choices on Mike's trial t choices. A log-linear model also estimates the interaction effects among the independent variables.

If the predictors are measured on an interval-level scale, logistic regression analysis can be used to analyze the data. Logistic regression is more general than log-linear analysis, but we still discuss log-linear analysis for historical and conceptual reasons. That is, by understanding the details of log-linear analysis, one can better understand the meaning of both a logistic regression analysis and an MLM analysis of a dichotomous outcome.

Table 14.2 presents the state-transition table for Mike and Sarah's choices over the 32 trials of the prisoner's dilemma game. The table is a

TABLE 14.2. State-Transition Table for 31 Prisoner's Dilemma Game Trials Ending in Mike's Choice

Prior choices		Mike t	
Mike $t-1$	Sarah $t-1$	C	D
C	C	8	1
C	D	2	5
D	C	1	7
D	D	4	3

Note. C, cooperate; D, compete.

three-variable (i.e., a $2 \times 2 \times 2$) state transition table. The three variables represented in the table are Mike's trial $t-1$ choices, Sarah's trial $t-1$ choices, and Mike's trial t choices. There are eight cells in this table, each representing the different combinations (2^3) of the three variables. The table is organized to reflect that the dependent variable is Mike's choice at trial t. There are two columns, one representing each of his choices (i.e., a C column and a D column). In the cells are counts for the number of times Mike made that choice following a particular configuration of Mike and Sarah's choices at trial $t-1$.

We need to refer to the cells of the table, and so we name them. The cell frequencies have three subscripts, arranged in the order of actor's prior response, partner's prior response, and the person's current response. A C choice is coded as 0, and a D choice coded as 1. Thus the first cell is f_{000} for "husband chose C (the last zero) following a trial in which both the husband (first zero) and wife (second zero) also chose C." For Mike, this cell has a count of 8 (top left cell under the C column in Table 14.2). To the right of this cell is f_{001}, the cell for the number of times Mike chose D on the trial following one in which both Sarah and he chose C. This occurred only one time for Mike and Sarah, and so f_{001} is 1.

Logit Model

We provide a detailed explanation of the logic of log-linear analysis of sequential data. We use a logit model that treats one variable as the dependent variable. For our example, that variable would be Mike's response at time t. We begin by computing the odds that he makes a competitive choice rather than a cooperative choice. For the condition in which both Mike and Sarah cooperated in the previous trial (the "00" condition), the odds are f_{001}/f_{000}, or 1/8. The next step is to take the natural logarithm of the odds, which is called the *logit*. The logit for the "00" condition is denoted as η_{00}. The conversion of the odds to log-transformed odds is required because the model is multiplicative. Thus, to make the model additive, we log transform the data. Logits, unlike probabilities or odds, can range in value from plus infinity to minus infinity. For example, the log-transform, or logit, of 2:1 odds is 0.693, the logit of 1:2 odds is –0.693, and the logit of 1:1 odds (i.e., equal probability) is 0. Logits, though statistically useful, can be difficult to interpret. Sometimes it is useful to convert a logit, denoted as η, into an odds by computing e^{η}, or to convert the logit into a probability by $e^{\eta}/(1 + e^{\eta})$, where $e \approx 2.718$.

Because it is possible that some cell frequencies might be zero and the logit could not be defined, it is advisable to add 0.5 to each of the cells. Table 14.3 presents the logit for all four conditions for Mike and Sarah. Note that for the "00" cell, the logit is $\ln(1.5/8.5) = -1.735$. A negative value indicates that cooperation was more likely than competition. The logit is also negative when both members competed on the previous trial, the "11" condition.

The logit log-linear model for the four conditions, based on four possibilities of prior responses, is

$$\eta_{11} = \mu + \alpha_1 + \beta_1 + \gamma_{11},$$
$$\eta_{10} = \mu + \alpha_1 - \beta_0 - \gamma_{10},$$
$$\eta_{01} = \mu - \alpha_0 + \beta_1 - \gamma_{01},$$
$$\eta_{00} = \mu - \alpha_0 - \beta_0 + \gamma_{00},$$

where, for example, η_{11} is the log odds of a 1 response for the "11" condition. We have a simple two-way ANOVA model (Maxwell & Delaney, 2004), with the effects summing to zero by rows and by columns. That is, the value of each cell is modeled to be a function of the grand mean of the logits, the deviation of the row mean from the grand mean (e.g., the degree

TABLE 14.3. The Log Odds, or Logit, of Mike Competing as a Function of Mike's and Sarah's Prior Responses

Parameter	Sarah cooperate	Sarah compete	Mean
Mike cooperate	–1.735	0.788	–0.473
Mike compete	1.609	–0.251	0.679
Mean	–0.063	0.269	0.103

to which Mike competes, more or less, after he has competed in the past), the deviation of the column mean from the grand mean (i.e., the degree to which Mike competes, more or less, after Sarah has competed in the past), and the unique effect of the combination of both Mike's past behavior and Sarah's past behavior. Observe that there is no error term in the model, because this model is a saturated model in that the sum of the parameters exactly reproduces the cell logits.

The four parameters in the model for Mike and Sarah are presented in Table 14.4. The first component is the mean, or μ, which equals $(\eta_{11} + \eta_{10} + \eta_{01} + \eta_{00})/4$. The mean can be viewed as the average logit. A positive score would indicate that Mike is more likely, on the average, to be competitive rather than cooperative. The average logit of choosing to compete (the D choice) on trial t is 0.103, which corresponds to a probability of competing of .53. A positive value indicates that the probability of Mike choosing D is greater than the probability of his choosing C.

Next we compute the husband actor effect, which is the temporal stability of his competitive responses. The actor effect, or α_1, equals $(\eta_{11} + \eta_{10} - \eta_{01} - \eta_{00})/4$. We can rewrite this formula as $\ln[(f_{111}/f_{110})/(f_{101}/f_{100})]/4 + \ln[(f_{011}/f_{010})/(f_{001}/f_{000})]/4$. Consider the term $(f_{111}/f_{110})/(f_{101}/f_{010})$; it contains a ratio of two odds and is therefore called an *odds ratio*. The actor effect involves the odds of the actor not changing versus odds of changing, averaged over the two possibilities of his partner's prior response. Mike's actor effect equals 0.576, which, because it is positive, indicates that there is temporal stability in Mike's choices—he is more likely to compete at time t if he competed at time $t - 1$.

Let us consider the actor effect in more detail. It is based on an odds ratio. Epidemiological findings are often reported in terms of an odds ratio; for example, that the odds of a smoker's getting lung cancer are 12 to 22 times greater than those of a nonsmoker. We can convert α_1, the actor

TABLE 14.4. Log-Linear Parameter Estimates for Mike's Behavior Based on His and Sarah's Prior Behavior over 32 Trials

Parameter	Estimate
Grand mean	0.103
Actor effect	0.576
Partner effect	0.166
Interaction effect	−1.096

effect estimate, to an odds ratio by computing $e^{2\alpha_1}$. Accordingly, the odds ratio of Mike's competing given that he has previously competed to his competing given that he has previously cooperated is 3.16.

The wife-to-husband partner effect is the next parameter. The estimate of β_1 is $(\eta_{11} - \eta_{10} + \eta_{01} - \eta_{00})/4$. The partner effect indicates that Mike reciprocated Sarah's use of the competitive choice, but the size of the effect is relatively small, as is evidenced by an odds ratio of only 1.39.

The last term in the model is the interaction effect. The estimate of γ_1 is $(\eta_{11} - \eta_{10} - \eta_{01} + \eta_{00})/4$. We can view this term as measuring how competitive Mike is when he and Sarah matched responses on the previous trial. It would be positive if Mike is more likely to be competitive following trials on which they matched, a strategy called *tit for tat* in the prisoner's dilemma literature. The interaction effect would tend to be negative if either person's use of the cooperative response option reduces the odds of Mike being competitive. If we reexamine Tables 14.2 and 14.3, the interaction is readily interpretable: We see that when Mike cooperated on the previous trial, his current trial response matches Sarah's prior response. Thus, if she cooperated, he continues to cooperate; but if she competed, he now competes. However, if he competed on the prior trial, on the current trial he does the opposite of what his wife did on the prior trial. He continues to compete if she cooperates, but he cooperates if she punished him by competing on the prior trial.

Significance Testing and Aggregation across Dyads

If one wishes to generalize findings for a particular dyad, a sufficient number of observations are needed to detect whether reciprocity, temporal stability, and the other parameters of the model are reliable. This issue parallels the situation in which individual is the unit of analysis and the number of individuals in the sample is a key determinant of the power to detect significant effects. For example, a correlation coefficient of .20 is not statistically significant in a sample of 25 individuals, but it is statistically significant in a sample of 200 individuals. The same situation holds for sequential analysis. The unit of analysis is not the individual but the number of observations of the dyad (i.e., time points or events sampled). However, even for very simple models involving only a few two-level codes, a large number of observations may be needed to provide sensitive and reliable estimates (Bakeman & Gottman, 1997).

A total of 32 trials of the prisoner's dilemma game is an insufficient sample size for making confident generalizations regarding patterns of interaction between Mike and Sarah (e.g., that Mike will generally recipro-cate Sarah's competitiveness). However, researchers are typically more interested in learning about patterns and dynamics that can be generalized beyond a particular dyad. In other words, the goal is usually to discover patterns that are characteristic of an entire group of people (i.e., the nomothetic research paradigm), not the particular relationship of just one couple (i.e., the idiographic paradigm). Toward this end, we can treat the sequential-analysis parameter estimates from each dyad as the input data for an analysis that aggregates across the whole sample of dyads. For example, the wife-to-husband partner effect estimates for each couple can be treated as scores, and we can compute the average across dyads. We can then use a one-sample t-test to evaluate whether the average wife-to-husband parameter differs from zero. In the example, this might tell us whether husbands generally tend to reciprocate their wives' competitive-ness in the prisoner's dilemma game.

Table 14.5 presents the averages of the sequential-analysis parameter estimates for 30 husband–wife pairs. The parameters for both the hus-bands and the wives are presented. Because these parameter estimates are means for the same parameters described in Table 14.3, there is no sub-stantive difference in the interpretations. However, we can generalize beyond the behavior of a single couple. Thus the first estimate reflects the average logit for husbands' D choice in the prisoner's dilemma game. The parameter equals 0.083 and reflects a probability of .52. A t-test is used to assess whether the mean is reliably different from zero. The results of this analysis suggest that there is no difference in the likelihood of husbands choosing C or D. The intercept for wives choosing D is also near zero and corresponds to a probability of .55. It, too, is not statistically significant.

The actor effects reveal an interesting difference between the behavior of husbands and wives. There is stability in husbands, but for wives the

TABLE 14.5. Mean Parameter Estimates for 30 Couples Using Log-Linear Analysis

Parameter	Husband	Wife
Intercept	0.083	0.216
Actor effect	0.155	−0.106
Partner effect	0.150†	0.156†
Interaction effect	−0.214*	−0.025

†$p < .10$; *$p < .05$.

effect is negative (0.150 and −0.106, respectively). Although neither of the actor effects differs reliably from zero, we can test whether they differ significantly from each other by subtracting one partner's actor effect from the other partner's actor effect for each dyad and testing whether the average of these differences differs from zero using a t-test. In the example, there is marginally significant evidence of greater temporal stability for husbands than for wives, $t(29) = 1.71$, $p = .098$.

The partner effect is interpreted as the person's tendency to reciprocate the partner's behavior. The two partner effects are similar in size for husbands and wives and are marginally statistically significant. Thus there is a trend for husbands and wives to reciprocate their partner's competitiveness. However, the partner effect is qualified for husbands, due to the statistically significant interaction effect. As was found for Mike, the interaction effect is negative, indicating that a husband's decision to reciprocate competitiveness is very much guided by consideration of his wife's prior choice. Furthermore, the difference between husbands' and wives' interaction effects is statistically significant, $t(29) = −2.33$, $p = .027$. The interaction is much stronger for husbands than it is for wives.

The Assumption of Stationarity in Time-Series Analysis

The goal of sequential analysis in particular, and time-series analysis in general, is to describe reliable temporal patterns in behavior. However, the pattern of behavior itself can change over time. For example, Gottman (1979) found different stages in marital problem solving. The first phase involves defining the problem, or what Gottman called *agenda building*. In the second phase spouses argue for their own position. The third phase involves negotiation processes, at least in relatively nondistressed couples. The question arises whether the pattern of interaction is the same across all three phases. If the sequential analysis measures the "average" pattern over the entire stream of behavior but the pattern is significantly different in the last phase than in the first phase, then this average effect is not an accurate assessment of the process in either phase.

There is good reason to question whether there is stationarity in the behavior of marital couples in the prisoner's dilemma game. Although we did not mention this earlier, the couples did not actually interact for 32 trials in a row. Rather, they interacted with each other in two distinct sets of 16 trials. It is therefore quite possible that the pattern of interaction was not the same in the second set as in the first set of trials. The test of stationarity is simply the test of whether any of the parameters reported in Table 14.4 differ across the two sets of trials.

To test for stationarity, an additional variable is added to the model, by which we predict one person's response using the person's prior response and the person's partner's prior response. This variable might be coded 0 for the first set of 16 trials and 1 for the second set of 16 trials. The central question is whether an effect interacts with this new variable. For instance, if the actor effect interacted with set, then that implies that the actor effect is changing from the first to the second set.

Beyond the Basic Analysis

Once the log-linear parameters for sequential analysis have been obtained from a sample of dyads, additional questions can be addressed. We have already shown that the behavior of partners can be compared within dyads. In addition, comparison between groups of participants is quite common. Such an analysis can determine, for example, whether spouses in distressed marriages are more likely to reciprocate negativity than spouses in nondistressed marriages (Gottman, 1979), or whether mothers of children with schizophrenia are more likely to reciprocate negativity than mothers of depressed children (Cook, Asarnow, Goldstein, Marshal, & Weber, 1990). The effects estimated from a sequential analysis can also serve as either the independent or dependent variable in either a correlation or a multiple regression analysis. For instance, it would be interesting to test whether people high in sensation seeking (Zuckerman, 1979) are more likely to reciprocate negativity than those who are low in the trait. As an example of using log-linear parameters as an independent variable, Gottman, Coan, Carrère, and Swanson (1998) suggested that people who not only reciprocate but also escalate negativity are more likely to get divorced.

In summary, sequential analysis is the most prevalent form of dyadic time-series analysis. It is appropriate when dyad members' behaviors are measured on a nominal or ordinal level. Statistically, one estimates the APIM for each dyad, and the unit of analysis is time rather than dyad. The log-linear parameters from the analysis of individual dyads can be aggregated across dyads to provide aggregate information, as well as information on subgroups. Thus it is possible to determine whether temporal patterns of interaction differ between groups and to correlate the parameters with other variables of interest.

STATISTICAL ANALYSIS OF SEQUENTIAL DATA: MULTILEVEL MODELING

Beginning in Chapter 4, we have emphasized the use of MLM for dyadic data. In this section, we discuss the use of MLM to estimate models for sequential data. In addition to the prior section on log-linear analysis (if only for familiarization with the example data), we advise the reader to read the section on cross-lagged regression analysis in the previous chapter.

As we discussed in the previous chapter, analyzing over-time dyadic data using MLM can be very complex. It is even more complicated when the outcome is dichotomous. In addition to problems inherent when individuals are nested within dyads and observations are nested within persons (i.e., repeated measures), there is the additional twist that we need to allow for the possibility that the two dyad members' scores at the same time point are related. For instance, in the Cook (1988) example, if the husband cooperates on a given trial, then the wife may also cooperate. More technically, we want to allow for the errors to be correlated. Finally, we need to allow for the fact that the responses are dichotomous and not continuous.

In terms of current software, SPSS cannot analyze mixed models with a dichotomous outcome. SAS can analyze such data using PROC NMIXED. However, NMIXED does not have the REPEATED option that we used in Chapter 13 to allow for the possibility that the correlation between errors is negative. The computer program HLM6 can analyze dichotomous outcomes (as well as counted, i.e., Poisson-distributed, outcomes). However, HLM6 does not allow for the repeated-measures option with dichotomous outcomes. Finally, MLwiN can handle dichotomous outcomes, but the approach, at least in the current version, is rather awkward.

This analysis uses the same data (Cook, 1988) that we discussed when we presented log-linear analysis. The HLM6 statistical program was used to estimate the model. We first determined the correlation of errors, or the residuals, in the husband's and wife's responses from the same trial. We saved the model's residuals and computed the correlation between husband and wife. Because that correlation is only −.028, it is reasonable to eliminate this parameter from the model.

One advantage of MLM over log-linear modeling is that a combined model for husbands and wives can be estimated. Because dyad members were distinguishable, we use the two-intercept approach that we first presented in Chapter 4 and used again in Chapter 13. Level 1 refers to dyad, and level 2 to time point. We created one variable called HUSBAND that was set at 1 if the observation was from the husband and 0 otherwise; the variable WIFE was set at 1 if the observation was from the wife and 0 otherwise. We then created the lagged actor, or LA, and lagged partner, LP, effect. We multiplied the HUSBAND and WIFE variables times the LA and LP variables to form HLA, HLP, WLA, and WLP. Finally, we multiplied LA times LP to form LAP, which is the actor–partner interaction, which we in turn multiplied by HUSBAND and WIFE to form HLAP and WLAP.

Initially, we allowed actor, partner, interaction, and intercept effects to be random and correlated. We found relatively small variances for the partner and interaction effects. Consequently, we estimated a model in which only the intercepts and actor effects were random; that is, these effects were allowed to vary from couple to couple. Note that in Figure 14.4, u_4, u_5, u_7, and u_8 are dimmed, meaning that their variances are fixed to zero. The setup for the HLM6 analyses is presented in Figure 14.4. The correlation of the husband (HUSBAND) and wife (WIFE) intercepts was .584, and the correlation between the actor effects (HLA with WLA) was .705. Given these high correlations, we might want to consider combining the two effects into a dyadic effect, but we did not do so in this example.

In Table 14.6, we present the MLM results for both husbands and wives. We first note that the results are generally similar to those found in the log-linear analysis in Table 14.5. For instance, in both analyses the

---

LEVEL 1 MODEL (bold: group-mean centering; bold italic: grand-mean centering)

$\text{Prob(COMPETE=1}|\beta) = \varphi$

$\text{Log}[\varphi/(1 - \varphi)] = \eta$

$\eta = \beta_1(\text{HUSBAND}) + \beta_2(\text{WIFE}) + \beta_3(\text{HLA}) + \beta_4(\text{HLP}) + \beta_5(\text{HLAP}) + \beta_6(\text{WLA}) + \beta_7(\text{WLP}) + \beta_8(\text{WLAP})$

LEVEL 2 MODEL (bold italic: grand-mean centering)

$\beta_1 = \gamma_{10} + u_1$
$\beta_2 = \gamma_{20} + u_2$
$\beta_3 = \gamma_{30} + u_3$
$\beta_4 = \gamma_{40} + u_4$
$\beta_5 = \gamma_{40} + u_5$
$\beta_6 = \gamma_{60} + u_6$
$\beta_7 = \gamma_{70} + u_7$
$\beta_8 = \gamma_{80} + u_8$

FIGURE 14.4. HLM6 setup.

interaction effects (HLAP and WLAP) are negative for both partners, and the actor effect is negative for the wife. The advantages of the multilevel approach are that we estimate the variability in the intercept and the actor effects and that we can estimate the correlation of these effects for husband and wife. In the example, the variances of both intercepts and both actor effects are statistically significant. The significant variance in the intercepts indicates that average levels of competitiveness for both husbands and wives varied from couple to couple. Similarly, the significant variance for both actor effects shows that the degree of stability in competitiveness for husbands and wives varied across couples.

We also tested for gender differences. We estimated a model with one actor, one partner, and one interaction effect and then examined whether these effects interacted with gender. The model is

$$\eta = \beta_1 \text{LagAct} + \beta_2 \text{LagPart} + \beta_3 \text{LagProd} + \beta_4 \text{Gender} + \beta_5 \text{GAct} + \beta_6 \text{GPart} + \beta_7 \text{GProd}.$$

The one statistically significant effect that we found was that the interaction effect was larger (i.e., more negative) for the husbands than for the wives, $\beta_7 = -0.124$, $p = .025$. For tests pooled across gender, only the interaction effect was statistically significant, $\beta_3 = -0.139$, $p = .013$. The partner effect was marginally significant, $\beta_2 = 0.111$, $p = .051$.

TABLE 14.6. HLM6 Analysis of the 30 Couples

	Husbands			Wives		
Effect[a]	HLM variable[b]	Estimate	t	HLM variable[b]	Estimate	t
Intercept	HUSBAND	0.027	0.115	WIFE	0.166	0.928
Actor	HLA	0.132	1.128	WLA	−0.073	−0.718
Partner	HLP	0.156	1.919	WLP	0.067	0.847
Interaction	HLAP	−0.263	−3.277	WLAP	−0.015	−0.190

Variance					
	Estimate	$\chi^2(27)$		Estimate	$\chi^2(27)$
Intercept	1.456	97.59		0.888	70.89
Actor	0.442	41.25		0.373	49.69

[a]Unit-specific effects.
[b]See Figure 14.4.

EVENT-HISTORY ANALYSIS

Some events, such as breaking up, having a first child, and death, occur for couples only once, at the most. For these events, we can record how long it takes for the event to occur. The analysis of such data has a variety of names, two of which are *event history* and *survival analysis*. We prefer the less foreboding and more general term of "event-history analysis." Our discussion of this topic is brief and should be considered introductory. We refer the reader to books by statisticians Cox and Oakes (1984), sociologist Allison (1995), and education researchers Singer and Willett (2003) for a more extensive discussion. However, these authors consider event-history analysis of individuals only, not dyads.

In some studies of dyads, both members are at risk of the event happening (e.g., becoming unemployed), whereas other events refer to the couple (e.g., breakup). We initially discuss dyad-level outcomes and later turn our attention to individual-level outcomes.

In the language of event-history analysis, each unit, in our case each dyad, is "at risk" of the event happening. The rate at which the event happens is called the *hazard rate*. Alternatively, we can consider the rate at which the event does not happen, or what is called the *survival rate*.

Consider as a hypothetical example a study of 200 couples who are followed for 10 years after marriage. For each couple we determine whether or not they broke up, and, if they did, we also determine when the breakup occurred. For instance, if a couple broke up during the fifth year of marriage in the middle of the year, their score would be 4.5—they were married four and a half years before breakup. Notice that one task in event-history analysis is defining time zero. For our example, it is defined as the day of marriage.

We might begin by determining the percentage of couples who have broken up after each year of marriage. In doing so, we might find that 93% remain together after 1 year and 55% after 10 years. We could then graph the decreasing percentage of couples who have not broken up for each of the 10 years of the study. Such a graph is called the *cumulative survival function*, and a hypothetical graph for the 200 couples is represented by the dashed line in Figure 14.5. The horizontal axis is time since marriage, and the vertical axis is the cumulative proportion of those who remain together. Note that this graph looks like a descending staircase and that each step is at the beginning of a year.

This first line in the graph treats time as a discrete variable, but we have a measure of breakup in continuous time. Instead of waiting to the

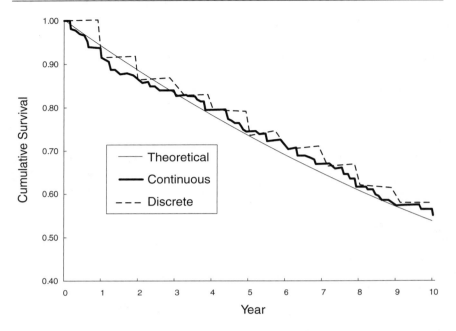

FIGURE 14.5. Cumulative survival function.

end of the year to update the percentage, we could update the percentages immediately. We are, in a sense, filling in information between the steps in the prior graph. The thick line in Figure 14.5 represents the continuous survival function. Notice that it is much smoother than the discrete cumulative survival function (the dashed line). However, even with a large number of cases, the function is still a bit jagged.

Thus far we have described the cumulative survival function estimated from data. We now consider an attempt to model that function. In the *exponential model*, we make the oversimplifying assumption that the risk does not change over time. The assumption, then, is that the risk of breakup is the same for the 1st year of marriage as it is for the 10th year. The functional form for the exponential model is $1 - p^t$, where p is the survival rate for one unit of time and t is the time unit.

We now return to the data in Figure 14.5. We have assumed an exponential model with a cumulative survival function in which the survival rate is .94 a year (the thin line). Thus with data we can create a cumulative survival function, and then we can find a theoretical survival rate that most closely matches the empirical survival function.

Obviously, the exponential model greatly oversimplifies the survival function. It assumes that the rate of breakup is the same throughout every year of marriage and does not allow for such phenomena as the "7-year itch." It also assumes that all couples would eventually break up if they lived long enough. There are more complex survival functions (see earlier cited texts), but the main purpose of event-history analysis is not to estimate the survival rate. Rather, the focus is on trying to understand factors that increase or decrease the survival rate. For breakup, we might ask the following questions:

- Are couples who marry younger at greater risk of breakup?
- Are gay and lesbian couples more or less likely to break up than heterosexual couples?
- If a baby is born, is there an increase or decrease in the risk of breakup?

These variables (age, sexual orientation, and baby's birth) are called *covariates* in event-history analysis. Notice that the predictor variable in the last question, birth of a baby, changes over time. This type of variable is referred to as a *time-varying covariate*.

In the proportional-hazards model (sometimes called the *Cox model*), we do not have to assume that the survival function takes on a specific form. Instead, we assume that the ratio of hazards is proportional. For instance, assume that the rate of breakup was greater for people who were not religious than for those who were religious. Now imagine that the breakup rate for religious couples was 80% of the breakup rate for nonreligious couples. In this case, the hazard ratio would be 1/.8, or 1.25. Thus the hazard ratio is assumed to be constant over time. Normally, the hazard ratio is logged, and we would compute ln(1.25), or 0.223.

Censored Scores

In event-history analysis, the "dependent variable" is the length of time for the event to happen—the breakup, in the example. The scores for the couples who have broken up range from 0 to 10, where time is measured in years. We would hope and expect that some couples would still be together after 10 years. Technically, for these couples, scores on the outcome variable are missing, or, in event-history analysis, they are said to be *censored*. We have given these couples a score of 10.5 on the outcome. We could have chosen 10.01 or 99.37. The key idea is to assign a value that is greater than the largest possible uncensored value.

We have not yet mentioned missing data. There are two major types of missing data. With *right-censored* data, the unit drops out of the study. It can be problematic to assume that the missing data are random. In fact, sometimes data are missing because the event has taken place: We have no further data for couples who broke up. If that were the case, it would be unreasonable to assume that the data are missing at random.

Sometimes data are said to *left-censored* in the sense that we do not know when the "clock started" for them, and we are missing their time-zero value. For instance, if we were to compare the rate of breakup of cohabitating couples with that of married couples, we would not have a date of "marriage" for the cohabitating couples.

To have satisfactory power for event-history analysis, we need many cases, but we also need the event to occur frequently. In other words, we need a reasonably large sample of cases in which the event has occurred. If we were looking at a rare event, for example, death of a partner in young couples, we would need more cases than we would if we were looking at a less rare event, such as the birth of a child.

Several unique issues arise when using event-history analysis with dyads. One potentially important question that occurs with distinguishable dyads is whether one type of member has more of an effect than the other on the hazard function. Therefore, if we are interested in estimating the effect of dyad members' age as a predictor of breakup, we include in the analysis the ages of the husband and wife at the time of their marriage. To determine whether the age of one gender is more important than the other, we would create two variables. For the first we compute the average age of the two members, and for the second we compute the difference in age, for example, husband's age minus wife's age. The sum and difference would then be predictors in the event-history analysis. If there is an effect of the sum, then we know that younger (or perhaps older) couples are at greater risk of breakup. If there were differential influence, then the difference score would be a predictor of the event, and one would conclude that the bigger the difference, the greater the likelihood of breakup. The direction of the difference effect tells us whose age has a stronger effect. If the effect is positive, then the age of the husband is more important than the age of the wife. If the effect is negative, then the age of the wife is more important. Note that if couple members were indistinguishable, then individual characteristics would be averaged. Thus, if we were considering gay or lesbian couples and we were looking at the effect of age on breakup, we would use the average age of the members of the couple at the start of the relationship.

Individual-Level Events

Earlier we stated that the event might occur for each of the members. For instance, we might have a study in which each member is at risk of "falling out of love." If dyad members are distinguishable, then we can run the analysis twice, once for each type of member. We know of no way to simultaneously estimate this model for both members—a repeated-measures event-history analysis. Moreover, it is not clear how the data would be analyzed if the dyad members were indistinguishable.

A version of event-history analysis can be applied to a single couple for events that happen frequently in a dyad. For instance, Griffin and Gardner (1989) considered the effect of a partner's behavior on one's own behavior: A husband may be at greater "risk" of gazing at his wife if his wife is gazing at him. An event-history analysis is performed on each couple, and then results are aggregated. Also Snyder, Stoolmiller, Wilson, and Yamamoto (2003) examined children's anger. They found that parents' ability to modulate their own emotions and negative behavior was associated with an increased latency for children's anger.

Discrete Analysis

Finally, we described earlier a discrete cumulative hazard function. Following Singer and Willett (2003), we can perform a discrete version of event-history analysis. First, we consider only cases for which the event has not happened at the prior wave. Consequently, if a couple first reported breaking up at year 5, we would have data for them at years 1, 2, 3, and 4. If 0 is used for staying together and 1 for breakup, then there would be a 0 for years 1, 2, and 3, and a 1 for year 4. If a couple never breaks up, then there would be 10 observations for them, all zeros, one for each year. Second, we run a logistic regression analysis on this data set, treating the event as the dependent variable. Interestingly and surprisingly for this data set, it is legitimate to ignore couple in the analysis. Observation would be the unit of analysis. Because the hazard function may vary over time, we would want to include time as a predictor variable. Keiley and Martin (2005) provide an extended illustration of a discrete event-history analysis.

SUMMARY AND CONCLUSIONS

The primary goal of this chapter was to introduce methods for analyzing discrete over-time dyadic data. As in other chapters, our discussion began with measurement issues, and we provided definitions of event and interval sampling. We then introduced sequential analysis, which models an individual's current behavior as a function of stability (i.e., what the person did in the past) and reciprocity or responsiveness (i.e., what the person's partner did in the past).

We discussed two very different approaches to the analysis of sequential data: log-linear analysis and MLM. Our presentation of log-linear analysis focused on the analysis of logit models, in which a logarithm of the odds for various behavior sequences (e.g., the odds that the husband competes after both partners cooperated in the prior turn) were modeled to be a function of a grand mean (i.e., the person's general tendency to behavior in a particular fashion across all trials), an actor effect (i.e., a person's tendency to follow his or her own prior behavior with similar behavior), a partner effect (i.e., a person's tendency to reciprocate his or her partner's behavior), and an interaction between actor and partner (i.e., a person's tendency to follow trials in which the two partners matched their behavior in a different way from the way he or she followed trials in which the partners differed). We then considered aggregation across dyads and significance-testing issues.

We next showed that specialized versions of MLM programs can be used to estimate essentially the same model as that estimated using log-linear modeling. We presented the models and estimates using HLM6, and we briefly discussed other programs as well. Finally, we included a brief description of event-history analysis.

As we noted at the beginning of this chapter, we have only presented a very brief introduction to what is a highly complex analysis. We refer the interested reader to Cox and Oakes (1984), Allison (1995), and Singer and Willett (2003). Some of the most important work in the study of relationships uses sequential analysis (Gottman, 1979; Hops et al., 1987). Thus the methods presented in this chapter are very important. However, as we have seen, this is a difficult topic. The combination of log-linear, multilevel, and dyadic analysis into one model is very complicated.

In the final chapter, we discuss neglected topics. Additionally, we also try to summarize the major themes of the book and provide guidance concerning the "dos and don'ts" of dyadic data analysis.

NOTE

1. In coding conversations, each speech act is coded as an event. It is possible that one member may produce two or more speech acts before the other member replies. In this case, the identity of the respondent is not switching with every event. Special coding rules are required for such situations. For example, if any of the husband's contiguous speech acts were coded as negative, one might code the whole set of his contiguous speech acts as negative. Such a coding strategy is based on the presumption that negative speech acts are more salient (and provocative) than positive or neutral speech acts, and so, if any in a series of speech acts were negative, that negative act is most likely to affect the partner's next speech act. Other solutions to this problem might be to code the husband's set of contiguous speech acts as the last in the set was coded, on the proposition that the most recent speech act drives the partner's next response.

15

Concluding Comments

In this final chapter we consider topics that we have not yet discussed in this book; specifically, we consider the analysis of specialized dyadic models and designs that go beyond the dyad. We also summarize several of the central themes that run throughout the book, and we describe what we call the "seven deadly sins of dyadic data analysis." Finally, we discuss several conceptual and practical issues in dyadic analysis.

SPECIALIZED DYADIC MODELS

We have tried to be comprehensive in our discussion of dyadic data. We have focused on models and designs that have been used in the literature. However, two additional dyadic models have been proposed and are sometimes used, and they are discussed here. No doubt there are other models. We strongly urge researchers to be creative in their choices of designs, models, and analyses and to choose according to the research question. For an example of a creative blending of dyadic models, the reader should consult Sadler and Woody (2003).

Mutual Influence

A model extensively featured in this book is the Actor–Partner Interdependence Model (APIM). The model was introduced in Chapter 7 and has been discussed in other chapters, particularly Chapters 13 and 14. Within the APIM, actor and partner effects model the interdependence of dyad members. The mutual-influence model (Kenny, 1996b) is similar to the

APIM in that we have two people who are both measured on outcome and predictor variables. However, in the mutual-influence model, the outcomes for the two people *directly* influence one another: There is reciprocal causation or feedback. For instance, how much person A likes person B may influence how much B likes A, and how much B likes A may influence how much A likes B. The model is one of bidirectional causation, or $Y_1 \leftrightarrow Y_2$. In the APIM there is influence, but that influence is indirect because it is mediated by X_1 and X_2.

A standard multiple regression analysis cannot be used to estimate the effects of the mutual-influence model because of the feedback (Kenny, 1979), which makes estimating the model much more difficult. There are two different strategies for estimating mutual influence paths. In the first strategy, reciprocal influence is estimated by assuming (1) that there are no other types of nonindependence and (2) equality of influence (i.e., how much person A affects B is equal to how much B affects A). The equality assumption is more reasonable when the dyad members are indistinguishable. If the intraclass correlation between the dyad members' outcome scores is denoted as r_I, then the reciprocal influence parameter equals

$$\frac{1 \pm \sqrt{1 - r_I^2}}{r_I},$$

using a formula given in Kenny (1979). There are two different solutions to this equation, and the solution that is greater than 1 is discarded. For instance, if the correlation between partners' marital satisfaction were .60, the reciprocal-influence parameter would be estimated as either 0.333 or 3.000. In this example the estimate of the reciprocal path would be .333, and the estimate of 3.000 would be discarded. For more elaborate models, structural equation modeling (SEM; see Chapter 5) can be used. Woody and Sadler (2005) provide an illustration that is a variant of the mutual-influence model.

When dyad members are distinguishable (e.g., husbands and wives) and we do not wish to force the paths to be equal, an instrumental-variable strategy (James & Singh, 1978) can be employed. As shown in Figure 15.1, there are two variables (X and Y) and two members in the dyad (1 and 2). It must be specified that X_1 causes Y_1 but not Y_2, and that X_2 causes Y_2 but not Y_1; that is, there are no partner effects. Thus the model assumes that there are actor effects but no partner effects, and this restriction permits the estimation of the mutual-influence effects. Note, too, that in this model (unlike the mutual-influence model without instrumental vari-

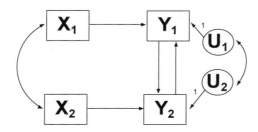

FIGURE 15.1. Mutual-influence model.

ables) the disturbances of the Ys are correlated. In this model X_1 serves as an instrumental variable to permit estimation of the path from Y_1 to Y_2, and X_2 serves as an instrumental variable to permit the estimation of the path from Y_2 to Y_1. (Less plausibly but theoretically possible, instrumental-variable estimation is possible if there are partner effects but no actor effects.) The absence of partner effects must be determined theoretically, not empirically. That is, one cannot estimate partner effects, find that they are zero, and then estimate a mutual-influence model. One advantage of the instrumental-variable approach is that the reciprocal paths need not be assumed to be equal for distinguishable dyads. This method also allows for the residual, or disturbance, effects to be correlated, and this correlation may represent a compositional effect (i.e., dyad members were not randomly paired together). Note, however, that the actor effects must be nontrivial in size in order for estimates of the reciprocal paths to be reliable, because the model is not identified (Chapter 5) if the actor effects are weak.

Perhaps the first use of instrumental-variable estimation of mutual-influence effects was by Duncan, Haller, and Portes (1968). In their study of schoolboys, each boy nominated his best friend to create a sample of dyads. The boys' parents' socioeconomic status served as the instrumental variable to estimate a feedback loop in which each boy's educational aspirations predicted the other's educational aspirations. Using a variant of SEM, they found evidence of substantial mutual influence in career aspirations. Neale, Eaves, Kendler, Heath, and Kessler (1994) have also discussed the use of this instrumental-variable approach for data from families, and Jennings and Stoker (2005) have used the model to study the mutual influence of husband's and wife's political attitudes. Finally, another version of the mutual-influence model, called the *endogenous feedback model* (Erbring & Young, 1979) allows for feedback between the disturbances of Y_1 and Y_2.

There are certain circumstances in which the mutual-influence model might be more plausible than the APIM. In these circumstances, the independent variable that serves as the instrumental variable is an individual-difference measure, and the dependent variable is a relationship-specific measure that would likely be predicted by the instrumental variable. For instance, a measure of person A's anxiety about close relationships in general could serve as the instrumental variable predicting person A's anxiety in relation to person B (i.e., relationship-specific anxiety). The corresponding measures would also be collected for person B's general relationship anxiety and his or her anxiety specifically in relationship to person A. Theoretically, any effect of person A's general relationship anxiety on person B would be mediated through person A's relationship-specific anxiety with person B, and there would be no partner effect for Person A's general relationship anxiety. The same condition would hold for person B. We estimated this model on husband–wife relationships using data from Cook's (2000) study of attachment security. Husband anxiety in relation to wife increases wife anxiety in relation to husband, $b = 0.337$; but wife anxiety in relationship to husband dampens husband anxiety in relation to wife, $b = -0.514$. However, neither of these paths were statistically significant.

An instrumental variable could be an experimentally manipulated variable (Smith, 1982). For example, a researcher might experimentally change how much each person likes the other by a similarity manipulation. To permit estimation, the manipulated variable should be mixed (i.e., not entirely within- or between-dyads). Thus, for some dyads, both members should have the same level of the manipulation, and for other dyads, they would have different levels. In such a way, the degree of reciprocal liking could be measured. If the dyad members are distinguishable, as in the case of opposite-sex dyads, then the relative degree of influence from men to women and vice versa can be assessed. If dyad members were indistinguishable (e.g., cousins), the analysis would become more complicated. We could use the Olsen and Kenny (2006) method of estimating SEM models with indistinguishable dyad members described in Chapter 5.

Common-Fate Models

In the common-fate model, the covariation between dyad members' scores is assumed to be due to some unmeasured factor that affects both dyad members. In this model, the two people do not influence each other, but, rather, the same external force influences both. The common-fate model has a long history, one older than the APIM. Kenny and La Voie (1985) were the first to present the common-fate model for the study of dyads and groups. Since then, several authors (Bowen & Huang, 1990; Gollob, 1991; Griffin & Gonzalez, 1995; Olsen & Kenny, 2006; Wilcox, 1994; Woody & Sadler, 2005) have made estimation suggestions.

The original common-fate model is presented in Figure 15.2. The variable X is assumed to be correlated with Y at two levels, the dyad and individual level. The dyad-level correlation assesses the degree to which the two individuals' shared tendency on X relates to Y, and it is shown as the relationship between latent X and latent Y in Figure 15.2. The individual-level correlation measures the degree to which a person's unique tendencies on X are related to that person's unique tendencies on Y. They are represented in the figure as two curved lines between the errors of X and Y, one for member 1 and another for member 2. The latent variables are assumed to be variables that affect both members of the dyad.

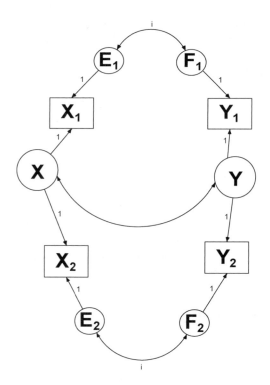

FIGURE 15.2. Original common-fate model.

One way of understanding the latent variables is that they represent something that is shared by the couple; hence the term *common fate*.

To make the model identified (Chapter 5), several restrictions are made. Specifically, the paths from the latent variables to the measures are fixed to 1; the individual-level correlations, denoted as i in Figure 15.2, between E_1 and F_1 and between E_2 and F_2 are set equal.

There are several ways to estimate the parameters for the common-fate model. We first consider ANOVA estimators of the dyad and individual correlations. The reader should consult Griffin and Gonzalez (1995) for a presentation of the pairwise estimates. To determine the dyadic and individual-level correlations, we compute MS_{BX}, MS_{BY}, MS_{WX}, and MS_{WY}, which are familiar mean squares that we introduced in Chapter 2 and have used throughout the book. Additionally, we need to compute MCP_{BXY} and MCP_{WXY}, which are the mean cross-products that we discussed in Chapter 6. To determine the dyad correlation, we compute

$$\frac{MCP_{BXY} - MCP_{WXY}}{\sqrt{(MS_{BX} - MS_{WX})(MS_{BY} - MS_{WY})}},$$

and the individual-level correlation is

$$\frac{MCP_{WXY}}{\sqrt{MS_{WX}\,MS_{WY}}}.$$

The individual-level correlation is a real correlation coefficient, but the dyad-level correlation is not an ordinary product–moment correlation. Rather, it is a latent variable correlation and has some unusual properties. The dyad correlation can be out of range (i.e., larger in absolute value than 1). To reduce the possibility of out-of-range solutions, dyad correlations should be computed only if both variables have significant between-dyads variance, which is indicated by a significant positive intraclass correlation for each variable. Moreover, if the correlation is greater than +1, it is reported as +1, and if less than −1, it is reported as −1. Kenny and La Voie (1985) provide more information on this subject. Bowen and Huang (1990), Gollob (1991), and Wilcox (1994) describe different estimators of the dyad-level correlation that have the advantage of not yielding any out-of-range estimates.

Because the individual-level correlation is a standard product–moment correlation, it can be tested using standard techniques. The degrees of freedom associated with the test are $n - 1$, where n is the number of dyads. The dyad-level correlation, on the other hand, cannot be tested for statistical significance using standard methods. Griffin and Gonzalez (1995) have proposed a test of this dyad-level correlation.

We think it best not to use ANOVA or pairwise correlations to estimate these models; instead, we suggest that researchers use an SEM program to estimate the model. Methods developed by Muthén and Muthén (2001), Woody and Sadler (2005), and Olsen and Kenny (2006) can be used to estimate these models.

A modified version of the common-fate model, developed by Griffin and Gonzalez (1995), is presented in Figure 15.3. There are three major changes to the model. First, there are paths, rather than correlations, at the two levels, and it is assumed that X causes Y at two levels. Second, the individual level refers to X and Y, not the "errors" in X and Y. Third, there is no latent variable for Y. The model in Figure 15.3 appears to be more theoretically interesting and easier to estimate than the model in Figure 15.2.

For both statistical and conceptual reasons, the APIM, first discussed in Chapter 7, has been used much more frequently than the common-fate model. It is an unfortunate commentary that there are more papers on how to estimate these common-fate correlations than there are papers that actually use those estimation formulas to test substantive hypotheses. However, there is one situation in which the common-fate model is by far more appropriate than the APIM. This is the case in which both members of the dyad report on the same variable. For instance, if the members of a married couple were asked to report on how each feels about the relationship, the APIM would be more appropriate, but if they were asked to report on how happy their child is, the common-fate model would be more suitable.

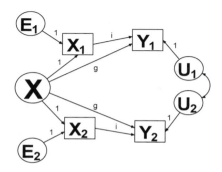

FIGURE 15.3. Modified common-fate model.

GOING BEYOND THE DYAD

Triads

Sometimes in the study of dyads we need to go beyond the pair and consider a triad. We have already discussed triads in this book. In particular, Chapter 9 extensively considered the perception of people in three-person groups (e.g., mother, father, and child). Also, in Chapter 10, we considered the one-with-many design, in which the "one" could be one person in a triad (e.g., the father) and the "many" could be the other two people in the triad (e.g., mother and child).

In some cases the measurements themselves might be triadic: For instance, Art may perceive how much Bob likes Chuck. Consider a model put forth by Bond, Horn, and Kenny (1997) that is a generalization of the Social Relations Model (SRM; Chapter 8) for triadic relations. We refer the reader to Bond and colleagues for the statistical details and to Kenny, Bond, Mohr, and Horn (1996) for an illustration. The model contains three people: a judge, an actor, and a partner. If Art judges how much Bob likes Chuck, Art would be the judge, Bob would be the actor, and Chuck would be the partner. We only state that there are 7 sources of variance (3 at the individual level, 3 at the dyadic level, and 1 at the triadic level) and 16 types of correlations (3 at the individual level, 9 at the dyadic level, and 4 at the triadic level). Although the model is quite complex, it answers some very interesting questions; for example, do group members agree about who is popular in the group?

Triadic effects can also occur when family members are asked to rate the relationships in their family. Bartle-Haring and colleagues (1999) considered such a model when members of three-person families (mother, father, and adolescent) were asked to rate the degree of differentiation of the six possible dyadic relations (MF, MA, FM, FA, AM, and AF). One potential model for such data is to apply the three-person SRM family model (Chapter 9) to the ratings of each family member and then allow for the factors to be correlated across ratings made by different family members. Alternatively, one could allow a second-order factor to cause the same factor across the three different sets of judgments. The reader should consult Bartle-Haring and colleagues for details concerning this and other possible triadic models.

Extensive triadic research has addressed the question of how members allocate rewards when they have different resources. For instance, person A may have 40 points to allocate, B may have 30, and C may have 20. The question, then, is how these persons ally themselves. The general view is that two people (e.g., B and C) form a coalition against the third (A).

Models beyond the triad are possible. For instance, a topic of interest might be the interactions between couples (one couple interacting with another couple). For a rather exhaustive treatment of these types of interpersonal models, the reader is advised to consult the triangle of interpersonal models (Bond & Kenny, 2002).

Groups

As shown in Kashy and Kenny (2000) and Kenny, Mannetti, and colleagues (2002), the APIM can be applied to group data. In this case, a person's outcome is influenced by his or her own X (an actor effect) and the mean of the other members of the group's X's (the partner effect). Thus for group data the actor effect has the same meaning that it has for dyadic data (i.e., to what degree the person's standing on X affects his or her own standing on Y). However, the partner effect differs for group data because it estimates the degree to which the average standing of the other group members on X affects the person's score on Y. Because the partner effect is the effect of an average of other group members' scores, with group data we can also consider weighting some members' scores more than others (i.e., we can compute a weighted mean for the partner effect).

Sometimes we might want to examine dyadic processes in groups by having persons make judgments of one another. In Chapter 8 we detailed the analysis of round-robin data in groups for which members are indistinguishable, and in Chapter 9 we detailed the analysis when members are distinguishable. Another strategy for studying groups is to consider each group as a variant of the one-with-many design. For instance, the question might be how members in the group view the group leader and how that group leader views the other group members. In this case, the leader would be the "one," and the other group members would be the "many."

Network Autocorrelation

Consider the following data set: There are 15 persons who are members of the same social network (Chapter 11), and each person is asked to name their two closest friends. Some of the pairs are mutual friends, but in other pairs, one person considers him- or herself to be a friend of the other, but not vice versa. For example, persons 1 and 2 are mutual friends, but person 3 is an isolate because person 3 nominates persons 1 and 7 as friends, but neither person 1 nor person 7 nominates person 3. In addition to nominating two friends, each person is measured on two variables, a predictor variable X and an outcome variable Y. For example, X might measure the person's agreeableness, and Y might measure psychological adjustment. The focus of the research is the degree to which agreeableness predicts adjustment. Values for X and Y, as well as each person's friend nominations for the 15 people in our hypothetical example, are presented in Table 15.1.

At issue in this design is the possibility that the network members' outcomes may be correlated due to friendship. For the example, this suggests that adjustment might be particularly similar for friends. The presence of this nonindependence biases the significance test of the effect of X on Y, and that bias is referred to as *network autocorrelation*.

To our knowledge, there is no general solution to the problem of network autocorrelation. We suggest two partial strategies. The first is to estimate the nonindependence in Y and then use generalized least squares (Draper & Smith, 1998) to estimate the effect of X on Y. The second is a method proposed by Kenny and Judd (1996) that can be used to estimate the nonindependence within the social network. That method selects all pairs of scores on the outcome variable and computes the squared differences. Some of those differences involve pairs of people who do not choose each other; other differences involve pairs who choose each other; and still others are pairs in which one member chooses the other, but that choice is not reciprocated. Kenny and Judd show how these squared differences on

TABLE 15.1. Network Autocorrelation Example

Person	X	Y	Friendship choices
1	3	6	2, 3
2	6	7	1, 5
3	7	6	1, 7
4	6	7	5, 6
5	5	8	2, 10
6	2	6	5, 15
7	4	4	6, 9
8	5	7	5, 10
9	6	8	3, 7
10	7	9	5, 11
11	8	8	12, 13
12	9	7	13, 14
13	4	4	14, 15
14	4	3	8, 15
15	6	5	13, 14

the outcome variable can be used to estimate the nonindependence in the data. Note that the nonindependence correlation should ideally measure nonindependence in the residuals of Y after X is controlled.

Once a measure of nonindependence is derived, generalized least squares can be used to estimate and test the effect of X on Y (e.g., the degree to which agreeableness predicts adjustment). Generalized least squares (GLS) is comparable to ordinary least squares, but it allows for correlated observations (as well as unequal variances). A drawback of this approach is that the method of GLS presumes that estimates of the nonindependence correlation are population values, not estimates.

As an alternative to using GLS, we could use a strategy to adjust the p-values for the bias due to nonindependence. This method adjusts the numerator and denominator of the F-test, as well as the degrees of freedom.[1] A major drawback with this approach is that the degree of nonindependence must be known a priori, which is almost never the case.

Returning to the data in Table 15.1, we used the method that adjusts the mean squares and degrees of freedom. Applying Kenny and Judd's (1996) method for estimating nonindependence, we find that the correlation for reciprocal friends is .451 and that the correlation for nonreciprocal choices is .159. If we were to ignore the nonindependence in the data when we test the effect of X on Y, we would obtain a $t(13) = 2.207$, $p = .046$. Using the adjustment methods, we find that the effective degrees of freedom are not 13 but rather 10.69. Moreover, the inferential test was biased by a factor of 0.952. Using these adjustment terms, the test of the estimated effect of X on Y is $t(10.69) = 2.318$, $p = .041$. Thus considering the nonindependence due to network autocorrelation does not affect the conclusion that we draw from the hypothetical data in Table 15.1.

Again, these approaches to network autocorrelation are not yet practical solutions. Ideally, the estimation of nonindependence and the estimation of regression coefficients, controlling for nonindependence, would be accomplished in one step. Because multilevel models allow for nonindependence, those models may eventually allow for network autocorrelation.

CONCEPTUAL AND PRACTICAL ISSUES

The Meaning of Nonindependence

We begin this section with a discussion of the different statistical meanings of nonindependence. In the second part of the section, we consider the theoretical or conceptual meanings of nonindependence.

Statistical Definitions

We have discussed the measurement of nonindependence for three different types of dyadic designs: the standard design discussed in Chapter 2, SRM designs discussed in Chapter 8, and the one-with-many design discussed in Chapter 10. Table 15.2 presents five different sources of statistical nonindependence and five sets of scores that represent these sources. We include in this discussion only those forms of nonindependence found in cross-sectional data. The meanings of actor, partner, relationship, and group correspond to components of the SRM, not the APIM.

The first source of statistical nonindependence is what we call *actor nonindependence*. When a person rates, judges, or interacts with two partners, the scores may be correlated. Normally, but not always, this correlation is positive, and in this case actor nonindependence can be treated as a variance. We discussed actor nonindependence in Chapters 8, 9, and 10.

The second source of nonindependence is what we call *partner nonindependence*. When the same person is rated by, judged by, or interacts with two partners, the two scores may be correlated. Again, this correlation is typically a positive value, and partner nonindependence is generally treated as a variance. We discuss partner nonindependence in Chapters 8, 9, and 10.

Group nonindependence occurs when the two scores represent four different individuals who are all members of the same group. In Chapter 9 we discussed family effects, which are a form of group nonindependence. Another form of group nonindependence is called a compositional effect. Compositional effects represent similarities among persons who make up the group.

The fourth source of nonindependence is *actor–partner nonindependence*. For this type of nonindependence, the two scores both contain person i, but i is the actor in the first score and the partner in the second.

TABLE 15.2. Five Different Types of Nonindependence in Dyadic Data

Source	Correlated scores
Actor	X_{ij} with X_{ik}
Partner	X_{ij} with X_{kj}
Group	X_{ij} with X_{kl}
Actor–Partner	X_{ij} with X_{ki}
Dyad	X_{ij} with X_{ji}

In Chapters 8 and 9, in presenting the SRM, we discussed this source of nonindependence. Basically, this nonindependence represents a form of generalized reciprocity.

The fifth and final source of nonindependence is *dyadic nonindependence*. It represents what we usually think of as nonindependence and represents the shared unique adjustment that each person makes to the other. Dyadic nonindependence has been discussed throughout the book.

It is important to note that in the standard reciprocal design, three different sources of nonindependence combine to form nonindependence between scores:

$$Dyad + 2(Actor\text{--}Partner) + Group.$$

Although we tend to think of nonindependence as only dyad non-independence, it could also occur because of actor–partner or group effects. Thus there is more than one interpretation of nonindependence in the standard reciprocal design. Only with SRM designs can we fully partition the various sources of nonindependence. With a reciprocal one-with-many design, we obtain a nearly complete partitioning, but we have to assume that there is no group nonindependence.

Conceptual Definitions

Conceptually, nonindependence has many different meanings. Following Cook (2003), we attempt to define conceptually the terms of interdependence, reciprocity, bidirectional influence, and synchrony.

The concept of interdependence is a central and defining concept in relationship science. Its roots are in the classic books by Thibaut and Kelley (1959) and Kelley and Thibaut (1978), and the two major applications are Kelley and colleagues (1983, 2003). Their approach presumes that social interaction can be modeled as a set of two-person games and that the outcomes of these games become inherently interdependent. As people develop an interaction history with their partners, the outcomes become more interdependent. Interdependence implies many forms of nonindependence, but it transcends any statistical definition.

Reciprocity has classically been defined in a sequential, or "tit-for-tat," process. Gottman and colleagues' (1998) negative spirals are good examples of reciprocity: Mary says something negative to Mike, and Mike then says something negative to Mary. Perhaps the best statistical definition of reciprocity is a partner effect in the sequential APIM that we discussed in

Chapters 13 and 14. Note that if the person responds in kind, we have reciprocity, but if he or she responds in the opposite manner (A is domineering and then B is submissive), we would have compensation. There are two measures of reciprocity for a dyadic sequential analysis: Person A's reciprocity of person B's behavior and person B's reciprocity of person A's behavior.

We should be clear that the SRM term *reciprocity* represents something quite different from the sequential definition. It corresponds to a simultaneous measurement of two responses. However, underlying this correlation of cross-sectional data is the assumption that reciprocity is the product of a temporally reciprocal (or compensatory) process. If one person reciprocates the behavior of the other, over time their rates will become similar and therefore correlated. Gottman (1979) has correctly criticized the use of correlations of raw scores (e.g., rates) to model reciprocity. It should be noted, however, that we believe that his criticisms do not apply to the reciprocity correlations in the SRM (Cook, 1994).

Bidirectional effects are frequently treated as though they are equivalent to reciprocity, but statistically they are not the same. Bidirectional effects are present when each person influences the other. For example, in the APIM, both of the partner effects must be present for there to be bidirectional influence. Reciprocity, on the other hand, can be inferred if only one of the partner effects is present (i.e., person A reciprocates person B's behavior). In the SRM, bidirectional influence can be operationalized at both the individual and dyadic levels of analysis. At the individual level of analysis, bidirectional influence exists if there is partner variance. Consider how much two coworkers trust one another. There is bidirectional influence if there is partner variance, because each person's trust depends on the specific partner, and so they both "influence" each other. Reciprocity at the individual level of analysis, however, would be indicated if the actor and partner effects are correlated: if one coworker's general trust of others leads others to trust him or her. Additionally, at the dyadic level of analysis, bidirectional influence exists if there is relationship variance because each makes unique adjustments to the other. Reciprocity is indicated by correlation in the relationship effects: If one coworker is especially trusting of another, is that trust returned?

Finally, we come to synchronicity. Here we are not referring to the psychological experience of being "in synch" but rather to the observation of temporally coordinated behavioral responses. We think that the best way of statistically operationalizing synchronicity is by the contemporaneous correlation of responses (e.g., coherence) and temporally based lag-lead relations among the responses, as discussed under the topic of spectral analysis in Chapter 13. In other words, the cocycling of two individuals' responses is the penultimate expression of synchronicity. Alternatively, the temporal coordination of behavior can be operationalized as the contemporaneous correlation of two individuals' responses within a time-series regression analysis (Chapters 13 and 14) and as partner effects among these variables. This analysis, however, should not be used if the responses of the individuals cycle. In either case, synchrony implies that the behavior of two people is coordinated (simultaneously or sequentially) on the basis of the same "clock."

Design and Measurement Issues in Dyadic Research

One of our strongest recommendations is that researchers gather reciprocal data. That is, researchers are best advised to examine the relationship from both persons' points of view. For the standard design, by having reciprocal data, we can index the degree of nonindependence in the dyad. That nonindependence describes the degree to which the pair has a relationship. Moreover, we can estimate the APIM and see how partner characteristics affect the person. If the dyad members are distinguishable, the different effects for the two members can be estimated. In some situations, only one member of the dyad might be the central focus. For instance, in a study of illness, the ill member of the dyad may be the central focus. Although the outcomes of the other member might not be of interest, it is still important to measure the characteristics of the healthy partner to see how those characteristics affect the outcome of the ill member.

Some SRM designs, such as the round robin, are inherently reciprocal. With reciprocal designs, a much more detailed measurement of reciprocity is possible. We can determine whether reciprocity is dyadic or generalized. Finally, with reciprocal one-with-many designs, one can recover all but one of the sources of nonindependence. Reciprocal designs provide the most detailed understanding of dyadic processes.

Besides the issue of measuring both members of the dyad, another key issue in the study of dyads is the measurement of the outcome variable. We have generally emphasized measurement at the interval level. However, we have tried to show that several questions can be answered at the nominal level of measurement. In Chapters 2, 3, 4, 5, 6, 7, 11, and 14, we have detailed the analysis of nominal (usually dichotomous) variables.

A related issue is the decision to measure the dyad at multiple time points. If the focus of the research were an idiographic analysis (e.g., measuring differences between couples in the size of the partner effect), then a longitudinal design would be necessary, because with a longitudinal design the effect can be measured for each couple. Although longitudinal designs can provide definitive answers to key theoretical questions, they are quite complicated designs to execute and quite difficult to analyze.

Recruitment and Retention

This book has not discussed one of the most difficult and perplexing problems in dyadic analysis: how to enlist dyads into studies. Most of the discussion of recruitment and retention of units concerns individuals. However, recruitment and retention of dyads is much more challenging. We provide only an introductory discussion of this important issue.

Very often couples are recruited by first obtaining one member and then asking that person to enroll the other member. No doubt a sample enlisted in this manner is different from a random sample of couples. Researchers should consider coding who the recruiting and recruited members are and determine whether there are differences between the two types of members.

There is some literature on the types of dating and married couples who tend to volunteer in relationship studies. The evidence seems to suggest that there is variance across couples, at least in terms of happiness. That is, the very happy and very unhappy couples tend to volunteer. A study by Bradbury (1994) suggests that being involved in a couples' study does not lead to any more relationship problems or difficulties than would ordinarily be expected.

If the study is longitudinal, couples can drop out for several reasons. Sometimes just one member of the couple drops out. Also, the couple may break up and no longer be a unit. Obviously, it is important to know whether the couple is still together at follow-up. It may be useful to treat the breakup of the couple as an outcome to be studied in its own right (see event-history analysis, Chapter 14).

THE SEVEN DEADLY SINS OF DYADIC DATA ANALYSIS

One of the purposes of this book is stop researchers from committing what we call the "seven deadly sins" of dyadic analysis. They are detailed as follows.

• *Sin 1: Assuming that dyad members are distinguishable (e.g., separate analyses for men and women) without testing whether such an assumption is warranted.* Chapter 6 details an analysis that statistically evaluates the assumption that dyad members are distinguishable. That is, it is possible to evaluate whether there are empirically meaningful differences between the members of the couple.

Obviously, there are some situations in which it is highly likely that there are differences. Nonetheless, we advise a test to determine whether the supposed differences are in fact present in the data at hand. Of course, finding no detectable differences for the variables being studied does not mean that there are no differences for other variables.

• *Sin 2: Assuming that a statistically significant effect for one member of the dyad (e.g., for men) but not the other (e.g., for women) implies that the effect varies across members (e.g., the effect varies across gender).* This is a common error. Essentially, it is one in which we assume that there is an interaction between a within-dyads factor and another variable without ever actually testing for that interaction. We detail in several chapters, most notably in Chapters 3 and 7, how to test for interactions with a within-dyads factor. One cannot infer that there is a gender interaction just because the effect is present for one gender and not the other. (We emphasize gender here, but our conclusions hold for any test of a within-dyads factor, e.g., parent–child, boss–employee, or student–teacher.)

Consider the following case: Assume that the same effect exists for men and women and that the power of the test is .5 for both. That is, there is approximately an even chance of obtaining a significant effect for men and for women. If we also assume that the two tests are independent, then one-half of the time we will find a statistically significant effect for one gender and not the other. Thus, in this case, even though the effect is exactly the same for men and women, half of the time we would conclude that the effect was different. Quite clearly, a statistically significant effect for one gender and not the other is not evidence of an interaction. We suspect that many reports in the literature of "gender differences" are not actual gender differences but rather the by-products of this mistaken strategy.

A related fact is that, if each test for men and for women has a power of .5, the power of the combined effect, given independence, is .75. There are considerable advantages to pooling a test across the sexes. Blindly assuming a gender difference can result in overlooking an important result.

• *Sin 3: Summing or averaging the scores of the two members of the dyad without any empirical justification.* At times, we think that the two members' scores can be combined into a single score—for example, marital satisfaction. Relationship researchers routinely combine couples' scores to form a single score. In Chapter 7, we described an empirically based strategy that can be used to decide whether to sum scores on causal variables. Thus, before thoughtlessly summing or averaging the scores of members of a dyad, a rather extensive and stringent statistical test should be performed.

If there were a couple-level independent variable in the study, then a sum score on the outcome would be created if we had equal paths to each member. For instance, if we have the causal variable of length of marriage and outcomes of marital satisfaction, then summing the two satisfaction measures would be permissible if the effect of length of marriage on satisfaction were the same for husbands as for wives. The decision to sum should not be made a priori; rather, it should be justified by a combination of a theoretical rationale, measurement theory, and empirical analysis.

• *Sin 4: Using a discrepancy score as a predictor variable without controlling for the main effects.* Consider the hypothesis that similarity in age leads to marital adjustment. The variable "similarity in age" is actually an interaction—the interaction of the husband's age with the wife's age. As detailed in Chapters 7 and 12, when testing an interaction, we must control for the main effects of the two persons' ages. To test for the effect of similarity in age, we would control for the effect of the husband's and wife's ages. If the discrepancy adds something beyond the main effects, then the relational concept of similarity is needed.

• *Sin 5: Pseudounilaterality, or assuming that one member causes the other without realizing that the other has influence.* This is a topic we mentioned in the very first chapter, but we have not explicitly discussed it until now. People who are members of a dyad mutually influence one another. We should never simply assume that one person influences the other. The prototypical example of this sin is research in developmental psychology. For years, the assumption was made that only the parent influenced the child. However, Bell's (1968) classic article finally provided explicit recognition that the child can influence the parent. We now understand that a parent's negative behavior may be caused by the child's personality and not vice versa.

Duncan and Fiske (1977) discuss this problem in the study of social interaction when a confederate or an accomplice of the experimenter is used. For instance, a confederate is instructed to act in a "warm fashion" with the participant. The assumption that only the confederate influences the participant and that the participant never influences the confederate is made erroneously. As discussed in Chapter 2, one solution to this problem is to use a computer program that appears to be another person, rather than having a real person be the partner. Although this strategy has been useful at times, it necessarily prevents any authentic social interaction from occurring.

The APIM, discussed in some detail in Chapters 7, 13, and 14, allows for bidirectional causation in naturally occurring situations. Moreover, in this chapter, we have presented a model of direct bidirectional causation.

• *Sin 6: Not including partner characteristics as predictors.* Chapter 7 details a model that emphasizes how a person can be influenced not only by his or her own characteristics but also by the characteristics of the partner. For example, Kurdek (1997a) examined how a person's relational outcomes were determined not only by that person's personality but also by the person's partner's personality. Recall, too, that to study the effects of partner characteristics, a dyadic data set often needs to be created.

• *Sin 7: Treating individual as unit of analysis.* Dyadic data requires making dyad, not person, the unit of analysis. Although there have been repeated alerts about using individual as the unit of analysis, the problem still continues.

In some ways, multilevel modeling (MLM) turns the unit-of-analysis issue into an empirical problem. We have extensively used MLM in Chapters 4, 7, 10, 13, and 14. Utilizing this analysis technique, we can simultaneously analyze relationship data at both the individual and dyadic levels of analysis. Typically, the analysis reveals important and meaningful variation at both levels. To look at only one level would be to miss something valuable.

THE LAST WORD

The seven deadly sins constitute negative advice: what to avoid doing. Now we provide guidance about what to do instead.

One general suggestion is to prefer simple analyses to more complex ones. This book has detailed many very complex analyses. Although complicated analyses are sometimes required, they can lead to errors; in part, these errors are due to the complexity of the analysis; in part, they are due to the ignorance of the analysts; and sometimes they are due to misinterpretation on the audience's part. At times, the simple analyses should not be reported, but doing them may be helpful nonetheless. By comparing the simple with the complex, we can gain an understanding of the validity of the results from the more complex analysis.

Another suggestion is to not ask too much of the data. Take into account the sample size, the strength of the relationships, and the number of parameters in the model. A more complex model is not necessarily a better model. Make sure the data are able to answer the questions that they are asked.

A further proposal is to associate the terms one uses for interpersonal processes with specific aspects of the statistical models used to test those processes. For many years, terms such as *mutual influence, reciprocity,* and *synchrony* have been used interchangeably. As noted earlier in this chapter, these terms do not have the same meaning when one considers how the corresponding processes are modeled and tested statistically. It has often been noted that we are so accustomed to speaking and thinking in terms of individuals that discussing relationships is sometimes awkward. The reason may be that relationships are two-sided, and the presence of interdependence means that mentioning one side of a relationship, even in isolation, implicates the other side. The development of a clear, concise, common language for relationship science is one of the challenges we face. By specifying the types of dyads (distinguishable vs. indistinguishable), the types of dyadic variables (within dyads, between dyads, and mixed), the types of dyadic designs (standard dyadic, one with many, and round robin), the types of dyadic models (APIM, SRM, mutual influence, common fate), and the sources of nonindependence (partner effects, reciprocity, dyadic feedback, synchrony, and temporal stability), we have attempted to contribute to the clarification of this language.

We hope that readers of this book will experiment with different methods of analyzing their data. All too often, researchers compute means and run a few ANOVAs or multiple regressions and feel they have completed their data analyses. There is often much more that can be done with the data. One theme of this book is that MLM and SEM can be profitably applied to dyadic data. We urge researchers to be even more adventurous. For example, if the design permits, perform a social relations analysis or an event-history analysis. Performing an analysis does not commit the researcher to publishing it. Believe it or not, the researcher might actually learn something from the analysis! We hope that by writing this book and presenting new methods, we have encouraged researchers to test new designs, models, and analyses of their dyadic data.

As a final point, the reader needs to realize that this book is not the last word on dyadic analysis. We have tried to provide a very general framework for asking and answering questions about dyads. We hope that there will be considerable theoretical, statistical, and computational progress on these issues. We would like this book to serve as a resource to help with the comprehension and utilization of future research. We certainly do not wish our book to straitjacket or limit the understanding and analysis of dyadic data.

About 20 years ago, Steve Duck asked one of us to write a chapter on dyadic data analysis. At that time, there was some question whether there would be enough material to fill a chapter. There was more than enough (see Kenny, 1988a). When we began to write this book, we wondered whether we could write a book-length manuscript. We soon found that we had ample material to write about. We are more convinced than ever that dyadic data analysis deserves a book-length treatment. It is our sincere hope that our book will provide our emerging field with the techniques that it requires to make new and exciting discoveries.

NOTE

1. A description of how to determine the bias and the correction to the degrees of freedom can be found on the website *http://davidakenny.net/dfbias.ppt*.

References

Acitelli, L. K. (1997). Sampling couples to understand them: Mixing the theoretical with the practical. *Journal of Social and Personal Relationships, 14,* 243–261.

Acitelli, L. K., Kenny, D. A., & Weiner, D. (2001). The importance of similarity and understanding of partners' marital ideals to relationship satisfaction. *Personal Relationships, 8,* 167–185.

Allison, P. D. (1995). *Survival analysis using the SAS system: A practical guide.* Cary, NC: SAS Institute.

Allison, P. D., & Liker, J. K. (1982). Analyzing sequential categorical data on dyadic interaction: A comment on Gottman. *Psychological Bulletin, 91,* 393–403.

Anderson, L. R., & Ager, J. W. (1978). Analysis of variance in small group research. *Personality and Social Psychology Bulletin, 4,* 341–345.

Anolli, L., Duncan, S. D., Jr., Magnusson, M., & Riva, G. (Eds.). (2005). *The hidden structure of social interaction.* Amsterdam: IOS Press.

Arbuckle, J. L., & Wothke, W. (2003). *Amos 5.0 update to the Amos user's guide.* Chicago: Smallwaters Corporation.

Argyle, M., & Dean, J. (1965). Eye-contact, distance and affiliation. *Sociometry, 28,* 289–304.

Attridge, M., Berscheid, E., & Simpson, J. (1995). Predicting relationship stability from both partners versus one. *Journal of Personality and Social Psychology, 69,* 254–268.

Badr, H. (2003). Chronic illness as a relationship challenge. *Dissertation Abstracts International, 63*(9-B), 4413. (University Microfilms No. 3064088)

Bagozzi, R. P., Ascione, F. J., & Mannebach, M. A. (2005). Inter-role relationships in hospital-based pharmacy and therapeutics committee decision making. *Journal of Health Psychology, 10,* 45–64.

Bakeman, R., & Beck, S. (1974). The size of informal groups in public. *Environment and Behavior, 6,* 378–390.

Bakeman, R., & Gottman, J. M. (1997). *Observing interaction: An introduction to sequential analysis* (2nd ed.). Cambridge, UK: Cambridge University Press.

427

Barabasi, A. L. (2002). *Linked: The new science of networks.* Cambridge, MA: Perseus.

Barcikowski, R. S. (1981). Statistical power with group mean as the unit of analysis. *Journal of Educational Statistics, 6,* 267–285.

Bartle-Haring, S., Kenny, D. A., & Gavazzi, S. M. (1999). Multiple perspectives on family differentiation: Analyses by multitrait multimethod matrix and triadic social relations models. *Journal of Marriage and the Family, 61,* 491–503.

Bell, R. Q. (1968). A reinterpretation of the direction of effects in studies of socialization. *Psychological Review, 75,* 81–95.

Bentler, P. M. (2004). *EQS structural equations program manual.* Encino, CA: Multivariate Software.

Berg, E. C., Trost, M., Schneider, I. E., & Allison, M. T. (2001). Dyadic exploration of the relationship of leisure satisfaction, leisure time, and gender to relationship satisfaction. *Leisure Sciences, 23,* 35–46.

Bernard, H. R., & Killworth, P. D. (1977). Informant accuracy in social network data: II. *Human Communication Research, 4,* 3–18.

Bernard, H. R., Killworth, P. D., & Sailer, L. (1980). Informant accuracy in social network data: IV. *Social Networks, 2,* 191–218.

Bishop, Y. M. M., Feinberg, S. E., & Holland, P. W. (1975). *Discrete multivariate analysis: Theory and practice.* Cambridge, MA: MIT Press.

Boker, S. M., & Laurenceau, J. P. (2006). Dynamical systems modeling: An application to the regulation of intimacy and disclosure in marriage. In T. A. Walls & J. L. Schafer (Eds.), *Models for intensive longitudinal data* (pp. 195–218). New York: Oxford University Press.

Boker, S. M., & Rotondo, J. L. (2003). Symmetry building and symmetry breaking in synchronized movement. In M. Stamenov & V. Gallese (Eds.), *Mirror neurons and the evolution of brain and language* (pp. 163–171). Amsterdam: John Benjamins.

Boker, S. M., Xu, M., Rotondo, J. L., & King, K. (2002). Windowed cross-correlation and peak picking for the analysis of variability in the association between behavioral time series. *Psychological Methods, 7,* 338–355.

Boldry, J. G., & Kashy, D. A. (1999). Intergroup perception in naturally occurring groups of differential status: A social relations perspective. *Journal of Personality and Social Psychology, 77,* 1200–1212.

Bolger, N., & Shrout, P. E. (in press). Patterns of covariance in dyadic diary data. In T. D. Little (Ed.), *Modeling developmental processes in ecological context.* Mahwah, NJ: Erlbaum.

Bollen, K. A. (1989). *Structural equations with latent variables.* New York: Wiley.

Bond, C. F., Jr., Dorsky, S. E., & Kenny, D. A. (1992). Person memory and memorability: A round robin analysis. *Basic and Applied Social Psychology, 13,* 285–302.

Bond, C. F., Jr., Horn, E. M., & Kenny, D. A. (1997). A model for triadic relations. *Psychological Methods, 2,* 79–94.

Bond, C. F., Jr., & Kenny, D. A. (2002). The triangle of interpersonal models. *Journal of Personality and Social Psychology, 83,* 355–366.

Bond, C. F., Jr., & Lashley, B. R. (1996). Round-robin analysis of social interactions: Exact and estimated standard errors. *Psychometrika, 61,* 303–311.

Bonito, J. A. (2002). The analysis of participation in small groups: Methodological and conceptual issues related to interdependence. *Small Group Research, 33,* 412–438.

Borgatti, S. P., Everett, M. G., & Freeman, L. C. (2002). *UCINET for Windows: Software for social network analysis.* Harvard, MA: Analytic Technologies.

Bowen, J., & Huang, M. (1990). A comparison of maximum likelihood with method of moment procedures for separating individual and group effects. *Journal of Personality and Social Psychology, 58,* 90–94.

Bowlby, J. (1949). The study and reduction of group tensions in the family. *Human Relations, 2,* 123–128.

Bowlby, J. (1969). *Attachment and loss: Vol. 1. Attachment.* New York: Basic Books.

Bowlby, J. (1973). *Attachment and loss: Vol. 2. Separation: Anxiety and anger.* New York: Basic Books.

Bowlby, J. (1980). *Attachment and loss: Vol. 3. Loss: Sadness and depression.* New York: Basic Books.

Bradbury, T. N. (1994). Unintended effects of marital research on marital relationships. *Journal of Family Psychology, 8,* 187–201.

Branje, S. J., van Aken, M. A., & van Lieshout, C. F. (2002). Relational support in families with adolescents. *Journal of Family Psychology, 16,* 351–362.

Branje, S. J., van Aken, M. A., van Lieshout, C. F., & Mathijssen, J. J.(2003). Personality judgements in adolescents' families: The perceiver, the target, their relationship, and the family. *Journal of Personality, 71,* 49–81.

Brauer, M., & Judd, C. M. (2000). Defining variables in relationship to other variables: When interactions suddenly turn out to be main effects. *Journal of Experimental Social Psychology, 36,* 410–423.

Brazelton, T. B., Koslowski, B., & Main, M. (1974). The origins of reciprocity: The early mother–infant interaction. In M. Lewis & L. Rosenblum (Eds.), *Effect of the infant on its caregiver* (pp. 49–76). New York: Wiley.

Bryk, A. S., & Raudenbush, S. W. (1992). *Hierarchical linear models: Applications and data analysis methods.* Thousand Oaks, CA: Sage.

Bui, K.-V. T., Peplau, L. A., & Hill, C. T. (1996). Testing the Rusbult model of relationship commitment and stability in a 15-year study of heterosexual couples. *Personality and Social Psychology Bulletin, 22,* 1244–1257.

Buist, K. L., Dekovic, M., Meeus, W., & van Aken, M. A. (2004). Attachment in adolescence: A social relations model analysis. *Journal of Adolescent Research, 19*(6), 826–850.

Butler, E. A., Egloff, B., Wilhelm, F. H., Smith, N. C., Erickson, E. A., & Gross, J. J. (2003). The social consequences of expressive suppression. *Emotion, 3,* 48–67.

Butterfield, R. M., & Lewis, M. (2002). Health-related social influence: A social ecological perspective on tactic use. *Journal of Social and Personal Relationships, 19*(4), 505–526.

Campbell, D. T., & Kenny, D. A. (1999). *A primer of regression artifacts.* New York: Guilford Press.

Campbell, L., Simpson, J. A., Boldry, J., & Kashy, D. A. (2005). Perceptions of conflict and support in romantic relationships: The role of attachment anxiety. *Journal of Personality and Social Psychology, 88,* 510–531.

Campbell, L., Simpson, J. A., Kashy, D. A., & Rholes, W. S. (2001). Attachment orientations, dependence, and behavior in a stressful situation: An application of the actor–partner interdependence model. *Journal of Social and Personal Relationships, 18,* 821–843.

Capitanio, J. P. (1984). Early experience and social processes in rhesus macaques (*Macaca mulatta*): I. Dyadic social interaction. *Journal of Comparative Psychology, 98,* 35–44.

Cappella, J. N. (1981). Mutual influence in expressive behavior: Adult–adult and infant–adult dyadic interaction. *Psychological Bulletin, 89,* 101–132.

Card, N. A., Hodges, E. V., Little, T. D., & Hawley, P. H. (2005). Gender effects in peer nominations for aggression and social status. *International Journal of Behavioral Development, 29,* 146–155.

Chaplin, W. F., & Panter, A. T. (1993). Shared meaning and the convergence among observers' personality descriptions. *Journal of Personality, 61,* 553–585.

Christensen, A., Sullaway, M., & King, C. E. (1983). Systematic error in behavioral reports of dyadic interaction: Egocentric bias and content effects. *Behavioral Assessment, 5,* 129–140.

Christensen, P. N., & Kashy, D. A. (1998). Perceptions of and by lonely people in initial social interaction. *Personality and Social Psychology Bulletin, 24,* 322–329.

Clark, M. S., & Mills, J. (1979). Interpersonal attraction in exchange and communal relationships. *Journal of Personality and Social Psychology, 37,* 12–24.

Cohen, J. (1960). A coefficient of agreement for nominal scales. *Educational and Psychological Measurement, 20,* 37–46.

Cohen, J. (1968). Weighted kappa: Nominal scale agreement with provision for scaled disagreement or partial credit. *Psychological Bulletin, 70,* 213–220.

Cohen, J. (1988). *Statistical power analysis for the behavioral sciences* (Rev. ed.). Hillsdale, NJ: Erlbaum.

Cole, D. A., & Jordan, A. E. (1989). Assessment of cohesion and adaptability in component family dyads: A question of convergent and discriminant validity. *Journal of Counseling Psychology, 36,* 456–463.

Collins, N. L., & Read, S. J. (1990). Adult attachment, working models and relationship quality in dating couples. *Journal of Personality and Social Psychology, 58,* 644–663.

Cook, W. L. (1988). Reciprocity of consistency: Implications for forecasting the outcome of relationships. *Dissertation Abstracts International, 48,* 1897. (University Microfilms No. 8722613)

Cook, W. L. (1993). Interdependence and the interpersonal sense of control: An analysis of family relationships. *Journal of Personality and Social Psychology, 64,* 587–601.

Cook, W. L. (1994). A structural equation model of dyadic relationships within the family system. *Journal of Consulting and Clinical Psychology, 62,* 500–510.

Cook, W. L. (2000). Understanding attachment security in family context. *Journal of Personality and Social Psychology, 78,* 285–294.

Cook, W. L. (2001). Interpersonal influence in family systems: A social relations model analysis. *Child Development, 72,* 1179–1197.

Cook, W. L. (2003). Quantitative methods for deductive (theory-testing) research on parent–child dynamics. In L. Kuczynski (Ed.), *Handbook of dynamics in parent–child relations* (pp. 347–372). Thousand Oaks, CA: Sage.

Cook, W. L. (2005). The SRM approach to family assessment: An introduction and case example. *European Journal of Psychological Assessment, 21,* 216–225.

Cook, W. L., Asarnow, J. R., Goldstein, M. J., Marshal, V. G., & Weber, E. (1990). Mother–child dynamics in early-onset depression and childhood schizophrenia spectrum disorders. *Development and Psychopathology, 2,* 71–84.

Cook, W. L., & Douglas, E. M. (1998). The looking-glass self in family context: A social relations analysis. *Journal of Family Psychology, 12,* 299–309.

Cook, W. L., & Dreyer, A. S. (1984). The social relations model: A new approach to the analysis of family–dyadic interaction. *Journal of Marriage and the Family, 46,* 679–687.

Cook, W. L., & Goldstein, M. J. (1993). Multiple perspectives on family relationships: A latent variables model. *Child Development, 64,* 1377–1388.

Cook, W. L., & Kenny, D. A. (2004). Application of the social relations model to family assessment. *Journal of Family Psychology, 18,* 361–371.

Cook, W. L., & Kenny, D. A. (2005). The actor–partner interdependence model: A model of bidirectional effects in developmental studies. *International Journal of Behavioral Development, 29,* 101–109.

Cook, W. L., Kenny, D. A., & Goldstein, M. J. (1991). Parental affective style risk and the family system: A social relations model analysis. *Journal of Abnormal Psychology, 100,* 492–501.

Cook, W. L., Strachan, A. M., Goldstein, M. J., & Miklowitz, D. J. (1989). Expressed emotion and reciprocal affective relationships in the families of disturbed adolescents. *Family Process, 28,* 337–348.

Corsini, R. (1956). Understanding and similarity in marriage. *Journal of Abnormal and Social Psychology, 52,* 327–332.

Cox, D. R., & Oakes, D. (1984). *Analysis of survival data.* London: Chapman & Hall.

Cronbach, L. J. (1955). Processes affecting scores on "understanding of others" and "assumed similarity." *Psychological Bulletin, 52,* 177–193.

Cronbach, L. J., & Gleser, G. C. (1953). Assessing similarity between profiles. *Psychological Bulletin, 50,* 456–473.

Curran, P. J., & Bollen, K. A. (2001). The best of both worlds: Combining autoregressive and latent curve models. In A. Sayer & L. M. Collins (Eds.), *New methods for the analysis of change* (pp. 107–135). Washington, DC: American Psychological Association.

Curry, T. J., & Emerson, R. M. (1970). Balance theory: A theory of interpersonal attraction? *Sociometry, 33,* 216–238.

Deal, J. E., Halverson, C. F., Jr., & Wampler, K. S. (1999). Parental similarity on child-rearing orientations: Effects of stereotype similarity. *Journal of Social and Personal Relationships, 16,* 87–102.

Delsing, M. J., Oud, J. H., De Bruyn, E. E., & van Aken, M. A.(2003). Current and recollected perceptions of family relationships: The social relations model approach applied to members of three generations. *Journal of Family Psychology, 17,* 445–459.

DePaulo, B., Kenny, D. A., Hoover, C., Webb, W., & Oliver, P. V. (1987). Accuracy of person perception: Do people know what kinds of impressions they convey? *Journal of Personality and Social Psychology, 52,* 303–315.

DePaulo, B. M., & Kashy, D. A. (1998). Everyday lies in close and casual relationships. *Journal of Personality and Social Psychology, 74,* 63–79.

Donner, A., & Bull, S. (1983). Inferences concerning a common intraclass correlation coefficient. *Biometrics, 39,* 771–775.

Donner, A., & Zou, G. (2002). Interval estimation for a difference between intraclass kappa statistics. *Biometrics, 58,* 209–215.

Draper, N. R., & Smith, H. (1998). *Applied regression analysis* (3rd ed.). New York: Wiley.

Duncan, O. D., Haller, A. O., & Portes, A. (1968). Peer influences on aspirations: A reinterpretation. *American Journal of Sociology, 74,* 119–137.

Duncan, S. D., Jr., & Fiske, D. W. (1977). *Face-to-face interaction: Research, methods, and theory.* Hillsdale, NJ: Erlbaum.

Duncan, S. D., Jr., Kanki, B. G., Mokros, H. B., & Fiske, D. W. (1984). Pseudo-unilaterality, simple-rate variables, and other ills to which interaction research is heir. *Journal of Personality and Social Psychology, 46,* 1335–1348.

Dunlap, K. D. (2002). Hormonal and body size correlates of electrocommunication behavior during dyadic interactions in a weakly electric fish, *Apteronotus leptorhynchus. Hormones and Behavior, 41,* 187–194.

Dunlop, W. P., Cortina, J. M., Vaslow, J. B., & Burke, M. J. (1996). Meta-analysis of experiments with matched groups or repeated measures designs. *Psychological Methods, 1,* 170–177.

Epstein, E., & Guttman, R. (1984). Mate selection in man: Evidence, theory, and outcome. *Social Biology, 31,* 243–278.

Erbring, L., & Young, A. A. (1979). Individuals and social structure: Contextual effects as endogenous feedback. *Sociological Methods and Research, 7,* 396–430.

Feeney, J. A. (1994). Attachment style, communication patterns, and satisfaction across the life cycle of marriage. *Personal Relationships, 1,* 333–348.

Feingold, A. (1988). Matching for attractiveness in romantic partners and same-sex friends: A meta-analysis and theoretical critique. *Psychological Bulletin, 104,* 226–235.

Felmlee, D., & Sprecher, S. (2000). Close relationships and social psychology: Intersection and future paths. *Social Psychology Quarterly, 63,* 365–376.

Ferrer, E., & Nesselroade, J. R. (2003). Modeling affective processes in dyadic relations via dynamic factor analysis. *Emotion, 3,* 344–360.

Fitzpatrick, M. A., & Dindia, K. (1990). Special vs. ordinary dyads: A round robin of interaction patterns analysis. In T. W. Draper & A. C. Marcos (Eds.), *Family variables: Conceptualization, measurement, and use* (pp. 179–196). Thousand Oaks, CA: Sage.

Fleiss, J. L. (1981). *Statistical methods for rates and proportions* (2nd ed.). New York: Wiley.

Fraley, R. C., & Waller, N. G. (1998). Adult attachment patterns: A test of the typological model. In J. A. Simpson & W. S. Rholes (Eds.), *Attachment theory and close relationships* (pp. 77–114). New York: Guilford Press.

Francis, D. J., Fletcher, J. M., Stuebing, K. K., Davidson, K. C., & Thompson, N.

M. (1991). Analysis of change: Modeling individual growth. *Journal of Consulting and Clinical Psychology, 59,* 27–37.

Franks, M. M., Wendorf, C. A., Gonzalez, R., & Ketterer, M. (2004). Aid and influence: Health-promoting exchanges of older married partners. *Journal of Social and Personal Relationships, 21,* 431–445.

Funder, D. C. (2001). Three trends in current research on person perception: Positivity, realism and sophistication. In J. Hall & F. J. Bernieri (Eds.), *Interpersonal sensitivity: Theory and measurement* (pp. 319–331). Mahwah, NJ: Erlbaum.

Gill, P. S., & Swartz, T. B. (2001). Statistical analyses for round robin interaction data. *Canadian Journal of Statistics, 29,* 321–331.

Glick, W. H., & Roberts, K. H. (1984). Hypothesized interdependence, assumed independence. *Academy of Management Review, 9,* 722–735.

Gollob, H. F. (1991). Methods for estimating individual- and group-level correlations. *Journal of Personality and Social Psychology, 60,* 376–381.

Golombok, S., MacCallum, F., & Goodman, E. (2001). The "test-tube" generation: Parent–child relationships and the psychological well-being of IVF children at adolescence. *Child Development, 72,* 599–608.

Gonzalez, R., & Griffin, D. W. (1999). The correlation analysis of dyad-level data in the distinguishable case. *Personal Relationships, 6,* 449–469.

Gonzalez, R., & Griffin, D. W. (2001a). A statistical framework for modeling homogeneity and interdependence in groups. In G. J. O. Fletcher & M. S. Clark (Eds.), *Blackwell handbook of social psychology: Interpersonal processes* (pp. 505–534). Malden, MA: Blackwell.

Gonzalez, R., & Griffin, D. W. (2001b). Testing parameters in structural equation modeling: Every "one" matters. *Psychological Methods, 6,* 258–269.

Gottman, J. M. (1979). *Marital interaction: Experimental investigations.* New York: Academic Press.

Gottman, J. M., Coan, J., Carrere, S., & Swanson, C. (1998). Predicting marital happiness and stability from newlywed interactions. *Journal of Marriage and the Family, 60,* 5–22.

Gottman, J. M., Levenson, R. W., Swanson, C., Swanson, K., Tyson, R., & Yoshimoto, D. (2003). Observing gay, lesbian, and heterosexual couples' relationships: Mathematical modeling of conflict interaction. *Journal of Homosexuality, 45,* 65–91.

Gottman, J. M., & Roy, A. K. (1990). *Sequential analysis: A guide for behavioral researchers.* New York: Cambridge University Press.

Gottman, J. M., Swanson, C., & Swanson, K. (2002). A general systems theory of marriage: Nonlinear difference equation modeling of marital interaction. *Personality and Social Psychology Review, 6,* 326–340.

Griffin, D. W., & Bartholomew, K. (1994). Models of the self and other: Fundamental dimensions underlying measures of adult attachment. *Journal of Personality and Social Psychology, 67,* 430–445.

Griffin, D. W., & Gonzalez, R. (1995). Correlational analysis of dyad-level data in the exchangeable case. *Psychological Bulletin, 118,* 430–439.

Griffin, W., & Gardner, W. (1989). Methods for the analysis of parallel streams of continuously recorded social behaviors. *Psychological Bulletin, 105,* 446–455.

Haggard, E. A. (1958). *Interclass correlation and the analysis of variance.* New York: Dryden.

Harvey, E. A. (2000). Parenting similarity and children with attention-deficit/ hyperactivity disorder. *Child and Family Behavior Therapy, 22,* 39–54.

Hatcher, L. (1994). *A step-by-step approach to using the SAS system for factor analysis and structural equation modeling.* Cary, NC: SAS Institute.

Havlicek, L. L., & Peterson, N. L. (1977). Effect of the violation of assumptions upon significance levels of the Pearson r. *Psychological Bulletin, 84,* 373–377.

Hazan, C., & Shaver, P. (1987). Romantic love conceptualized as an attachment process. *Journal of Personality and Social Psychology, 52,* 511–524.

Hindy, C. G., & Schwarz, J. C. (1994). Anxious romantic attachment in adult relationships. In M. B. Sperling & W. H. Berman (Eds.), *Attachment in adults: Clinical and developmental perspectives* (pp. 179–203). New York: Guilford Press.

Hoff, P. D. (2005). Bilinear mixed-effects models for dyadic data. *Journal of the American Statistical Association, 100,* 286–295.

Holland, P. W., & Leinhardt, S. (1981). An exponential family of probability distributions for directed graphs. *Journal of the American Statistical Association, 76,* 33–50.

Hops, H., Biglan, A., Sherman, L., Arthur, J., Friedman, L., & Osteen, Y. (1987). Home observations of family interactions of depressed women. *Journal of Consulting and Clinical Psychology, 55,* 341–346.

Hox, J. (2002). *Multilevel analyses: Techniques and applications.* Mahwah, NJ: Erlbaum.

Hu, L., & Bentler, P. M. (1998). Fit indices in covariance structure modeling: Sensitivity to unparameterized model misspecification. *Psychological Methods, 3,* 424–453.

Hubbard, J. A., Dodge, K. A., Cillessen, A. H., Coie, J. D., & Schwartz, D. (2001). The dyadic nature of social information processing in boys' reactive and proactive aggression. *Journal of Personality and Social Psychology, 80,* 268–280.

Ickes, W., Buysse, A., Pham, H., Rivers, K., Erickson, J. R., Hancock, M., et al. (2000). On the difficulty of distinguishing "good" and "poor" perceivers: A social relations analysis of empathic accuracy data. *Personal Relationships, 7,* 219–234.

Jackson, D. (1972). A model for inferential accuracy. *Canadian Psychologist, 13,* 185–194.

James, J. (1953). The distribution of free-forming small group size. *American Sociological Review, 18,* 569–570.

James, L. R., & Singh, B. K. (1978). An introduction to the logic, assumptions, and basic analytic procedures of two-stage least squares. *Psychological Bulletin, 85,* 1104–1122.

Jennings, K. M., & Stoker, L. (2005). Political similarity and influence between husbands and wives. In A. S. Zuckerman (Ed.), *The social logic of politics: Personal networks as contexts for political behavior* (pp. 51–74). Philadelphia: Temple University Press.

Jöreskog, K. G., & Sörbom, D. (1993). *LISREL 8: Structural equation modeling with the SIMPLIS command language.* Hillsdale, NJ: Erlbaum.

Jung, T. (1999). A new look at moderator variables of agreement: The role of target standing. *Dissertation Abstracts International, 59*, 5167. (University Microfilms No. 9906550)

Kanfer, A., & Tanaka, J. S. (1993). Unraveling the web of personality judgments: The influence of social networks on personality assessment. *Journal of Personality, 61*, 711–738.

Karney, B. R., & Bradbury, T. N. (1997). Neuroticism, marital interaction, and the trajectory of marital satisfaction. *Journal of Personality and Social Psychology, 72*, 1075–1092.

Kashy, D. A. (1992). Levels of analysis of social interaction diaries: Separating the effects of person, partner, day, and interaction. *Dissertation Abstracts International, 53*(1-B), 608–609. (University Microfilms No. 9215414)

Kashy, D. A., Campbell, D. T., & Harris, V. A. (2006). Advances in data analytic approaches for relationships research: The broad utility of hierarchical linear modeling. In A. Vangelisti & D. Perlman (Eds.), *The Cambridge handbook of personal relations* (pp. 73–89). New York: Cambridge University Press.

Kashy, D. A., & Kenny, D. A. (1990a). Analysis of family research designs: A model of interdependence. *Communication Research, 17*, 462–482.

Kashy, D. A., & Kenny, D. A. (1990b). Do you know whom you were with a week ago Friday? A reanalysis of the Bernard, Killworth, and Sailer studies. *Social Psychology Quarterly, 53*, 55–61.

Kashy, D. A., & Kenny, D. A. (2000). The analysis of data from dyads and groups. In H. T. Reis & C. M. Judd (Eds.), *Handbook of research methods in social psychology* (pp. 451–477). New York: Cambridge University Press.

Keiley, M. K., & Martin, N. C. (2005). Survival analysis in family research. *Journal of Family Psychology, 19*, 142–156.

Kelley, H. H., Berscheid, E., Christensen, A., Harvey, J. H., Huston, T. L., Levinger, G., et al. (1983). Analyzing close relationships. In H. H. Kelley, E. Berscheid, A. Christensen, J. H. Harvey, T. L. Huston, G. Levinger, et al. (Eds.), *Close relationships* (pp. 20–67). New York: Freeman.

Kelley, H. H., Holmes, J. G., Kerr, N. L., Reis, H. T., Rusbult, C. E., & van Lange, P. A. (2003). *An atlas of interpersonal situations*. New York: Cambridge University Press.

Kelley, H. H., & Thibaut, J. W. (1978). *Interpersonal relations: A theory of interdependence*. New York: Wiley.

Kenny, D. A. (1979). *Correlation and causality*. New York: Wiley-Interscience.

Kenny, D. A. (1987). *Statistics for the social and behavioral sciences*. Boston: Little, Brown.

Kenny, D. A. (1988a). The analysis of data from two-person relationships. In S. Duck (Ed.), *Handbook of interpersonal relations* (pp. 57–77). London: Wiley.

Kenny, D. A. (1988b). Interpersonal perception: A social relations analysis. *Journal of Social and Personal Relationships, 5*, 247–261.

Kenny, D. A. (1990a). Design issues in dyadic research. In C. Hendrick & M. S. Clark (Eds.), *Research methods in personality and social psychology* (Vol. 11, pp. 164–184). Thousand Oaks, CA: Sage.

Kenny, D. A. (1990b). What makes a relationship special? In T. W. Draper & A.

C. Marcos (Eds.), *Family variables: Conceptualization, measurement, and use* (pp. 161–178). Thousand Oaks, CA: Sage.

Kenny, D. A. (1994). *Interpersonal perception: A social relations analysis.* New York: Guilford Press.

Kenny, D. A. (1996a). The design and analysis of social-interaction research. *Annual Review of Psychology, 47,* 59–86.

Kenny, D. A. (1996b). Models of nonindependence in dyadic research. *Journal of Social and Personal Relationships, 13,* 279–294.

Kenny, D. A., & Acitelli, L. K. (1994). Measuring similarity in couples. *Journal of Family Psychology, 8,* 417–431.

Kenny, D. A., & Acitelli, L. K. (2001). Accuracy and bias in the perception of the partner in a close relationship. *Journal of Personality and Social Psychology, 80,* 439–448.

Kenny, D. A., & Albright, L. (1987). Accuracy in interpersonal perception: A social relations analysis. *Psychological Bulletin, 102,* 390–402.

Kenny, D. A., & Bernstein, N. (1982). *Interactions between opposite-sex strangers.* Unpublished manuscript, University of Connecticut.

Kenny, D. A., Bolger, N., & Kashy, D. A. (2002). Traditional methods for estimating multilevel models. In D. S. Moskowitz & S. Hershberger (Eds.), *Modeling intraindividual variability with repeated-measures data: Methods and applications* (pp. 1–24). Mahwah, NJ: Erlbaum.

Kenny, D. A., Bond, C. F., Jr., Mohr, C. D., & Horn, E. M. (1996). Do we know how much people like one another? *Journal of Personality and Social Psychology, 71,* 928–936.

Kenny, D. A., Calsyn, R. J., Morse, G. A., Klinkenberg, W. D., Winter, J. P., & Trusty, M. L. (2004). Evaluation of treatment programs for persons with severe mental illness. *Evaluation Review, 28,* 294–324.

Kenny, D. A., & Cook, W. (1999). Partner effects in relationship research: Conceptual issues, analytic difficulties, and illustrations. *Personal Relationships, 6,* 433–448.

Kenny, D. A., & DePaulo, B. M. (1993). Do people know how others view them? An empirical and theoretical account. *Psychological Bulletin, 114,* 145–161.

Kenny, D. A., Horner, C., Kashy, D. A., & Chu, L. (1992). Consensus at zero acquaintance: Replication, behavioral cues, and stability. *Journal of Personality and Social Psychology, 62,* 88–97.

Kenny, D. A., & Judd, C. M. (1984). Estimating the nonlinear and interactive effects of latent variables. *Psychological Bulletin, 96,* 201–210.

Kenny, D. A., & Judd, C. M. (1986). Consequences of violating the independence assumption in analysis of variance. *Psychological Bulletin, 99,* 422–431.

Kenny, D. A., & Judd, C. M. (1996). A general procedure for the estimation of interdependence. *Psychological Bulletin, 119,* 138–148.

Kenny, D. A., & Kashy, D. A. (1994). Enhanced co-orientation in the perception of friends: A social relations analysis. *Journal of Personality and Social Psychology, 67,* 1024–1033.

Kenny, D. A., Kashy, D. A., & Bolger, N. (1998). Data analysis in social psychology. In D. T. Gilbert, S. T. Fiske, & G. Lindzey (Eds.), *Handbook of social psychology* (4th ed., Vol. 1, pp. 233–265). Boston: McGraw-Hill.

Kenny, D. A., & La Voie, L. (1984). The social relations model. In L. Berkowitz (Ed.), *Advances in experimental social psychology* (Vol. 18, pp. 142–182). Orlando, FL: Academic Press.

Kenny, D. A., & La Voie, L. (1985). Separating individual and group effects. *Journal of Personality and Social Psychology, 48*, 339–348.

Kenny, D. A., & Lowe, C. (1979). *Judgments of roommates*. Unpublished manuscript, University of Connecticut.

Kenny, D. A., Mannetti, L., Pierro, A., Livi, S., & Kashy, D. A. (2002). The statistical analysis of data from small groups. *Journal of Personality and Social Psychology, 83*, 126–137.

Kenny, D. A., Mohr, C., & Levesque, M. (2001). A social relations partitioning variance of dyadic behavior. *Psychological Bulletin, 127*, 128–141.

Kenny, D. A., & Winquist, L. A. (2001). The measurement of interpersonal sensitivity: Consideration of design, components, and unit of analysis. In J. A. Hall & F. J. Bernieri (Eds.), *Interpersonal sensitivity: Theory and measurement* (pp. 265–302). Englewood Cliffs, NJ: Erlbaum.

Kilduff, M., & Tsai, W. (2003). *Social networks and organizations*. London: Sage.

Kline, R. B. (2005). *Principles and practice of structural equation modeling* (2nd ed.). New York: Guilford Press.

Klump, K. L., McGue, M., & Iacono, W. G. (2000). Age differences in genetic and environmental influences on eating attitudes and behaviors in preadolescent and adolescent female twins. *Journal of Abnormal Psychology, 109*, 239–251.

Krackhardt, D. (1987). Cognitive social structures. *Social Networks, 9*, 109–134.

Kraemer, H. C., & Jacklin, C. N. (1979). Statistical analysis of dyadic social behavior. *Psychological Bulletin, 86*, 217–224.

Krippendorff, K. (1970). Bivariate agreement coefficients for reliability of data. In E. F. Borgatta (Ed.), *Sociological methodology* (pp. 139–150). San Francisco: Jossey-Bass.

Krueger, J. (1996). Personal beliefs and cultural stereotypes about racial characteristics. *Journal of Personality and Social Psychology, 71*, 536–548.

Kurdek, L. A. (1997a). The link between facets of neuroticism and dimensions of relationship commitment: Evidence from gay, lesbian, and heterosexual couples. *Journal of Family Psychology, 11*, 503–514.

Kurdek, L. A. (1997b). Relation between neuroticism and dimensions of relationship commitment: Evidence from gay, lesbian, and heterosexual couples. *Journal of Family Psychology, 11*, 109–124.

Kurdek, L. A. (1998). Developmental changes in marital satisfaction: A 6-year prospective longitudinal study of newlywed couples. In T. N. Bradbury (Ed.), *The developmental course of marital dysfunction* (pp. 180–204). New York: Cambridge University Press.

Kurdek, L. A. (2000). The link between sociotropy/autonomy and dimensions of relationship commitment: Evidence from gay and lesbian couples. *Personal Relationships, 7*, 153–164.

Kwan, V. S., John, O. P., Kenny, D. A., Bond, M. H., & Robins, R. W. (2004). Reconceptualizing individual differences in self-enhancement bias: An interpersonal approach. *Psychological Review, 111*, 94–110.

Lakey, S. G., & Canary, D. J. (2002). Actor goal achievement and sensitivity to partner as critical factors in understanding interpersonal communication competence and conflict strategies. *Communication Monographs, 69,* 217–235.

Landolt, M. A., & Dutton, D. G. (1997). Power and personality: An analysis of gay male intimate abuse. *Sex Roles, 37,* 335–358.

Lashley, B. R., & Kenny, D. A. (1998a). Power estimation in social relations analyses. *Psychological Methods, 3,* 328–338.

Lashley, B. R., & Kenny, D. A. (1998b). *Significance testing for block SRM designs.* Unpublished paper, University of Connecticut.

Laurenceau, J. P., & Bolger, N. (2005). Using diary methods to study marital and family processes. *Journal of Family Psychology, 19,* 86–97.

Leonard, K. E. (1984). Alcohol consumption and escalatory aggression in intoxicated and sober dyads. *Journal of Studies on Alcohol, 45,* 75–80.

Lester, B. M., Hoffman, J., & Brazelton, T. B. (1985). The rhythmic structure of mother–infant interaction in term and preterm infants. *Child Development, 56,* 15–27.

Levenson, R. W., & Ruef, A. M. (1992). Empathy: A physiological substrate. *Journal of Personality and Social Psychology, 63,* 234–246.

Levesque, M. J., & Kenny, D. A. (1993). Accuracy of behavioral predictions at zero acquaintance: A social relations analysis. *Journal of Personality and Social Psychology, 65,* 1178–1187.

Levinger, G., & Breedlove, J. (1966). Interpersonal attraction and agreement: A study of marriage partners. *Journal of Personality and Social Psychology, 3,* 367–372.

Li, H., & Loken, E. (2002). A unified theory of statistical analysis and inference for variance component models for dyadic data. *Statistica Sinica, 12,* 519–535.

Little, R. J., & Rubin, D. B. (1987). *Statistical analysis with missing data.* New York: Wiley.

Liu, H. J., & Detels, R. (1999). An approach to improve validity of responses in a sexual behavior study in a rural area of China. *AIDS and Behavior, 3,* 243–249.

Locke, H. J., & Wallace, K. M. (1959). Short marital adjustment and prediction tests: Their reliability and validity. *Marriage and Family Living, 21,* 251–255.

Malloy, T. E., & Albright, L. (1990). Interpersonal perception in a social context. *Journal of Personality and Social Psychology, 58,* 419–428.

Malloy, T. E., & Albright, L. (2001). Multiple and single interaction dyadic research designs: Conceptual and analytic issues. *Basic and Applied Social Psychology, 23,* 1–19.

Manke, B., & Plomin, R. (1997). Adolescent familial interactions: A genetic extension of the social relations model. *Journal of Social and Personal Relationships, 14,* 505–522.

Maxwell, S. E., & Delaney, H. D. (2004). *Designing experiments and analyzing data: A model comparison perspective* (2nd ed.). Mahwah, NJ: Erlbaum.

McBride, C. K., & Field, T. (1997). Adolescent same-sex and opposite-sex best friend interactions. *Adolescence, 32,* 515–522.

McClelland, G. H. (2000). Increasing statistical power without increasing sample size. *American Psychologist, 55,* 963–964.

Messick, D. M., & Crook, K. S. (1983). *Equity theory: Psychological and sociological perspectives.* New York: Praeger.

Miller, L. C., & Kenny, D. A. (1986). Reciprocity of self-disclosure at the individual and dyadic levels: A social relations analysis. *Journal of Personality and Social Psychology, 50,* 713–719.

Moffitt, T. E., Robins, R. W., & Caspi, A. (2001). A couples analysis of partner abuse with implications for abuse prevention. *Criminology and Public Policy, 1,* 5–36.

Mohr, C. D., Averna, S., Kenny, D. A., & Del Boca, F. K. (2001). "Getting by (or getting high) with a little help from my friends": An examination of adult alcoholics' friendships. *Journal of Studies on Alcohol, 62,* 637–645.

Murray, S. L., Holmes, J. G., & Griffin, D. W. (1996). The benefits of positive illusions: Idealization and construction of satisfaction in close relationships. *Journal of Personality and Social Psychology, 70,* 79–98.

Murstein, B. I., & Beck, G. D. (1972). Person perception, marriage adjustment, and social desirability. *Journal of Consulting and Clinical Psychology, 39,* 396–403.

Muthén, L. K., & Muthén, B. O. (2001). *Mplus user's guide.* Los Angeles: University of California.

Myers, J. L. (1979). *Fundamentals of experimental design* (3rd ed.). Boston: Allyn & Bacon.

Neale, M. C. (1991). *Mx: Statistical modeling.* Richmond: Virginia Commonwealth University.

Neale, M. C., Eaves, L. J., Kendler, K. S., Heath, A. C., & Kessler, R. C. (1994). Multiple regression with data collected from relatives: Testing assumptions of the model. *Multivariate Behavioral Research, 29,* 33–61.

Newcomb, T. M. (1961). *The acquaintance process.* New York: Holt, Rinehart & Winston.

Newsom, J. T. (2002). A multilevel structural equation model for dyadic data. *Structural Equation Modeling, 9,* 431–447.

Neyer, F. J., Banse, R., & Asendorpf, J. B. (1999). The role of projection and empathic accuracy in dyad perception between older twins. *Journal of Social and Personal Relationships, 16,* 419–442.

Niederhoffer, K. G., & Pennebaker, J. W. (2002). Linguistic style matching in social interaction. *Journal of Language and Social Psychology, 21,* 337–360.

Nunnally, J. C., & Bernstein, N. (1994). *Psychometric theory* (3rd ed.). New York: McGraw-Hill.

Olsen, J. A., & Kenny, D. A. (2006). Structural equation modeling with interchangeable dyads. *Psychological Methods, 11,* 127–141.

Orina, M. M., Wood, W., & Simpson, J. A. (2002). Strategies of influence in close relationships. *Journal of Experimental Social Psychology, 38,* 459–472.

O'Rourke, N., & Cappeliez, P. (2003). Intra-couple variability in marital aggrandizement: Idealization and satisfaction within enduring relationships. *Current Research in Social Psychology, 8,* 206–225.

Park, B., & Judd, C. M. (1989). Agreement on initial impressions: Differences due to perceivers, trait dimensions, and target behaviors. *Journal of Personality and Social Psychology, 56,* 493–505.

Patterson, G. R. (1976). The aggressive child: Victim and architect of a coercive system. In L. A. Hamberlynck, L. C. Handy, & E. J. Mash (Eds.), *Behavior modification and families: Theory and research* (Vol. 1, pp. 267–316). New York: Brunner/Mazel.

Pearson, K., & Filon, L. N. (1898). Mathematical contributions to the theory of evolution. *Transactions of the Royal Society of London (Series A)*, *191*, 259–262.

Raghunathan, T. E., Rosenthal, R., & Rubin, D. B. (1996). Comparing correlated but nonoverlapping correlations. *Psychological Methods*, *1*, 178–183.

Rasbash, J., Steele, F., Browne, W., & Prosser, B. (2004). *A user's guide to MLwiN version 2.0*. London: Institute of Education.

Raudenbush, S. W., Brennan, R. T., & Barnett, R. C. (1995). A multivariate hierarchical model for studying psychological change within married couples. *Journal of Family Psychology*, *9*, 167–174.

Raudenbush, S. W., & Bryk, A. S. (2002). *Hierarchical linear models: Applications and data analysis methods* (2nd ed.). Thousand Oaks, CA: Sage.

Raudenbush, S. W., Bryk, A. S., Cheong, Y. F., & Congdon, R. T. (2004). *HLM6: Hierarchical linear and nonlinear modeling*. Chicago: Scientific Software International.

Rayens, M. K., & Svavardottir, E. K. (2003). A new methodological approach in nursing research: An actor, partner, and interaction effect model for family outcomes. *Research in Nursing and Health*, *26*, 409–419.

Rempel, J. K., Holmes, J. G., & Zanna, M. P. (1985). Trust in close relationships. *Journal of Personality and Social Psychology*, *49*, 95–112.

Reno, R., & Kenny, D. A. (1992). Effects of self-consciousness and social anxiety on self-disclosure among unacquainted individuals: An application of the social relations model. *Journal of Personality*, *60*, 79–94.

Roberts, L. B., & Searcy, W. A. (1988). Dominance relationships in harems of female red-winged blackbirds. *Auk*, *105*, 89–96.

Robins, R. W., Caspi, A., & Moffitt, T. (2000). Two personalities, one relationship: Both partners' personality traits shape the quality of their relationship. *Journal of Personality and Social Psychology*, *79*, 251–259.

Robinson, W. S. (1957). The statistical measurement of agreement. *American Sociological Review*, *22*, 17–25.

Rosenthal, R., & Rosnow, R. L. (1991). *Essentials of behavioral research: Methods and data analysis* (2nd ed.). New York: McGraw-Hill.

Ross, H., Stein, N., Trabasso, T., Woody, E., & Ross, M. (2005). The quality of family relationships within and across generations: A social relations analysis. *International Journal of Behavioral Development*, *29*, 110–119.

Ross, H. S., & Lollis, S. P. (1989). A social relations analysis of toddler peer relationships. *Child Development*, *60*, 1082–1091.

Ross, L. (1977). The intuitive psychologist and his shortcomings: Distortions in the attribution process. In L. Berkowitz (Ed.), *Advances in experimental social psychology* (Vol. 10, pp. 173–220). New York: Academic Press.

Roter, D. L., Geller, G., Bernhardt, B. A., Larson, S. M., & Doskum, T. (1999). Effects of obstetrician gender on communication and patient satisfaction. *Obstetrics and Gynecology*, *93*, 635–641.

Rusbult, C. E. (1980). Commitment and satisfaction in romantic associations: A test of the investment model. *Journal of Experimental Social Psychology*, *16*, 172–186.

Rusbult, C. E. (1983). A longitudinal test of the investment model: The development (and deterioration) of satisfaction and commitment in heterosexual involvements. *Journal of Personality and Social Psychology*, *45*, 101–117.

Sabatelli, R. M., Buck, R., & Kenny, D. A. (1986). A social relations analysis of nonverbal communication accuracy in married couples. *Journal of Personality, 53*, 513–527.

Sackett, G. P. (1979). The lag sequential analysis of contingency and cyclicity in behavioral interaction research. In J. Osofsky (Ed.), *Handbook of infant development* (pp. 623–649). New York: Wiley.

Sadler, P., & Woody, E. (2003). Is who you are who you're talking to? Interpersonal style and complementarity in mixed-sex interactions. *Journal of Personal and Social Psychology, 84*, 80–96.

Sampson, S. F. (1968). *A novitiate in a period of change: An experimental and case study of social relationships.* Ithaca, NY: Cornell University. (University Microfilms No. 690575)

Satorra, A., & Saris, W. E. (1985). Power of the likelihood ratio test in covariance structure analysis. *Psychometrika, 50*, 83–90.

Satterthwaite, F. W. (1946). An approximate distribution of estimates of variance components. *Biometrics Bulletin, 2*, 110–114.

Scott, J. (1991). *Social network analysis: A handbook.* Thousand Oaks, CA: Sage.

Shechtman, Z., & Kenny, D. A. (1994). Metaperception accuracy: An Israeli study. *Basic and Applied Social Psychology, 15*, 451–465.

Shilits, R. (1987). *And the band played on: Politics, people, and the AIDS epidemic.* New York: St. Martin's Press.

Shrout, P. E., & Fleiss, J. L. (1979). Intraclass correlations: Uses in assessing rater reliability. *Psychological Bulletin, 86*, 420–428.

Simpson, J. A., Rholes, W. S., & Nelligan, J. S. (1992). Support seeking and support giving within couples in an anxiety-provoking situation: The role of attachment styles. *Journal of Personality and Social Psychology, 62*, 434–446.

Singer, J. D. (1998). Using SAS PROC MIXED to fit multilevel models, hierarchical models, and individual growth models. *Journal of Educational and Behavioral Statistics, 23*, 323–355.

Singer, J. D., & Willett, J. B. (2003). *Applied longitudinal data analysis: Modeling change and event occurrence.* New York: Oxford University Press.

Smith, E. R. (1982). Beliefs, attributions, and evaluations: Nonhierarchical models of mediation in social cognition. *Journal of Personality and Social Psychology, 43*, 248–259.

Smith, P. B., & Bond, M. H. (1994). *Social psychology across cultures: Analysis and perspectives.* Boston: Allyn & Bacon.

Sneeuw, K. C., Albertsen, P. C., & Aaronson, N. K. (2001). Comparison of patient and spouse assessments of health related quality of life in men with metastatic prostate cancer. *Journal of Urology, 165*, 478–482.

Snijders, T. A. B. (2002). Markov chain Monte Carlo estimation of exponential random graph models. *Journal of Social Structure, 3* [Online]. Available at *http://citeseer.ist.psu.edu/snijders02markov.html*

Snijders, T. A. B., & Bosker, R. J. (1999). *Multilevel analysis: An introduction to basic and advanced multilevel modeling.* Thousand Oaks, CA: Sage.

Snijders, T. A. B., & Kenny, D. A. (1999). The social relations model for family data: A multilevel approach. *Personal Relationships, 6*, 471–486.

Snyder, J., Stoolmiller, M., Wilson, M., & Yamamoto, M. (2003). Child anger regulation, parental responses to children's anger displays, and early child anti-social behavior. *Social Development, 12,* 335–360.

Steiger, J. H. (1980). Tests for comparing elements of a correlation matrix. *Psychological Bulletin, 87,* 245–251.

Steiger, J. H., & Lind, J. M. (1980, May). *Statistically based tests for the number of common factors.* Paper presented at the annual meeting of the Psychometric Society, Iowa City, IA.

Stevens, S. S. (1946). On the theory of scales of measurement. *Science, 103,* 677–680.

Stevenson, M. B., Leavitt, L. A., Thompson, R. H., & Roach, M. A. (1988). A social relations model analysis of parent and child play. *Developmental Psychology, 24,* 101–107.

Strauss, J. P., Barrick, M. R., & Connerley, M. L. (2001). An investigation of personality similarity effects (relational and perceived) on peer and supervisor ratings and the role of familiarity and liking. *Journal of Occupational and Organizational Psychology, 74,* 637–657.

Tabachnick, B. G., & Fidell, L. S. (2001). *Using multivariate statistics* (4th ed.). Boston: Allyn & Bacon.

Thibaut, J. W., & Kelley, H. H. (1959). *The social psychology of groups.* New York: Wiley.

Thomas, G., & Fletcher, G. J. (2003). Mind-reading accuracy in intimate relationships: Assessing the roles of the relationship, the target, and the judge. *Journal of Personal and Social Psychology, 85,* 1079–1094.

Thompson, A., & Bolger, N. (1999). Emotional transmission in couples under stress. *Journal of Marriage and the Family, 61,* 38–48.

Thomson, P. C. (1995). A hybrid paired and unpaired analysis for the comparison of proportions. *Statistics in Medicine, 14,* 1463–1470.

Tukey, J. W. (1949). One degree of freedom for non-additivity. *Biometrics, 5,* 232–242.

van Duijn, M. A. J., Snijders, T. A. B., & Zijkstra, B. H. (2004). p_2: A random effects model with covariates for directed graphs. *Statistica Neerlandica, 58,* 234–254.

Vazire, S., & Gosling, S. D. (2004). e-Perceptions: Personality impressions based on personal websites. *Journal of Personality and Social Psychology, 87,* 123–132.

Wakimoto, S., & Fujihara, T. (2004). The correlation between intimacy and objective similarity in interpersonal relationships. *Social Behavior and Personality, 32,* 95–102.

Walster, E., Walster, G. W., & Berscheid, E. (1978). *Equity: Theory and research.* Boston: Allyn & Bacon.

Warner, R. M. (1998). *Spectral analysis of time-series data.* New York: Guilford Press.

Warner, R. M., Kenny, D. A., & Stoto, M. (1979). A new round robin analysis of variance for social interaction data. *Journal of Personality and Social Psychology, 37,* 1742–1757.

Wasserman, S., & Faust, K. (1994). *Social network analysis: Methods and applications.* Cambridge, UK: Cambridge University Press.

Watts, D. J. (2003). *Six degrees: The science of a connected age.* New York: Norton.

Wendorf, C. A. (2002). Comparisons of structural equation modeling and hierarchical linear modeling approaches to couples' data. *Structural Equation Modeling, 9,* 126–140.

Wilcox, R. R. (1994). Estimating winsorized correlations in a univariate or bivariate random effects model. *British Journal of Mathematical and Statistical Psychology, 47,* 167–183.

Wilhelm, P., & Perrez, M. (2004). How is my partner feeling in different daily-life settings? Accuracy of spouse's judgements about their partner's feelings at work and at home. *Social Indicators Research, 67,* 183–246.

Williams, L. J., & Hazer, J. T. (1986). Antecedents and consequences of satisfaction and commitment in turnover models: A reanalysis using latent variable structural equation methods. *Journal of Applied Psychology, 71,* 219–231.

Winquist, L. A., Mohr, C. D., & Kenny, D. A. (1998). The female positivity effect in the perception of others. *Journal of Research in Personality, 32,* 370–388.

Woody, E., & Sadler, P. (2005). Structural equation models for interchangeable dyads: Being the same makes a difference. *Psychological Methods, 10,* 139–158.

Zimbardo, P., Banks, W. C., Haney, C., & Jaffe, D. (1973, April 8). The mind is a formidable jailer: A Pirandellian prison. *New York Times Magazine,* pp. 33–60.

Zuckerman, M. (1979). *Sensation seeking: Beyond the optimal level of arousal.* Mahwah, NJ: Erlbaum.

Index